RECREATION BUSINESS

RECREATION BUSINESS

JOHN R. KELLY
University of Illinois

JOHN WILEY & SONS
New York
Chichester
Brisbane
Toronto
Singapore

Library of Congress Cataloging in Publication Data:

Kelly, John R. (John Robert), 1930–
Recreation business.

Includes index.
1. Recreation—North America—Management. 2. Recreation —North America—Finance. 3. Business. I. Title.
GV181.3.K44 1985 790′.06′9 84-11965
ISBN 0-471-89491-5

Printed in the United States of America

10 9 8 7 6 5 4 3 2 1

About the Author

John R. Kelly is Professor of Leisure Studies at the University of Illinois. He has been a consultant to research firms and American and Japanese corporations in recreation marketing, product development, and market research. The federal government has supported his research into leisure and aging, planned communities, benefits of recreation, and leisure styles. He is the author of two other books on leisure and over fifty published papers. His graduate degrees are from the universities of Oregon, Yale, and Southern California.

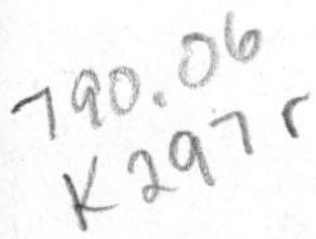

PREFACE

Recreation business is the market sector response to the demand for enabling goods and services. In a market economy many of the goods and services required for recreation participation are supplied through the private, or business, sector of the economy. These goods and services are a complement to those offered through the public sector. However, there are important differences in the aims and operations of business and public enterprises. In the functional approach of this book both differences and similarities will be introduced in the dual contexts of business and recreation studies.

Commercial recreation businesses are more than public programs with a profit. They not only have different aims and procedures related to finance and marketing but reach people quite untouched by the public sector. Recreation businesses are a pervasive part of the lives of most North Americans from the cradle to the grave. Yet both recreation business marketing and public sector programming are based on the leisure participation patterns and orientations of the populations to be reached. Business competence without a grounding in leisure/recreation studies is likely to lead to missing significant opportunities. A background in recreation without business skills is usually a prelude to failure. The intent of this book is to bring together the two fields in an introduction to this developing area.

The author would not claim unlimited knowledge in either field. Approaching the formidable task of creating a new synthesis from a background in the social science study of leisure and recreation, I have drawn on the experiences of a number of old and new friends who are engaged in recreation-related businesses, as well as several years of occasional engagements in marketing and product development consultation with a variety of regional, national, and international firms. However, a major benefit of the preparation has been a systematic study of basic business literature. My aim has been to integrate a knowledge of leisure with current business scholarship and experience.

However, this is only an introduction. It does not include "all you need to know" about either recreation or business. Further, as the field develops, other analysts will contribute to our understanding of many of the issues and practices touched on here. It is my hope that this inaugural effort will be found to be a substantial base on which to build.

A number of themes run through the book:

1. Businesses operate in a market economy that in turn exists in a complex and interrelated system of institutions that impact on every aspect of a business. The intent is to be realistic rather than ideological about the business environment.
2. Business is approached functionally. The question is, What must a business accomplish in order to succeed? Issues of finance, marketing, management, and operations are dealt with in the context of recreation businesses that face real decisions and dilemmas.
3. Vocational opportunities in the field are introduced in the analysis of the functions of a variety of types of businesses. The range of interests and skills that may be employed in the field is so vast that no simple list or line of preparation can begin to encompass the possibilities.
4. Recreation business opportunities fill the spectrum from the international conglomerate to the one-person service and from specialized skills to a general recreation background. Entrepreneurial imagination combined with informed analysis may open new lines of products and services that reach or create markets. This book provides a framework for analysis of what might be as well as what is now.
5. Fundamental to any analysis is an understanding of what people do and how they do it in their leisure. There is no substitute for a thorough grounding in the considerable knowledge that has been developed in the past decade and is continually receiving significant additions.

Therefore, to enter the field of recreation business well prepared a person should know more about both business and recreation than can be offered here. Those who read this book with a thorough grounding in business, through experience or academic preparation, should augment this beginning with further exploration of leisure studies. Those who come with a recreation background will need to augment this introduction to the functions of finance, marketing, and management with further course work and field experience.

Writing this book has been a learning experience for me in many ways. I am grateful to many persons who shared their experiences to provide case material. This is, after all, a beginning for those of us who are trying to contribute to an important new field and perhaps for many who will direct their lives toward this mode of enabling others to enrich their lives through engagement with leisure.

JOHN R. KELLY
University of Illinois

CONTENTS

1 OVERVIEW—RECREATION BUSINESS IN AMERICA

ISSUES

What is the scope of recreation business in contemporary society?

What are the most useful definitions of leisure, recreation, and recreation business?

Which recreation resources are market-supplied?

What is the place of leisure in consumer purchasing?

What is the place of recreation in overall consumption patterns?

Are there significant changes and trends in recreation markets?

Is supply always a response to demand?

How do market-supplied resources for recreation differ through the life course for those in the Preparation, Establishment, and Reintegration periods of life?

Are public recreation and recreation business competing or complementary?

The products of recreation businesses are everywhere. In North America they are found on the street and in the playground, in the home and the forest, on the water and in the air, in the sports arena and the school, and even in church and in the shopping center. There are many kinds of equipment that facilitate participation in games, sport, hobbies, the arts, and a variety of social occasions. There are magazines, books, and guides that prepare for and promote participation. There are media that entertain in the home and in public places. There are events that draw us away from home and varieties of entertainment and learning that are delivered into the home. There are all the services that enable us to travel, learn, and recollect.

Recreation business finds its markets with all types of people. Toys for children are hung in the crib, and homebound retirees consume entertainment media and employ equipment to pursue leisure interests. Most gifts to children are related to play in some sense, whether the activity requires disciplined preparation or only a little time and interest. Both the vacation trip and the weekend for the child-rearing family employ countless supplies and services purchased at a price. For most people, there is seldom a day that is untouched by recreation business provisions for some activity, present or anticipated.

Just think about these questions:

- How could we travel to visit friends or some attractive environment without the support services that exist?
- How would public and school recreation programs continue without the equipment and supplies produced and distributed by recreation businesses?
- Where would students gather in our communities if every commercial place providing food, drink, and entertainment closed next weekend?
- How would we fill most evenings if all commercial opportunities to watch television, listen to music, and read were taken from us?
- How would we plan next year's vacation or remember last year's if there were no travel guides, brochures, motels, near-shore services, agents, picture postcards, or photography supplies?
- How would we plan any special evening if all the restaurants, bars, nightclubs, theaters, traveling shows, and other places of entertainment were closed? Or what if they were open but unable to inform us of their offerings through some form of advertising?
- How many new residential developments attempt to attract purchasers by promoting their recreation opportunities rather than their floor plans?

Just examine the texture and fabric of ordinary life. It requires no compilation of statistics or testimonies to make clear this simple fact: Our lives have some elements of recreation-related business woven through the timetables and the locales of who we are and what we do.

TYPES OF BUSINESS PROVISIONS

No single book can describe every kind of recreation-related business, much less analyze the past, present, and future of every specific producer and distributor of goods and services. For example, in a few years business enterprises designing, manufacturing, promoting, packaging, franchising, and retailing electronic games have spun off from other enterprises, proliferated, consolidated, combined, grown or failed, and moved into a variety of new markets. Specialization has developed for the in-home market, the secondary market in which games are placed in a variety of retail stores, and the direct market for electronic games in new arcades. The market has developed from a few replacements for mechanical pinball machines into a worldwide industry with producers of microcomputers and microchips combining with game distributors to promote products that are only a little different in style or cost from several others. In a span of two or three years, companies opened, closed, combined, and made or lost large amounts of investment capital. A full analysis of even the first five years of this industry, from the application of weapons-aiming microchips to machine games to a still-developing industry incorporating every element of business on a world scale, would require years of research and hundreds of pages. Recreation business is not a simple phenomenon.

Nevertheless, some framework of classification can help sort out the variety and complexity: In general, there are two types of recreation business. The first type is the *direct* supplier of goods and services related to recreation. The second is the *indirect* provider.

Direct suppliers provide the equipment and environments that make recreation activity possible. They include the manufacturers, wholesalers, and retailers of recreation equipment and apparel. They offer campsites for rent, swimming pools and sport clubs for membership or daily fees, resorts at which to stay, athletic contests to watch, concerts to attend, and tourist attractions to visit. They bring the circus to town, operate the cruise ships, open the racetracks, operate the bowling alleys, and plan the floor shows. They build marinas, organize tours, and offer a week on a ranch, health spa, or tennis camp. They combine lodges with ski tows and parking lots with lift tickets. They rent the raft, provide the guide, and bus clients back to their cars upriver. They are businesses, large and small, that deal directly with the customer.

Indirect suppliers are a step removed from our experience with the recreation occasion. For example, they advertise the products, edit trade periodicals for the business managers, and provide capital for new and expanding businesses. They develop the locales in which the direct providers operate, the shopping malls and centers or the residential locations for the community pool or golf course. They are the businesses that depend on holiday trade for their success—providers of food, drink, lodging, travel by air or rail, car rental, airport speciality shops, and even the supermarket down the road from a public campground. They are all the business services along the highway leading to a national park, including those where cars are repaired, equipment fixed, and sundries purchased. They are the infrastructure of the market econony that makes available the many articles required to take the leisure trip, visit the leisure locale, or engage in the recreation activity. In turn, they have a viable market because people are investing time and resources in some form of leisure. They exist because of the recreation, and often make it possible.

LEISURE, RECREATION, AND BUSINESS

Before proceeding to the variety and scope of recreation business in North America, three basic terms should be defined:

Leisure The two dimensions of leisure that have persisted into modern times have been relative freedom and intrinsic satisfaction. The simplest definition available is, "Leisure is activity that is chosen primarily for its own sake."[1] That is, leisure is distinguished from what *has* to be done. A leisure activity is *chosen* at least in the sense that it did not have to be done and that there were alternatives. Further, the motivation is largely intrinsic rather than being chosen for some external aims or purposes.

There are a number of variations on the two themes of freedom and intrinsic meaning. For example, Joffre Dumazedier, a French sociologist, stresses the distinction from obligation and the positive functions of "relaxation, diversion, or broadening . . . knowledge and spontaneous social participation."[2] Kenneth Roberts recognizes that leisure is commonly distinguished from work and defines it as "relatively freely undertaken nonwork activity."[3] John Neulinger, a psychologist, emphasizes the experiential nature of leisure by proposing the perception of freedom, intrinsic motivation, and noninstrumentality.[4] A social psychologist, Chad Gordon, combines the elements of doing something, activity, with a self-contained meaning when he takes an action perspective and calls leisure "discretionary personal activity in which expressive meanings have primacy over instrumental themes."[5]

Note that there are several defining elements in common:

- All reject the "spare time" definition by focusing on the meaning of an experience that can occur at almost any time and place.
- All reject a simple work-leisure dichotomy that divides the world of action into necessity and freedom.
- All reject attempts to list activities that by their form or context are always leisure.
- All define leisure by the quality of the experience rather than the form, timing, or location of the activity.
- All define leisure *inclusively* in ways that can include daydreaming as well as disciplined rigor, moments of expressivity as well as scheduled events, and solitary as well as social action.

Recreation Just as the origin of the term *leisure* is from the Latin and denotes freedom, so recreation stems from the Latin *recreatio* and refers to restoration or recovery. Recreation contains the idea of purpose, usually the restoration of the wholeness of body, mind, and spirit. It presupposes some other activity or realm of life for which the individual is prepared. Recreation, then, has the social purpose of restoring the participant for something else, for being a worker or citizen or parent. It has social purpose.

Further, recreation is organized behavior. It is intended to be beneficial to participants and, at least indirectly, to benefit the society. Therefore, recreation is organized institutionally within a social system with positive outcomes intended. Neil Cheek and William Burch argue that recreation is more than restoration of the individual.[6] Rather, recreation is a social phenomenon that provides a social space for the development and expression of primary relationships. Recreation contributes to the maintenance of family, personal communities, and other social institutions.

When the dimensions of organization and social purpose are recognized, "recreation is defined as voluntary nonwork activity that is organized for the attainment of personal and social benefits including restoration and social cohesion."[7] A more humanistic approach would stress the individual benefits rather than social aims. However, in any case, recreation is provided within a society by its sanctioned institutions because it is presumed to benefit the society and its members. Recreation is one kind of leisure, an important kind, but only part of the expressive activity that is leisure.

Business Of course, everyone knows what "business" is—it is General Motors and Pop's Lunch Counter. It is the hamburger chain and the steel plant. It is also the bank and the advertising agency, the discount house and the shoe repair shop, the truck on the highway and the ski instructor, and so on. Business is defined in the dictionary as commerce, and vice versa. Both terms are so taken for granted that many economics textbooks define neither. That's how thoroughly business is embedded in our world.

So let's begin on the ground floor. Within any social system there is the necessary production and distribution of goods. Some goods are necessary for survival, some just considered useful, and others desired but of questionable usefulness. In a modern society there are two primary sectors: the public and the private. The public, or government, sector produces and distributes some goods and services, usually those considered basic, necessary, or that require the resources of the state. The private sector produces and distributes other goods and services. Public sector goods and services are paid for through the government's power to obtain material and labor directly or to gain capital to pay for them. The common means is taxation. The private sector has to obtain the materials and labor by paying for them with the returns from supplying the goods and services. The usual means is by distributing only to those who pay. That is, goods and services are provided through the *market*. Business, then, engages in some part of the production and distribution of goods and services through the market. Business—or commerce—pays for materials, labor, and capital from the price received in exchange for the goods or services.

Further, participation in the private or market sector of the economy requires, at least over a period of time, that the price received be adequate to pay for the investment capital necessary to operate the business. Money costs money, in interest paid or foregone. Therefore, a business must operate with a return above costs, a profit, to reward the investment of capital, the money necessary to begin and maintain the business *before* and at the time that income is received through participation in the market.

Business, then, is characterized by the following:

- It is in the private or market sector of the economy.
- It provides goods and/or services through the market at a price.
- It requires a return adequate to pay for materials, labor, and investment capital.

Therefore, *a recreation business provides goods and/or services for organized leisure through the market sector of the economy.* A recreation business is organized to obtain a price for goods and services adequate to pay the costs of materials, labor, and capital plus an incentive to engage in the business, a profit.

Considerable leisure requires no external provisions, public or market. It consists of imaginative activity, interaction with companions, and resource-free forms of play. The resources required for other leisure are supplied publicly, by the recreation agencies of the government. However, considerable leisure does depend on market provisions, on recreation business. It is that sector of recreation that we will introduce in the next section.

THE VARIETY OF RECREATION BUSINESS

Two books that introduce contemporary leisure and recreation in North America, *One Third of Our Time?*, by Michael and Holly Chubb,[8] and *Leisure*, by John R. Kelly,[9] have sections outlining the variety of commercial recreation resources. We begin by simply listing classifications of such business from each book.

From Chapter 12 of *One Third of Our Time?*:

Shopping Facilities
- Conventional stores
- Other retailers: catalog sales, markets, etc.

Food-and-Drink Services
- Food and beverage stores
- Fast-food establishments
- Cafés and coffeehouses

- Restaurants
- Bars and nightclubs
- Refreshment services at sites and events

Participatory Facilities
- Dancing establishments
- Sports establishments

Amusement Parks
- Traditional
- Theme

Museums, Gardens, and Parks

Shows, Towers, and Tours
- Traveling shows
- Overlooks and tours

Stadiums and Racetracks

Camps, Hotels, and Resorts
- Campgrounds and marinas
- Hotels and boarding houses
- Self-contained resorts: seasonal
- Spas and beauty resorts
- Sports resorts
- Travel clubs
- Cruise ships
- Mobile resources: river, lake, back-country

Farms and Estates

Native People's Enterprises

Camps and Schools

Products and Services
- Recreation products
- Professional services
- Rentals

This approach concentrates on resources, especially those that involve some sort of travel or special geographical resource. However, the importance of business provisions that are used for recreational purposes within a community includes sites in which leisure activity is only one purpose, such as restaurants and shopping centers. It is important to recognize that the design of such retailing centers increasingly provides for informal meeting and interaction as well as trade shows and exhibitions.

Leisure has separate chapters on sports, travel, popular culture, and the arts. Therefore, the commercial provisions related to those types of leisure are introduced separately. They include:

Travel
- Direct providers: air, water, and land
- Arrangers: travel agencies
- Support services: hotels, campgrounds, service stations, en route food and drink businesses, automotive, etc.

Sports
- Spectator: professional, school, etc.
- Participatory: facilities, equipment, teaching, support
- Television: networks, information, publicity, etc.
- Information: magazines, newspapers, guides, programs
- Gambling: government controlled, extra-legal

Popular Culture
- Printed media: books, periodicals
- Visual media: television, movies
- Auditory media: records, tapes, concerts

The Arts
- Performing
- Graphic
- Literary
- Community theaters
- Instructional programs

Of course, many of the resources in all these areas are public- rather than market-provided. The overlap seems to involve both competition and complementarity. The chapter entitled "Commercial Recreation" lists many types of enterprises that are likely to be overlooked:

Convention programs and provisions

Second homes and related real estate businesses

Liquor package stores

Secondary support services including repairs and resales

Financial services including loans for purchases and for recreation businesses

Market research

Advertising

Contracting for "family rooms" and residential patios

Services supporting gardening and landscaping

Holiday businesses: Christmas decorations, etc.

However, the more traditional categories are:

Destination attractions

Indoor sport provisions

Outdoor sport provisions
Travel support
Spectator sports
Skill acquisition
Outdoor resource sites
Popular culture
"High" culture
Gambling: legal and illegal
Equipment manufacturing
Specialty publications
Employment preparation and services

Further, any specific list is outdated before it is published due to the rise and fall of various business enterprises. There are always the "fads" that last a few months or years and then disappear. There are also businesses that gain new markets rapidly, peak, and then recede to a stable, more modest level. The essence of the market is change, and the hope is usually for a quick return on investment.

Whatever the rate of change, recreation business is characterized by considerable variety. That variety is partly shaped by technology. In this century alone, two technological developments have transformed resources for leisure. First, the private automobile changed the locale of leisure opportunities from home and neighborhood to community and metropolitan area. Most away-from-home leisure now presupposes access to a car. The car is more than transportation to playing fields, stores, and meetings; it is an entire realm of freedom for those seeking privacy and new environments, especially teens. Together with the network of highways and diverse destinations, it is a world of freedom and autonomy for adults who experience considerable constraint in the home, shop, and office.

Second, television has brought into the home an array of entertainment beyond the dreams of those who depended on the buggy, books, and an occasional traveling show early in the 20th century. Any account of leisure that predates the omnipresence of television is of only historical interest. Research on time use demonstrates the dominance of nonwork time by television. The car vastly enlarged the accessible world of leisure; now television has brought images of that vast world into the home at only nominal cost.

There are always predictions of the next technological breakthrough related to leisure. In the beginning it is difficult to distinguish trends from fads and dominant technologies from interesting gadgets. Certainly the microchip and modern electronics will add to the variety and impacts of television. However, those who predict that computer games will transform leisure patterns need to know first how many people, and in which periods of the life course, play interactive games with regularity. The likelihood is low of any single technology having the impact of the car or of television. Why? Because such an impact requires pervasive change in the institutional structure of the society and must overcome considerable inertia both in institutions and in the value structures of individuals.

However, from a business perspective, technologies that complement existing patterns of leisure behavior or that can be marketed to obtain a rapid return on investment are of considerable interest. Recreation-related manufacturers are always looking for a new or revised product that can capture a share of an existing market and use that base to create a new one. Technologies as simple as the replacement of wood by fiberglass in boats, skis, and countless other products have opened formerly limited markets to new growth. Technology is one important element in recreation business, but only one.

RECREATION BUSINESS AND THE ECONOMY

There are two equestion that together introduce the place of recreation business in the American economy:

1. What place do recreation expenditures have in the total purchasing schemes of consumers?
2. What is the proportion of recreation-related business within the economy as a whole?

RECREATION EXPENDITURES: PERSONAL CONSUMPTION

The U.S. Bureau of Economic Analysis has developed tables that suggest trends in personal expenditure for recreation. They are based on such items as purchases of toys and sporting goods, admissions to entertainment events, and reading materials. The problem is that such totals omit some of the major expenditures. For example, not included are:

1. The proportion of car expenses attributable to recreation when we know that over 25% of total miles are for outdoor recreation, entertainment, and sightseeing and over 36% for visiting.
2. The proportion of housing costs related to indoor and outdoor space for recreation such as the television, gardening, entertaining, children's play areas, and privacy for reading.
3. The proportion of other travel expenses that are for leisure, especially as part of trips with some business aim or family purpose.
4. The proportion of the household clothing expenses that are intended for leisure settings and activities.

TABLE 1-1 Recreation Expenditures—1960, 1970, and 1980

	1960	1970	1980
Total recreation expenditures	$17,855,000,000	41,322,000,000	105,414,000,000
Percent of personal consumption	5.5	6.6	6.4
Selected items from total:			
Magazines, newspapers, music	$2,164,000,000	4,005,000,000	8,881,000,000
Nondurable toys and sport supplies	$2,477,000,000	5,474,000,000	14,017,000,000
Wheel goods, durable toys, sports equip., boats, aircraft	$1,976,000,000	5,146,000,000	15,446,000,000
Radios, televisions, records, musical instruments	$3,003,000,000	8,436,000,000	21,602,000,000
Admissions: sports, movies, theater, etc.	$1,652,000,000	3,210,000,000	6,424,000,000
Participation: bowling, dancing, riding, swimming, golf, amusement parks, etc.	$1,200,000,000	2,189,000,000	6,150,000,000

5. The costs of eating out, a major leisure activity for middle- and upper-class families.
6. Other kinds of recreation costs hidden in expenses such as grocery bills, energy costs at home, and miscellaneous trips to the shopping center.

However, even with these serious limitations, the direct-cost figures are useful in analysing trends:

There are a number of trends worth noting:

- Except in times of war or prolonged recession, the proportion of expenditures directly for recreation has not changed radically. It has leveled at about 6.5%.
- The greatest growth segments, except for mass media, have been in expenditures for toys and sporting equipment. Sporting goods include equipment, clothing and shoes, and major items such as boats.
- In-home entertainment is a major expense. However, despite the multiple TV sets in many homes, more is spent for flowers, seeds, and potted plants than for TV repairs.

- The relatively stable percentages of total consumption allocated directly to recreation suggest that any new business, especially with a new product or service, must compete with other recreation businesses for a share of the market. During the period 1970 to 1980, the economy flourished with an average annual growth rate in new capital expenditures for business of 8.4% from 1970 to 1975, and of 13.4% from 1975 to 1980. Retail sales increased from $391,800,000,000 to $523,900,000,000 in constant dollars. However, the proportion devoted to recreation did not change.

Growth in Recreation Services Retail businesses vary in their patterns of growth. The statistics for different types of enterprises are not comparable. However, some examples give an idea of the magnitude of the markets as well as trends:

	1972	1977
1. Retail nurseries, lawn, and garden supply stores:		
Number with payrolls	3,800,000	6,900,000
Total sales	$695,000,000	$1,584,000,000
2. Mobile-home dealers:		
Number with payrolls	7,800,000	5,500,000
Total sales	$3,601,000,000	$3,709,000,000
3. Radio, TV, and music stores:		
Number with payrolls	20,200,000	26,100,000
Total sales	$4,365,000,000	$7,705,000,000
4. Eating places:		
Number with payrolls	208,900,000	237,700,000
Total sales	$29,313,000,000	$54,406,000,000
5. Drinking places:		
Number with payrolls	78,400,000	70,900,000
Total sales	$5,735,000,000	$6,901,000,000
6. Sporting goods, bicycle shops:		
Number with payrolls	12,400,000	17,100,000
Total sales	$2,284,000,000	$4,172,000,000
7. Hobby, toy, game stores:		
Number with payrolls	4,300,000	6,600,000
Total sales	$811,000,000	$1,554,000,000
8. Camera, photographic supply:		
Number with payrolls	3,300,000	3,600,000
Total sales	$736,000,000	$1,111,000,000

9. Bookstores:		
Number with payrolls	5,000,000	7,600,000
Total sales	$854,000,000	$1,722,000,000
10. Retail trade—total:		
Number with payrolls	1,264,000,000	1,303,600,000
Total sales	$440,222,000,000	$699,635,000,000

(*Source:* U.S. Bureau of Economic Analysis)

During the five-year period 1972 to 1977, a period that encompassed an economic slump in 1975 but was a time of overall economic growth, how did retail recreation businesses fare?

- Types of business that did much better than the overall retail growth were

  Nurseries, garden, and lawn suppliers
  In-home entertainment suppliers
  Restaurants and other eating places
  Sporting goods stores
  Toy and hobby stores
  Bookstores

- Those that did not do as well were

  Drinking places: bars and nightclubs
  Mobile-home builders
  Photography suppliers

The photography retail problem may have reflected a market saturation and competition from other suppliers such as discount stores. There is more behind such gross figures than demand for the product or service. However, it is important to note that the recreation market is a differentiated one. Some types of business do better than others in any period. Such relative success or failure reflects a number of factors including changes in the total demand, competition, market saturation, and the state of the economy. Relative position in the overall recreation-related market also reflects changes in the tastes of the consumer, an issue to which we will give further attention.

CHANGES IN RECREATION PARTICIPATION

To be well grounded, a business investment takes into account the present and potential market for the goods or service. One indicator of the potential market is the trend of activity that employs the goods or service. For example, if participation in downhill skiing were found to be decreasing, with the decrease especially marked among those aged 18 to 21, then increased future demand would seem unlikely.

The possible problem with such a simple conclusion would be that downhill skiing might be declining during a given period due to factors such as weather or poor snow conditions, high unemployment rates among the age group most likely to ski, overcrowded ski areas and consequent dissatisfaction, and other temporary constraints. Further, at least in a given market area, a new resource that is significantly different from those currently available may change participation rates. A new possibility, well advertised and at a price that makes the sport accessible to a larger market, may create new or larger markets for the recreation resource. Business may create trends as well as follow them.

Nonetheless, tastes do change. Particular activities that are based on new products or resources may have a rapid growth in participation that eventually levels or even declines. Markets can be saturated and people can be satiated. Trends need to be examined carefully.

These figures indicate a general increase in outdoor recreation. Further data indicate that tennis experienced rapid growth between 1970 and 1975, with a leveling off in the latter half of the decade. The number of sailboats owned doubled, but inboard power boats showed only a modest increase. The popular indoor sport of bowling, on the other hand, had an increase in organized participation unaccompanied by a growth in the number of bowling alleys or total of lanes.

The snowmobile phenomenon is one of the most dramatic examples of the participation response to a new product that reached a point of market saturation in a few years. In 1960 there was no recognized snowmobile market. Within ten years that market had peaked as a result of product development and promotion. Studies have shown that dual use of the product in rural areas—for winter sport and transportation—accounted for most of the sales. Then a com-

TABLE 1-2 Participation in Selected Recreation Activities: 1960 and 1980

Activity	1960	1980
Golf: 15 rounds or more	4,400,000	13,000,000
Tennis: players	5,000,000	32,000,000
Bowling: establishments	8,997	8,591
Bowling Congress members	5,538,000	9,595,000
Boating: Inboard boats	900,000	1,200,000
Outboard boats	4,100,000	6,800,000
Sailboats	500,000	1,000,000
Snowmobiles: Sales in U.S. (1970)	405,000	129,000

Source: Statistical Abstract, 1981

bination of saturation, warm winters, and other elements of disenchantment led to a leveling of the market at about 30% of its peak.

During the same period, from 1960 to 1980, spectator sports also increased in attendance:

- Major league baseball more than doubled, from 20,261,000 to 43,746,000.
- Professional basketball grew from 1,986,000 to 10,677,000.
- Professional football increased from 4,054,000 to 14,017,000, not including playoffs. College football attendance in the same period rose from 20,403,000 to 35,541,000.
- Horse-racing attendance went from 46,879,000, to 74,690,000.
- National Hockey League admissions grew from 2,387,000 in 1960 to 10,534,000 in 1980.

Both active participation in sports and attendance of sporting events were areas of growth. As a consequence, business investors have recognized the significance of the actual and potential markets. The key word is *potential.* Such long-term trends do not identify those activities that are growing most rapidly from a small base. In 1977 there were an estimated 3 to 4 million cross-country skiers, only about 30% of the total of downhill skiers, but the number has grown from insignificance in a very few years. Locating a potential market requires being alert to short-term trends as well as more established ones. An example of a general trend is that there seems to be a greater increase in nonmotorized equipment sales than in motorized, especially since the costs of fuel have escalated.

Also important for discerning markets is the composition of the participation aggregates. Is the increase in participation among population segments that are growing, such as those over 55, or among those becoming relatively smaller, such as those of school age? Or are there signs of growth in participation in certain kinds of activity across the life span? The point is that trends are not fixed in concrete and may change as tastes, values, resources, and opportunities are altered.

In any case, the scope of recreation is suggested by Table 1-3.

Note that even very small percentages represent rather large numbers of participants. The 7% who engaged in downhill skiing is equal to almost 12 million individuals. The small percentage who sailed five or more times, 5%, are a market of almost 8 million. The golf market of current participants is 27 million. Further, over 50 million people went camping at least once.

Market research firms attempt to track changes even more closely than the federal government. For example, the A. C. Nielsen Company conducts a recreation market survey that is useful for identifying possible short-term trends. For example, they found that from 1979 to 1982 the number of participants in their sample who engaged in snow skiing increased 27 percent. Snowmobiling in-

TABLE 1-3 Outdoor Recreation: 1977 Participation Percentages

Activity	One to four times in the past year (%)	Over five times (%)	Percent total
1. Visiting zoos, fairs, parks, etc.	34	39	73
2. Picnicking	23	49	72
3. Driving for pleasure	12	57	69
4. Other walking or jogging for pleasure	11	57	68
5. Swimming in pools	14	49	63
6. Sightseeing	26	36	62
7. Attending outdoor sports events	17	44	61
8. Other outdoor sports or games	13	43	56
9. Fishing	17	36	53
10. Walking to observe or photograph nature	14	36	50
11. Bicycling	8	39	47
12. Other outdoor swimming or sunbathing	11	35	46
13. Outdoor concerts, etc.	19	22	41
14. Other boating	14	20	34
15. Tennis	9	24	33
16. Camping in developed areas	18	12	30
17. Hiking or backpacking	12	16	28
18. Offroad vehicles or motorcycles	6	20	26
19. Sledding	9	12	21
20. Camping in primitive areas	12	9	21
21. Hunting	5	14	19
22. Kayaking, canoeing, river running	11	5	16
23. Waterskiing	8	8	16
24. Golf	5	11	16
25. Ice skating	7	9	16
26. Horseback riding	7	8	15
27. Sailing	6	5	11
28. Snowmobiling	3	5	8
29. Downhill skiing	3	4	7
30. Cross-country skiing	1	1	2

Source: J. R. Kelly, *Leisure,* 1982:407.

creased 23 percent; soccer, 23%; roller skating, 19%; racquetball, 14%; and boating, 11%. During the same period their figures show a 7% drop in bowling, 28% in table tennis, 10% in baseball, 53% in handball, and 17% in ice hockey. The sample consisted of 3,025 households.

If these findings are reliable, then some interesting trend information is revealed. For example, the enormous increase in racquetball participation from 1976 to 1979 has begun to level off. The phenomenal growth related to increased opportunities may have reached a more stable level because of the costs associated with participation for those other than students. Further, the most popular activities, such as swimming, bicycling, walking, hiking, and camping, are relatively stable.

Two points should be emphasized:

1. Provisions create markets. A new product such as a snowmobile, increased facilities such as racquetball clubs, new technologies such as fiberglass boats, or lowered costs as with ski equipment can enlarge previous markets or create new ones. Supply creates demand, especially if accompanied with an effective promotion program.
2. Insofar as participation reflects preferences, people do change. These changes are reflected in long-term trends such as the overall increase in participation in outdoor activity. They are also reflected in "product cycles" in which initial enthusiasm for new activities or products wanes in time and initiates fail to become devotees. At the same time there is considerable stability in participation rates among well-established activities for which opportunities are general and of relatively low cost. Further, not only do aggregate rates change, but individuals change through the life course.

MARKET PROVISIONS THROUGH THE LIFE COURSE

Distinguishing between "children" and "adults" does not begin to identify the significant changes in the use of recreation business provisions through the life span. The life course can be divided into three main periods and a number of sub-periods.

THE PREPARATION PERIODS

In Western cultures a third or more of a seventy-five-year life span is spent primarily in preparation for later "production periods" of family and work life. These early years are a time of learning, anticipation, and of being continually evaluated for later roles. During this period much of life is structured as "socialization," the learning of role expectations, cultural values, and skills considered necessary for social functioning. In earliest childhood most of this socialization takes place in the family. However, in time, peer groups, school, and organized community activities take over part of the socialization responsibilities. Among these, recreation may have an important place.[10,11]

In leisure, critical development of selfhood may take place. Both children and adults work out who they are to themselves and to others, defining their personal and social identities.[12] In play settings, the child develops self-definitions of physical and social competence. In leisure away from the supervision of adults, the adolescent begins to work through what it means to be a man or a woman, establishing sexual identity in an often ambiguous social world. In fact, in the Preparation period, leisure may often be more central than school in crucial social learning.

What, then, is the place of recreation business in the Preparation years? A few examples will have to serve to suggest the countless ways in which market provisions are part of this period.

- Crib toys, whether designed only to get attention or to provide an opportunity for physical manipulation, begin market provisions for play.
- Before children are one year old, sex-differentiated toys are available that contribute to the socialization process. The market supplies a variety of dolls, for example, that can begin role identification early in life.
- Throughout childhood, toys, sport equipment, games, costumes, books, and other paraphernalia are employed in play with peers and family.
- Commerical television that captures the largest number of at-home hours for children of almost any age.
- Sports and arts introduced in neighborhood and school are carried on with the support of private teaching programs, equipment sales and rental, and a multitude of live and media programs that attract interest and demonstrate competence.
- Family vacations with children, a special time for many families, are supported by a variety of commercial providers of goods and services.
- And even possession itself, the value placed on acquisition in a capitalist society, may be learned through recreation-related goods as well as in games of which the classic Monopoly is only the most durable.
- Later in the Preparation period, during the teen years, the central developmental tasks revolve around acquiring sexual and work-related identities. Especially the exploration, affirmation, and often reorientation of sexuality takes place largely in leisure environments. Among these, eating and drinking places, concerts and special events, shopping centers, and other places where teens can meet away from close adult supervision are significant. Almost every community has a history of teens abandoning adult-

provided recreation centers and "taking over" some commercial area, sometimes to the dismay of the proprietors.

- For students away from home, the "campustown" provisions are woven into the daily routines of life, and not only supply goods and services but also meeting places and activity settings. On many campuses far more students go shopping on Saturday than go to the football games.
- Although the future-oriented elements of student life are of greatest concern to parents and teachers, much of life is focused on the present. This is the part of life that tends to be most expressive, most shaped by symbols of group identification, and most materialistic.[13] Clothing, cars, music, and vocabularies are all part of the expression and interaction of students, whether at a party or the dorm, on the street or in a bar. Recreation business is seldom out of sight when students gather.
- Insofar as the term *courting* still has meaning for the development of lasting relationships between men and women, recreation markets provide many of the places, common activities, and mutual entertainments in which the relationships are begun, enriched, and expressed.

THE ESTABLISHMENT PERIODS

People do not stop playing when they leave school, marry, or take full-time employment. However, their leisure does have different contexts when they move from school quarters to their first established residence. The social context of leisure is altered by the commitment of marriage. The resources, constraints, and aims of leisure are shaped by being parents, and even by the ages of the children. The dissolution of a marriage, especially one with children, closes off the fundamental context of leisure for one parent (at least most of the time) and increases the constraints for the other.

In this production period, people choose or drift into work roles. They find that expectations are associated with these roles that influence the schedules and often the investment of leisure. They may seek a place in the community through affiliation with groups and institutions, some of which may be recreation-based. And as parents they may find that considerable nonwork time becomes invested in the recreation commitments of their children. Again, a few examples will serve to suggest the importance of recreation business in this central period of life:

- Although some postschool adults who remain single aim their life investments primarily toward careers, many employ a variety of leisure locales for the exploration of same and other-sex friendships.
- More of leisure takes place at home for established adults. Therefore, the recreation businesses that supply and service in-home media, entertain-

ment, and indoor and outdoor "do-it-yourself" materials for home projects become more important in this period.

- All the goods and services associated with recreational travel find major markets among the younger adults who may have some truly discretionary income for the first time. Further, equipment formerly supplied by the school must now be rented or purchased.
- Most of those who marry have children. Family leisure tends to revolve around the children, so the suppliers of toys, game equipment, away-from-home amusement areas, and vacation resources become central to adult leisure as well as for the children.[14] Cost may be an important consideration due to the heavy demands on lower-income families. However, time is also a scarce resource for most parents.[15]
- Leisure goods may also have meaning for status symbolism in suburban communities where work roles are in distant locales and often only vaguely known. The exotic locale for a vacation, the second home, the major toys parked visibly in the driveway, and the recreation-related clothing with the right labels may be chosen to confer or confirm social status as well as for use.
- In recreation as well as in parenting and work, midlife adults may seek some demonstration of "performance." They want to do well and receive some confirmation of success. As a result, leisure may become somewhat reoriented toward activities that yield signs of positive results. Some parents seek such signs through their children, who are urged to do well in sports, scholarship, or the arts. Others develop latent skills. In such cases, recreation businesses are expected to have available the quality of equipment that will facilitate skill improvement and some recognition of competent performance. Note the middle-year men who change golf clubs or tennis racquets every time something new and "better" hits the market. Some participants escalate their level of equipment as skills are increased, while others begin with expensive purchases.
- As children reach the age of leaving home, parents may seek some compensatory recreation investment to take the place of the time formerly focused on the children. Again, travel support is a common business contribution to this period in life.

As the relative demands and salience of various work, family, and community roles change through the life course, leisure changes as well. Not only what people do, but what they seek in their leisure changes through the years. For some, recreation activities and locales are primarily a place to meet new people and form new relationships. For others, family nurture is the main aim of recreation. There are individuals who seek their own development and expression in a particular leisure investment. Some desire change and relaxation rather than anything strenuous, mental or physical. For others, the first meaning of leisure is being with other people. As people move through the middle years of the life course, all these meanings and orientations wax and wane. As a result, the employment of market resources is characterized both by variety and by change.

THE REINTEGRATION PERIOD

The later years of life course are characterized by the attempt to "put it all together," to achieve some integration of investments, relationships, and meanings. During this period there are some significant transitions that impact leisure and all of life. They include the "launching" of children, preparation for retirement, retirement, and widowhood. Life is, after all, somewhat different when we recognize that it is two-thirds or more over, and it is time to sort out what is important.

As a result of such reevaluation, leisure may change. Some activities and interest may be laid aside as no longer worth the investment. Often, old interests are renewed and leisure takes on an increased salience in priorities of time and resource allocation. For example:

- Postparental leisure is characterized by a release of time and financial resources for new possibilities. The recreation market for those in their 50s may involve some "big ticket" items such as camping trailers, boats, second homes, and major trips that had been postponed during the child-rearing years.
- At the same time, concern with health and physical condition leads some later-life adults to reenter worlds of regular physical activity. However, they are less common than those who settle into routines that do not involve strenuous activity other than that required around the house and yard.
- Especially two-income adults may now eat out more, entertain in more costly ways, and plan their weekends for activities that require blocks of time seldom available when children lived at home.
- As the years go by, in-home recreation becomes more and more important. Not only mass media but also reading, informal social interaction, and hobbies and games may be given more time and attention. In many cases, continued interaction with adult children and with grandchildren may return older adults to the toy store and the amusement park.
- Most adults, usually women, find themselves without a marriage partner for some period of their later years. The contribution of recreation to rebuilding social contexts for leisure and to supplying a network of regular interaction is under study. In any case, leisure is called on to supply more than time-filling activity. Leisure may be central to expressive identities,

self-definitions of competence, and social integration. The recognition of such aims by recreation businesses has not been fully developed.

The market provisions for the leisure of later-life adults are given much less attention than the potential share of the market merits. Ours is an aging population in which 15% of the population will be over 65 by the year 2020. Further, those who reach later life in the coming years will have greater educational and financial resources than those over 65 now. They will have experienced the satisfactions of more varied leisure through the life course. Also, they will have fewer adult children and grandchildren to occupy their attention. They are a significant market segment now and will be more important in the future.

RECREATION BUSINESS AND PUBLIC RECREATION

It has been common among those engaged in the public sector of recreation to refer to "commercial recreation" in value-laden ways as somehow second-rate, tainted by the profit motive, and even peripheral to the leisure of children and adults. Even in this introduction it should be apparent that market-provided recreation resources are much more pervasive in the leisure patterns of North Americans than are public provisions. However, it is not a matter of which is first and which is second; nor is the question one of quality.

Certainly, community resources for recreation may be scarce, crowded, degraded, poorly managed, and replete with problems of group conflict, discrimination, and even danger. All public recreation is not of high quality, and/or is it equally accessible to all potential users. Poverty and travel costs alone bar many citizens from enjoying some of the richest experiences possible in special programs or environments. In the same way, recreation businesses may be so oriented toward immediate profits that the long-term damage done to resources and to people is ignored. The market is no guarantee of quality. Further, the price of marketed recreation resources inevitably denies the opportunity to some in a society with a wide range of incomes and considerable poverty.

However, once the invidious stereotypes are laid aside, an analysis of the relationship of public and business recreation provisions begins with their essential complementarity. Consider some examples:

- Equipment for community sports programs is obtained through local retail businesses. However, playing fields and outdoor facilities are public provisions.
- Recreation businesses often sponsor special public events such as bicycle races, 10,000-meter runs, and softball tournaments.
- For-profit schools and academies take musicians, artists, gymnasts, dancers, and others who began in public programs and train them at higher levels of performance. In turn, graduates of such programs often provide the leadership for the public offerings.

- Commerical campgrounds complement public provisions by accommodating overflows, providing special facilities for families or locations where trailers may be left all season, locating along travel routes where no public camping is available, and catering to special groups.
- Recreation business provides most of the essential services near remote public attractions such as the Grand Canyon, at Corps of Engineers reservoirs, and historic sites such as Philadelphia's Liberty Square.
- Businesses lease sites on public land to build and manage recreation resources such as ski runs and marinas.
- Travel services handle the arrangements for many trips that have public destinations.

The point is that supplying recreation resources in North America is not a matter of public versus commercial interests. In a mixed economy and a society that combines the public-welfare concerns of the state with market distribution of many goods, public and business recreation are frequently complementary. They depend on each other. However, there may be instances of competition. Certainly there are occasions of friction in which the policies of one sector are seen as a threat by the other. However, current recreation practices require both public and market sectors of resource provision, more often in a complementary than competitive relationship.

Further, it is important for those who will be planning and managing public recreation programs and resources to understand the nature of the market sector. Seeking a profit is not necessarily better or worse, but it is different. Accounting for public responsibility is somewhat different from accounting to meet the requirements of investors, lenders, and the Internal Revenue Service. Planning that has to take into account the interest costs of a line of credit is different from planning from a tax base assured for two or five years. Calculating the potential paying market for a resource is different from evaluating whether or not populations of special need are being adequately served.

Whatever the philosophical premises or the economic ideology of the recreation provider, ours is a system that combines public and market modes of the production and distribution of goods and services. Therefore, we need to try to understand both parts of that system.

PREVIEW OF THE BOOK

This book is an introduction to recreation business. While it does not presuppose previous preparation in business and economics, it is based on a contemporary understanding of business and economy. Recreation business is a major segment of the economy in its own right and is treated as such here. It is not an appendix to "real business," nor is it secondary to "real recreation," that utilizing public resources. And at this point it should already be evident that recreation business is a complex and varied phenomenon that cannot be exhaustively presented in any one volume.

In chapter 2 we will attempt to describe how the economy of the United States works. The approach will be neither highly technical nor ideological. Many will disagree with some aspects of the description because it probably will not agree with their idea of how the economy ought to work or what they have experienced. Nevertheless, we believe it is important to try to place this particular kind of business in a context of the whole economy with its problems, trends, and conflicts, and, indeed, in the context of the interrelated economies of the world market.

The next chapter will introduce the major aspects of business: marketing, finance and planning, accounting, and personnel and operations management. This chapter is no substitute for more intensive course work and experience in the field. It is not "all you need to know" about business functions. However, it is intended to enable the nonbusiness major to enter into conversation about how businesses operate. It introduces essential vocabulary, concepts, and issues that will be amplified and illustrated in the following chapters.

The second major section of the book consists of eleven chapters that focus on major types of recreation business. These are chosen out of the immense variety of businesses because they are common, employ personnel whose primary interest is in recreation rather than the details of business management, and are within the experience of most students. The brief case studies contained in the chapters have been selected to illustrate central issues in planning and managing such enterprises. However, the chapters should not be taken as "how to" formulas for the successful operation of such businesses. Like the rest of the book, they are introductory, descriptive, and analytical, not complete handbooks or guides.

Finally, chapter 15, "Recreation Business in a Changing Society," sums up the main issues of the book. It includes some sociological material on institutional change in the society and implications for recreation business.

Every reader of the book probably will know more about some aspects of the subject than the author. Students will have had experience as consumers and often as front-line personnel in retail businesses. Those engaged in public recreation will be familiar with details of the relationship between market and non-market provisions in their community or area. In most cases, they will find that the general level of analysis in this book only partly corresponds to every detail of their experience. And those with a business background will find that the business administration and economics basis of the book is somewhat thin in comparison with completing a major course of study in the field.

Nevertheless, this book does bring together material and areas of study that have been, for the most part, separated in the past. It is intended for those who are investigating the potential of the field of recreation business for their own vocational exploration. It is also for those who are trying to understand this major but often overlooked element in both the economy and in recreation resources. For any reader, it is intended as a springboard to further study and experience rather than as an encyclopedia of market-provided recreation resources.

SUMMARY OF ISSUES

Recreation business is a major segment of the American economy.

Leisure may be defined as activity chosen primarily for its own sake; recreation is leisure organized for personal and social benefits; and recreation business supplies resources for leisure through the market sector of the economy.

An inclusive view of recreation business in contemporary society demonstrates its diverse and pervasive character.

Even the narrowest approach to recreation business indicates a set of expenditures of over $100 billion a year. More inclusive estimates range up to $300 billion. Government estimates suggest a fairly stable 6.5% of personal consumption is spent directly in recreation.

New resources create markets, and preference patterns may be altered by access to new opportunities. Technological, resource, and taste changes may alter market patterns.

Markets for recreation business are also related to the developmental aims and changing resources of the three major life course periods.

Use of many public recreation provisions depends on complementary resources obtained through the business suppliers.

DISCUSSION QUESTIONS

1. List all the recreation business provisions you have utilized in an average weekday. An average weekend day.
2. How would such a list differ for young parents? For single adults age 20 to 30? For preretirement adults? For those age 65 to 70? 75 to 80?
3. How is real estate development a recreation business? Automotive design? TV advertising?
4. If leisure is defined in terms of the experience of freedom and intrinsic meaning, is recreation business more of a resource or barrier to such leisure?
5. Does the necessary profit of a business limit the kinds of recreation opportunities that can be provided? How?

6. What are growing recreation markets? Shrinking ones? Why?
7. Would you invest in a recreation business? If so, in which sectors of recreation?

REFERENCES

1. Kelly, John R. *Leisure,* p. 23. Englewood Cliffs, N.J.: Prentice-Hall, 1982.
2. Dumazedier, Joffre. *Toward a Society of Leisure,* pp. 16–17. New York: Free Press, 1967.
3. Roberts, Kenneth. *Contemporary Society and the Growth of Leisure,* p. 3, London: Longman, 1978.
4. Neulinger, John. *The Psychology of Leisure.* Springfield, Ill.: Thomas, 1974.
5. Gordon, Chad, and C. Gaitz. "Leisure and Lives: Personal Expressivity across the Life Span," in R. Binstock and E. Shanas, eds. *Handbook of Aging and the Social Sciences,* New York: Van Nostrand, Reinhold, 1976.
6. Cheek, Neil, and William Burch. *The Social Organization of Leisure in Human Society.* p. 224. New York: Harper and Row, 1976.
7. Kelly, 1982:27.
8. Chubb, Michael, and Holly Chubb. *One Third of Our Time?* New York: Wiley, 1981.
9. Kelly, 1982.
10. Kleiber, Douglas, and John R. Kelly. "Leisure, Socialization, and the Life Cycle," pp. 91–137, in S. Iso-Ahola, ed. *Social Psychological Perspectives in Leisure and Recreation.* Springfield, Ill. Thomas, 1980.
11. Kelly, 1982:138f.
12. Kelly, John R. *Leisure Identities and Interactions.* London: G. Allen and Unwin, 1983.
13. Kando, Thomas. *Leisure and Popular Culture in Transition,* 2nd ed. St. Louis, Mo.: Mosby, 1980.
14. Rapoport, Rhona, and Robert N. Rapoport. *Leisure and the Family Cycle.* London: Routledge, 1975.
15. Kelly, 1982:144.

2 HOW THE ECONOMY WORKS

ISSUES

Why is an understanding of how the economy works relevant to business operation?

What are the major historical trends leading to the current economic structures and orientations?

How does the American economy work theoretically and in actuality?

How do market and state economies differ?

What are the basic operating principles of a market economy?

How do problems such as resource limitations, inflation, unemployment, and income distribution impact on a business?

What major changes are now going on in the economy? How do interdependent world markets, service sector growth, corporate power, and political priorities affect the business environment?

What are implications for recreation businesses of investment balance, long- and short-term decisions, resource allocation, and fundamental labor policies?

No economy works equally well for all people at all times. Nevertheless, unless the economy of a social system operates to produce and distribute necessary goods in some way, the society will eventually fail. One problem is that modern economies have become so complex that even a rudimentary sorting out of the factors in their operation becomes a formidable assignment. Further, there is something less than full agreement as to just what those factors are and how they affect each other. Major elements such as the role of government, supply of money, reality of competition, function of labor, sources of growth, roots of recession, and creation of investment capital are all subject to argument among economists. And such argument cannot isolate any national economic system—the American, Soviet, or Zambian—from the rest of the world economy. Whatever the system—capitalist, socialist, or mixed—it exists in relation to an increasingly interrelated world system of production and distribution.

CASE: A LOCAL BUSINESS IN A WORLD ECONOMY

Suppose your analysis of business opportunities in your community located what appeared to be a gap in the supply of a service. At the local airport the major car rental chains are represented by the "Big Three or Four" franchises who specialize in business customers who fly in. Downtown the major auto dealers offer long-term leases to businesses that find it economical and tax-efficient to lease rather than purchase their sales and managerial fleets. But there does not appear to be an adequate service for the "ordinary" local resident who may need to rent for special purposes. For example, households with small, fuel-efficient cars may need to rent larger cars for special vacation trips; members of one-car families occasionally need to travel separately; students or urban apartment dwellers without their own cars may need one for special occasions; and so on. Now, on the surface, that would seem to be a very local business. Or is it?

First, if new vehicles are to be purchased or leased, then you are dealing with a corporation that sells and often manufactures in every part of the world, especially General Motors, Ford, or Chrysler. Further, the marketing practices of those firms have been changed by the years of competition from, first, the European manufacturers such as Volkswagen and, today, companies from the Orient such as Toyota. In fact, Ford produces a car that has parts manufactured in Japan, Spain, Brazil, Italy, Great Britain, Taiwan, and Germany as well as the United States. The prices, models, and availability of cars you want to employ in your new service place you in the world market structure.

Second, the costs of doing business require you to deal with the government in such matters as taxation, employment policies, safety, pollution control, and licensing. Your little business is now in competition with at least one multinational conglomerate corporation. Your prices are based not only on the costs of your doing business but also on the advertised rates of franchises set 1,000 miles away. The price you pay for your cars, a major factor in your pricing of the service, is influenced by tariffs on steel shipped from one country to another, wage packages negotiated for an industry two years ago, and production decisions made in a board room 7,000 miles away. Fuel costs reflect political conflicts halfway around the world. Labor costs are affected by the state of the economy. And so on.

Third, the potential customers you believe you have identified—your market—have their use for your service influenced by weather, the scheduling of events to which they might travel, the public school timetables, and variations in their incomes.

In short, what seemed like a very local service responding to a localized need is entangled in a world of economics and even politics. And there may actually be an answer to the rhetorical question, "What does that have to do with the price of tea in China, or at least Japan?"

THE AMERICAN ECONOMY: A HISTORICAL OUTLINE

The American economy has a history of change as well as growth. The growth has been phenomenal: In 1776 a population of about 2.5 million produced goods and services worth about $500 million. A little over 2 centuries later, 225 million people produced a gross national product of over $200 billion, 400 times as much as in 1776.[1] In a land with great natural resources, a people of great resourcefulness produced such economic growth.

However, the growth was not in the economy alone. The population grew as America was seen as a new opportunity for millions from Europe; the land resource grew in the westward expansion; and new technologies transformed production processes. Growth was accompanied by change in how and where people lived as well as in how and where they worked.

AN AGRICULTURAL ECONOMY: FROM THE BEGINNING TO 1865

The economic stories of the early colonies combine hardship, scarcity, failure, and venture capital. Several early settlements failed, some with tragic results. Even those in Massachusetts and Virginia that survived underwent periods of great difficulty marked by disease, shortages, and famine. These colonies were usually commercial enterprises funded by venture capitalists who expected to make a profit on their initial investment in ships, supplies, and securing land charters.

Most colonies became agriculturally self-sufficient quickly and began to enter into cross-Atlantic trade within a few years. By the time of the Revolutionary War, such trade had been going on for close to 150 years. In fact, taxation and trade restrictions were one of the central issues over which the conflict began. From the first, business interests were a factor in political action.

Following the Revolutionary War and in the early period of independence, there was a rapid expansion of both business and territory. Business was for the most part based on agricultural production. At the same time, the Westward push was under way, first into the Ohio Valley and then leapfrogging from the Mississippi and Missouri rivers over the Plains to the far West. Again, this expansion required political action to secure title to the new lands.

Alexander Hamilton, first secretary of the treasury of the new republic, assumed the debts of the colonies and established the Bank of the United States in 1791. A measure of fiscal reliability and order gave stability to the currency and made possible business exchange within the country and with other economies.

In the early nineteenth century, the resource base of the new land was expanded to the Pacific Ocean. Transportation became a paramount need, so a system of canals was developed in the East and followed by railroads. By 1860 there were over 30,000 miles of track. Westward expansion required a means of transporting manufactured goods to the West and bringing raw materials and agricultural products to the East. During the same period, technological innovations such as the gin to clean cotton and the first manufacture of interchangeable parts to replace individual craftsmen were the beginning of the mechanization of the production process and of the factory. Steam power, transportation, and the division of labor, these were the precursors of the Industrial Revolution and the transformation of the old agricultural economy.

INDUSTRIALIZATION: 1865–1900

The Industrial Revolution was not only marked by the growth of the factory and nonagricultural production, it was a revolution of scale as businesses began operating nationwide.

The first factor was technology. Railroads went ocean to ocean in 1869 and eventually formed a network of tracks. The grain of the West, cotton of the South, and textiles of the Northeast could be taken to market anywhere in the country. Steel became a major industry where the rivers met and coal and iron ore were brought to the furnace. Now there were coal power, water and rail transportation, raw materials, steel, and the new technologies of manufacture. What more was needed?

First, the factories and mines required a concentration of labor. So, the new cities rose—Pittsburgh where the rivers met, Chicago and Cleveland along the lakes, New York and Newark near ports, and so on across the land. Factories and mines spawned their company towns. Immigrants worked in the lofts, never saw a contract, and forfeited their health without consideration or compensation. Tenements were packed with people and language groups banded together for mutual support.

Second, there were the entrepreneurs. Partly through the railroad and banking combines, men learned to turn money into more money through investment. These were the hunters and gatherers of capital, the organizers of their own money and that of others. They founded the great industrial combines—Rockefeller and Standard Oil, Carnegie and steel, J. P. Morgan and banks. Despite the Sherman Antitrust Act of 1890, they consolidated businesses to operate on a scale that brought them enormous power as well as wealth. They believed that capital deserved to have the highest rewards and that labor was only a cost, a factor of production along with the machine.

By 1900 less than 10% of the population owned 75% of the nation's wealth. Children were still working in mines for $2 a day and young women in shops for $3–5 a week. In the steel mills men with broken health were lucky to stay on as sweepers for 75 cents a day. Attempts to organize labor were met with force, the National Guard and private armies. Between 1880 and 1900 there were over 2,000 strikes, but few succeeded in achieving major improvements in the conditions or rewards of work.[2] However, in time the unions gained some power, work hours shortened, factory conditions improved, and labor costs became something more than a pittance. Then the efficiencies of new technologies became less costly than labor and another element of change emerged.

WARS AND DEPRESSION: 1900–1950

The revolution went on. Steel production rose from 100,000 tons in 1870 to 25 million tons in 1910. The 10 million tons of coal produced in the 1850s increased to 500 million by 1910. Railroads carried 10 billion ton-miles in 1870 and 150 billion in 1910.

During the first half of the twentieth century the population of the United States doubled to 150 million, life expectancy increased from 50 to almost 70 years, per capita income went from $246 in 1900 to $847 in 1929 and to almost $9,000 by 1980. The workweek declined on average from 84 hours in 1800 to 60 in 1900 and about 40 by 1950. The gross national product rose from $18.7 billion in 1900 to over $100 billion in 1929. In 1979 it totaled $2,369 billion.[3]

In 1902 Henry Ford began to produce the first low-cost automobile. In a few decades the industry was the nation's largest. In 1913 Eli Whitney began the first assembly line. Mass production was on its way. In 1919 General Motors introduced a variety of car models, challenged the Ford Model T, and began an era of marketing. The creation of the Federal Reserve Bank in 1913 regularized bank loans, and practice of borrowing for homes and, eventually, consumer goods was inaugurated.

In the meantime large corporations broadened their ownership through the sale of stock to raise capital. American Telephone and Telegraph built a national telephone service while selling shares to individual investors. Consumer credit, public sale of voting shares in corporations, marketing and advertising, competitive pricing, mass production, and myriad combinations of technology, financing, and organization—so much that we now take for granted—were all developed in the early 1900s.

During this period major events had their effects on the American economy. World War I was a disruption and a learning experience as the economy was mobilized under government direction. The Great Depression shattered many dreams of progress, brought forth many critiques of capitalism, and also spurred government action to mitigate some of its effects on people and business. When World War II required another mobilization, the depression was past but not forgotten. The issues of economic cycles and government action remained. Again, new technologies and forms of organization were developed during the war. The consumer drought of wartime was ended in a period of expansion during the years that followed. Despite periods of recession and the beginnings of localized failure to meet competition in the world markets, business and government were seen as partners in economic growth and a resulting rise in the overall standard of living.

Coming into the contemporary period, a number of salient factors had emerged:

1. An expectation developed that the government would use its financial resources, regulatory powers, and direct participation in the economy to stabilize fluctuations and mitigate the consequences of market shifts. Even the most conservative proposals have been for changes in how the government supports the market rather than for a withdrawal of participation.
2. There has been a return to concern about economic cycles and the extent to which periodic rise and fall in the economic system is inevitable or can be controlled.
3. The distribution of income remains an issue. In 1977 the lowest 20% of workers received less than 2% of the total earnings, with the top 20% receiving over 48%.[4] The bottom 40% received only 10% of the total income, with the top 40% gaining 75%. The social costs of such uneven distribution as well as the inability of the lowest 20% to participate effectively in the market as consumers pose enduring problems for the society and the economy.
4. The problems of industrialization have not all been left behind. Various forms of pollution of the environment, job-related health hazards, regional unemployment as older factories lose their place in the system due to inefficiency, and residual problems related to urbanization remain. Now the society must cope as well with an economy that is moving into a "post-industrial era" with the majority of workers in service rather than production, and various forms of automation, cybernetics, and electronic communication and control eliminating vast numbers of production, clerical, and information-processing positions.

5. Without attempting a list of legislation in any area, the increase of regulation of business in the United States has been significant in the period since 1900. Antitrust regulation and laws prohibiting the "restraint of trade" have expanded into laws protecting the health of consumers, requiring "truth" in packaging and advertising, limiting the amount of damage an industry can do to the environment, and a variety of laws attempting to ensure that the exchange of money, stocks, and other financial transactions are carried on with a minimum of advantage to "insiders" and a maximum of public disclosure. Dealing with such regulations has become a major fact of doing business in every modern economy.
6. Finally, the auto industry is not the only one that has come to a realization that it exists in a world economy. Even the smallest retail store selects stock from suppliers around the world whether the item is a calculator, tennis shoes, or a stereo cassette. Variations in labor costs, production processes, transportation modes, and economic systems are all factors in how a local firm participates in the market.

THE ECONOMY TODAY: HOW DOES IT WORK?

What kind of economy now exists in the United States? Is it *capitalist* because it provides for a return on investment capital, money making money? Is it *socialist* because the state is a major factor in determining how production and distribution will be carried out? Is it a *market economy* because prices are allowed to vary according to demand? Is it a *mixed economy* because the state acts directly in some matters such as banking and utilities, indirectly in regulating other economic processes, and leaves some areas of the economy relatively free? Or do all the labels obscure what is really going on?

CLASSIC ECONOMIC THEORY

The two extremes of economic theory have their roots in the writings of Adam Smith and Karl Marx. Although the ideas of both have been subjected to considerable revision by their followers, the centrality of the market or the state remains fundamental.

Adam Smith wrote *The Wealth of Nations* in 1776.[5] He based his proposals for maximizing the growth of a national economy on four basic theses:

1. Private property—the freedom to own and control property including resources for production.
2. Free choice in the market—the right of the consumer to decide on the relative value of goods.
3. Competition among suppliers through a free market.
4. Freedom from government interference in the system.

DEFINITIONS:

Gross National Product: The total market value of all goods and services produced by an economy in a given time, usually one year.

Labor: The human resources used to produce goods and services: the physical and mental contribution of people to production.

Capital: All the machines, tools, and buildings used to produce goods and services; the cost of all man-made factors of production.

Market: The negotiated exchange of an economic good:

1. The organized exchange process.
2. For the firm, the buyers to whom it can sell a product.
3. For the household, the firms from whom a product can be purchased.

Smith believed that the market in which goods were exchanged employing a regularized medium, money, would provide the basis for the most efficient use of the resources of production—labor, machines, and capital. Writing in the early days of industrialization, he decried any attempts to interfere in the process by the state, however well meaning the attempts to mitigate the short-term results of competition. The system should allow for failure rather than cushion its costs.

Karl Marx, on the other hand, developed a critical analysis of early industrialization that was in part a social protest, in part an economic analysis of capitalism, and in part a political program. The first volume of his major work, *Capital,*[6] published in 1867, proposes that capitalism will in time fall under the weight of its inherent contradictions. The drive to lower production costs will reduce the income of workers to a level that prevents them from participating in the market. The economy will collapse from overproduction and a failure to distribute wealth adequately to support consumption. Further, rewarding capital investment rather than labor produces an inequitable system in which many suffer and few gain disproportionate wealth, power, and privilege. He believed that a just economic system required control by the workers rather than by those who owned and controlled the means of production, the capitalists. Therefore, socialism is based on ownership and control of basic industries by the state acting on behalf of the workers or on a system in which workers exercise economic control through some political means.

Of course, neither classic theory has remained intact through all the changes of the past century. All but a few proponents of capitalism admit that the state must participate in the economic system to provide some stability and systematic flow of information and capital. Further, just providing for the "common defense and order" and basic welfare services makes the government a major element in the economy. Still further, few would want Adam Smith's competitive market to be open to any form of deceit, manipulation, or coercion that might benefit a few at the expense of the system itself.

At the same time, market economies have proven much better able to adapt to change, limit production, and reward the worker than Marx predicted. The growth in production in Western economies, whatever the early costs to labor and the remaining costs to the economies of third world countries, has given a large proportion of the population more of a stake in the system in terms of material rewards than Marx anticipated. Further, the concentration of economic power has not prevented democratic political processes from mitigating many of the consequences of unregulated competition. Children are now in schools rather than factories and mines, and the financial manipulations of the early entrepreneurs are largely in check.

Nevertheless, the fundamental debate remains between those who rely on the market to determine the way the economy works and those who believe that the state must control the processes in behalf of the members of the society. "Pure" economic systems do not exist in the modern world. Capitalists want government protection and assistance. Socialists turn to the world market for sources of capital to develop industry and rely on the free enterprise of "the second economy" for production and distribution of some agricultural goods and services. This may not be a time of the "end of ideologies." Systems of ideas still have considerable influence in the world. However, any economic system must cope with fundamental problems of production and distribution, adapt to changing technologies, and respond to the value systems of the society in which it exists.

THE AMERICAN ECONOMY

What follows is both highly simplified and argumentative. Nevertheless, businesses exist in economic systems. Those systems, however complex and changing, are the context of economic activity. To understand or try to operate a business without some grasp of the context is equivalent to swimming in a river without knowing its temperature, pollution content, boat traffic, or direction and strength of current.

Functions of the Economy An economic system has two functions: the production and distribution of goods. An economic *good* is any product or service needed or valued enough so that users will exchange something of recognized value. Such a good may be a necessity such as food, clothing, or shelter; or it may be a service such as flute lessons or a car wash. "Good" does not imply moral worth or even benefit. In a barter economy, goods are exchanged directly. In a money-based economy, some medium of exchange is accepted as representing such value and permits indirect exchange. The value of the money rests primarily on the relative strength of the economic system employing it. A war, for example, may render a currency valueless as with Confederate dollars after the Civil War.

> **DEFINITIONS:**
>
> *Public Sector:* That portion of the economy in which principal decisions are made by the central authorities, the government and its agencies.
>
> *Private Sector:* That portion of the economy in which decisions are made largely by households and firms, the market part of an economy.
>
> *Profit:* The excess of the value of the output over input in a business, the money remaining after all expenses of production and distribution have been paid.
>
> *Capitalization:* The cost of the capital factors of production, usually long-term costs of business.

Public and Private Sectors Production and distribution may be undertaken by the public sector, the state. When the public sector dominates the process, the system is said to be some version of socialism. The aim of socialism is to maximize participation in production and provide a high degree of equity in distribution. When the private sector dominates the process, then emphasis may be on production. In a capitalist system the central feature is the control of the economy by investors and the rewards from such investment. In a market-based economy, distribution is primarily through an exchange system in which prices for goods are governed by relative demand and supply. In theory, as the supply of a good increases and demand remains steady or falls, the price per item should be lowered. When the price falls below a level at which the good can be delivered with a profit to reward the investment, then production and the supply will decrease. In time the smaller supply will cause prices to rise at a level attracting investment.

In actuality, all modern economic systems have some combination of the public and private sectors involved in both production and distribution. In the socialist economies of Eastern Europe, private enterprise and the market supply many personal services, considerable retail distribution, some elements of agricultural production, and even some basic goods through international trade. In a capitalist economic system, often energy is produced by the public sector and private utilities have their prices regulated. Transportation is usually partly supplied by the public sector, partly subsidized, and partly regulated. The state may produce some goods, manage some resources, act as a price-setting producer or consumer in some markets, and engage in considerable regulation that shapes the operation of the market.

Nevertheless, most economic systems can be classified according to relative reliance on the market. The economy of the United States incorporates many elements of public sector participation. However, most of the products of the economy are distributed through a market system in which ries are not predetermined by the state. It may be a mixed system, but it is far from state-controlled socialism.

How the Economy Is Expected to Work Exchange began with the "specialization of labor" in which some members of a social system, perhaps hunters, traded their produce for some other goods or services, the protection of the warrior, the blessing of the priest, or the implement of the metalworker. Such specialization is often efficient and allows individuals to concentrate on what they do best. Such exchange now generally employs money rather than a direct exchange.

Factors of production include materials, implements of production such as machines, power, capital, and labor. Most workers sell their labor in some phase of production or distribution and receive wages in return. These wages are then used in the market to purchase selected goods. In a condition of relative scarcity, the allocation of goods is through the market. Price is a variable factor that allocates goods and services when the supply is less than could be consumed.

Three groups operate in this market: households, firms, and central authorities. The *household* is the basic consumption unit and consists of all those living in a single residence who coordinate their financial decisions. Households decide, in some fashion, what to buy and what to forego. Households also supply labor for the system. *Firms* are the producing units. The firm is the supplier of goods and seeks to provide goods or services through the market at a price that covers costs and a profit, the return over and above the costs of production and distribution. *Central authorities* are all the public agencies that exercise control over households and firms and that influence the operation of the market.

Markets are where goods are traded, an arena—face to face or electronic—in which producers and purchasers negotiate the terms of exchange. In product markets, firms sell their goods. In factor markets, households sell their labor and other firms sell materials and services necessary for production. In a condition of "perfect competition," the decisions of households and firms control the process. In theory, the market process moves toward a balance of supply and demand through the pricing mechanism. In a "command" or "state" economy, decisions are made by a central authority. In a mixed economy, decisions involve both the public and private sectors in some combination.

Adam Smith, in 1776, wrote of *price* as the "invisible hand" that would guide the system and keep it moving toward equilibrium.[7] When the supply exceeded demand, prices would fall until profits ceased and production was reduced. When demand exceeded supply, prices would be forced up and production increased as the anticipation of profit was recognized.

Macroeconomics The working of the economy as a whole is the province of

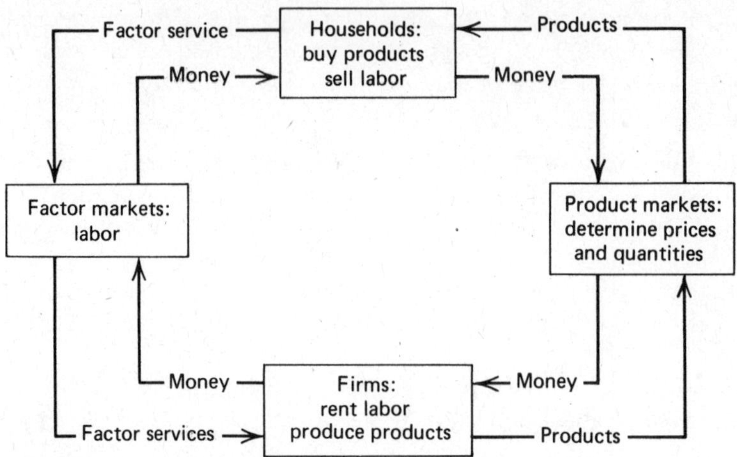

FIGURE 1 Macroeconomics: The Double Circle

macroeconomics. In the theory underlying a market economy, there is a double circular flow. In one direction, firms produce goods and services that are distributed through the market at a price to households, who in turn supply their factor services to the firms for a price, wages. The reverse flow is that of money, the medium through which the exchange is priced in the negotiations.[8]

Of course, there is more to the system than this. Households must pay taxes to support state services. Households also save for the future by withdrawing money from the direct-consumption cycle. Firms save, and invest in potential factors of production. Further, there are additions to the system by government spending that add to the income of households and firms.

> **DEFINITIONS:**
>
> *Factor Markets:* The markets in which households sell their services, labor, to firms.
>
> *Product Markets:* The markets in which firms sell their output of goods and services.
>
> *Consumption:* Using commodities to satisfy wants; household purchase and use of goods and services.
>
> *Demand:* Ability and willingness of consumers to buy specific quantities of a good at a given time; the taste, income, population, and price factors in determining decisions to purchase.

Microeconomics The determination of prices and quantities of goods and services in the markets is the province of microeconomics. Demand is said to be determined by "tastes," the preferences of members of a society, the amount of income that can be directed toward consumption, the number of potential consumers, and the supply and prices of competing goods. Goods and services may be competing when one can substitute for another, or complementary when used jointly in such a way that the reduction in the price of one can raise the price of the other. For example, two types of transportation between cities are competing, with price being a factor in choice. On the other hand, if a household allocates a certain amount for private transportation, a reduction in the price of gas may release income for the purchase of a higher-priced car, a complementary product.

In the market, it is assumed that the demand for any good will increase as prices fall. However, an increase in the income of potential consumers should also increase the effective demand and increase the price at a given supply level. Demand is made up of factors of taste, population, and income. Supply is determined by the goals of the firms who are the suppliers, by technology, the costs of production, the effective demand at a price, and the supply of other goods. In theory, price is determined by demand and supply in the market. *Elasticity* is the degree to which the quantity demanded changes with changes in the price. Elasticity is determined not only by the direct market but also by the prices of substitute goods, income changes, and alternative methods of securing the good or service.

DEFINITIONS:

Competition: Alternative suppliers of goods and services that enable consumers to make choices; price and quality differences in available commodities.

Elasticity: Responsiveness of quantity supplied or demanded to a change in price; percent change in quantity ÷ percent change in price.

Utility: The satisfaction a buyer derives from consuming a good or service.

Marginal Utility: Additional satisfaction from consuming one unit more of a good.

Household Consumption Behavior Price is not commensurate with value. A household may spend only a few dollars a year for water and $10,000 for a second car. *Utility* is the satisfaction received from consuming a commodity. The *marginal utility* is that satisfaction received from consuming one more unit. Such marginal utility is presumed to diminish so that the utility of one's first car is much higher than a third car, which may actually pose a storage problem. Therefore, the demand for any product is reduced as the supply is great enough that further consumption by households yields little or no marginal utility. A high marginal utility is usually associated with scarcity.

Further, utility is calculated at a price. Utility for a second car, a vehicle especially useful for camping trips, may stimulate a purchase at a price of $2,000 but not at $5,000. The marginal utility at the higher price cannot compete with another good, perhaps adding a screened porch to the residence or investing for children's education. However, a change in income—a substantial raise or an unexpected legacy—may alter the calculation. What a household wants is shaped by tastes, but actual decisions involve resources (income), marginal utility at a price, and alternatives.

This highly simplified description assumes that the household is some kind of rational decision-making group. Of course, that is seldom the case. Rather, differential power within the household, emotional attachments, impulses, compensation for frustrations, response to various marketing strategies, and many other factors enter into decisions. Further, there is an elasticity in presumed resources due to the possibilities of buying with yet unearned income, that is, on credit obtained by obligating future income. The budget of the household is much more complex than just a given income per month or week. There are payments for past expenditures, savings in anticipation of future consumption, and incursions into the rational budget due to uncalculated purchases.

Nevertheless, it is possible to examine the consumption behavior of households relative to their demonstrated tastes and rates of income to anticipate probable demand for goods and services. Further, that probable demand is price related. At the early price of $200 per unit, the demand for pocket calculators was quite small. At a later price of $6.95 a unit, the calculated marginal utility exceeded the price for millions of consumers so that many households now have several. This demand elasticity is especially significant for recreation expenditures. Since there are almost always substitute goods, price becomes a major factor in demand. When equipment for inaugurating an activity can be purchased for $20, the possible demand is likely to be far greater than for $200 or $2,000. Consumers simply rule out of consideration skiing trips to the Swiss Alps when actual household choices consist of calculating the marginal utility of eating hamburgers at a local fast-food establishment.

Production Costs *Cost* is the value of the factors of production for a good or service. Costs must be assigned to such production so that resources can be employed to gain the greatest long-term profit. Materials, labor, and capital are the fundamental costs of production. However, there is always the *opportunity cost,* that is, the benefit foregone in order to produce the good. For example, in order to raise production in a one-person shop, a worker may give up a family trip to work through the weekend. The opportunity cost of the business is in the leisure and companionship foregone. On the other hand, the opportunity cost of the trip might be rejecting a firm order for his product, a cost that can be assessed in current dollars as well as potential loss of a client.

Each factor of production must be assigned a cost so that in the long term a firm shows a positive opportunity cost, a profit. This includes the cost of money, income foregone on investment capital or interest paid for borrowed money, and the depreciation of buildings and equipment used for production. Prices,

> **DEFINITIONS:**
>
> *Cost:* The value of factors—capital and labor—used to prepare a good.
>
> *Opportunity Cost:* The value of resources used for a given purpose, usually measured by the utility or revenue given up by not using them for another alternative.

then, reflect not only the relative demand and the prices for competing and substitute goods but also production costs. If supplying goods or services does not produce a profit over a reasonable period of time, the opportunity cost outweighs the gain and the business operates at a loss. There is, therefore, always a risk in going into business. The risk is not only financial, the capital invested, but also the personal risk of giving up other opportunities for rewarding work.

PROBLEMS IN THE SYSTEM

That is roughly how the system works—in theory. If that were all, then the system would always move toward an equilibrium. Producing units would calculate their costs and direct their efforts toward providing goods and services for which there is a demand at a reasonable rate of profit. High profits would bring competitive producers into the market and lower prices. Low profits or losses would reduce the number of competing firms and allow prices to rise to a level that covers opportunity costs.

From the consumption end, households would calculate the relative marginal utility of those goods and services and allocate their resources to maximize satsifaction. The aggregate demand, made up of the decisions of all those households, would reflect such decisions so that production would respond to utility decisions. In a growing economy, incomes would increase, demand grow, and business expand to provide goods and service. The market, then, is the mechanism through which information is exchanged and the costs of production and demand meet at a viable price.

But it isn't that simple. To begin with, economies do not inevitably expand and grow. Further, there appear to be a number of difficulties that prevent such equilibrium from being approached, much less attained. To be realistic about the context of business, we have to address some of those problems.

Lester Thurow, an economist, has discussed such limitations on the distribution systems and the possibilities for economic change.[9] The underlying problem is simply the lack of growth. Industrial productivity in the United States rose only 1% a year from 1972 to 1978 as compared to almost 4% in West Germany and over 5% in Japan.[10] In the early 1980s a worldwide slowdown in growth affected even those economies that had been expanding most. This means that the rising standard of living that had been taken for granted by Americans came to a halt. Further, in an economic system with widely different levels of reward—salaries, wages, and other income—the living standard of those with lower incomes may be impacted in ways that affect housing, transportation, food, education, and other necessities.

In recent history, the American economy grew most rapidly in the 1940s, when it was run as a "command economy" for wartime mobilization, and in the 1960s.[11] During the 1960s the government expanded a wide range of welfare services that added considerable income to the economy but was paid for largely by taxation on growing incomes and profits.

Now things are different. Higher energy costs, inflation, unemployment, environmental degradation, costs of regulation, and increasing income differences between minorities and majorities are all rendered acute because economic growth no longer obscures their effects. Thurow argues that resources are not infinite, that ours is a "zero-sum society" in which solutions to one problem may intensify another.

The issues are those of distribution. The obvious example is relative poverty. If the incomes of the poorest 20% of the population are to be increased above marginality, then some other segments will have to give up a measure of their income. Agreement that equity requires raising the income floor for 20% does not necessarily lead to agreement as to who receives less. Further, since taxation is the likely means of redistribution, the decision is political as well as economic.

We are not arguing here that the problems are insoluble or that there will be no change in the economic situation. In fact, changes are occurring that will alter the structures as well as the processes of the system. However, either ignoring the problems or doing something about them requires action that interrupts the self-regulation of the market economy.

For example, a majority of the people in the United States are female. A proportion of women are demanding that their chances in life, for economic opportunity and reward as well as for a wider set of choices, be brought to the same level as those of men. If there are only so many jobs in the range of occupations, then more opportunity for women would mean less for men. If the costs of production have presupposed that women are paid less than men for the same work, then equalization in an industry where prices cannot be raised will require paying men proportionately less.

A majority of the people in the world are nonwhite. In general, a vastly disproportionate amount of wealth has been controlled by those who are white, with a resulting higher standard of living. Unless there is great growth in the world economies, any shift toward equality in resources and standard of living will come at the expense of those who are white.

The resources for economic growth in the world may not be fixed—a "zero sum"—but they are also not infinite. In a condition of limits, environmental improvement, raising the living standards of the poor, increasing educational opportunities, or widening employment opportunities will come at some cost. Those costs will affect every kind of business enterprise.

INFLATION

In recent years, one major factor in inflation, the rise in prices for goods, has been the increased cost of energy. Energy is required for every aspect of production and distribution, so that increased costs are compounded through the process. Thurow points out that when the price of a good goes up, those who purchase it then have less for other consumption; however, the seller has more. Inflation, then, has differential impacts.

Inflation has had several causes. Energy costs, the costs of wars, government debt and the costs of servicing it, and "racheting." A rachet is a mechanical device that prevents backward movement. Economic racheting is seen in labor contracts that increase wages to meet inflation but not lower wages in times of recession, or in transfer payments such as social security that can rise with the cost of living but not be reduced. Prices can go only one way when costs cannot be reduced.

No industry operates in isolation from others. Workers in electronics know what wage rates are in steel or the automobile industry. They demand relative equality or better. Also, contracts that index wages to some cost-of-living measure build in inflation. As costs of housing, food, and other goods go up, wages rise proportionately.

There is a way of slowing or stopping inflation. It requires allowing total income in an economy to stabilize. One means is control by the state. Another is to reduce the total cost of labor by allowing unemployment to rise.

UNEMPLOYMENT

The second problem, then, is unemployment. If an economic slowdown is the price of reducing inflation, then one consequence is a higher rate of unemployment. The official rates include only those who are involuntarily without a job and are still looking for one. Excluded are many older workers, women, and others who have given up. Further, overall unemployment rates are deceptive because they hit some so hard. An overall rate of 8% may often be translated into 50% unemployment of inner-city nonwhite men between the ages of 18 and 24. When firms lay off a proportion of their union workers, seniority rules may impact younger workers, the fathers of young children. In technical and white-collar occupations, older workers—age 50 and up—may be terminated with little chance of reemployment later. Perhaps most critical, entry-level positions for those completing school preparation may be closed so that the work career begins with disappointment and frustration.

A second result of high unemployment rates is the loss in purchasing power in the economy. The circular flow of exchange is interrupted and demand for many goods reduced. A third consequence is that government spending is increased for programs that provide some kind of income floor for households that have no one fully employed. This in turn may raise the costs of borrowing as the federal treasury has to borrow more to pay the costs of support programs.

Higher interest rates then make it more difficult for businesses to borrow to expand or enter new product lines that might reduce unemployment. The costs are both economic and human.

The root problem, of course, is the state of the economy itself.[12] When productivity rates in an industry are not high enough to allow for effective competition on the world markets, that industry will in time cut back and leave former workers without jobs. Also, the demand for most products and services is reduced when the economy is in a no-growth or cutback period.

Some unemployment may be cyclical, the result of temporary excess of supply over demand. The American economy has gone through major and minor cycles. Such waves of unemployment may be one element of a market-based economic system. If so, then the state can act to mitigate temporary social and human consequences in periods of recession. Other unemployment is structural, the result of changes in the economic conditions that are not likely to improve. For example, a particular industry may have to increase efficiency of production to compete in the world market. Such increased productivity comes at the cost of reducing the work force and making the production process more mechanized and automated. Unless the changes capture a much improved share of the total market, the job loss is probably permanent. The same loss may occur when the total demand for a product is reduced as was the case with horse-drawn buggies 70 years ago or school textbooks more recently. Such unemployment is called *structural.* A solution requires overall economic growth and shifting of the workers to other sectors of the economy.

INCOME DISTRIBUTION

The distribution of income in the American economy is more than a problem of social ethics. Whether or not it is acceptable in what is still a relatively resource-rich economy for as many as 20% of the households to be marginal or below in purchasing power is one question. The economic consequences remain an issue separable from the costs in terms of human potential and development. In the United States, the top 20% of the population have almost 80% of the total wealth as well as 44% of total income.[13] The top ½ of 1% own 43% of all common stock, and the highest 1% receive 11% of all income.

One study found that many people are poor simply because they are not employed. Rather than a permanent class of the poor, many households move in and out of poverty that requires assistance for maintenance when they obtain or lose jobs.[14] Others are poor in ways that are not likely to change, due to combinations of health impairments with age or the difficulties of supporting young children on a small or nonexistent income.

Whatever reasons, when the lowest 20% of households receives less than 5% of the income, their participation in the economy is reduced.[15] They are able to purchase little except low-cost food, unreliable transportation, crowded housing, and cheap entertainment. Even those items often require some subsidy from various levels of government. Much of that income is in transfer payments from the state that stave off starvation and exposure to the elements.

At the other end of the spectrum, the spending patterns of the upper 20% with almost 45% of the income are quite different. They are a major portion of the market for designer clothing, luxury levels of housing and transportation, expensive leisure goods, and high-cost travel. Their children are most likely to attend private summer camps, receive instruction in the arts, and go to expensive private universities. They can employ their resources to purchase a wide range of services and to try out possessions or activities that suggest they might prove some pleasure. They also are most likely to invest their income and provide a source of business capital directly and indirectly.

Economic results of this distribution pattern pervade the entire system. Investment is skewed toward high-profit goods and services for the upper-income markets. Markets for many kinds of durable goods such as refrigerators and cars are reduced. The ability to prepare for many kinds of economic participation and contribution are limited to a preselected part of the population. Government resources are required to maintain even the low standard of living of the poor as well as to provide a range of services. And, for a number of reasons built into the social system, particular population segments experience a disproportionate share of the negative results, especially those who are black, Hispanic, female, young, old, or some combination of these factors. Further, change in this distribution pattern since 1970 has been negligible.[16]

ECONOMIC GROWTH

The American economy has undergone considerable examination in recent years. One reason is that there has been a new combination of factors, inflation combined with relatively high unemployment and reduced growth. Previous theories, some based on the work of the late J. M. Keynes, offered the proposition that increased government activity in economy could "prime the pump" in times of stagnation and get the economy onto a higher level of production, employment, and consumption.[17] Several new factors have brought that approach into question. One is that the economy of any nation is more subject to the effects of changes in the world markets than formerly. Competition is not just among firms in an economy but among firms in a worldwide distribution system. Further, costs of production may be altered by uncontrollable changes such as increases in energy costs when Middle East Oil sources combined to raise prices. Therefore, labor costs, productivity rates, technological efficiency, and the results of research and development anywhere in the world are all determinative factors in the viability and profitability of many businesses in the United States. The market for competing and substitute goods is now a world market.

As a result, solutions of problems of inflation, unemployment, and the distribution of income must be worked out in a condition of limited economic growth. Redistribution of goods and resources seems to require lowering the economic power or rewards of one segment of the population in order to better the position of another if the economic system remains largely unchanged.

There may be other possibilities. One is that a major restructuring take place in the relative position of the private and public sectors of the economy. A greater share of production would then go into state-subsidized production of goods such as housing and transportation and services such as education and health. The problem is where the capital would come from when the rest of the economy is not growing.

Another possibility is that the national economy adjust to a new position in the world market system. Research and development would be oriented toward new technologies that would strengthen the American place in production and distribution in relation to other national economies. The problem is that a reduction in returns in other economies would then result in reduced markets for American goods.

A third possibility is that the third world economies be assisted to develop their resources in ways that make them more active participants in the world markets, as producers and consumers as well as sources of raw materials. Then, there might be overall economic growth in a world system in which national economies specialize in what they can provide best. The problem of mitigating consequences such as structural unemployment when entire industries close is a serious one. However, one long-term benefit might be a world that becomes so interdependent that war can be inaugurated only after recognizing that all participants will lose in both the short and long terms.

All this may seem far afield from an introduction to recreation business. However, no business exists in an economic vacuum. Even the most localized enterprise is affected by the general economic conditions of its market area, its local community. Further, the possibilities of competing and substitutable goods and services from across the country and across oceans are increasingly probable. While no one can accurately forecast the details of the future of the American or world economies, some idea of both theory and issues may assist in identifying the factors that are critical in the success or failure of any particular enterprise. And one sure prediction can be made: Economic conditions are changing now and will continue to change.

ECONOMIC CHANGE

Most of the changes have already been mentioned. However, some of their ramifications for the context of recreation businesses may be introduced more fully.

THE INTERDEPENDENT WORLD MARKET SYSTEM

One difficulty with traditional texts in economics and business is that they do not always recognize the extent to which national economies have become interdependent. Any discussion of markets is inadequate that does not take into account the competition from producers throughout the world and the reorganization of major corporations into multinational enterprises that buy, sell, and trade around the world. Just go to your local discount house and check out the manufacturers' labels to verify this fact. Clothing made in Korea, Hong Kong, and even China; auto parts from West Germany, Japan, and Spain; cameras from Portugal and East Germany; and shoes from almost anywhere fill the shelves of discount stores in Alabama and Iowa as well as New York and California.

The trade goes both ways. In the ski business the American shop promotes skis from Norway and Japan while in Switzerland jackets and even Tyrolean caps come from Minnesota. The American market is important to sporting goods suppliers throughout the world, but American brands carry prestige in the same towns where competing goods are manufactured. Further, in some industries much of the growth in markets has been outside North America as economies in countries such as West Germany, the Netherlands, Sweden, and Japan provide higher per capita incomes.

The interdependence is demonstrated further by the import and export figures from 1980 (Table 2-1).

Note the imbalance of imports over exports from the OPEC countries that is not quite balanced by the export surplus in trade with Western Europe. Energy is the major single element in imbalance. Note also the importance of trade with the less developed countries of Africa, Asia, and South America. This trade, almost in balance overall, is the second largest segment of U.S. world commerce.

The goods exported in greatest quantity and value from the United States are machinery and food; imported most heavily are fuels and raw materials. For example, most "strategic metals" necessary for the manufacture of heavy machinery, aircraft, weapons, and some tools are imported from Asia, Africa, South America, and Australia. However, these areas are also markets for the goods manufactured.

Further, the interdependence of currencies, investment markets for stocks and bonds, and financing arrangements means that disruptions in any major economy has impacts on all the others. In 1982 the American recession and high interest rates produced slowdowns in all developed countries. Earlier, the escalating costs of oil from the Middle East drastically changed the balance of payments of all fuel-dependent economies, rich and poor.

Nor can we assume that there will be little change from present conditions. The oil embargo was a dramatic demonstration that formerly dependent countries, directed by perceived national interests, will no longer accept dictation

TABLE 2-1 Imports and Exports of the United States in 1980

	Canada	W. Europe	Japan	Other developed	OPEC	Other less developed	Communist
Exports (%)	18.3	29.9	9.7	3.1	8.3	26.5	4.2
Imports (%)	18.4	20.2	12.7	2.6	20.4	24.5	1.2

Source: U.S. Department of Commerce, Overseas Business Reports, 1980.

from the major powers without attempting to exercise their own economic muscle. Just as important for our purposes, however, is the significance of the world market. Few, if any, industries are isolated from this complex phenomenon.

For example, a European-based airline may decide to invade some of the vacation-related markets such as round trips from major American cities to Switzerland with fares of only 60% of the excursion fares of established carriers. This competition has a number of results: The established carriers lose business and try to make up the loss on other routes. Skiers find that they can go to Switzerland for a week on the slopes for only $200 more than the cost of going to Colorado or Utah. Travel agencies develop low-cost packages based on the low fares. Flying with full planes booked well in advance, the invading airline expands its services. At the same time, ski resorts in North America may lose just enough high-tariff business to turn profit into loss for the season. Also, skiers traveling to Europe may purchase some of their new clothing and gear in Europe rather than Vail, Aspen, or even Omaha. Like it or not, the entire range of ski-related businesses is affected by one single addition to the world market.

SERVICE SECTOR GROWTH

The second major change in the economic system is the major shift toward the service sector. Some summarize this change by saying that ours is now a "postindustrial economy" in the sense that over half of employment is now in services rather than production. The trend has been under way for decades, but has accelerated since World War II. A little less than 30% of the man-hours added to the economy from 1965 to 1972 was in services. From 1972 to 1980, it was 47%. Almost half the extra services were in health care. Decline was in mining, construction, and utilities.[18]

Service occupations include not only public sector work, such as education, social welfare, police and fire protection, recreation, public health, and management of public resources, but also the private sector employment other than manufacturing. The greatest increases have been in health services, retail sales, finance, and business services. The proportion of employment by the federal government has not increased in the last thirty years. Productivity rates of many industries have not increased, but the demand for services has.

There are a number of results. One is that an economy undergoing such a shift may have difficulties competing in the world economy. Overall productivity is reduced. Further, less and less of national income is reinvested in productive industries. The industries that do continue to compete in the world economy must employ the most efficient technologies for production as well as engage in research and development that will provide new goods and create new markets. The economy in general must be strong enough to support the increase in services.

Further, there will be more and more workers whose employment will have to be reimbursed by the productivity of a smaller and smaller number in industries producing goods for the world market. This means that unless the economy is growing at a rate that can support the growth in services, competition will become increasingly sharp in *service markets.*

Further, most new employment will be in services of some sort. Unless there is a marked redistribution of resources between the public and private sectors of the economy, new employment will be largely in private sector services. The increasing proportion of the federal budget that goes for income and health services to older citizens—the Social Security System—makes the increase of resources for other services difficult in the period 1980 to 2020 as the proportion of older citizens grows and the unfunded support obligations increase drastically.

Therefore, there will be two consequences for recreation businesses. First, there is the likelihood of increased competition among recreation enterprises to attract users and purchasers. Second, such competition will be among services and goods with different activity bases and resource requirements as well as among those who seek to supply the same market. Home-based recreation items may be competing with those that are travel-related, not just tennis shops with other tennis shops and athletic-shoe stores with other footwear suppliers. Third, more people will be attracted to recreation-related business, even in such a competitive condition. And, fourth, businesses will have to be well managed to survive, even when viable markets are established.

MICROECONOMICS: A SUPPLIER'S MARKET

Several years ago John Kenneth Galbraith published an analysis of the operation of the market in an economy dominated by industrial giants that reversed the demand-and-supply flow.[19] The thesis is simple: The investment costs of producing and distributing a new product are so high that a corporation cannot afford to wait and see if there will be a demand. Also, the planning nd development time sequences require that decisions on new or enhanced products be made far in advance. Therefore, the corporation does everything possible to ensure that there will be a demand, to create a market. This is done through advertising, by controlling wholesale and retail outlets, and by a measure of control over the market structures related to the good. Such anticipation and control are not perfect. Many products of even the strongest corporations are not successful. Further, in today's world economy competing products may reach the market before production and launching costs of even an initially successful product are returned and a profit realized.

The point is that there is much more to providing a product or service at a profit than locating a latent demand and trying to fill it. Take the following simple example, video games.

CASE: DEVELOPMENT OF A MARKET

The development of the first electronic games was for the market of stores, bars, arcades, and other retail outlets. The traditional suppliers of such games, previously mechanical, dominated the markets. However, the transistor and miniaturization soon made possible consoles and programs that enabled such games to be played on the home television screen. This brought new suppliers into the market, those who had previously been manufacturers and developers of other kinds of electronic products and those who had been in the home-based game business all along.

At first the emphasis was on the appeal of particular games, usually those with established clienteles in the retail arcades. However, similar games were soon developed as substitutes. Competition developed over price as well as over the nature of the games themselves. All this time the suppliers were developing new markets, not competing for established ones. Production technologies enabled new firms to lower prices and to offer low-cost substitutes for the "name brand" games. In time consumers were no longer first-time buyers but users making decisions about the "marginal utility" of another game or console at a given price. What had originally been a process of supply creating demand moved toward a market situation in which consumer decisions gained more salience. In the process many suppliers could not compete in the new market conditions and either retrenched or gave up the business entirely.

At first a very small number of producers took a new technology—the weapons-aiming silicon chip—and created a demand. Technological improvement in both the product and the production processes allowed for price reductions and competition based on price as well as product differences. Eventually, the possibilities of a continual creation of new demand were drastically reduced and potential supply exceeded probable demand. Then firms had to make decisions about how to increase or consolidate their share of the market or to withdraw in favor of creating demand for other products.

Add to this complication the likelihood that different firms do not have the same access to capital or distribution mechanisms. The more established firm has a greater likelihood of producing its own investment capital from other lines of enterprise, a history of obtaining credit from financial institutions, and the possibility of adding to its capital by selling more shares. Further, a corporation that supplies other key goods to retailers has more leverage in getting its products on the shelves and before the consumer. Also, its brand name may create some recognition and confidence for its new product. As a result, the large corporation has any number of advantages in creating and developing markets for new products. And, when necessary, it has the capital to lease or purchase the new technology developed by a smaller and more innovative company.

MACROECONOMICS: CAPITAL AND LABOR

The concept of a market company rests on the power of the buyers collectively to create demand and govern the decisions of the suppliers. As we have seen, the producers have more power to determine the nature of the market than the theory suggests. Further, there has been a consistent development of large corporate structures in the economics of North America and Western Europe. These multinational conglomerates participate in the markets of the world by producing and distributing a variety of goods and services. By their very size and domination of some markets they have inordinate power to enter and participate in other markets.

First, they have power in obtaining labor. By the scope of their operations they can exercise local influence over labor markets as well as having access to alternative sources. If the cost of labor becomes too high in one area, they can transfer production to another state, another country, or even another continent. While such choices are limited by previous investments in plants, machinery, and training, there are alternatives possible.

Second, they have power to determine the costs of their materials because they are a major segment of the purchasing market. They can enter into long-term contracts, assist financing the development of suppliers in return for special considerations, and even become their own suppliers when it is advantageous. They thus control more and more of the production process.

Third, as already mentioned, they have access to capital in a variety of ways. They have long-established lines of credit with banks. They can use capital from one section of the corporation for investment in newer or struggling enterprises. They can go to capital markets with an established record and with vast assets. In short, they have many ways of solving that major problem of business, adequate capitalization.

Finally, in the case of major producers, they have considerable control over distribution systems and retail outlets. When an IBM or Xerox begins to consider the development of a new type of business or home computer, they begin from a completely different base than the group of electronics engineers who are thinking about forming a new company. They already know how their product will reach the markets.

Some critics of the system have added another factor. Mammoth corporations, whether a Philips in the Netherlands or Exxon in the United States, also have access to considerable political power. The various departments of the federal and regional governments tend to be closely tied to such major corporations. Personnel from the business may work for the government as advisors. Technical information about the industry comes from the corporation to the government. The corporation becomes a major factor in producing items necessary for the defense programs of the nation. Even the departments of state of the nation often have as a major aim the development of conditions that facilitate the growth of the corporations in other countries.

The result of all this is that major corporations may not operate in a "free market" economy at all. Rather they so dominate their industries that they are in a position to determine price structures, shape the markets, and reduce the possibilities of competition that will endanger their long-term interests. For those contemplating participation in any major aspect of business, especially those related to the production or distribution of goods, the race may not be exactly even. All do not have the same starting position or access to resources along the way.

POLITICAL ISSUES

One problem with any purely economic approach to understanding how any economic system works is that political and economic factors are inseparable. One major element in business decision is taxation. Without estimating the tax consequences of any decision, a business manager cannot choose between alternatives of how to raise capital, whether to replace or repair equipment, whether to sell off inventory or carry it into another tax year, calculate profit or loss on any segment of the business, or whether to expand some product line or service.

Further, the regulatory functions of the government impact business decisions in hiring personnel, disposing of waste materials, providing parking for customers, wage rates, necessary insurance, safety rules for employees, the length of time perishable items can be on the shelves, and the cost of retirement programs. More regulations have been developed because some group needed protection from others in the society. Such regulations change, and it is the responsibility of the business operator to know and adhere to regulations that affect the firm. As a result, regulations may not only add to the cost of doing business directly but also to the time required to keep up with their application, engage in required accounting, and respond to schedules for reports.

However, dealing with such regulations is only the microlevel of political impacts on business. The macrolevel is less concrete but just as important. For example, taxation policies that support consumption such as allowing income tax deduction for interest paid on consumer debt is a major factor in the purchase of durable goods and the ownership rather than rental of housing. This means that a major portion of income in the United States or any country with similar policies is likely to go into the purchase of housing, partly as an investment, and into servicing consumer debt. That leaves less discretionary income for short-term purchases and for services. It also relieves the tax burden of those able to make such purchases and to borrow. On the other hand, tax policies that support investment, such as reducing the double taxation on income that is then reinvested and gains income as interest and dividends, make the capitalization of a business easier.

Another macrolevel issue is the relative balance of the public and private sectors of the economy. A policy of relying on the market for all feasible services rather than stressing the equity and efficiency bases of public services skews resources toward those goods and services most likely to produce a return on investment. The equity basis for public services is that those resources necessary for the maintenance and development of a full life should be available to all. Therefore, basic health services, education, space for children to play in, and decent housing cannot be denied to those at the bottom of the income spectrum.

The efficiency basis of public services is closely related to equity. It is just not efficient for a private group to own and control expensive and scarce urban playing fields or beaches near a city. Resources that are used only occasionally can provide the maximum utility when publicly operated and made available to the widest possible number. Relying on the market to provide softball fields in most urban areas would mean having them stand unused while potential users had no place to play.

However, the distribution of national income to public goods and services becomes a political question. How much of the Gross National Product should be appropriated by taxation and allocated to public services? Which services take priority, health protection or higher education, the conservation of forests or the provision of water for cities, fire protection or daycare for children? Such decisions, with all their economic ramifications, are fought out in the political arenas.

A final macrolevel matter is the preservation of the system. For example, decisions as to resource allocation for daycare and university research are much easier when the economy is expanding and there is more national income to tax each year. However, the political decision about whom to tax and how much may have repercussions on the ability of the economy to grow. Without investment capital, expansion is unlikely. Without profits to turn toward research and development, gaining new world markets is unlikely. Therefore, both the viability of a national economy and the support of public sector services may require taxation policies that do not stifle investment and that encourage research and development by both private and public agencies.

Even more fundamental is the use of the state to ensure the stability of a system that provides a viable context for corporate enterprise. Major corporations doing business in other parts of the world support governmental action and inaction that promises to yield a stable context for international business. Particular arrangements for the purchase of critical materials are especially important to many international corporations. Political instrumentalities, including military forces and various forms of direct aid, are seen as the means to economic ends.

In general, the same is true for domestic policies. The basic orientation of corporate influence in the government is toward stability, the maintenance of a political-economic-social system that enables the multinational conglomerate to do business. Sometimes special conditions or support are sought by a particular industry. However, the deeper level is that the Washington representatives of banks and financial institutions, manufacturers, and distributors want the same thing, namely, system stability. As a result, their political influence tends to inhibit change unless that change self-evidently provides some long-term advantages to business in general.

ONGOING CRITICAL ISSUES

Briefly, then, four persistent issues will be introduced that have particular relevance for recreation business.

THE INVESTMENT BALANCE

Is economic return the only significant return on investment? It is possible, for example, to calculate the economic return on having a literate population that can learn economic tasks and participate in the economic processes as producers and consumers. It is possible to calculate the economic value of particular discoveries of university research centers that were supported by federal grants. There are straightforward economic arguments for many kinds of public sector spending.

Even simpler, how would goods move to markets without publicly built streets and highways, publicly dredged ports and waterways? How would health standards be maintained without a public supply of relatively pure water? It is possible to support such public sector services on purely economic grounds.

But what about the return on human investment? Can we calculate the economic value of the opportunity for a child to play, the chance for a New York City youth to have high-level training in some musical skill, the counseling that helps a mother deal with the problems related to some traumatic event, or the natural environment where a family may experience and express a different dimension of bonding? One problem with many public programs is that their results are incalculable.

In a condition of abundance, this may not be a problem. Providing access to a beach or community orchestra seems self-evidently a good, if for no other reason than that people use the opportunity. But in a condition of scarcity, when supporting one program means either less support for another or a level of taxation that lowers the supply of investment capital available for business, human investment may lose out. The balance of resource allocation too easily goes toward programs and resources with measurable economic payoff. And in the very long run, if able and creative people are the greatest resource of any society, such allocation may be very costly.

LONG- AND SHORT-TERM DECISIONS

It is not easy to start a business and keep it profitable enough to survive and grow. Many times decisions have to be made that maximize short-term gain at the possible cost of long-term development. After all, the business must have enough return to keep going in the short term or there will be no long term. However, this, too, presents problems. One is simply the difficulty of avoiding decisions that close off future potential in order to pay the bills and retain a viable credit rating. That is a business problem.

However, another problem is related to resources. What if the intensive use of a land resource for five years seriously damages its quality for 50 years? What if disposing of wastes leads to immediate solutions that are inexpensive but produces the eventual degradation of the very water resource necessary for the business? What if a decision to leave the downtown for a new shopping mall may be critical in the failure of a costly redevelopment program for the heart of a community?

A business manager may respond that there was no economic alternative. Capitalization limitations, operation costs, or being where potential clients gather may have been overriding considerations, especially when the survival of the business is in doubt. Nevertheless, the dilemma remains. And the long-term social costs of short-term business decisions may mean that others pay the bill. The costs may be borne by the "downstream children"—those who literally or figuratively must live in or with the damaged resource, the dangerous condition, or the unsafe product.

DISTRIBUTION OF INCOME AND RESOURCES

There are two sides to this issue. First, what are the long-term economic costs of having 20% of the people in a nation with income so limited that theycannot provide adequate housing, nutrition, and support for child development? Or what are the results of having over half the people in the world in such a condition? Second, what are the costs to the people themselves in their failure to become what they could be in physical, mental, emotional, and social dimensions of life? Can a condition of vastly inequitable human opportunities be accepted indefinitely on any grounds?

The economic costs of such a skewed income distribution are manifold. A major segment of the population of the nation is unable to participate fully as consumers. As a consequence, there is a reduced market for all kinds of goods. Further, the children from such families are less likely to be prepared to make the fullest possible contribution to the economy. They do not develop skills commensurate with their abilities.

When we realize such costs from having 20% of the U.S. population in a condition of relative poverty, then the magnitude of having over half the world in destitution becomes a little more comprehensible. There are stark contrasts between the few living in their secluded villas and wearing their Paris clothes and the swarms of undernourished and disease-ridden children trying to survive in the streets and fringe shacks in the cities of Asia and Latin America. Whether the contrasts are between the general standards of living of "developed" and "underdeveloped" nations or between the elites and the poor majorities within nations, the loss in human potential is incalculable.

It seems unlikely that such inequities in access to resources will continue indefinitely. In an increasingly interdependent world economic system the dispossessed will find ways to exercise their economic and political leverage to bring about change. In the meantime, until most people in the world can participate fully in their economies, economic systems will be strained to provide some minimum basis for existence for those who are not given the opportunity to contribute to the economy. And businesses and services providing recreation opportunities have only a fraction of their potential market.

QUESTIONS ABOUT PEOPLE

The disparities in income and resource distribution are only one problem related to people in contemporary economic systems. Some are also tied to the place of recreation business in the overall scheme of distribution.

One issue focuses on the possible use of recreation provisions to distract people from fundamental problems. The most common approach is to begin with the vast literature on alienation. In many ways people have been found to be cut off from much of their own potential development as beings who can create, produce, and relate to other beings. They are, at least in part, alienated from a full and productive life by social and economic structures that deny them control over their own lives. Neither their work nor their leisure is free, creative, and responsive. They are unable to relate to other persons in the fullest communication and sharing of which they are capable.

Some social critics have proposed that leisure may be one of the rewards of economic participation that obscures such a lack of freedom. Especially when leisure that can be purchased on the market—consumptive leisure—is defined as the appropriate reward for continuing alienated employment and futile political participation, then leisure may be an instrument of social control that steals rather than offers freedom.

The next phase of this argument is that the operation of the market economy reinforces such an emphasis on consumptive leisure in order to increase markets for cost-intensive products and services. Through advertising, producers attempt to convince the potential consumer that there is a direct correlation between satisfaction and money spent. Only when doing the "right" (costly) thing in the "right" place with the "right" equipment and wearing the "right" apparel can leisure be truly satisfying. If people become convinced that this is true and that they are rewarded with enough income to purchase their share of such leisure, then they are more likely to accept their place in the economic system and continue to do routinized work without protest.

In this way the system is protected from disruption by those who might recognize that they are being used for the benefit of those who gain the major benefits of the system, the investors. Workers are utilized for production and distribution tasks, rewarded with wages, and convinced that being able to purchase a set of possessions that will provide pleasure is all they might want out of life. Further, many kinds of leisure that are relatively cost-free yet yield great satisfaction—an evening walk with a friend for example—are not promoted or encouraged by such a system. Rather, the consumption aspects of leisure are consistently given prominence in all the media that communicate their messages about what is "the good life."

There is, of course, no reason why recreation businesses cannot be providers of a variety of experiences. Nor is the market always a device of manipulation. People do make choices based on past experiences of enrichment or dissatisfaction. However, the basic thrust of a business competing through the market to provide goods or services at a price is to *sell.* Any business must do enough business to recover its production costs including the cost of capitalization. Therefore, business tends to promote cost-intensive rather than cost-free leisure.

The basic human issue may be the fundamental freedom of the individual. Are we manipulated by market forces to choose leisure that is oriented toward the possession and use of *things?* Or do most people retain enough autonomy to participate in recreation markets in ways that are based on their own judgments as to the kinds of experiences that are most rewarding? Do we retain our humanity amid all the attempts to shape our behavior so that we are free enough to choose leisure that is expressive of our full beings, develops our greatest potential, and relates us to other persons in real community?

After all, recreation business is only one factor in all the forces and institutions that are brought to bear on our lives. As a single factor, one part of a business that captures about 6% of our total budget seems unlikely to be *the* factor that misdirects our freedom and robs us of our humanity. Rather, within the economic options available to us, we participate in recreation markets as we do in other markets, aware of their limitations and seeking to discover provisions that make a significant contribution to our lives. Perhaps in the long run those businesses will survive that do the best job of enabling clients to have the fullest experiences of satisfaction and community.

SUMMARY OF ISSUES

Any business exists in an economic climate that opens and closes markets, allocates resources, and defines opportunities. Economic changes alter both the profitability and viability of any business.

The American economy has developed from simplicity to complexity in dimensions of scope, production, distribution, government relations, and finance.

The theory of an economy that is self-directed through the market has been amended by a series of developments and interventions.

The theory of a worker-directed economy has also been transformed by the realities of functioning in the real economic and political world.

In even a modified market economy the potential production plans and markets are reshaped by resource limitations, the distribution of purchasing power impacted by unemployment and inflation, and the basic reward system.

No business is untouched by competition from other economies, the shift toward service sector employment, the power of corporations to create and determine markets, and political actions of taxation, regulation, and business support.

There are fundamental economic issues such as the balance between public and private sector investment, long- and short-term considerations in resource distribution, and productivity and alienation factors of labor conditions that have implications for the basic aims and opportunities of recreation businesses.

DISCUSSION QUESTIONS

1. What were the earliest recreation businesses in America? How did they develop? Look at F. R. Dulles' *A History of Recreation* for information.
2. What are the arguments for and against government regulation of business? What would happen if all regulations were abolished? Why do businesses want some regulation and government participation in the economy?
3. Why do workers who do not own or control the companies for which they work often believe that they have a stake in the system? How is leisure a factor in this belief?
4. What is the "utility" of recreation? How does demand for recreation goods differ

from the demand for food? Housing? Education? How does increased income change the demand for recreation goods?

5. What is the opportunity cost of taking time off from work for a vacation trip? Does leisure always have an opportunity cost?
6. Is household consumption a rational calculation of relative utility? Give examples that can be analyzed.
7. How would changes in distribution shifting move income to lower-income segments alter the shape of recreation business?
8. Give examples of the impacts of the supply of goods from overseas on American recreation markets. What does the future seem to hold?
9. In what kinds of recreation businesses are large corporations most able to dominate markets? Why?
10. How does the United States economic system determine the kinds of recreation resources available to different population segments?
11. Does American society have about the right balance between public and private provision of recreation resources? How would you argue for more public or market sector provisions?
12. Are market leisure resources more a source of freedom or of bondage to alienating economic participation?
13. How are consumers persuaded that costly leisure is more satisfying than cost-free leisure?
14. How free is contemporary leisure?

REFERENCES

1. Rachman, David J., and M. H. Mescon. *Business Today,* 3rd edition. New York: Random House, 1982.
2. Bettman, Otto L. *The Good Old Days—They Were Terrible.* New York: Random House, 1974.
3. Rachman and Mescon, 1982.
4. Thurow, Lester C. *The Zero-Sum Society: Distribution and the Possibilities of Economic Change,* p. 201. New York: Basic Books, 1980.
5. Smith, Adam. *The Wealth of Nations,* 1776.
6. Marx, Karl. *Capital,* 2nd edition, 1873.
7. Smith, 1776.
8. Lipsey, Richard G., and Peter V. Stein. *Economics,* 4th edition, p. 66. New York: Harper and Row, 1975.
9. Thurow, 1980.
10. Ibid., p. 5.
11. Ibid., p. 8.
12. Ibid., p. 42.

13. Pechman, Joseph A., and B. A. Okner. *Who Bears the Tax Burden?* Washington, D.C.: The Brookings Institution, 1974.

14. Duncan, Greg J. *Years of Poverty, Years of Plenty.* Ann Arbor, Mich.: Institute for Social Research, 1984.

15. Thurow, 1980:163.

16. Ibid., p. 56.

17. Rachman and Mescon, 1982:84.

18. Thurow, 1980:88.

19. Galbraith, John K. *The New Industrial State.* Boston: Houghton Mifflin, 1967.

3 BUSINESS FUNCTIONS

ISSUES

What are the functions required to operate a business?

What steps are necessary to form a business?

What are the advantages and disadvantages of partnerships and corporations?

What are the essentials of marketing? What is contributed to a business by market identification, segmentation, market research, analysis of consumer behavior, promotion, and advertising? How is the "product life cycle" important to recreation businesses?

Is there more to operations management than telling employees what to do? How does the law shape the context of doing business?

What are the main elements of short-term and long-term financing? How is accounting much more than bookkeeping?

How are computers changing business operations?

Business is that part of the economy that operates through the mechanisms of the market. Business is buying and selling, production and distribution, managing and financing. The fundamental question for this chapter is, How does business work?

Books designed to introduce students to business in North America usually run about 600 pages . . . and they are only introductions! Therefore, in these relatively few pages it is impossible to present "all you need to know about business." However, the "need to know" criterion will be applied. Before we embark on a description and analysis of various types of recreation business, what do we need to know? Just how much vocabulary and conceptual apparatus is necessary to get started?

One approach is the functional one. A *function* is an operation or task necessary for continued existence. Business functions are those operations required for the survival of the business. A business may go through a sequence of stages from inauguration through development, growth, and a variety of crises and contingencies to success or failure. In each of these stages general functions related to management and finance must be carried out. Failure to accomplish these functions will lead to the failure of the business.

In a market economy the general criterion of success is profit. Profit is not some extra reward for the lucky, skillful, or unscrupulous. Rather, in an economy in which investment comes from private sources, profit is necessary to attract capital. Capital is necessary to purchase labor and other means of production on the market. So, the rate of profit—the surplus of income over the costs of doing business—is a primary standard of business functioning.

However, there are others. Depending on the aims of the business, other criteria of success may be efficiency, worker satisfaction, or service to clients. In any case, fulfilling such aims requires a functional integration of a number of elements of finance and management. Details and illustrations of these functions for recreation businesses will be offered in chapters 4 through 14. In this chapter we will try to become familiar with some terms and concepts so basic that it is difficult even to describe a simple business without them. They will be presented under four headings:

Formation

Marketing

Operations management

Financial management

BUSINESS FORMATION

When a business is begun, an initial choice has to be made. What form of organization will be selected? There are four kinds of business organization: sole proprietorship, partnership, corporation and cooperative. Each has certain advantages and disadvantages. Once the choice is made, many other issues are determined including tax reporting, legal liabilities, borrowing procedures, property ownership, and terms of dissolution. The choice has both business and legal ramifications, so that an attorney competent in business law is usually engaged.

FORMS OF BUSINESS

Several issues are involved in the form of business. They include the identification of control, costs of formation, taxation and capitalization questions, owners' liability, and what would happen if the initial owners died or were incapacitated. Each form has somewhat different relationships with government agencies and regulatory bodies.

Sole Proprietorships Such a business is owned, financed, and operated by a single individual who has complete authority and responsibility. This is the most common form for small business, especially in retail services and agriculture. About 80% of all American businesses have this simple form. Advantages include easy formation, low costs of formation, undivided profits, direct control for the owner, maximum freedom from government regulation, no special taxation, and simplicity of dissolution. Disadvantages include unlimited liability in which the assets of the owner can be attached for business debts, difficulty in raising capital, instability in case of owner's incapacity or death, limited management, and difficulties in attracting employees. In general, the sole proprietorship has both the advantages and problems of simplicity.

Partnerships A partnership is defined as an association of two or more persons who are coowners of a business. In a *general partnership* partners share in management and profits, ownership of assets, and are subject to unlimited liability for debts and contracts. In a *limited partnership* one or more partners have unlimited liability and one or more partners have liability for debts limited to their capital contribution. Limited partnerships allow owners to raise capital by offering a share in profits to limited partners, who avoid the risk of losing assets in case of bankruptcy. A *joint venture* is a special type of partnership that is begun for a specific project and a limited period of time.

Advantages of partnerships are ease of formation, greater capital availability, the diverse skills and experience of partners, flexibility, and relative freedom from regulation. Disadvantages are the legal responsibility of partners for the acts of all partners, unlimited financial liability, the problem of stability if a partner dies or leaves, sharing profits, and difficulties of transferring partnership equity. Partnerships and proprietorships pay no income tax, but do report on the division and distribution of profits.

Corporations A corporation is a "legal person" established by the laws of a state with a charter to do business. A corporation can hold property, make contracts, and engage in legal activity. It can buy and sell, enter into binding agreements, sue and be sued, and pay taxes.

A corporation consists of incorporators, stockholders, directors, and managers. The incorporators are the organizers who establish the company, sign the charter application, decide on its name and purpose, and determine the initial amount of ownership shares. Stockholders are the owners of a proportional interest determined by the number of shares owned. Stockholders are entitled to vote at annual meetings, receive dividends when declared, elect directors, and sell or transfer their stock. Directors, elected by the stockholders, set corporate policies, elect officers, and oversee operations and finances. Managers, generally officers of the corporation, conduct the regular business of the corporation under the authority given by the directors.

There are many advantages to the corporation form of business. Owners have liability limited to the amount invested. Their personal assets cannot be seized to pay corporate debts or judgments. Ownership can be transferred and, when there is a market for the shares, sold. A corporation has stability because it is not dependent on named partners. And it can raise capital by selling more shares.

There are also disadvantages. Despite many proposals to change the system, corporations are currently subject to a corporate income tax. Since income distributed to owners is also taxed, profits are doubly taxed. Formation of a corporation is more costly and complex. Regulation is also much more complex. For example, selling stock shares requires registration with the Securities and Exchange Commission. Both federal and state regulations may require reports of transactions.

Historically, corporations have constituted about 15% of all firms doing business in the United States, but have generated over 80% of business receipts.[1] The trend toward centralization and size has continued, with corporations such as General Motors employing 750,000 in 1981 and Exxon having sales of over $100 billion. Further, conglomerates that conduct many different kinds of business under one corporate and financial structure have become more common during the 1970s. Finance is the core of such corporation policies with products and services shaped by financial goals.

Cooperatives A cooperative is an association of persons or businesses formed to obtain greater market power in buying or selling. Members of cooperatives pay an annual fee and receive a proportionate share of any profits. There are no stockholders who receive profits.

Coops may be formed to achieve economics of scale in purchasing merchandise or equipment. They may provide leverage when selling by combining the products of different firms. A cooperative may own property and do business but does not have the tax disadvantages of a corporation.

REQUISITES FOR FORMING A BUSINESS

What does it take to begin a business? First, the business has to have something to place on the market, something for which others will pay. That product, service, or "line" may be technical expertise, a new or competitive device, a different method of distribution or sale, or a service that does something that others cannot or prefer not to do for themselves. It has something to sell or rent.

Second, the business needs an idea or concept. The concept may center on the "something" to sell or on a mode of marketing. The concept should contain some special advantage that will enable it to obtain a market, to compete for money now being employed in other ways.

Third, the business requires some physical and personnel resources. It needs a place of business, a location for production and distribution. And there have to be the people who can carry out the functions of the business.

Fourth, the firm needs relationships with those outside—sources of capital, banking services, communications such as mail and telephone, suppliers, distributors, transportation, and usually accountants, advertising services, and advisors.

Fifth, there have to be clients, those who will order and purchase the service or product.

For a recreation business, the product or service is most often developed out of familiarity with a particular resource or activity. Technical know-how is more often related to recreation than to business. Therefore, the analyses that follow will give considerable attention to business functions.

Seed capital is the investment needed to cover the initial costs of developing the business. Even when time is donated by the business initiators, there are costs such as letterheads, legal advice on formation, a mailing address or location, costs of prototype fabrication and patenting for a product, needed permits and registrations, and basic equipment. That is before the start-up costs of marketing are under way. Most often seed capital comes out of the savings or assets of the founders. The biggest investment may be in opportunity costs, the time and effort not devoted to another enterprise that could yield income.

CAPITALIZATION

There is an old adage that "it takes money to make money." Actually, it takes much more, namely, a concept for a business that can reach a viable market and the organization to get the product or service to that market. However, there is almost always the need for *capital,* money invested in the business in the hope of receiving a return greater than the amount invested.

Loans from banks or other institutions usually involve reserving some assets from disposal to secure the loan. Such *collateral* may be real estate, personal property, investments, insurance, or some assets of the new business. The move from personal financing of a business to obtaining outside capital involves both risk and costs. The capital loaned will call for initial fees, usually a percentage of the loan principal, called *points,* and a repayment schedule of principal plus interest.

A second source of funds is *venture capital,* money invested in new companies by those willing to take a high risk in the hope of high profits if the business is successful. For the founders, the problem with such venture capital is that the ownership interest given is quite high in relation to the investment, perhaps a share for only $2. Further, the founders give up a share of both ownership and control to obtain the funds.

There are many reasons why new businesses fail.[2] Among the most common are starting with too little capital to launch the business, having too much capital and overspending, borrowing more than can be repaid in the time frame, not allowing for the ongoing expenses of doing business and running short of cash, giving too much credit when operating on borrowed capital, underpricing, not allowing for enough time to develop a market, and using business income for personal expenses. Note how many of the problems involve money and the costs of capital.

MARKETING

Marketing is the process of getting goods and/or services to people willing and able to pay for them. It involves the "four P's" of product, price, promotion, and placement. First, there is a product or service to market. Second, a price schedule is determined that will yield a profit. Third, promotion informs prospective customers about the product and its availability. Fourth, the product is placed or distributed to the customer.

Two styles of marketing are common. The first, *consumer orientation,* is based on identification of those people most likely to buy the product or service. When they are defined with profiles of their characteristics of age, sex, income, location, and media habits, the marketing strategy concentrates on reaching them with an attractively presented offering. The aim is to reach the consumers with what is wanted or what they can be persuaded to want.

The second, *goal orientation,* is based on the aims of the firm. Such factors as profit margins, company image, product identification, investment in technologies, and long-term product development are combined in to a marketing concept. The firm develops products consonant with its history and capacities to market at a profit-producing price with promotion that announces the values for those with whom the product is placed.

In the *marketing mix* the "four P's" are combined in a marketing program that serves the interests of the company. When a major corporation introduces a new product, it is designed to complement the production capacities of the firm. Promotion will differentiate it from other goods and bring it to the attention of the targeted consumers. Pricing from the producing company enables wholesalers and retailers to offer the product at a final price that is attractive to the identified potential consumers. The *promotional mix* consists of advertising, sales promotion through trade shows and other displays, and publicity that utilizes any news possibilities in the product and its introduction. Marketing, then, is a broad and inclusive concept that can be applied not only to selling a specified product but also to developing the image of a firm, promoting some cause or public service, and building the reputation of an institution.

MARKET IDENTIFICATION

Who are the potential consumers of a product or service? How can they be identified and contacted?

Market segmentation is the process of defining those in the population most likely to respond to the marketing. For example, the figures on hunting participation indicate that hunters are almost all male. Further, particular kinds of hunting may be divided by income categories, with the more distant and esoteric types generally reserved for those who can afford the time and financial cost of travel. Therefore, a marketing approach will utilize male-oriented images in advertising in media read primarily by males, such as newspaper sports pages and sports periodicals. Products are developed for the market segments of males under 50 years of age with pricing stratified to reach both middle- and upper-income segments. Markets in general are segmented by age, sex, income, geographic location, and, more recently, by some life-style characteristics. The markets may be segmented further according to use characteristics such as regular or occasional use, the benefits anticipated, such as health or physical attractiveness, and patterns of introduction to the product.

Market segmentation in North America depends on *demographic variables.* These are the readily available census items of age, sex, education levels, occupation, income, and household composition. For example, the once simple product of blue jeans has become highly specific with marketing from design to advertising aimed at particular age and sex classifications. Demographic analyses of nations, regions, states, cities, counties, and SMSAs (Standard Metropolitan Statistical Areas) are available in a variety of publications within a few years after each national census.

However, more and more types of market segmentation have been employed. There have been found to be different styles of travel, different orientations to television and other media, and a variety of leisure patterns. Education is an important index of many kinds of interest and taste. *Psychographics* is a set of methods for categorizing the psychological profiles of consumers in terms of their orientation to a variety of ways of investing time and money. *Identities* are those self-definitions that are developed and demonstrated in particular contexts and that lead to life-styles that involve somewhat predictable consumption patterns.[3]

Product differentiation is the process of distinguishing one firm's products or services from others. Such differentiation may be accomplished in any of the functions of marketing—by price, product, promotion, or placement: "Our exercise set costs $100 less than competing brands." "Our bass boat trolls slower and runs faster." "Our service and parts are available in all fifty states." Or some promotional slant may seek to give the impression of a difference when there is none: Pain relief product X is "pure aspirin."

Marketing positioning is the placement of a product or service in the general market. Positioning follows market segmentation or product differentiation. The product is priced or promoted in a way designed to reach a particular market segment. For example, high-end positioning is aimed at the upper-income segment and combines a high price with some aura of prestige, exclusivity, or quality. Positioning for a general purpose home computer, on the other hand, may stress availability and low price to position the product for middle-income nontechnical market segments: "The simple and affordable home computer for the entire family."

MARKET RESEARCH

Research is often required in order to identify market segments and position a product. Such research may be carried out by specialists from outside the firm, advertising agencies, or departments of the producing company. Some market research is quite simple and direct, such as examining the sales trends or observing product users. Other market research may become quite complex and sophisticated, utilizing existing literature and both primary and secondary data. The aim is to identify possible consumers of a product or service, the magnitude and characteristics of the market, and what types of appeals may be most effective.

In many fields sales trends differentiated by region and types of product are available from national trade organizations. More general economic trend information is available from publications of the federal Department of Commerce. States and even cities often have economic analyses that indicate retail sales trends by categories. Other secondary data, such as employment patterns in the trade area, housing starts and locations, and household composition, can be obtained in most public-library reference departments.

Primary data are collected directly from the source. *Secondary data* are obtained from sources such as government agencies, research bureaus, trade associations, and university research departments. The aim of market research is to put together the information needed in order to make marketing decisions. Research requires knowing what is available, what is reliable, and what requires developing primary data. Further, market research has the specific end of informing marketing decisions rather than the scientific aim of explanation. However, good science can be the basis of good market research.

Methods vary. The traditional survey of markets using some kind of self-report instrument with a representative sample of the total population is useful for exploration. Telephone surveys are probably the most common method of determining interests and consumer behavior. However, focused group discussions and psychographic analysis are often more useful for discovering just which elements of a product or service may be appealing to whom and *why*. The essence of useful market research is to know what kind of information is needed in order to develop the marketing strategy. Then, the research program can be efficient, sound, and useful.

CONSUMER BEHAVIOR

The composite decision processes and purchasing acts of people are called *consumer behavior*. The decision whether or not to buy or rent is seen as a problem-solving task. It may be ordinary and routine or singular and complex. The elements and sequences of decision are the other end of marketing, the response or lack of it to a particular marketing program.

Consumer behavior may be analyzed on two levels. Some decisions are best understood as those of individuals seeking in some way to maximize their satisfaction. Other decisions are more those of the household, a group sharing common residence and interacting regularly. The household, whether a family or not, usually engages in some consumer decisions as a unit. Food, household supplies, appliances, transportation, and other items may be bought by one person. However, that person either represents the household or takes the resources and needs of the household into account when making a decision. Therefore, considerable analysis of consumer behavior takes the household as the basic unit in the society. It may be a more accurate approach for washing machines and automobiles than for recreation equipment or entertainment.

The problem-solving approach to consumer behavior may be quite complex. A decision about a vacation trip involves the schedules, past experiences, social attachments, recreational skills, interest hierarchies, and financial resources of all involved—usually a family or other group of intimates. Some kind of sequential decision tree may be adopted formally or informally in order to sort out all the factors that have to be considered. Further, the vacation decision for a household often takes place over a considerable period of time.

At the other extreme are the routine purchases that are almost reflex actions. Some kind of "brand loyalty" may combine with frequent purchase so that pulling a familiar package off a shelf is done almost without thought. Probably most common are the consumer decisions that are limited by resources and availability and shaped by some past purchases and decisions but do call for some investigation and even comparison of products.

Marketing, then, is the function of getting a product to the consumer. The exchange process in a market economy involves decisions made by both producing firms and consuming households and individuals. The producer will usually develop a marketing strategy that identifies target markets for products or services that fit the capabilities and aims of the company. Marketing involves the entire process of bringing the product to the purchaser.

ADVERTISING AND PROMOTION

Promotion is the process of informing and persuading target markets about a product or service. Along with advertising, the *promotional mix* includes retail selling, use of informational and news media for publicity, and any other techniques that call attention to the product. In some cases, the key to promotion is at the retail level with such elements as placement of stock, window displays, community promotional projects, and institutional relationships. The general visibility and reputation of retail outlets may be more important than the product itself.

The promotional mix differs with products that depend heavily on corporate image— "It's a Sony!"—and new products of firms with little established reputation. The nature of the product, the composition of the market segments, and the costs of promotion are all factors in deciding on a promotion strategy. However, in almost every promotional program, advertising takes some part.

Major corporations that market consumer-oriented products may spend half a billion dollars a year on advertising. In 1980 over forty corporations spent over $100 million apiece on advertising.[4] Such a commitment indicates that there is a powerful belief in the necessity of advertising in a mass market economy.

There are many kinds of advertising. *Institutional advertising* is designed to create a favorable image for the company itself. *Advocacy advertising* attempts to persuade about some issue that is of importance to the firm. *Pioneer advertising* introduces and announces a new product or service. *Comparative advertising* in some way stresses the superiority of one product over others. The appeals of advertising are manifold: endorsements of experts or celebrities, association with attractive environments or people, statistics of use or quality, comparative tests, repetition of slogans or phrases to grind into the memory, humor and the use of quaint characters, sex appeal, tapping emotions of personal inadequacy or the need for change, fear and anxiety including dread of death, social success or embarrassment, and so on.

Advertising, whether in print media or electronic, has aims of credibility, information, attraction, timing, and attention. Its aim is to contribute to a directed decision in the consumer-behavior process. However, advertising is only one element in marketing and of no value unless all the functions are fulfilled.

THE PRODUCT LIFE CYCLE

In recreation there have been a number of fads in the past years, products or activities that gained considerable media attention and participation in a short

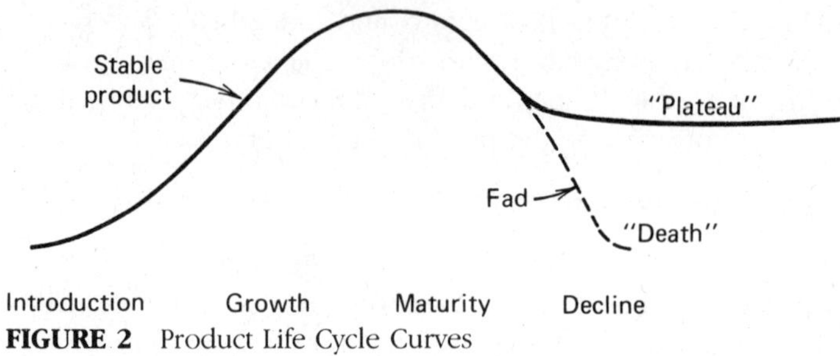

FIGURE 2 Product Life Cycle Curves

time and then waned as rapidly. In marketing some sort of *product life cycle* has been found to be common for almost any commodity. A product will be introduced, have a period of growth in sales, a time of maturity, and decline. The length of the periods may vary greatly. A fad has a rapid growth period and short maturity, followed by a quick decline to death. A product that fits into consumer use patterns better will have a relatively long maturity and then decline to a plateau of use rather than fall to oblivion.[5]

The aims of marketing strategies change through the product life cycle. During introduction the main aim is to develop outlets and announce the existence of the product. Since most of the profit will be obtained during the growth and maturity periods, distribution and advertising seeking to widen markets will characterize the growth period. During maturity marketing costs may be reduced to maximize profits. Another strategy is to position the product in the overall market to minimize decline. The marketing aim during decline is to identify and stabilize consistent markets so that a plateau will be reached at a viable level of production. There will be an attempt to foster "brand loyalty," differentiate the product from its competition, and solidify distribution systems.

OPERATIONS MANAGEMENT

There are four functions of *management* as well as of marketing. They are planning, organizing, directing, and controlling. In a business these are the organizational tasks necessary to carry out the objectives of the firm. They may be simple and unified in a small proprietorship and beyond comprehension in a massive conglomerate. However, the development of an organization that can accomplish the aims of the business still is required if the inaugural concept is to yield a long-term profit.

PLANNING

The objectives of a business seem simple: to establish a market for a product or service and to deliver the product at a profit-producing price. However, the specific goals change through various stages of the development of a firm just as marketing aims change through the product cycle.

Planning usually begins with a general purpose related to the kind of business being developed. The purpose consists of *objectives,* the broad or general goals of the organization, and *policies,* the guidelines according to which the objectives are to be realized.

In the short term, management consists of procedures, practices, rules, and budget.[6] *Procedures* instruct employees as to what to do in given circumstances. *Practices* are more general methods for dealing with particular problems. *Rules* are the prescribed procedures for a specified situation. A *budget* is a financial plan that allocates resources of the firm for a period of time.

Planning is looking ahead, anticipating decisions, developing needed resources, avoiding problems, and setting policies. It is preparation for what is to come. Planning may focus on different organization tasks at different periods in the life of a business. Getting a service established and announced calls for planning different from dealing with the personnel and financial requirements of a growth period. In general, *planning* is that operation that ties together the goals of a company with its operations for a period in the future.

ORGANIZING

Once goals are set and general plans outlined, the structures have to be in place to carry out the plans. *Organizing* is the process of arranging resources, including personnel, in a functional and consistent structure. An organization needs to be flexible and responsive to change. However, it is necessary that tasks and responsibilities be assigned, decision-making authority designated, and communication channels understood.

The *division of labor* is the assignment of tasks and authority within an organization. It may be task based, with the operations of production, sales, distribution, and management designated to specified persons or offices. Complex tasks are divided for efficiency or to minimize training in multiple skills. Carrying this to extreme means that employees become replaceable units of production. Or the division of labor may be authority based and defined by the power granted to make and carry out decisions. *Authority* is the power granted within the organization to "do things." It is recognized and stable.

There are a number of approaches to the personnel organization of a business. In the early days of industrialization, task division was developed to increase productivity for the factory. However, more recently there have been questions about the long-term effectiveness of rigid divisions and quite specific tasks. One proposal is that workers have more control over their jobs with some authority to shape the particulars of their working situation. There is also the attempt to coordinate tasks so that workers have some sense of accomplishment, of producing something from beginning to end. There are quality-of-life approaches that involve workers in limited decision making. There are theories that stress the attachment of the worker to the firm, its goals, and its community of employees. However, in the end the purpose seems to be that of Adam Smith's first division of labor: greater productivity or output per worker.

The purpose of organization is to "get the job done." Organization by definition is to be functional. Procedures and rules may be mitigated by a variety of lines of communication within an organization to build commitment to goals and to increase flexibility. However, organizing is for a purpose, the creation of consistent ways of directing and doing the tasks required for the business.

DIRECTING

Directing is the function of getting personnel to do their jobs, to carry out their tasks within the organization. Direction consists of two functions: motivating and leading. *Motivation* is instilling an attitude of willingness within the workers, giving them reasons to do the work. *Leading* is the means of demonstrating how the tasks are to be done.

There are several leadership styles. Each has implications for motivation in the organization. An *autocratic* style uses authority to require compliance with directives. It can be quite efficient, but often at the cost of worker commitment and contributions. A *democratic,* or participatory, style involves personnel in decision making and stresses two-way communication. Willingness and maximum contribution of ideas and energies are the advantages but may be countered by slowness and confusion as to decisions and lines of authority. *Laissez-faire* leadership is a style of cooperation and consultation that puts aside authority of office and positions. It is often more effective at stimulating ideas than carrying them out.

Motivation is more complex than merely leading. What are the most successful ways to instill in others a commitment to their share of the total work of an organization? Leadership style is one factor. Having some autonomy within the work setting is another. Seeing some connection between what one does and an outcome of value to others is a third. Communication and companionship on the job is a fourth. Giving a sense of contribution, being valued, and being part of a team are others. However, the reward structure is still central to motivation. People seek the rewards of prestige and financial gain, factors in motivation for which there is seldom any adequate substitute. As a consequence, the organizational structure of a business is a basis for motivation as well as accomplishing business tasks.

CONTROLLING

Control in a business organization is the process of measuring the extent to which objectives are being met and taking actions to correct deficiencies or deviations. Within an organization there are *standards,* measurable objectives for units of the business or for individuals. In a rational organization these standards are known and agreed on in advance of performance.

Standards for sales may be set in dollar volume per month. Standards for production may be so many "widgets" per hour. In order for the manager to evaluate according to those standards, there must be some *feedback* or information system that accurately records and reports on performance. When the information is received and processed, control calls for a response to the employee. The manager may inform, warn, discipline, penalize, encourage, or dismiss the worker. Or some action may be taken that enables the employee to work more effectively. Leadership merges with control when the manager seeks to understand the reasons for failure to meet standards and to implement actions to correct the problems.

WHO ARE THE MANAGERS?

Managers are those in an organization with the authority to make and implement decisions. In a complex firm there may be hierarchy of management. Top managers make and implement policy. Operating managers supervise the functions of a particular area or function of the firm. Middle managers implement policy and supervise operations managers in a more complex organization.

Management calls for a number of skills. There are technical skills, those necessary to carry out the functions of the position. There are human relations skills of communication and cooperation with others. There are conceptual skills of understanding the processes of planning and management and of developing strategies for uniting goals and methods into a cohesive process.

A number of approaches to management are in the business administration literature. There are *scientific* approaches that present a rationalized set of techniques to accomplish the objectives of the firm. there are *systems* approaches that stress functional organization, lines of authority and communication, and flows of information. There are approaches that emphasize the personal style and charisma of the manager. In any specific situation it is likely that an effective management approach is a blend of the requirements of the particular organization with a systematic and functional structure, a viable means of communication and assessment with the personal style of leaders, consistency with flexibility, and long-term planning with day-to-day attention to operations.

MANAGEMENT AND THE LAW

In every society business is carried on within the framework of law. Laws effecting business operations are varied and complex. They differ from state to state as well as from country to country. However, it is important at least to be conversant with the types of law that permit and regulate how business may be conducted.

First, there is the *common law* that is based on the decisions of the courts rather than established by legislative action. *Statutory law,* on the other hand, is written and enacted by local, state, or federal legislative bodies. When there is conflict between common law and statutory law, the statute *as interpreted by the courts* prevails.

Among the types of law that impinge on the management of a business are the following:

The Uniform Commercial Code A form of statutory law that has been adopted in every state but one to facilitate doing business in more than one jurisdiction.

Contracts An exchange of promises that is enforceable by law. In a contract an offer is made and accepted under the principle of mutual acceptance and some item of value or consideration is given by each party competent to enter into a contract. The form of the contract has to be in a legal form and the conditions subject to law.

Breach of contract A breach occurs when a contract agreement is broken. In case of breach, there may be a discharge from contractual terms, damages awarded as a result to loss to one party, or specific performance required of the party not fulfilling the terms.

Agency In agency law one party authorizes another to act in his or her behalf. The *agent* has legal power to enter into contracts for the person or organization making the authorization. Written authorization is called *power of attorney.*

Tort law A *tort* is a noncontractual act resulting in injury to a person, property, or reputation for which there is legal right to compensation. Libel, for example, is injury to another's character or reputation. In *product liability* a business is responsible for damages done by its product or service even though there was no negligence or knowledge of the potential danger. *Negligence* is failure to exercise reasonable precautions against damage or injury to others.

Property law Property law includes two types of documents related to real property. A *deed* grants legal interest in real property. A *lease* grants use of the property for a period of time. A lease is granted by the owner or landlord to the tenant, who may then use the property according to the terms of the lease. In the transfer of ownership, *title* or legal possession of the property is given by one party to another in exchange for some consideration. A *sale* occurs when title is transferred from one owner to another, from vendor to buyer, at the time consideration is received by the vendor.

Bankruptcy This is the legal procedure in which a business or person, unable to meet financial obligations, receives a court judgment ending those obligations and dividing assets among creditors. Bankruptcy proceedings initiated by creditors are called *involuntary bankruptcy.* In the more common *voluntary bankruptcy,* a person or business can be declared bankrupt if liabilities exceed assets and total debt is over $1,000. Under one provision of bankruptcy law, a firm unable to meet its obligations can be reorganized under court order without relinquishing ownership of its assets or control of the business. Bankruptcy is then utilized as a method of getting a new start with a business that has become overextended financially but still has a viable market for its product or service.

FINANCIAL MANAGEMENT

Finance is a management function, that of obtaining and using money. A business firm deals in *revenues,* the money income received from sales and rentals. However, some money is also obtained by sharing ownership through the sale of *stock,* or shares of ownership, and by borrowing money or *credit.*

The functions of financial management involve both finance and controls. *Financial planning* is necessary so that revenues and expenditures can be predicted and held in some balance. Tax management involves estimating tax obligations and implications for business decisions and actions. *Custody* of company funds, credit and collection activities, insurance against risks, and financial relations with creditors and investors are other finance functions.

Control functions require a number of records and reports. *General accounting* is the formal record of a firm's assets and liabilities. *Cost accounting* is a full record of expenses. *Internal audits* verifying financial records are conducted regularly, and *external audits* by accountants outside the firm are completed at least once a year. *Planning and budgeting* involves a systematic anticipation of expenses and revenues.

Assets are all items of value owned by the firm including money, real property, equipment, stock, and other tangible goods. Intangible assets such as a brand name or patents are included in accounting reports if salable. *Liabilities* are the money, goods, or services the firm owes other businesses or persons. Liabilities include both long and short-term debts. *Owners' equity* is the portion of assets remaining when all debts have been satisfied.

SHORT-TERM FINANCE

Short-term finance is usually defined as all financial business to be completed in a year or less. *Long-term finance* involves time periods of more than one year.

A key concept in short-term finance is *cash flow,* the total amount of money, both income and expenditures, needed to operate a business over a period of time. Cash flow predictions are critical because a negative cash flow for more than 30 days may require the business to borrow to meet obligations. And, of course, borrowing adds to the cost of doing business.

Current assets are those that can be exchanged for cash in a year or less. They include cash, savings and other deposits, and accounts receivable. Accounts receivable, the money owed the firm for goods or services purchased and delivered, are often discounted a percentage for the likelihood of bad debts.

Liquidity is a measure of the speed with which current assets can be turned into cash. Some kinds of securities are almost as liquid as cash. On the other hand, real estate held for long-term appreciation can be converted into liquidity only at a loss in potential gain.

Several short-term finance problems revolve around the fact that "money costs money." To borrow, often through a *line of credit* at a bank in which the company may borrow up to a certain amount and repay at any time, can be quite expensive. Interest rates on line-of-credit borrowing tend to be high. On the other hand, a business that must incur considerable cost to build up an inventory to sell or to prepare equipment for a later service will have to borrow unless previous revenues have put it in a strong cash position. Capital, the money for doing business, may be a major cost.

There are many sources of short-term financing:

1. *Trade credit* such as open-book accounts in which payment is delayed for goods received and promissory notes stating terms of future payment.
2. *Financial institution loans* such as unsecured and secured bank loans and the sale of accounts receivable. Loans may be secured through a personal pledge of repayment or the pledge of assets such as real estate, equipment, or inventory.
3. *Investor loans* such as "commercial paper," the direct borrowing from or through financial sources such as investment funds or individuals. Usually only large and well-established firms are able to raise capital in this way.

The most common sources are open-book credit in which payment for goods is delayed and institutional loans secured by some assets of the company. When such loans are unpaid, the collateral promised as security can be seized by the loaning institution. When accounts receivable are the collateral, the bank will have to notify those whose debts are payable before collecting directly. When loans are unsecured, they are based on the general business history of the firm borrowing and usually require that a proportion of the loan amount remain on deposit in the loaning institution.

LONG-TERM FINANCE

For a business to function over a period of time, it must have capital. Some capital is obtained from *undistributed profits,* the excess of revenues over expenses from previous years. Corporations also obtain capital by selling bonds, known as *debt capital,* and by selling stock, called *equity capital.*

Bonds are certificates representing the loan of money to the issuing firm and stating the terms of repayment and interest. A bond consists of an amount borrowed, the *principal;* a rate of interest paying the bondholder for the use of the money at a fixed or variable rate; and a *maturity date,* when the company must repay the principal. Bonds may be secured with particular real estate, equipment, or mortgages. Unsecured bonds, also called *debentures,* are based on the general credit of the company. A recent trend has been to offer bonds at interest rates that vary with some standard such as the interest rate of U.S. Treasury securities.

Stocks, shares of ownership in the corporation, are also major sources of capital. A stockholder owns a share of the company that is a proportion of all stock issued and evidenced by a stock certificate. The maximum number of shares that can be issued is the *authorized stock*. *Issued stock* are those shares sold and held by stockholders. Profits distributed to shareholders are called *dividends*. *Preferred stock* has priority in the payment of dividends distribution of assets but generally does not include full voting rights in the corporation. *Common stock* is voting stock, but holders of common stock received dividends only after preferred stockholders have received their distribution. That is, common stock has a *residual right,* or last claim, on profit distribution and on assets in case the corporation is dissolved. Stockholders have two sources of return on their investment, dividends and capital appreciation when the firm is successful and the value of shares increases.

SMALL-BUSINESS FINANCE

What are the elements in the finance plan of a small business? A brief introduction may place the various parts of the function in an integrated perspective.

Gaining and Managing Capital A business, usually a retailing firm of some sort, will gain part of its operating capital through *trade credit*. Furnishings and equipment may be provided by a dealer who offers some extended payment terms at low interest. Once paid for, such equipment may be used as collateral for a modest loan to assist with operating expenses and cash flow. Cash flow conditions are enhanced by offering a discount price to customers who pay cash on delivery. Once a business is operating, many suppliers will offer a line of credit—up to 90 days to pay for goods. On the other hand, a firm may take advantage of discounts and pay cash during periods of a positive cash flow.

Short-term bank loans are a necessity for most businesses. Therefore, the banker is usually consulted and informed about the development of the business. Having security even for short-term loans will reduce the interest rates and often the "points," or initial costs, of obtaining the loan. Obtaining loans requires submitting complete financial statements and often marketing plans to the bank. A demonstration of sound planning and stability may be as important as collateral in obtaining a loan. The line of credit, or maximum the bank will loan during the year, is not only a method of handling uneven cash flow but also a means of establishing a reputation of reliability with financial institutions.

Small businesses seldom issue stock at first. More often, personal savings are invested and capital is borrowed by putting assets of the owners at risk. Home mortgages may be rewritten to provide initial capital. Life insurance can be a source of borrowed funds. The key to establishing a business and keeping it operational is financial planning that anticipates capital requirements as well as operating expenses and is realistic about both the amount and timing of revenues.

FINANCIAL CONTROL: ACCOUNTING

Accounting is more than just financial record keeping; it is an instrument of control and assessment for the financial management of a business. Considerable accounting is accomplished by employees who use accepted accounting procedures to produce a firm's financial records. However, *public accountants* are employed from outside the firm to provide a number of accounting services. Among these are independent audits of finances, tax return preparation and advice, consultation on accounting systems and procedures, assistance with loan applications and securities registration, and the design of accounting systems. A *private accountant* is employed directly by a firm with the task of providing information to the managers. *Certified public accountants* (CPAs) have met the standards of a state and are designated as competent for certain independent review and evaluation functions such as corporate audits.

Accounting procedures include a number of operations. The basic recordkeeping functions include recording data on income and expenditures, posting data on transactions to the proper accounts, and making the consequent adjustments to those accounts. Such procedures are usually termed *bookkeeping* and may be performed by anyone trained in the procedures.

Reporting the transactions and their consequences involves preparing trial balances, financial statements, income statements, balance sheets, and reports of financial position alterations.

A *trial balance* is a display of financial transactions for a period that is used to sort and classify receipts and expenditures and other business exchanges.

The *balance sheet* shows what a firm owns, assets, and what the firm owes, liabilities. An *income statement* displays profit or loss over a period. Also, a *statement of changes in financial position* may be produced to summarize shifts in capital positions.

Assets, anything owned by a business, include *fixed assets,* which are long-term, and current assets. The basic *accounting equation* is assets = liabilities + owners' equity.

Double-entry bookkeeping is based on the accounting equation. Every transaction or exchange requires two entries, one to record a *debit,* which shows an increase in assets and a decrease on the side of liabilities and owners' equity, and one to record a *credit,* which decreases assets and increases liabilities or owners' equity. For example, when a firm purchases equipment, a debit pair of entries record the asset increase and also increased liability of the price owed for the purchase, resulting in a decreased owners' equity.

Most businesses keep some type of *general journal,* the initial recording of transactions in chronological order. A *general ledger* takes the journal entries and categorizes them according to *accounts* such as cash, sales, salaries, accounts receivable, and others. Recording the data is called *posting*. Frequently the general journal and ledger are today being replaced by some form of electronic processing that incorporates the transaction data into an accounting program. Such a program is able to produce a *balance sheet* in printed form ("hard copy") that summarizes the financial position of the firm.

An *income statement* is a summary of revenue and expense activities over a given period of time. *Revenues* are all the receipts from sales and rentals, interest earnings, royalties, and dividends. Expenses include the *operating expenses* of marketing costs and the expenses of delivering products or services and *administrative expenses* of salaries, depreciation of equipment and furniture, office supplies, rent, insurance, and interest paid. The "bottom line" of the income statement records *net profit after taxes,* the amount the firm has made or lost during the period.

Accounting has a number of functions. It is required for tax reporting and for a yearly accounting to shareholders of corporations. Further, it is necessary in order to report the financial state of the business to any interested parties. However, its most central function is for the business itself. Accounting is a method of analyzing and assessing the financial state of a business so that the business can be managed to yield a return on its investments of capital and labor.

COMPUTERS AND DATA PROCESSING

Many operations and financial management functions are now carried out with the assistance of computers. The details of computer and microprocessor prices, capabilities, sizes, and programs change almost by the month. There are two possibilities for the smaller business. The first is to purchase a small computer with a set of programs that can be readily adapted to such functions as inventory control, payroll, tax computation, and accounting. The second is to subscribe to a service that uses somewhat more complex computers to supply similar services to a number of firms. The decision as to which approach is better depends on the computer interests and skills of the business managers, the tasks that need to be done, local availability of services, and relative costs.

What Computers Do A *computer* is an electronic machine that can store and sort information, both quantitative and verbal, perform a variety of arithmetic, and mathematical manipulations with quantitative data, and assemble and analyze nonquantitative data. The speed, capacities, and availability of computers have increased geometrically since the introduction of UNIVAC in 1951. *Information processing* has now become a prime growth industry in its own right as well as an invaluable tool for other businesses and institutions. The major change in the 1980s has been miniaturization with the use of the microchip, which contains thousands of circuits on minute bits of silicon. Because of the greater availability, portability, and lowered costs, there is now a new generation in the work force to whom the computer is as familiar an instrument as was the book to previous generations.

The functions of a computer are fivefold: input of data, storage of data, control of processing, processing, and output of information. The computer *hardware* consists of input devices such as terminals, processing units including a central processing unit (CPU), output devices such as printers for "hard copy," and storage units of *memory* such as tape and disk drives. *Software* consists of the devices that instruct the hardware to perform any operations. Computer software introduces *programs* of integrated processing instructions through *languages* of instruction that are translated into the *machine language* that controls the hardware processing.

Batch processing utilizes programs that receive groups of categorized data, and performs a sequence of operations. *On-line modes* directly link the user to the computer with processing done at that time through interactive input and output devices. *Time-sharing* is the sharing of one computer by several users with multiple input devices in a system through which the user pays for computer time actually used.

The most common input/output device is the *terminal,* which transmits messages to the computer and receives messages in return. A "hard-copy" terminal is like a typewriter, and a cathode-ray-tube (CRT) terminal is like a television screen. However, information may also be submitted from card readers, magnetic tapes, and magnetic disks.

The central processing unit (CPU) is directed by its machine language to process data according to a system of arithmetic logic. The CPU also contains a *main memory* to store the data being processed as well as systems of instruction. The basic storage unit is called a *bit,* which is combined into units called *bytes* representing numbers or letters. A "K" is 1024 bytes of information. Computers use a binary counting system in which the basic symbols are simply 0 and 1.

Communication with the computer is through *job control language* (JCL), which connects the processing unit with the applications programs. *Applications programs* that direct the actual operations called for are in a variety of "languages" such as FORTRAN, BASIC, COBOL, PASCAL, ADA, and others.

Business Use of Computers What will computers do for the business? Essentially, they process information at a high rate of speed. The major advantage is that once data is in the memory of a computer programmed to complete certain operations, an incredible number of things can be done with that information. Comparisons, statistical analyses, the combining and recombining of items of information in any number of schemes, and retrieval of past data can be accomplished in minutes once the data are entered and the programs are in place.

The computer can store, categorize, and display many kinds of information that the manager may need for planning (*data management*). Data can be stored in small spaces and retrieved in seconds, rather than being locked away in the stacks of file cabinets in the back of an old store room.

Management applications include personnel records, production and inventory control, payroll, and scheduling the sequences of operations in a complex production or marketing operation.

Marketing applications are especially useful in complex pricing decisions as well as evaluating the return from various promotional programs and advertising investments.

Financial and accounting applications include paying bills, managing accounts receivable, budgeting, and virtually everything that involves the manipulation of numbers. The ongoing accounting system of a firm can be computerized so that any information needed for current decisions can be retrieved at any time rather than waiting for monthly reports. The computer makes accounting even more of a decision-making tool than traditional methods. Break-even analysis, cash flow calculations and projections, and all sorts of ratio analyses can be programmed into the records system to enable a manager to know more in an hour than was previously available from an accounting service once a year.

SUMMARY OF ISSUES

The main forms of business include sole proprietorship, partnership, corporation, and cooperative. Each has a number of advantages and disadvantages.

Beginning a business requires something to market, a concept, physical and personnel resources, outside relationships, clients, and capital.

Marketing—delivering goods or services to those who will pay—involves the four P's of product, price, promotion, and placement.

Market research may identify those market segments that are the most likely clients for products or services. Research into consumer behavior can specify the decision processes and factors in purchasing of such market segments.

Advertising is only one element in promotion, informing and persuading target markets about a product or service.

The product life cycle varies for different goods, so that marketing strategies change in periods of introduction, growth, maturity, and decline.

Operations management includes planning, organizing, direct-

ing, and controlling. The division of labor requires that personnel be prepared, directed, and motivated in ways that carry out the functions of the business.

Contract, agency, tort, property, and bankruptcy are only some of the types of law that provide a framework of doing business.

Finance is the function of obtaining and using money. A firm plans, manages, and records revenues, expenditures, credit, and capitalization through systems of accounting.

Accounting not only records but also controls and assesses the finances of a business in accordance with accepted procedures.

Computers may perform a variety of data management tasks for a business, including personnel and payroll records, production and inventory control, scheduling, pricing, budgeting, and many kinds of analysis on a demand basis.

DISCUSSION AND EXERCISES

Use the following terms in an account of a recreation business operation in such a way that the meaning of the term or terms is illustrated:

Business Formation

Sole proprietorship
Partnership
Limited partnership
Corporation
Stockholders
Directors
Cooperatives
Liability
Seed capital
Capitalization
Venture capital
Loan

Marketing

Consumer orientation
Marketing mix
Promotional mix
Market segmentation
Product differentiation
Market positioning
Market research
Consumer behavior
Promotion
Advertising
Pioneer advertising
Product life cycle
Demographic variables
Primary data
Secondary data
Household
Brand loyalty

Operations Management

Planning
Organizing
Authority
Property law
Procedures
Budget
Contracts
Agency
Product liability

Directing
Control
Managers
Common law
Statutory law
Tort law
Division of labor
Productivity
Motivation
Lending
Standards
Feedback
Deed
Lease
Title
Sale
Bankruptcy
Negligence

Financial Management

Finance
Custody
Control
General accounting
Cost accounting
Short-term finance
Long-term finance
Capital
Revenue
Credit
Audits
Operating expenses
Hardware
On-line
Budgeting
Public accountants
Bookkeeping
Balance sheet
Income Statement
Fixed Assets
Double-entry bookkeeping
Assets
Liabilities
Owners' equity
Cash flow
Administrative expenses
Software
Time-sharing
Current assets
Liquidity
Line of credit
Collateral
Bonds
Debentures
Stock
Dividends
Trade credit
Credit
Debit
Computer
Programs
"Language"

REFERENCES

1. Gitman, Lawrence J., and Carl McDaniel, Jr. *Business World,* p. 59. New York: Wiley, 1983.
2. Rachman, David J., and Michael H. Mescom. *Business Today,* p. 101. New York: Random House, 1982.
3. Kelly, John R. *Leisure Identities and Interactions.* London and Boston: George Allen and Unwin, 1983.
4. Gitman and McDaniel, 1983:303.
5. Udell, Jon G., and G. R. Laczniak. *Marketing in an Age of Change,* p. 272. New York: Wiley, 1981.
6. Rachman and Mescom, 1982:125.

4 RETAIL RECREATION SUPPLIERS I

ISSUES

What are the most common problems for retail recreation businesses?

How does the business concept lay the basis for a new business?

How do established and created markets offer business opportunities?

What are the main start-up costs for a retail business?

What are the critical factors in selecting a location?

What are the advantages of a franchise?

How can new markets be identified?

What are the dimensions of a viable trading area?

How can a recreation fad be recognized?

Where is inexpensive market research information available?

The first line in the overall spectrum of recreation businesses is the retail suppliers of goods and services. In this chapter we will begin to examine the businesses that provide recreation equipment and related services in the local community. Some specialize in retail sales, some in services, and some combine the two. Some retail recreation suppliers concentrate on equipment for one activity such as camping, while others offer products over a wide range of sports, arts, and other types of activity. Some are dealers for a particular brand, and others stock a number of competing brands. Some are part of a chain of stores, some are franchised outlets, and others are locally owned and operated. What they have in common is the retail sale of recreation supplies, equipment, apparel, or product-related services.

In chapter 6 we will introduce activity centers that offer opportunities to participate in some activity, learn skills, and use special equipment or facilities. We will not include here the sale of food and beverages except as an auxiliary part of a recreation business. Although restaurants, bars, nightclubs, and refreshment stands are often leisure locales serving people who have chosen to come with orientations and aims that reflect social leisure more than nourishment, they are a special kind of business and cannot be given adequate treatment in a book focusing on recreation.

A study by the U.S. Department of Commerce analyzed the relative size of a number of kinds of retail business. Among them were a number of recreation supply categories:[1]

These 1972 percentages may have changed in the last decade. Sporting goods and games would show some increase in their share of personal spending as well as gross dollar volume. As indicated in chapter 1, the dollar volume increase from 1960 to 1980 has been rapid in several categories: 560% for non-durable toys and sports supplies and 750% for durable sports goods, toys, wheel goods, boats, and aircraft. During the 1970s retail growth in recreation-related product sales was especially strong. On the other hand, the total proportion of

TABLE 4-1 Relative Size of Recreation Merchandise Categories

Type of retail outlet	Percent of personal income spent in category	Percent of annual total retail sales
Radio, TV and music	0.3	1.0
Eating and drinking places	2.6	8.0
Florists	0.7	2.2
Sporting goods and bicycles	0.1	0.6
Book stores	0.5	0.2
Hobby, toy and games	0.4	0.2
Camera and photo supply	0.4	0.2

personal income spent directly on recreation and leisure has not changed drastically but has remained at about 6–7%. Recreation is a substantial segment of the total economy. However, it is divided into many different kinds of goods and services. The variety in leisure interests and investments is reflected by the diversity of recreation retailing at the community level.

The Small Business Administration prepared a special report on outdoor recreation and tourism enterprises in 1974.[2] The report focused on retail sales and service businesses, most of which are small businesses. The report outlined a number of problems that impact such businesses:

1. *Capital* Recreation businesses face the common difficulty of all small firms, obtaining adequate capital. They may not be able to get long-term financing at all or must pay extremely high rates for loans when they are obtained. They are often judged a poor credit risk by local lending institutions.
2. *Seasonality* Many recreation activities are seasonal, so that the selling season is short. This problem may be compounded by sensitivity to weather conditions and environmental changes.
3. *Management* The report asserts that recreation businesses are often poorly managed. In a small business the quality of management is crucial to success. Owner-operators more interested in the recreation activity than the business may not devote the attention required for good management. The study found that between 20% and 30% of such businesses were operating at a loss. For the others, the average margin of profit was about 5% of gross sales as compared to 10% for firms not in outdoor recreation and tourism.

There is no universal and sure-fire model for business success. However, the establishment and operation of any business calls for the fulfillment of a number of business functions. Such functions provide the framework of the analysis of recreation retailing. In order, we will introduce the business concept, formation, product development, marketing plans, market research, operations management, financial management, and dealing with change. One type of retail business, a sporting goods store, will be used as an example as we go through the outline. Other cases will be included to illustrate various problems and approaches. However, the process of building a viable retail business is always specific to the particular products and services, the market area, and the composition of the population whose recreation is the basis for the business. Further, different styles of retail management may prove successful when they fit the style of the manager and the culture of the community.

THE CONCEPT

The beginning of a business is an idea, a clue about the potential fit between the product or service to be offered and the interests of a number of people in the area to be served. In the case of a retail supplier, the concept will usually take form when some product or service needed for recreation participation is seen as difficult to obtain.

The concept for a retail business may be based on an established market or a created one. An *established market,* say, for sports or arts equipment or bicycle repairs, already exists in current participation. Further, there is already available some source of retail supply. The concept for a new business may be that the supply is inadequate, that the market can be enlarged by a new business, or that a different approach will enable another supplier to secure a viable share of the market. In an established market the concept becomes primarily one of marketing, of a better way.

A *created market* is one that does not now exist. It will come into being only when the concept is developed and implemented. A new product will be so appealing that customers will buy it and employ it in their recreation. The market may be created by a new resource such as a nearby reservoir that makes possible several kinds of boating that previously could be engaged in only after a long trip. Or some combination of promotion and services will facilitate participation in some recreation activity that is now perceived as too costly or difficult by most potential participants. The created-market concept is the most difficult to assess but may also present the best opportunity in an area where traditional recreation-related retailing is well established.

In recreation retailing, location is a primary determinant of the type of business. Some retailing takes place at the point of origin, the residential community. Community retailing usually concentrates on supplying goods and services for local participation. However, increasingly the special needs of those who leave the local area for some form of recreation are met at home. Backpackers, skiers, boaters, campers, and others prefer to prepare for the trip at home, where they can obtain service, have an ongoing relationship with the supplier, and obtain recourse in case of some product failure. Further, they can shop more carefully, spread equipment purchases over a longer period of time, and enjoy the leisure experience of planning and purchasing for anticipated recreation.

On the other hand, resort or use-area recreation retailing at the participation site presents quite a different set of opportunities and limitations. The resort retailer has a kind of captive market, but only for a short time. At the use-area store the customer will come for convenience "I forgot" items, lost or broken equipment, repairs, and perishable supplies. Further, the use-area manager may design the shop so that those who come for such small goods and services may be attracted to other recreation-related purchases. However, the resort supplier has to cope with both the seasonability of the demand and the likelihood that many customers will be there for only a short period. Also, in high-demand recreation areas, competition may be acute.

THE STORE IMAGE

The physical appearance of a place of retail business is quite important. There are uninviting stores with hidden doors, littered entryways, dark interiors, back-street locations, and faded or gaudy signs. However, such obvious factors are only the beginning of the store image.

In residential community stores the image becomes a matter of common knowledge. It is more than appearance but is built up over time by the total marketing and management concept and operation. At the beginning of the life of a business some of that image is announced. Part of the announcement is physical—the location, decor, stock arrangement, and featured merchandise or services. Part of the announcement is in the orientation of initial promotion in which the concept and anticipated appeal of the business is stated quite directly. For example, the image may be based on the reputation of a particular brand of merchandise: "Your new supplier of Brand Z running shoes!" It may stress self-selection and a wide assortment of goods or brands: "For ALL your art supply needs!" It may emphasize service in an area of recreation requiring some expertise: "Where those who KNOW can help you decide!" Or it may be based on an image of reliability: "Your HOMETOWN store!"

The store image shapes how the concept is realized in the minds of present and potential shoppers.[3] Components include

1. Quality, price, and assortment.
2. Merchandise, service, physical facilities, general atmosphere, post-transaction satisfaction, and convenience.
3. Sales elements such as advertising, salesperson attention, and exterior displays.

Each set of elements can be broken down into a number of components. For example, in a use-area business where initial appearances may be crucial in attracting customers who do not know the long-term reputations of competing shops, stress may be placed on location and street-front decor. The entrance, signs, displays, lighting, colors, and brand announcements may be given special attention. On the other hand, in a smaller community with less competition the image emphasis may be more on the interior and product attributes of quality, assortment, dependability, and personal service. One of the advantages of a franchise business is the "instant image" it is given by the established label and known mode of doing business.

In recreation-related retailing, a fundamental image element is whether the supplier is comprehensive or focused in approach. The trend in retailing has seemed to diverge. Comprehensive stores that offer a range of recreation items, often in one part of a large display area, have been increasing. Especially the so-called discount operations have taken a major share of most retail markets. But there is also the more focused concept, usually attached to a particular activity or environment. A store may offer equipment for fishing or camping only, for racquet sports or golf, for ceramics or dance. At the focused business, some expertise and a high level of personal service usually accompany the merchandise. And a major problem that the focused concept must overcome is in image—that of the presumed higher prices.

CASE: SPORTING GOODS—THE BEGINNING

In this case the owner of a now successful sporting goods store began with retailing experience. A salesman-buyer for a locally owned men's clothing store believed he was ready to start his own retail business. He already knew much of what was required since he had been part of the growth of a specialty store's clientele and expansion of its lines of merchandise. He knew the details of buying, financing stock, sales, and records keeping from several years of experience. Further, he had developed a reputation in the community as being able and reliable.

Rather than go into the same type of business somewhere else, therefore, he sought an unmet demand in the town where he had built his reputation. During the past years he had watched the sportswear lines in the clothing store capture a larger share of the business. In a town experiencing moderate growth as an outer-ring suburb, all predictions were for an increasing population base. At this time there was no comprehensive retail supplier of sports equipment and apparel in either the town or any satellite area. Nor was there any really first-rate outlet on the most-used highways into the city.

On the other hand, could a town of eight thousand support such a business? Were there enough sports participants to yield a demand? The first task was to identify potential markets. The most evident were the following:

- Students at the small college in the town
- Participants in public school sports
- Children being introduced to participation by families and friends
- Children in the modest public recreation programs
- Adult sport participants
- Possible institutional sales to schools, etc.

Of course, students—in this case about eight hundred in residence on the campus—are a high-demand market for equipment due to their high participation rates and the easy-access facilities of a college. Programs for children seemed to be on the increase in the community as local voluntary organizations joined with the public recreation program to sponsor sports programs. A strong age-group swimming program was already established. While facilities for adults were modest by suburban standards, adult recreation might become an area of growth. On the other hand, the prospective entrepreneur found that school sales involved competitive price bidding and would produce a low margin of return. The key was the recreational sports market.

Encouraged by informal conversations with residents and key informants, he began to investigate possibilities of securing financial backing. To his surprise, he found that his reputation in the community together with the lack of competition in the field were enough to secure a bank loan.

The concept was simple: It was based on current recreation participation and lack of direct competition. The concept was for a comprehensive retail store with the possibility of capturing some of the sportswear market in selected lines that clothing stores carried only as a sideline. In this case the beginning was the desire to enter into independent retailing. The entrepreneur was interested in sports but was not a known expert in any and did not have a reputation as a coach or star performer.

OTHER CONCEPTS

Often recreation businesses begin with involvement in the activity or sport rather than from a retailing history. In such cases the key may be to learn what business formation involves and to employ the previously acquired knowledge of the equipment or services needed for participation in the activity.

For some entrepreneurs the options are limited. Available capital, locations, experience, and competition clearly define what is possible. However, there may be alternatives. For example, a retail outlet often has to decide between *high-end* and *low-end* strategies. A high-end strategy is one that seeks the higher-price end of the product spectrum. It includes a high-rent location, elaborate decor and fixtures, services such as credit and delivery, a high sales attention approach with a larger staff, stress on quality rather than price, and locating most merchandise in the back room.

The low-end strategy stresses price and seeks to serve those with the widest range of incomes. In general, locations are chosen to minimize rent, few services are offered, decor and fixtures are minimal, merchandise is displayed for self-service, the interior is crowded, and staff kept small. The promotion is price-oriented.

In recreation businesses the competition must be assessed carefully. In urban areas there will always be competition for low-end markets from a variety of discount outlets. Their merchandise selection is usually based on what is available at low cost from manufacturers rather than on a balanced selection, but the markup is low. To position a new retail business requires recognizing which segments of the total market are not being served and creating a store image that will attract those segments.

A Resort Specialist Getting there first has the advantage of not having to face established competition. For this reason a couple with business experience elsewhere opened a ski apparel store on the main street of the town around which new ski resorts were being opened. However, the advantage came at some cost. They were there before the high-income skiers decided to try the new area. As a result, even though their eventual aim was to develop a high-end strategy for name-brand goods, in the early seasons they stocked a wide range of merchandise. They also offered user supplies such as laces, socks, wax, and waterproofing to bring new customers into the store. Theirs was a strategy that called for a narrowing as the overall market grew. Further, they stocked and advertised a few quality-brand apparel items to begin to establish the high-end image that was their goal.

A Limited Service A small but successful business began when its owner-operator was laid off from his previous job. He was a devotee of the only motorcycle then manufactured in the United States and was involved with others who shared his passion. Having experienced difficulties in obtaining parts and securing repairs, he opened a little repair service on a side street in an inexpensive building near his home. With no ambitions to expand or become a major cycle dealer, he soon found himself quite busy. By staying focused, capitalizing on his own experience and skills, staying in touch with the consumer group, and knowing what was needed, he turned an initial investment of $500 into a thriving business. He met a need for service that was ignored in the marketing schemes of other motorcycle shops. Even the threat of ceasing production of the American bike did not create a problem because it would increase the need for parts for and repairs of the aging machines.

A Business Philosophy It has been suggested that the concept of a business rests on a seldom-announced philosophy. What is the aim of the business? It may be more than just paying salaries and earning a return on investment capital. For those in recreation businesses, there is often also a desire to facilitate recreation experiences, to provide needed supplies *well*.

The retail establishment is a business, but it is also a resource. Western societies rely on the market sector of the economy to supply many resources necessary for participation in fulfilling leisure—whether in the arts, sport, outdoor activity, or regular social interaction. Not only is it necessary to respond to the participation basis of a recreation business, but the business may take an "enabling" approach to its marketing.

There are many kinds of examples of how a business may be oriented toward enabling participation through resource supply. A special display of low-cost equipment for children may help introduce those with limited financial resources to an activity. Sponsorship of programs for younger participants may be more than business promotion. A careful selection of merchandise can take into account user requirements that lower thresholds of satisfaction. Reliable repairs on equipment and do-it-yourself tools can minimize the interruptions in participation that sometimes lead to discontinuation. Cooperation with public programs can facilitate beginners in starting an activity with minimum investment.

It can be argued that in the long run all these are good business strategies. In recreation, that may be especially true. The best strategy is one that helps people *do* the activity, that is, get into it with the least constraint, and stay in it in the most satisfying way. However, there may be times when the short-term maximization of profit is in conflict with long-term enabling of recreation through resource supply. Then the philosophy underlying the business concept can make the difference.

BUSINESS FORMATION

Starting a business is more than just having an idea and defining potential markets. A business also requires structure.

FORMS OF RETAIL BUSINESS

As outlined in chapter 3, there are several forms that a business may take. Each has certain advantages and disadvantages. While the form can be changed later, it is usually best to begin with a formation structure designed for the mature stages of the business.

For a relatively small retail business, the advantage of a sole proprietorship is that all control rests with the single owner. It maximizes flexibility in the early stages of the business. However, the owner is also responsible for the debts of the business and puts personal assets at risk. Many small businesses are begun in just this way, with personal assets as the security behind any credit obtained.

At the other extreme, a corporation protects the owners' personal assets. It also allows assets to be held by the corporation as a tax reduction. Owners can pay themselves salaries, hold useful assets such as cars and equipment in the corporation, and have the option of raising capital by selling stock in ways that do not relinquish control of the business. On the other hand, a corporation must pay taxes, be formed and registered in ways that usually require legal counsel, and file annual reports. Incorporation is a state transaction and may require additional registration to do business in other states. Details of incorporation and corporate taxation vary from state to state and are subject to legislative alteration at any time. However, the protections and continuity in case of the death of a principal are significant advantages. The business accounting and reporting required are not a major burden to a business operated with adequate records for its own management purposes.

Increasingly, businesses are being formed as limited partnerships. In a limited partnership two classes of partners are created: general partners, who have a vote but also assume liability for debts, and limited partners, who are excluded from voting and liability but share in ownership. Such a business form is simpler than incorporation and only the income of the partners is taxed. However, it has the disadvantages of unlimited liability for general partners, dissolution if a partner dies or withdraws, and complications in raising outside capital. The avoidance of corporation taxes is attractive as long as the ownership and management of the business is relatively stable and free of conflict. However, long-term flexibility is enhanced by incorporation with its options of tax reporting, holding of assets, securing outside investment, and protection in case of failure.

COSTS OF BEGINNING

All analysts of small-business success and failure agree that a major cause of failure is undercapitalization. The U.S. Department of Commerce estimated in 1975 that it required $50,000 investment capital with $15,000 start-up cash to open a recreation, entertainment, or travel business. Figures for local retail enterprises are about the same. Translated into current dollar values, it means that few entrepreneurs are able to begin a business out of their own savings and resources. Why is this the case?

The start-up costs of a local retail recreation supply business vary according to the costs of merchandise and equipment, size and location of the business, need for advertising and other promotional efforts, and the size and experience of the initial staff. While a one-person repair shop may open in a garage with $500 invested in tools and parts, a recreation vehicle store with expensive merchandise and indoor and outdoor show space and storage may require at least $200,000 capitalization in a prime location.

Some of the factors that must be considered in estimating such costs are the following:

- Leasing space and remodeling
- Acquiring stock on 30-day and 90-day accounts
- Staff salaries during a slow opening period
- The impact and timing of seasonal sales variation
- The cost of obtaining loans, interest, and fees
- Legal costs in forming the business
- Costs of extending credit when there is no income from backlogged accounts
- Equipment needed for transporting and storing merchandise
- Utilities including deposits and installation
- Advertising and promotions
- At least maintenance income for the owner-operators
- Repairs, especially if used equipment and furnishing are used.

- Insurance
- Write-off of perishable merchandise

This does not include any margin for error. Most new business managers make mistakes in judgment usually related to inventories and an inability to estimate future sales accurately. Optimism, necessary in the very idea of opening a business, has to be tempered with realism about the costs. A careful estimate of costs for the first year is necessary in order to begin with enough investment capital to enable the business to be run well and to develop its potential markets.

LOCATION

In retailing, location is often a major factor in the outcome of the enterprise. Deciding on a location is a two-step process. First, a trading area is selected and, second, a specific location in the area is chosen.

The trading area selection is based on an evaluation of the potential and manifest markets for the goods and services proposed within an area. A market-center town may draw customers from a radius of 100 miles in the Great Plains. On the other hand, a shopping center on the edge of a city may be cut off from customers by a railroad or river in a 60°C to 180°C arc around the location, limiting the trading area to a few square miles. Good geographical analysis is required to define the trading area. Factors in evaluation of a trading area include:[4]

Population: Trends, income distribution of income, social strata, recreational sytles, age distribution, cultural backgrounds and education levels.

Community environment: Taxes, competition, zoning and other legislative restrictions, transportation facilities, banking and credit facilities, insurance rates, availability of employees, recreation opportunities, and future recreation development.

Business growth: Present and planned industries, business trends, cooperative business agreements and promotions, real estate costs and availability, and regional growth patterns.

For some types of recreation business, some minimum market base might be established. In *One Third of Our Time?*, Michael and Holly Chubb estimate from an analysis of the state of Michigan the market requirements for various recreation resources.[5] For example, they estimate that a population base of over five hundred thousand and a market area of over 200 square miles is needed for a major shopping mall, but a bowling center can be supported by a population of less than twenty-five thousand and a small market area. Such general estimates may serve as a beginning for analysis. Some market areas are just too small to consider. Others are too competitive. However, recreation patterns do change, new resources create the need for suppliers, and superior business concepts capture markets. Each trade area analysis is specific to the business contemplated and the time of investigation.

The particular location of a store or service after a trading area is selected involves a different set of variables. To begin with, a location may be either freestanding, separate from other business locations in a neighborhood, or on a highway. More often, locations are "business-associated." They are in one of the following:

Center or fringe of a downtown business area

Neighborhood business district

A secondary business district with at least one major store

Along a highway business string

A planned shopping center: neighborhood, community or regional

Factors in such a decision involve access for potential clients as well as costs. Is the location visible to the population of the trading area by being along a transportation route or in a major shopping center? Is it located near magnet businesses such as major stores or food markets? Is there direct or indirect competition in the vicinity? Or are there complementary businesses nearby? Is the location accessible to recreation-use areas or along the way to related resources? Are the recreation target populations likely to find the location convenient? Is the business onc that is location sensitive or will it draw its clientele from almost anywhere in the trading area because of its unique goods and services?

And there are also cost elements in the decision. While a central location in an established shopping mall may be both visible and accessible, it may also require a high-cost lease and expensive remodeling. On the other hand, a recreation business for which there is a demonstrated market may be able to draw customers to a low-cost location where there is more space for the services offered. In many cases, the amount of up-front capital available places such constraints on the options that only one or two locations are possible. In other cases, alternatives lead to quite different definitions of the business, its offerings, markets, image, and potential for growth.

In any case, there are a few simple questions that must be answered:

What volume of business will be required to support the location?

Is the location accessible to the target markets?

Is there flexibility in financial arrangements, amount and use of space, and agreements on the use of the building?

What will be the costs of preparing the location for use?

Does the location benefit from existing transportation patterns?

CASE: LOCATION OF A SPORTING GOODS STORE

In a relatively small town the location decision may be simple when only one location is available. Fortunately for the young retailer opening the town's first sporting goods store, that location was between the main entrance to the campus and the post office three blocks away. It was on the way to Main Street for students, but in an old building requiring remodeling. Since the town provided no off-street parking, people were accustomed to walking the sidewalk from one store to another.

The major location decision came several years later. The store had now outgrown its space, even with the shoe section in what had been a storage area and the old basement used for storage. When the local Penney's outlet was closed after the opening of a big new store in a shopping center halfway to the city, the building was available at a reasonable rent. It had the space and was still near the campus. However, there were a number of questions:

Was the business volume large enough to justify the acquisition of all the fixtures and display cabinets needed for the larger area?

The location was not on a heavily traveled pedestrian route. Was the business now established well enough so that customers would walk a block or two to get there?

What about the loss of impulse buying triggered by the window displays?

How much additional staff would be needed to cover the tripled display space and guard against shoplifting?

And what about the competition of the shopping centers? The downtown street was barely surviving while several shopping centers of various sizes and configurations dotted the routes to the city. A major comprehensive-store chain planned a new center on the edge of town. Was it wise to commit the store to a downtown location where there is now no supermarket, no drugstore, and limited facilities for food and drink?

The owner, partly because of the importance of the campus trade and partly to support the downtown area of the community, decided to stay and invest in remodeling the old Penney's store. For the first year it seemed like a good decision as business grew slightly even in a recession. Then, three more stores a block away closed and fire gutted the three small shops between the store and the main banking corner.

Looking back, the owner reviewed the history of his enterprise. What did it take to begin such a store and nurse it to health? In this case the capital came relatively easily through the bank's cooperation. The basic knowledge of retailing, lacking so often when coaches or artists open retail recreation businesses, had been acquired through several years of hands-on experience. The other factor was personal. The store had from the beginning required incredible attention, dedication, and scheduling. At first it had been a seven-day-a-week proposition because there was no one else who could do more than routine floor selling. Time with young children, time for singing in the church choir, time for community participation, time for the house and yard—all had to be squeezed out of the demands of the business. Even after gaining some stability and success in ten years, the business was always there. Something more always needed to be done. Even more than capital, time remained the scarce resource. Up and down the highway were the remnants of stores opened by entrepreneurs who had wanted to be part-time managers. Retailing was not for the timid or the half-hearted.

ALTERNATIVES IN FORMATION

The variety in recreation businesses suggests that there is no one way to form successful enterprises. Even a decision such as location can include alternatives other than finding an available building and renovating it to suit the particular type of business.

Gaining Experience How do you get started in retailing when you have the desire and interest but little experience except for two summers at a fast-food outlet? The first step may be to work in an established store or department as close to the anticipated product or service line as possible. This may involve commuting to another trade area or even moving for a time. A second method is to get experience in the anticipated trade area, but in a different line of retailing. This establishes some relationships and develops an understanding of the markets.

A third possibility for someone with little capital is to persuade an established business to add a recreation-related line. Especially when a store has space that is not being profitably employed, such a proposition can be quite attractive. In some cases the beginning entrepreneur may work out a sharing arrangement to obtain inventory and divide profits. One problem with this arrangement is that it will usually include an agreement not to start up a competing business in the same trade area at a later time.

If the magnet of a successful shopping center is considered essential for the new business but costs of a lease are prohibitive, there is an alternative being tried more frequently. Some comprehensive stores, regular or discount, will sublease space for a semiindependent department. The new business may be a department in the larger enterprise with its own inventory, accounting, staff, and services. Advertising and checkout counters may or may not be shared. Obviously such an arrangement requires a contract that anticipates sources of conflict and misunderstanding of expectations. However, as space costs escalate, such an arrangement can be quite attractive.

Further, initial investment can be reduced by renting or leasing equipment, fixtures, and even some services. The problem with leasing is that it may place a strain on the cash flow, especially in a seasonal business with year-round leases. Nevertheless, borrowing capital to purchase equipment is also costly and locks the business into the original concept when flexibility may be more desirable as the markets take shape over time.

The formation of a retail business involves a set of interrelated decisions. Often the concept of a service will dictate the amount of capitalization needed or the location required. In other cases limitations on borrowing power will place strict limits on how the business can be started. A plan for formation may require the entrepreneur to work backward from a predetermined goal, the concept. For example: "If the service is to attract on-site business, then it must be located on the main highway. The only rental location available there is at 1800. Its size precludes having a major display area." And so on.

ANOTHER ALTERNATIVE: THE FRANCHISE

There are many kinds of franchise recreation businesses. Campgrounds, motels in resort areas, food chains, fitness centers, and travel agencies may be franchises in which the concept, image, merchandise, and retailing style are predetermined. Here we will focus on franchises in recreation retailing.

Retail recreation franchises include stores with identical merchandise and image but local ownership. Some concentrate on a single brand of merchandise, such as the athletic shoes of a major manufacturer. Others have only one line of goods, such as shoes, music, art, or camping equipment. Some specialize in rentals for recreation purposes with a standardized line of goods and services. A franchise consists of a contractual relationship between a franchiser, who contributes a trademark, image, reputation, products, and mode of operation, and a franchisee, who adds operating capital and operates the local business.

The advantages of franchising to the franchiser are related chiefly to the opportunity for expansion without having to make the investments or have a widespread management operation. Further, the risk is largely assumed by the franchisee, but the profits are shared by the franchiser. When the contract provides a high initial fee, the franchiser profits whether or not the local business prospers. Some franchisers have concentrated so much on selling contracts that they develop a reputation for a high failure rate and the entire operation collapses.

The advantages to the franchisee can be considerable when the franchiser does not overemphasize growth at the expense of developing a sound network of outlets. In a good franchise, the local owner gains a reduced risk through a tested and established product or service, regional or national promotion and advertising, training in how to run the business, consultation in formation decisions, and often some advantages in obtaining credit and capital. In general, the franchisee begins with a head start: an image and product that is known, methods of organization and operation that have been tested and refined, and a ready-made identification with potential consumers. In a resort-area business, where a high proportion of business is new and not local, a franchised identification may be all-important.

Perhaps the greatest disadvantage of the franchise for the retailer is its lack of flexibility Since no two market areas are exactly alike, the formula that has succeeded elsewhere may place costly restrictions on the local entrepreneur. In some retail franchises the inventory, store layout, and advertising are all prescribed. An attractive complementary line of merchandise or service cannot be added to the formula. A special market segment cannot be given special attention. The same standardization that may attract some customers may also turn away others.

There are several types of franchises that offer some flexibility. A *straight product distribution franchise* is one in which a firm is given a contract as one or the only retail outlet for a brand of products in the area. The local business is a licensed distributor for the supplier. The contract usually requires that certain services be provided by the wholesale supplier and the retail merchant.

A *product license franchise* enables the local business to actually produce or modify the product. The local owner usually pays an initial fee plus a percentage of gross revenue to market the product or service.

Trade name franchises license the use of the trade name but exercise little control. In some cases the arrangement involves only the purchase of certain equipment. If leased, there is a monthly fee. The franchisee, however, may use the trademark of the product or equipment in the business.

CASE: FRANCHISING DIVERSIFICATION

When the concept was developed, the idea was linked to a trade name. Knowing that shoes were the most rapidly growing market in sporting goods and that they have a relatively high markup, a young entrepreneur decided to specialize in athletic shoes. The prospect of a year-round market based on different sports in their season was a major attraction. However, identification of the specialized business could be a problem.

The solution seemed to be to attach the business to a known brand name through a product distribution franchise. In order to use the name and trademark of the world's prestige sports footgear as the name and trademark of the local store, an exclusive contract was executed. The store would sell tennis, basketball, running, and other shoes distributed only by that one supplier. The supplier authorized use of the brand identification but promised no exclusivity in the market area. Other stores would continue to carry the same merchandise.

The arrangement continued for five years. The business, due to its location in a prime market area, did well. A bonus turned out to be the growing custom of wearing running shoes for everyday use by students and others courting an athletic image. Further, the brand carried had a kind of aura or prestige that enhanced such sales.

However, through the years other suppliers continued to call and offer inducements to add their line of shoes. Also, despite the good profit yield of shoes, another opportunity was intriguing. Since shoes were displayed mostly on walls and one at a time to prevent stealing, they require little floor space. That space could then be used for various kinds of apparel to attract impulse buying in season.

The decision was whether or not to abandon the exclusive contract and also the established name of the business in order to diversify in shoes and other merchandise. The argument for the change was that the business now had its own local identity and no longer needed the prestige of the known trademark.

EVALUATING A FRANCHISE

From the perspective of the prospective franchisee, a number of questions are important in evaluating the advantages and disadvantages of the arrangement:[6]

How long has the franchising firm been in operation and what is their history of success?

What is the francisher's reputation for honesty?

Is there a high or low rate of discontinued franchises?

Will the franchiser assist with management and employee training, public relations and advertising, and obtaining capital?

What is the program for selecting locations and are the trade areas protected against later competition?

What are the results of examining audited accounts from other franchisees in similar locations?

Just what can the franchise do for the business that cannot be done locally?

And are those benefits cost-effective?

What are terms of ending the contract in costs and limitations?

How much capital is required and what margin of profit is necessary to pay the continuing franchise fees?

Do the advantages outweigh the loss of independence of action and decision?

Is the product market in that trade area likely to increase in the future?

Will the franchise identification be a major factor in the potential increase?

Will the franchise give an advantage over present and future competition that is worth the cost?

Is the expertise of the franchiser essential to starting the business at all?

What are your lawyer's and banker's judgments about the terms of the franchise contract?

Can the contract be modified for your circumstances?

How carefully has the franchiser evaluated you and your ability to operate the business successfully? (Too little caution on the part the franchiser may be a warning that interest is primarily in the initial fee rather than long-term service.

The decision as to whether or not to consider a franchise includes many factors such as personal business experience, the nature of the trade area, the drawing power of the franchise image, and alternative concepts.

CAPITALIZATION AND MARKETING

The capitalization requirements of a business vary widely. However, two elements are both important and closely related to each other. The first is the capital needs are for more than opening the business. It takes time to build up a market and secure an adequate cash flow. The financing plan of any business has to look forward past the first month or season.

In order to obtain outside capital, either by borrowing or from investors, it is necessary to present a plan that indicates a reasonable chance of successful operation over time. In chapter 6 an outline for a comprehensive marketing plan is presented. In the section that follows below, a number of issues central to such a plan for a retail recreation business are introduced. The point is that all these business functions are dependent on the others. The concept is the beginning. However, implementation calls for some capitalization. In order to interest investors, whether partners or corporate shareholders, or to gain the confidence of lenders, it is necessary to analyze the market and present a plan for implementation of the concept. "Formation" consist of more than getting an idea and money.

PRODUCT DEVELOPMENT

Some recreation businesses produce the product for sale. Others distribute the product of others. In early stages some businesses combine the functions. In any case, there is a *product line* of goods and/or services that is offered to the public at a price. This product line is the heart of the concept for the retail business.

SERVICES

Most often a retail recreation service business evolves out of previous experience with the activity and equipment used in obtaining the experience of participation: A skier who wants to live near the slopes opens an equipment repair shop; a backpacker extends experience with equipment into a rental and repair shop; a tennis player strings racquets.

Perhaps even more common is the service offering of instruction. An exercise physiologist opens an exercise and fitness center, teaching techniques that can later be employed privately. Artists teach others their art form, sometimes beginning in a public program and then taking their following to a private studio. An interest in jazz leads to programming for a local food and drink establishment and then to the management of artists. A boater finds that there is no local repair and parts service and opens one that develops from a weekend and summer business into a year-round enterprise.

In all such cases participation in recreation precedes the business. Knowledge of the product comes first, and a service business follows. However, even in such modest beginnings there are requirements for organization. The smallest business needs records, tax procedures, liability insurance, some space to work, a business account and telephone, and some means of announcing its existence. The functions of business soon surround even the simplest service.

PRODUCT SALES

More common is a business concept involving some product sales. The one-person repair shop soon becomes a parts supplier for the equipment being repaired. Retail sales, even when it primarily consists of ordering parts and opening cartons, calls for transmitting sales taxes, keeping records, balancing accounts, and building a business image.

A retail sales business matches a product line to the market. Some selection is made about the type of product to be sold, the range of brands and accessories, the size of the inventory, and the support services to be included. For example, does sales imply service of the products sold? If so, what about servicing other items for customers? In retailing, one thing seems to lead to another.

CASE: MARKET CHANGES

The business began when a young clerk in a hardware store in New England proposed a way to increase winter sales. The store, in a city of a hundred thousand, had a major trade in building supplies for both contractors and do-it-yourselfers. However, this trade fell off by 60% in the winter. The clerk had noted the growth of a new industry in the area, skiing. What began as a minor local avocation had developed into a major recreation activity with some local activity and a great deal of driving north into the mountains.

So the hardware store began to handle skis, boots, and related gear. The trade prospered and in time took over the entire back third of the store from October through March. The clerk, now manager of the ski shop, expanded from a few ski lines to a large inventory. Having the shop in a year-round business enabled the store to keep prices relatively low. Instead of competing with the ski resort shops, the hardware store sold basic equipment at prices below those that could be charged at a shop that was closed most of the year. It was a "no frills" operation that in time attracted buyers from a large area.

Then came competition. Two specialty shops opened in the city. The first was run by a former Olympic skier who went after the committed skiers oriented toward high skill development. They met at the store, exchanged advice, planned weekends, and fraternized with the "star." The second store was a branch of a national chain that stocked a full range of skis and equipment in a supermarket mode and was able to keep prices low with their national purchasing leverage.

The hardware store had lost its exclusive markets. They could not compete with the Olympian for the high-end and pro-oriented market. They could not compete with the chain in price or inventory. Should they get out of the business after 15 years or identify market segments that were still unmet?

Two alternatives were developed by the ski shop manager to present to the hardware store owner. The first was to capitalize on their reputation for reliability. While their prices and inventory were not directly competitive with the chain, they could promote the image of customer confidence: "We have stood behind everything we sell for 15 years." "You *know* you can trust Smith's." "We sell only what we believe in." "We have met your ski needs for 15 years." This strategy was designed to retain old customers rather than open new markets. However, it might enable the business to continue on a reduced basis.

The second alternative was stumbled on by the manager. Several customers had inquired about the likelihood of adding a new line, cross-country skis and equipment. The manager began to investigate the potential of the market by talking to skiers, visiting areas where the activity was reported to be increasing, and quizzing sales representatives as to sales trends elsewhere. In time he developed a concept that was more than a minor change. He proposed turning the ski shop into a well-advertised center for the developing sport. It was to take their established reputation for ski equipment and translate it into a new speciality, to become *the* center for Nordic skiers. The risk, of course, was much greater than the first alternative; but the market potential might also be much greater. Further, southern New Hampshire was good terrain for Nordic skiing, so that there would not be competition from the on-site retailers who still sold much of the Alpine ski gear.

This case illustrates two techniques for recreation retailing. The first is to open a new product line in an established business. Such an expansion of concept is especially attractive when there are seasonal complementarities such as:

Bicycles in summer and cross-country skis in winter in Wisconsin.

Motorcycles in summer and snowmobiles in winter in North Dakota.

Boat repair in summer and storage in winter.

Camping gear in summer and ski equipment in winter.

Rental services that follow the seasons.

Golf items in summer and outdoor apparel in winter.

Recreation vehicles in summer for local use and rental and travel arrangements for sun-seekers in winter.

Of course, a store with a full line of items will follow the seasons as a matter of course. Just as the three hundred Little Leaguers hang up their spikes for the summer, four hundred soccer enthusiasts are getting equipped for the fall. Anticipating inventory needs and keeping in close touch with the public and private organizers of such programs is a central part of the business.

MANUFACTURER'S REPRESENTATIVES

Just as the physician receives much current information about drugs from the "detail men" sent out by the manufacturers, so the recreation business manager relies on company representatives. In general, their purpose is to increase the distribution of their own product lines. Further, they are in competition with each other.

Nevertheless, taking into account their own aims and orientations, they can be valuable sources of information. They can provide product mix figures from similar stores; they can identify trends in consumer buying patterns; and they can be of assistance in scheduling orders for the retailer who is new in the business. Further, they serve as middlemen who can also represent the retailer to the manufacturer. If product quality is a problem, the representative should be available to reduce the cost to the retailer of honoring guarantees and warranties.

How is it possible to evaluate the information from such representatives? The first rule is to ask for data. When figures are given on product mix and sales trends at other stores in different trade areas, it is not costly to call and check them out. The reliable representative will encourage clients to talk to each other. The rep who is always offering unsubstantiated information on a confidential and unverifiable basis is likely to be giving an account that is biased toward his own product lines.

CASE: THE POWERFUL NEW PRODUCT

A boat dealer was offered a great new opportunity, to be the first and exclusive dealer in the area for a product that might drive outmoded products off the market. The product was a new form of outboard motor that incorporated a means of propulsion with several alleged advantages: It was simpler and should be low-maintenance. It was more powerful and economical, at least in the high power ranges. It was offered by an established manufacturer who had invested $500,000 in its development. It was not a modification on the traditional system but required a complete purchase. It would appeal to the American penchant for having the "latest thing."

However, the dealer was cautious. With the sales staff, an analysis was done of types of sales for the past five years and of the kinds of boating done by customers. First, the analysis showed that "high-power" boaters were only 30% of their market by number of sales and 45% by dollar volume. Many family boaters, fishing enthusiasts, and sailors for whom the motor was auxiliary were also customers. Further, the risk seemed great in case the product did not prove successful technologically or in market development. The dealer decided to remain more diversified and forego both the risk and the opportunity.

In the subsequent years caution was rewarded. The new propulsion system proved less reliable than predicted and also more limited. Further, the recreational boating markets became more and more diversified. Then, when the cost of gasoline soared, the "high power" end of the market dropped even more. Now the dealer is considering stocking equipment for windsurfing.

CASE: MARKET SITUATION

What do you do when the market seems saturated? For years during the period of housing expansion, the contractor who specialized in selling and installing in-ground residential swimming pools had done well. Sales had increased every year for six years. Four installation crews were busy six months of the year. From handling all the sales herself, the owner now employed a sales department with a manager and three weekend salespersons.

Then, in a year, it all seemed to come apart. New-home building in the area dropped off considerably, largely because the available land was filled and developers had moved further out. At the same time a period of recession had affected the market for those who had been in their homes for a few years and wanted to enhance at-home recreation for their families.

What were the options open? One was just to wait out the recession in hope that the recreation-addition market would come back and that competitors would have left the area to follow the new building. This plan involved reducing the size of both construction and sales staffs, at least for a time.

A second option was to reorient the business toward service, to try to become *the* pool supply, maintenance, and repair firm for the market area. Then, they would also be in a good position to exploit any period of economic recovery.

The third option was to identify a new market area where residential building was being planned and to try to transfer the experienced staff to that area. The old location could be closed or reduced to a service business. This was the most costly option, the one with the highest risk, and the one calling for head-to-head competition with other firms who had made the same decision.

A fourth option, never considered by the owner, was to diversify. Were there other at-home recreation product lines that would be complementary in seasonality and clientele? Rather than go on with a line that would in time lead to another situation of saturation, why not use the established local store image to sell different products to the same residential markets?

RELATION TO PUBLIC PROGRAMS

Especially for those who have been professionally involved in public or school recreation, supplying such programs is an obvious market opportunity. There are two elements in such markets. The first is to sell directly to the recreation department or school. While such sales are one market, in most areas they cannot support a business. The general sporting goods store introduced in this chapter did only 4% of its gross sales to the local school system. Further, such sales were on a very small profit margin.

The problem is twofold: First, the public agency is usually required by law and practice to secure competing bids for orders of any size. As a consequence, to supply equipment to such a program calls for a willingness to operate at little profit. The remainder of the business supports the public sales rather than the reverse. Second, the public agency has a wide range of possible suppliers. More than the individual customer, the institution is besieged with catalogs and bulk-order discounters ready to respond to the competitive quick delivery from their warehouse direct to the agency or school. They are severe competition in both price and convenience. However, because they are not in the locality, they do not provide easy repair and replacement, service for small orders, and responsiveness to special local needs.

The second aspect of responding to institutional recreation programs is to supply the participants rather than the institutions. Here the local retailer has several advantages. By maintaining close contact with those who plan the recreation for public agencies and the schools, the local business can be ready to cope with changes and expansion. If the local soccer program is adding a new age group, the local business will be there to have appropriately sized equipment on hand before the season begins. The local supplier can work with program officials and coaches to examine the possibilities for new uniforms and participation gear. The local retailer can initiate as well as respond to the market changes.

In general, any program in recreation—arts, sports, outdoor experience, skill acquisition, or social—depends on local retail business to supply goods to participants. The product lines of businesses should not only complement the public resource offerings but also utilize their ongoing flow of customers. Recognizing that most people, especially children, do many things as recreation, the store can often use low-profit sales to interest consumers in products for other activities. The clue to complementarity in product development is to understand complementarity in recreation. One important question is, What is the other recreation of those who are already coming into the store? Supplying participants in public programs can be the key to developing markets for other recreation goods and services.

MARKETING PLANS

For some recreation businesses there is only one market segment. A specialized business may supply only equipment for one form of one activity, high-end shoes and costumes for ballet dancers or trophies for local sports leagues. However, more often a retail business is designed to reach a number of market segments and has some diversification in product lines.

CASES: IDENTIFYING NEW MARKETS

In a community of some size a prospective entrepreneur identified what appeared to be an untapped market segment—tennis-playing women. While men might shop at a pro shop, a traditional expert-oriented old shop, or through the mail, women might respond to a different approach. A pleasant store staffed by women who could provide advice on equipment and apparel would be more attractive. Further, tennis shoes, dresses, and warmups were worn many places other than at the courts. The increasing interest of women in the sport might well be compounded into sales for general wear as well as for participation use. In time, the market segment identification proved to be accurate. There was a market there, but it did not develop to be large enough to support the store. However, a complementary market was later identified, for exercise and fitness program participants who needed the special shoes, leotards, leg-warmers, and other apparel for such programs both in and out of the residence. In many cases those attracted by one line became markets for the other.

A dealer in recreation vehicles—both camping trailers and self-propelled—found business limited by the price factor. There were many campers who seemed interested in the comfort and convenience of camping and traveling with such amenities along, but they just couldn't handle the high cost. Especially those who had only a week or two each year for such travel just did not make the purchases. Therefore, the dealer soon established a rental program with the addition of rent-purchase options. It provided a method of trying out such vehicles for those who were unsure as well as responded to the interests of those who would not make the purchase. The problem with this market plan was the high cost of maintaining a fleet of mobile homes and trailers that were no longer available to those customers who wanted a new product. This was partially solved in a program that enabled those who made a purchase to use a rental vehicle while waiting for their factory order to be filled.

ISSUES IN RETAIL MARKETING

The first essential of developing a market plan is to identify potential markets. Elements of such analysis include the delineation of the trading area, consumer trends, the recreation participation base, product cycles, competition, and changes in the area, such as increased recreation resources and population composition shifts.

One outline of market identification for a local retail recreation business would include the following:

What are the patterns of current recreation participation?

Are there trends in participation change?

What is the size and shape of a viable trading area?

What is the competition in retail product and service distribution in that trading area?

Are there goods and services for which the market is now saturated? For which there is an undersupply? That are not supplied at all?

What changes are now manifest? In new products and their use cycles? In recreation resources? In the population of the trading area? In recreation and leisure styles?

Will a new or augmented supplier be likely to increase participation and the related markets for goods and services?

CURRENT RECREATION PARTICIPATION

A retail recreation business begins with what people do for recreation. While national and regional statistics are useful in delineating general trends and suggesting possibilities of change, there is no substitute for participation data from the trading area. The problem is that there is not likely to be any single source of data. However, there are some sources with which one may begin.

Public Recreation Reports Most public recreation programs keep account of participation in their various programs. For facilities the statistics may be only the number of entries and season passes sold. For some specific programs there are enrollment figures. Comparing such numbers over time can yield some idea of trends. However, there are inherent limitations to such data. First, there is usually no identification of repeaters. Five thousand entries into a pool per week may represent only one thousand individuals, most of whom swam every day. Further, user figures are a response to opportunity and do not represent the potential market for other activites.

Business Statistics Most businesses can supply at least an estimate of the number who use their facilities. One problem may be that a club or activity center with a pro shop may want to discourage competition. For this reason, getting data from similar communities may be necessary.

Leisure Research Reports Although not completed in the trading area, a number of studies that are household-based are invaluable in developing an overall profile of recreation. Only research that moves off the location of participation to the residence can encompass the full spectrum of leisure. Much of the retail market is not tied to either public or commercial resources but is developed by the living unit—the family or household—and utilizes equipment, special clothing and shoes, and other items obtained from retail outlets. The backyard, living room, car, neighborhood, and vacation itinerary all produce part of the retail recreation market.

Industry Sales Figures Although they must be treated critically and applied to a specific locality with care, industry figures do provide an idea of trends in retailing and often untapped marketing possibilities in a trading area.

Informal Sources One of the best sources of data is "hanging around." Any retailer should get out of the store and into the locales where people gather to ask questions about interests, constraints in obtaining goods and services, and hopes for future recreation participation. However, it is necessary not to allow the bias of particular locations to outweigh more reliable information.

Especially important is being attuned to trends. Recreation is not a static phenomenon. New resources and styles are always being developed, demonstrated in singular areas, picked up by the media, and spread to other areas. Some are fads; others are based in established patterns and interests but enhance opportunities that are now limited. Last year's sales figures are not always the best guide to orders for next year's inventory.

THE ECOLOGY OF THE TRADING AREA

A retail business is located in a particular place. Its trading area is shaped by a number of factors including distance, means of transportation, access from roads and highways, barriers such as rivers and railroads, residential dispersion, and current retail shopping habits. Factors in choosing locations have already been discussed. However, the nature of the trading area cannot be overstressed in defining markets.

For example, a retail store will usually find that 50% to 70% of its trade comes from within a primary trading area. In a city that may be a neighborhood, in a separate town it may include all or most of the community; in a shopping center location it may include only those whose regular shopping patterns for food and repeat services bring them to that center. A secondary trading area, providing 15% to 25% of sales, will be defined as those areas for which there is no barrier except distance. The remaining customers will come from the fringe trading area.

A recreation specialty store possessing the only inventory of some type of equipment may have a wide trade area and obtain a higher proportion of its business from fringe areas. In an area where competition is intense, the primary trading area may produce 90% of the business volume. Therefore, in delineating a trading area both the nature of the business and the shape of the area itself must be considered. However, this analysis has major implications for the precise location of the business. For a dispersed trading area with considerable fringe trade, location convenience to major highways and freeways and adequate parking are critical. For a business with a highly concentrated trading area, centrality may be more important.

Current patterns can be estimated by finding the frequency with which customers in a geographical area shop at a particular store, their average purchases, and the concentration of credit card holders in a given area.[7] For a satellite business in recreation retailing that depends on the drawing power of major department stores and supermarkets, such information is important in selecting a specific location.

The Bureau of the Census offers considerable data about areas that can serve as the basis for analysis. Further information can be obtained from the *Survey of Buying Power, Editor and Publisher Market Guide,* the marketing departments of local newspapers, regional planning boards, public utilities, chambers of commerce, and shopping center developers. The population size and characteristics, availability of labor, the economic base, competitive situation, location availability, taxes, and regulations are all part of trading area analysis.

Overall trends in a trading area should also be taken into account. One persistent issue is the common decline of older central retailing districts and the rise of shopping centers accessible by car. For example, in San Diego less than 1.5% of goods are sold in downtown stores.[8] In Cleveland downtown sales declined over 26% from 1967 to 1976 and in Atlanta by 35% from 1958 to 1972. However, in Minneapolis downtown sales grew over the same period due to a massive renovation of the central retail area. The point is that in any trading area a location decision can be made only when what is going on is accurately understood. Then an entrepreneur who decides to go against a trend does so knowing that a marketing plan will have to bring people to the location rather than count on the location to produce trade.

COMPETITION

Measuring competition for a retail recreation store involves more than counting listings in the Yellow Pages. Here are only a few examples of competition for local retail recreation business:

- Direct competition in the trading area
- Direct competition outside the primary trading area but accessible by making a special trip or en route to some destination. An outlet along a route heavily traveled by commuters may be directly competitive even though miles away.
- Discount stores: Almost all kinds of recreation equipment and apparel are offered in some discount outlets. Stock may be limited, but the assumption of lower prices is a difficult image to counter.
- Departments in comprehensive stores: Many major retailing chains such as Sears have their own recreation product lines. They are able to advertise nationally and attract business to local stores through name recognition. In some cases mass purchasing and distribution through established channels can create formidable price competition.
- On-site outlets: For recreation goods that are often used away from home there are usually some retail outlets at or near the participation site. They seldom compete in price but are right there when consumers are actually engaged in the activity. They may also be able to take advantage of a more consumption-oriented atmosphere in the recreation locale.
- Mail-order businesses: One of the fastest-growing types of retail business is mail-order. Mail-order retailing has many advantages. Advertising can be specific to the product by using specialized periodicals such as *Tennis* or *Field and Stream.* Catalogs can offer the convenience of in-home purchasing and a wide range of items. Since a mail-order business can be located in a warehouse area away from high rents, space costs may be relatively low. Credit cards and telephone ordering now speed the process and add to convenience. Mail-order firms offer serious competition to the local store. Especially when the stock and expertise of the local business is used to gain knowledge and make a decision but the purchase is made by mail at a price the local store cannot match, the mail-order competition actually exploits the services of the retailer.

Sometimes sales representatives can provide nonconfidential figures on the sales levels of competitors. However, the "missionary man" whose job it is to secure new outlets for a firm's product may underestimate the competition. Comparative sales figures are difficult to obtain in reliable ways.

However, the breadth of competition needs to be taken into account in assessing markets. What firms advertise in newspapers and other media received locally? How much of the trading-area population commutes regularly to other and larger areas for work? How much of the recreation participation is at sites where there are retail suppliers? How much of the market is price-sensitive, shopping carefully for suppliers and sales in order to reduce the financial investment in recreation activity? In the relevant product lines, to what extent does service bring in sales business and vice versa?

ESTIMATING SATURATION AND UNDERSUPPLY

Obviously the trick is to avoid products and services in saturated markets and concentrate on those for which there is an evident undersupply. All that the market plan approach introduced is relevant. Recreation participation, population size and characteristics, trading area, and competition are the primary factors in assessing saturation.

If some product or service is totally lacking in the trading area, then the key factor is use—recreation participation that requires the resource. In the case of goods with multiple suppliers, quite specific analysis of the offerings of existing suppliers may locate a number of gaps. Certain brands, price levels, auxiliary goods or services, or new technologies may be missing. Or there may be segments of the population that are not attracted to the images and formats of the current retail firms. Some of the types of market research suggested in the next section may be employed to target such specific supply gaps.

CHANGES IN PRODUCTS

Some recreation supplies are relatively permanent, lasting for years and requiring replacement only under rare circumstances. For example, a fiberglass sailboat hull is almost indestructible. Other supplies have a limited usage life and must be replaced every season or after a period of use. A sailboat hull may outlast several sets of sails, which are good for 5 to 10 years. Some supplies are perishable and need replacement several times a season or even after each use.

A marketing plan for a recreation supplier should divide products among the three categories: *long-term* investment, *periodic* replacement, and *perishable*. Such identification is important in quite basic ways. A store layout may place perishable items in a location that requires the customer to walk through attractive displays of periodic items. Regular patronage for perishable merchandise is utilized to build interest in periodics.

An additional element in such product identification is technological or style change. Recreation is, after all, often a matter of display as well as play. Apparel for the activity is especially subject to style change. The rate of replacement can be increased considerably by marketing. Along with style, there is technological change. Equipment is developed that is safer, lighter, more convenient, or that may improve performance. A wooden tennis racquet that loses resilience after only three seasons may be replaced after a year by a graphite model that promises some advantages for volleying. In some cases dissatisfaction with performance leads consumers to seek new technologies that are quite irrelevant to the problem. Nevertheless, sales are generated by the production and promotion of altered equipment.

Retail marketing in recreation involves response to product changes. Stocking new items and being able to display and explain their advantages is part of selling. Knowing style shifts often means the difference between a good sales volume and having a large quantity of outmoded items to be disposed of at below-cost sales.

CASE: USING PRODUCT CHANGES AND CYCLES

A tennis shop In a highly competitive area a retail tennis specialty shop based its entire marketing strategy on one simple concept. It sold tennis balls at cost, not only at sales but all the time. The idea was to use the perishable item to create a permanent flow of tennis players into the store. Balls were kept behind the counter so that the purchaser had to interact with a salesperson on each occasion. Further, by making the price leader fixed, customers were less likely to stock up for months during a limited-time sale. They were repeatedly exposed to displays and discussion of new lines of racquets, shoes, clothing, and other high-profit items when they came for another three cans of balls.

The attraction of services Another marketing strategy was to use essential services to draw potential buyers into the store. A racquet-stringing service providing quality at a low cost brings a consumer into the store twice at a time of equipment failure. Sail mending does the same for those who already own sailboats. A parts supply for motorized equipment is another type of service attraction.

Advertising In some types of recreation new technologies attract considerable attention. An alert entrepreneur can advertise the new product not only to announce its availability and enhance the store image but also to use the interest to bring new customers into contact with the general line of supplies.

CHANGES IN RECREATION STYLE

The most dramatic recreation change in the past decade has been the increased involvement of women in activities that were formerly male dominated. This change has not only enlarged the markets for equipment and apparel but also altered some styles of participation. Major lines of recreation goods have been developed to meet the opportunities of this new market. Less dramatic changes are always in process. Each may offer new market opportunities. At the same time failure to recognize such stylistic shifts may be quite costly in both the overstocking of declining goods and the failure to have what customers seek.

The only way to be in touch with such trends is to be tied into the participation patterns in some way. In single-activity shops the manager is usually a participant. More comprehensive stores supply a number of sources of information. Trade journals and sales reps may help. Hiring salespeople who are participants in activities different from those of management can be invaluable. Keeping in touch with key informants is also necessary. Local retailing success is partly a matter of being *in* the community, of knowing its life patterns and customs. Absentee management always presents the danger of recognizing stylistic trends only *after* inventories have become unbalanced.

The product-life-cycle concept is also useful in the evaluation of changes. However, in the case of recreation the product life cycle is based on participation cycles. Almost any activity will have a period of introduction followed by growth, maturity, and decline. Sales of related equipment and the need for services will follow that cycle. The question is not whether or not such a rise and fall will occur, but what will be its rate and shape? Will a new product stimulate a demand that peaks rapidly and falls sharply? Or will the rise be more gradual and the decline level off to provide a continuing market of importance? A number of factors will affect the product life cycle in recreation:

1. *The breadth of participation* A product being sold to a narrow spectrum, especially in age, is most likely to be a fad with a quick cycle of growth and decline.
2. *Product specialization* A product that is used only in a special context unrelated to other recreation is most likely to be a fad. On the other hand, a product that complements other recreation skills or is used in a variety of environments more often retains a viable market.
3. *Satisfaction contribution* Different types of recreation activities provide different types of satisfactions. If the product is found to increase common satisfactions in an activity with a sizable participation base, then demand will usually grow and remain significant.
4. *Social contexts* Much recreation is chosen in order to provide a context for mutual activity. If the product contributes to the social meanings of an activity or locale, then it generally will find an ongoing market. If it requires a break in usual social groupings, then its life cycle will be brief.

CASE: SPORTING GOODS MARKETING

On what basis are orders developed for a local retail sporting goods store? Remembering that orders are placed up to 6 months in advance of delivery for the season, how is it possible to look that far ahead?

1. Careful records are kept year by year that distinguish brands, sizes, price levels, and items that must be reordered. The trends revealed are the basis of new orders.
2. Changes in resources are monitored so that increased demand can be anticipated. Doubling the size of community soccer program is a dramatic instance in which failure to anticipate the demand will damage the store's image as well as lead to lost sales.
3. Innovation is worth some risk. New products, lines, developments, and styles are important to stimulate demand, especially in those periodic replacement categories.
4. Response to the product and style changes already introduced.

As the store increases its sales and inventories, sales trends reveal the remarkable significance of athletic-shoe sales. Shoes are high-profit items, replaced with some regularity and used outside the specific sports for which they were designed. Ordering has to ensure an adequate supply of the brands and styles that have acquired considerable product loyalty. New items could be introduced slowly, yet in ways that are responsive to the variety of uses.

MARKETING AND PROMOTION

When market segments have been identified and product lines have been stocked that are responsive to their participation needs, how are they reached and informed of the supply resource? The first answer to come to mind is advertising. In chapter 9 there is an introduction to the kinds of advertising media available to a local business. The advertising mix is selected in an analysis of the market segments to be reached in relation to cost.

The limitations of advertising are as important as its promotional values. For some businesses the selection of media is simple. A business organizing a rock concert or retailing records and tapes will advertise heavily on radio stations that program for the teen audience. Sporting goods stores will employ ads in the sports sections of local newspapers. Basic displays in the Yellow Pages, announcement-type ads on bus posters, outdoor billboards, and signs on company trucks and at the store itself are useful. However, a retail business cannot afford to allocate much more than 2–3% of its gross sales revenues on advertising and remain competitive in price and service.

Further, the results of advertising tend to be quite fleeting. In some cases a special sale or the addition of a new product line justifies an unusual expenditure on advertising. The event or change in store image has to be announced if it is to have an impact on potential customers in the trade area. But advertising can seldom create interest in products where none existed. Further, the base of recreation retailing is still participation. The ad will not create new markets, but it will announce an opportunity. In the long term the general image of the store, an awareness of its product lines and services, and—especially in urban areas—telling people where it is located are the basic aims of advertising.

Nevertheless, a number of promotional devices can be used to increase trade, both for a specific event and over time. Again, the beginning is to identify the market segments that may be attracted by a particular promotional device or strategy. Here are a few examples:

- A sporting goods store has sponsored teams in the community recreation leagues consistently enough so that membership on those teams carries added prestige. The image of quality has been valuable to the general image of the store.
- A community-oriented hall that brings outside entertainment to an ethnic urban neighborhood bases its promotion on community involvement. The only advertising is by posters in front of the place of business and distributed around the neighborhood. Merchants display the posters in return for regular business from the entertainment entrepreneur. The strategy is to be very visible in the neighborhood and to make the nightclub a place to meet as well as one that caters to the musical tastes of the Hispanic clientele. The manager tries to say yes to everything from Scout troops to the promotions of other merchants to obtain reciprocal support.
- Cooperative retail promotions have been used almost monthly in the old downtown retail area to bring customers to the district. Sidewalk sales, midnight "pajama sales," and a variety of musical and other entertainment events are sponsored jointly to attract people to the locale. Such events have been increased since the opening of a second shopping center on the edge of the town.
- Sales are still an important combination of promotion and marketing. The end-of-season, start-of-season, mid-season and out-of-season sales of recreation goods and apparel have more than one aim: They help reduce inventories in slow-selling items; they increase the cash flow and lower the debt servicing charges for maintaining inventories; and they bring customers into the store who often purchase items other than those on sale. In order to achieve all these aims the sales need to be designed in ways that combine advertising, store layout and displays, and combinations of sale merchandise to attract buyers who do not visit the store regularly. Market segment identification is central to the strategy development.
- Price leaders are another promotional strategy that involves selling one or more popular items at little or no profit in order to attract customers. The price leaders are chosen for breadth of interest, possibility of obtaining a quantity at a reduced wholesale price, brand reputation, and contribution

to store image. For example, advertising a price leader in tennis racquets may involve selecting a major style and brand with the hope of introducing those attracted to the virtues of others displayed all around the price leader. Often advertising costs can be minimized when the store is in a visible location by utilizing storefront posters and maintaining the price promotion over an extended period of time.

The ultimate aim of promotion is sales. However, the intermediate aims are to attract attention, inform, and draw the consumer to the store. Different types of promotional strategy emphasize one or more of those aims. A new business will stress creating a store image. An overstocked firm may merely want to move out a lot of merchandise at any price approximating cost. A business in a highly competitive trading area may be in a constant battle to retain an edge for specific market segments. Further, the seasonal nature of much recreation requires anticipating needs and maximizing what may be a relatively brief sales season.

The *promotional calendar* of a recreation business may be especially important to developing promotional strategies. The promotional budget, promotional calendar, and merchandising budget should be prepared together. An integration of recreational use periods with holidays and other sales dates makes possible a long-term strategy of promotional allocation.

The promotional plan may stress "hot items" to maximize sales in season and draw traffic into the store. Prestige brands may be featured to undergird the general prestige of the store. Price or some other element of value may be featured and is effective when prices tend to be known by consumers. Cooperative advertising can be arranged with manufacturers through their representatives or the regional distributor.

And, finally, every promotion should be carefully evaluated. Coupons may be used in advertising with codes that signal their source. Changes in sales patterns during a promotional period are compared to previous years. Salespersons can informally ask customers, especially new ones, how they were attracted to the store. Often just the initial question, "Can I help with something in particular?", will elicit valuable information. However, systematic reporting is necessary if the information is to be evaluated. In the end any promotional strategy has to be cost-effective, that is, to produce more than it costs. A strategy that isn't working can always be replaced by another.

MARKET RESEARCH

Most local retail stores do not do much market research. The very idea sounds expensive and difficult. Further, most retailers tend to believe that they "know their markets" and that market research will be of little help in their day-to-day decisions.

The next chapter has a fuller introduction to the steps and procedures of market research. Here we will only suggest some varieties of market research that are especially useful for the local retail recreation business.

The participation basis of the business has already been stressed. Many local sources of participation data can be tapped with enough regularity to keep in touch with trends.

Recreation as organized leisure activity usually requires certain facilitating resources—special space and environments, skill-acquisition programs, organized events, special access for those with abilities limited by age or some incapacity introduction to resources and opportunities, and regular scheduling of the social organization needed for participation. The recreation business may not only respond to changes in the resource opportunities but also initiate and implement them. Market research that taps interest and barriers to participation can lead to aggressive programs in which a business takes the lead in expanding opportunities. For example, sponsorship of special arts or sports programs for special populations may open new participation opportunities that also produce a new market segment.

The previous section on marketing plans included a number of current sources on statistical information about the trade area. The reference section of a good public library can offer considerable information and leads on other sources. This is particularly important for a recreation supplier because of the high correlations between certain population variables and participation. While there are many indications that barriers are falling to many types of participation formerly discouraged for children, middle- and late-life adults, women, and ethnic groups, traditional market segments still are the core of sales for many goods and services. A business that is not conscious of population trends such as the decrease of school-age children and the increase of middle-aged adults with grown children runs the risk of marketing only for the shrinking segments.

CASE: SIMPLE MARKET RESEARCH FOR RETAILERS

An art supply shop The store began as a summer business. The community was one that had tripled in size during the summer due to its nearby lakes and 200-mile distance to a metropolitan center. Since the area attracted a number of artists, especially painters, the shop was opened in the afternoons four days a week to sell painting supplies paper, paints, brushes and so on. In its small space and including tax write-offs for the owner, it immediately paid for the summer for the nonresident operator.

Stage two emerged when the building next door lost its tenant. The owner persuaded the art-supply manager to consider moving to the larger space and adding to the business by displaying and selling the work of local artists on a consignment and commission basis. The possibility was made attractive by a two-year lease at a low introductory rent and the interest of two of the store owners's nieces in working in the summer.

Again the concept proved successful. A market developed for paintings and some local handicrafts. Many who visited the area in the summer were eager to take home some attractive reminder of its beauty. In time the store even became a meeting place for artists and those interested in their products. The coffee corner was seldom empty and developed the reputation of being the most lively spot in town for conversation. Contributions to the "coffee fund" far exceeded costs.

Then, in a conversation one day, the owner was presented with another plan for expansion. For those who came to the vacation area as renters, there was often not enough space to engage in their arts production. The proposal was to use the back room as a rental studio in which good light, space, easels, and perhaps pottery wheels and a kiln would be available for a fee. Both the social and arts-production resource were attractive to the little group of seasonal visitors. But was there a large enough market to justify the expense and management costs?

The shop owner developed a market research instrument that was offered to all who came to the shop for a month. It asked information about length of stay, interest in art as a consumer and producer, possible use of a common studio, desire for instruction, and plans for future summers. From the results she was able to make a decision about the new business opportunity.

Evaluating a new market possibility An art supply store in a large southern city considered opening a second store. However, its success in the first location was due to the sizable community of productive artists in the community. Would there be a viable market in a more conventional city? A market survey was considered to find the number of amateur or professional artists who would be potential customers. However, a research advisor examined national figures and determined that the percentage of the general population in this market segment was so small that a survey would be extremely expensive.

As an alternative, national surveys were examined and profiles of arts participants drawn. Education was found to be the critical factor. Then, weighting this variable strongly, the population of the city was examined to estimate the probable size of the arts market.

However, the entrepreneur was not satisfied with the estimation procedure and wanted an enhanced basis for the decision. The market research consultant then made a series of phone calls to the main manufacturers and distributors of art supplies. Although some of the research conducted by such firms was not released to any outside firm, even a potential retail outlet, there was considerable evidence that the art supply business had demonstrated a national increase of almost 20% a year.

Estimates of the supplies needed by amateurs and professionals over the course of a year combined with the population analysis and growth figures led to a decision that a potential market existed in the city.

Finally, an in-store survey was employed at the first location and used as the basis for a marketing plan for the second store. It was found that shopping for art supplies was usually a planned trip rather than impulse shopping. Customers showed a high degree of store loyalty, drove to the store, and spent over $100 annually on supplies. The indication was that location should be accessible to transportation routes rather than in an expensive magnet location.

A further analysis of the population of the city, its geography, and institutional structure revealed significant market information. A private university was near the intersection of three major traffic arteries. The neighborhoods around the university contained a disproportionate number of college graduates. Further, the university itself had no outlet offering a full line of art supplies. The question of location seemed to be narrowed considerably.

Note that no expensive market research endeavor was launched for this project. Except for the simple in-store survey, the analysts relied on available data. Their contribution was in knowing sources and identifying the critical issues for the retailer.

Tools of the Trade The basic tools of simple market research are neither costly nor esoteric. They include a detailed map of the market area, a business directory to locate competing and complementary businesses, time to visit such firms to observe and ask questions, the library and local business organizations such as newspapers that have already gathered information about the area, a willingness to use available informants, such as customers, recreation participants and providers, and some trade sources

Most important is knowing what you need to know. What are the decision criteria for identifying markets, evaluating their current size and potential, and developing a business concept and marketing plan? Such questions are general, but the answers are specific to the business concept, trade area, and composition of the recreation market.

SUMMARY OF ISSUES

New recreation businesses have to deal with the problems of capitalization, seasonality, and management skill.

The concept of a new business may offer a different entry into an established market or seek to create a market. The created market offers both greater risk and potential.

The store image includes much more than physical appearance.

An enabling approach to recreation business supports participation through the supply of needed resources.

Start-up costs of a business require calculation of capital needs and cash flows over at least a full year.

Locating a business is based on the concept and marketing strategy as well as the identified trade area.

Franchises offer many recognition and management advantages, but at the cost of considerable flexibility.

A retail business finds many market opportunities in relation to public programs and resources.

Recreation participation is the basis of markets. Identifying new markets begins with participation as well as delineating market areas and competition.

Continual change in recreation styles includes both trends and fads. Viable markets are most often established on participation that is consistent with established styles and commitments.

The promotional calendar integrates recreation seasons with the necessity of anticipating buying patterns.

Market research is oriented toward practical questions such as the criteria for identifying markets.

DISCUSSION QUESTIONS

1. What are the advantages and disadvantages of specialty and comprehensive retailing approaches in recreation?
2. Which types of retail stores are best with high-end strategies and what recreation outlets should adopt low-end approaches?
3. How would you develop an argument to a bank loan officer supporting credit for a new recreation business?
4. Where would you locate various kinds of recreation businesses in your community? Why?
5. How would you decide whether or not to drop the franchise in the "Franchising Diversification" case?
6. What alternative in the swimming pool "market saturation" case seems most promising? Why?
7. One case suggests that women may have been an overlooked market in tennis goods. Are there other such overlooked market segments? How would you locate them?
8. Identify possibilities of market saturation in your area. What businesses might be in jeopardy?

9. In the recreation activity you know best, how have new products created new demand?
10. Describe retail promotional efforts that seem to have been particularly effective. How do they reach important market segments?
11. How is a retail promotional calendar related to a recreational calendar?

EXERCISES

1. Analyze the physical store image of a local recreation retail outlet.
2. Characterize the marketing and merchandising style of a local store.
3. Outline a loan application for a new retail recreation business.
4. Interview successful retail entrepreneur to find out what they believe it takes to succeed.
5. Outline a retail merchandise plan based on the needs of participants in a public recreation program in the community.
6. Analyze national participation trends to try to identify recreation retail market segments.
7. Using public data sources, develop a market profile for your trade area. What are the variables that are most important for particular recreation markets?
8. Outline a market research plan for a new recreation specialty store in a growing city.

REFERENCES

1. Marquardt, Raymond A., J. C. Makens, and R. G. Roe. *Retail Management,* 2nd ed., p. 159. Hinsdale, Ill.: The Dryden Press, 1979.
2. Skeirik, Kaleel C. "Small Outdoor Recreation Businesses: Pleasure or Profit?" *Leisure Today.* November–December, 1975:2.
3. Berman, Barry, and J. R. Evans. *Retail Management: A Strategic Approach,* p. 395. New York: Macmillan, 1979.
4. Marquardt et al., 1979:123.
5. Chubb, Michael, and Holly Chubb. *One Third of Our Time?,* p. 408. New York: Wiley, 1981.
6. Steinhoff, Dan, B. A. Deitzer, and K. A. Shilliff. *Small Business Management: Cases and Essays,* p. 86. Columbus, Ohio: Grid, 1975.
7. Berman and Evans, 1979:197.
8. Ibid., p. 225.

5 RETAIL RECREATION SUPPLIERS II

ISSUES

What is required to move merchandise from the loading dock to the customer?

Is there more to personnel management than hiring and firing?

How does the law shape retail business operations?

Is recreation expertise important for retail business personnel? What are the elements of selling? How is service important to retail marketing in recreation businesses?

Marketing merchandise is more than stocking shelves. How do demand changes, seasonality, and product life cycles affect such merchandising strategies?

What are the main elements of a financial plan?

How are pricing, credit programs, and cash flow interrelated?

How does accounting contribute to management in a retail business?

What are the kinds of economic, social, and market changes that have impacted retail recreation businesses?

The previous chapter discussed business concept, formation, product development, marketing plan, and market research. This chapter deals with how the retail business is run, operations and financial management, and coping with change. It presupposes bringing together a product or service concept with viable market segments. However, it takes more than ideas and potential clients to operate a retail business.

CASE: "CLIMBING THE WALL"

The business concept involved more than retailing supplies for particular kinds of resource-based outdoor recreation. It also involved an ideology, a concept of how people should work and live together. The business title, "Climbing the Wall," referred not only to rock climbing as one recreation activity requiring special equipment, but also to a deliberately personal mode of operating the business. Systematic bookkeeping and marketing designed for a maximum profit were considered petit bourgeois by the four partners who began the business. Their aim was to provide a community service, making available high-quality equipment along with the advice of experienced devotees to those engaged in rock climbing and backpacking. They would stock only the best materials, personally evaluate everything sold in the store, and even help arrange—at no fee—group trips to the mountains and instructional experiences. They believed in the value of the activities for which they offered supplies.

In their area, northern California, lived many participants who were intrigued by the style of the business and enjoyed the interaction with other climbers and packers at the store both during and after regular hours. Low rent in a transitional neighborhood, word-of-mouth advertising, the absence of salaries and wages—since the four shared the operation—and the cooperation of sympathetic manufacturers' representatives enabled the business to return an adequate income for maintenance for the first two years.

Then some troubles began to develop. Two of the partners had increased household support responsibilities and questioned the financial return in relation to the time invested. Since there were no records other than taxes paid off cash register receipts, invoices, and sums distributed to the partners, it seemed impossible to reconstruct the basis for any analysis of the costs of doing business in relation to sources of income. Markdowns and sales had been a matter of agreeing on items that had been in stock too long and their changing the tags.

Further, a few of the practices had raised other problems. The register was available to all partners as a source of cash. Some of the IOU notes placed there did not even give the dates when cash was removed. No record existed of trades and substitutions in hours at the store, so that some partners thought they had worked extra hours that had never been balanced. And there was the partner who had hooked up his van to the store electricity and maintained this temporary living arrangement for eight months.

The central problem was that four individuals were now asking questions about equity and opportunity costs. They had invested themselves for two years, enjoyed the experience, seen the clientele grow, and didn't know how to figure out why the financial return had been so meager. Small items such as buying beer for after-hours out of the cash register, allowing regulars to use the repair shop and then not being able to find tools, and a general aversion to keeping records might have compounded the difficulty. Now all they had was an uninventoried stock of goods, very little cash, and a fair amount of goodwill. The question was whether the business could be changed to provide enough of a return to support the partners and if the changes would destroy the spirit of cooperation and trust. Further, they didn't know where to begin to find out either where their income came from or where it was going.

THE TASKS OF RETAILING

What has to be done in order to operate a retail business? The partners from "Climbing the Wall" had recognized only that they needed merchandise to sell, customers to sell to, a place of business, and someone to handle sales and help customers. They found that there were other functions that had to be completed if the business were to be *managed.*

Specifically, there are at least nineteen tasks:[1]

Buying merchandise
Shipping merchandise
Receiving merchandise
Checking income shipments
Marking merchandise
Inventory control
Preparation of merchandise displays
Customer research
Customer contact
Personnel management
Repairs and alterations of merchandise
Billing customers
Handling cash receipts

Credit operation
Wrapping and packaging
Delivery
Return of merchandise to vendors
Sales forecasting
Coordinating

Some of these may be simplified. Some take place entirely in the store and are part of the routine of selling. However, note that these functions are only those of operating the store and do not include financial management. As the partners discovered, there is more to it than goodwill and knowledge of the product line.

In a business of some size the allocation of tasks is a part of management. The aim is to divide the functional assignments in ways that take advantage of complementarity in time use, skills, and locations. *Back-room* tasks may combine both receiving and shipping merchandise. *Floor* tasks include preparing and maintaining displays as well as direct selling. *Inventory* tasks include ordering, forecasting, and control. In a small business one or two people may do it all. Therefore, it is no wonder that beginning such a business requires a high investment of self.

As a business grows in size and complexity, organization becomes more and more of an identifiable task itself. Here only some of the issues of organization can be introduced. Further, the styles of management vary with the specific situation, aims of the firm, and history of relationships among personnel. However, a number of principles are common in the literature on retail organization.

1. Concern for employees includes plans to improve job satisfaction, recognize contributions and accomplishment, provide for advancement, allocate rewards fairly, and incorporate the input of employees into the operation.
2. Lines of authority should be clear so that everyone knows to whom responsibility is directed.
3. Generally an employee should report to only one supervisor. However, various kinds of employee-management "councils" can provide opportunity for more inclusive participation.
4. Each person in the organization should have the authority to accomplish designated responsibilities.
5. Some fair and recognized system of evaluation is necessary. Even though authority may be delegated by owners, the final power to evaluate is in the ownership structure of the corporation or partnership. At each level employees should be clear about the criteria of evaluation as well as the tasks assigned.

6. Supervision should not become too comprehensive for effective assistance, direction, and evaluation. A supervisor can only direct so many employees.
7. Organization for its own sake should be avoided. Simplicity is not only efficient but maintains more of an understandable business structure.
8. Everything in the business is not on the organization chart. Any organization has an informal structure in which information is transmitted and some decisions made. Failure to recognize the developed lines of communication and histories of problem solving may lead to conflict and disaffection.

Some organizations are task-oriented. Others tend to be oriented more toward the needs of the people who make up the organization. When efficiency is the sole criterion of performance, an organization may be disrupted by personnel turnover and lack of motivation. When satisfying staff is the main aim, customers may find their needs are not being met and take their business elsewhere. A retail store is in a business that brings together goods and services with people through other people, the staff. None of the three elements can long be ignored.

BUSINESS AND THE LAW

Business operates within a social system of law. The law impacts on the operation of a retail business in so many ways that only an outline can be introduced here. Business is both supported and regulated in the United States. Many fundamental financial services, product development and testing, protection against theft and fraud, and recourse against violations are provided by the government. Business could not exist without the services and infrastructure of the state. However, the same law that protects the business from chaos also protects others against the business. Businesses are regulated, sometimes to the point that meeting the requirements of the law seems to be a major part of operating a store.

Retailing and the Law

I. STORE LOCATION AND OPERATION

Zoning laws governing locations
"Blue laws" restricting days and hours of types of operation
Local ordinance on fire protection, smoking, animals, capacity, external signs and displays, etc.
Personnel laws requiring fair procedures in hiring, promoting, and firing of personnel
Antitrust laws regulating business mergers and combinations
Contract law on franchises and other agreements

Real estate law on leases, mortgages, transfer of property, property title, etc.

II. PRODUCTS AND SERVICES

Patents and copyrights giving exclusive rights for a period of time
Trademarks governing rights to names and symbols
Robinson-Patman Act restricting large retailers from obtaining discounts in acquiring merchandise
Product safety laws prohibiting sale of products not tested or declared unsafe
Product liability setting conditions of legal redress for defective or misrepresented products
Warranty and guarantee laws setting standards for assurance of product quality and means of redress
Mail and telephone sales restrictions
Delivery laws exacting penalties for late deliveries
Inventory regulations requiring an adequate stock in order to hold a sale
Labeling law requiring correct price and designation

III. PROMOTION

Truth in advertising, labeling, and packaging law on accuracy and completeness
Truth in credit requiring full disclosure of terms and equal opportunity
Loss leaders in some areas are prohibited even with full disclosure
Bait-and-switch prohibition of pressure to buy a higher-priced item than advertised
Door-to-door sales restrictions, i.e., "Green River" ordinances
Cooling-off laws providing a cancellation without penalty period for certain kinds of sales
Advertising restrictions on some items

IV. PRICING

Unit pricing law calling for display of price per unit of measure
Correct marking requiring the correct price to be on each item
Dual-pricing prohibition of old and new items being priced differently
Collusion restriction against discussing selling price with competition
Sales law designating a price reduction and nothing else as a "sale"
Fair-trade laws formerly required all retailers to sell such items at the same designated price, not now in force.

Some such regulation is obviously for the benefit of the consumer. Some protects the retailer as well by prohibiting unfair or dishonest competition. Further, there are laws that regulate the impact of the business on the environment. The visual environment cannot be "polluted" by oversize signs or offensive displays. Noise levels are regulated. Disposal of wastes must be according to health standards and out of sight of the public. Air pollution from smoking within the place of business or through some "smokestack" effluents may be prohibited or limited by certain standards.

All of these are only the beginning. Any community has a set of extralegal standards developed over time and based on custom. A local business that violates those customs will be subject to many kinds of penalty, not the least being the alienation of potential customers. In general, the laissez-faire approach to business has long been set aside in modern social systems in favor of regulation that provides some assurance to those entering into business transactions. For the most part the intent is to provide for a stable context for doing business as well as to protect consumers.

Credit legislation is an example of how such regulation developed out of a recognized need. "Truth-in-lending" acts are based on such technical matters as the different kinds of interest calculation that make a simple "10% interest" statement almost meaningless. Further, some businesses took advantage of ambiguities to place creditors in jeopardy when they did not fully understand the terms of their borrowing. In much the same way civil rights legislation was a response to evidence that those identified as part of particular racial or ethnic groups were being denied opportunities available to others by both public and private organizations. Now a variety of practices that have discriminated against women are also being controlled by a combination of regulation and court action. Renewed concern about retirement, health and safety, and union management is also leading to consideration of new legislation. Even those who prefer a minimum of regulation by the state seldom support the tragedy of old-age poverty due to a pension-fund bankruptcy or the death of children from asbestos poisoning.

CASE: SERVICE AND RETURNS

The sporting goods store described in the previous chapter had discovered that its highest-profit item was also its largest merchandising problem. Shoes were essential to the business but also were most likely to be defective. Further, the "defects" often seemed to be identified only after the shoe had been worn for some time. The first problem was that of placing some limit on the store's responsibility, especially when a pair of shoes had obviously had a fair amount of use before being returned. Could a warranty include a measurement of "tread depth" as with auto tires? The possibility of losing customers had to be weighed against costs of replacement.

The second problem was that the suppliers had different policies. Two of the manufacturers simply accepted the retailer's report on a defective item and replaced it. One required that the shoes be set aside for inspection by the company representative who might come by only four times a year. The fourth supplier, one that advertised widely in the region and sponsored well-known performers, produced the shoes with the most defects, required the most documentation on returns, and was slowest to replace them.

Could the retailer drop the line even though many customers asked for that brand? Could he assign a different replacement policy for that brand? Was a compromise possible in which a fair and even generous store policy on returns would be enclosed in every purchase, explained, and then consistently enforced? Or in this trading area was the only way of coping to use a pricing policy that reflected the additional service required? That way the fourth supplier might have a $1-a-pair markup added due to the costs of servicing the product. Each alternative had to be evaluated for legality as well as impact on the image of the store.

PERSONNEL MANAGEMENT AND SELLING

Recreation businesses tend to be labor-intensive. They not only employ sizable staffs for the volume of business but also are expected to employ personnel knowledgeable about the product and the activity in which it is employed.

The principles of organization outlined earlier are only the beginning of personnel management. For a recreation retail business, whether a leased department in a comprehensive business establishment or a small specialty shop, a key element of the enterprise is expertise. There is an expectation of service that is more like that of a dealership than a department store. In a modern department store or discount outlet, sales personnel are not expected to know anything about the merchandise except price and how to write up a purchase. In a recreation business, salespeople will be expected to know about sizes, weights, styles, and brands of equipment. After all, without such assistance the customer might as well try the discounter and just shop for price.

As a consequence there is a strong service component in a recreation business. Both personal attention and knowledge are part of the service. A mother wants to know the correct size and weight of a racquet for a ten-year-old beginner. The runner believes she needs shoes that provide heel support and cushioning for hard pavement. The backpacker wants to cut weight and retain warmth in sleeping bags. What is the right product? What are the relative advantages and disadvantages of waxless skis, graphite racquets, waffled soles, aluminum bats, and the latest shoe-repair glue?

This kind of service takes time. In the calculation of the costs of doing business, there will have to be a relatively high calculation for sales time and personnel. Also, the personnel will have to be selected with consideration for more than merely the ability to perform the tasks, deal with customers, and meet the trust criteria of the business. Every person hired should add to the expertise of the current staff, either by strengthening a high sales line or complementing current expertise. A store carrying a product line and without anyone adept in that form of recreation would seek to add such experience and knowledge. Again, selling recreation equipment is one aspect of providing a resource for an activity. The meaning of the activity is the experience. To sell the equipment, it helps to have shared the experience.

Of course, there are also other criteria for hiring. For a small business one major turning point is the decision to expand the staff to the point where specialization in job description divides and delegates responsibilities. Then both personnel selection and personnel management become a major part of the work of general management. There is a temptation to remain small and simple rather than rely on others to carry out the functions of the business. On the other hand, economies of great size in a competitive environment may be too significant to resist. Bigger is not necessarily better or cheaper, but small is not always efficient.

FUNCTIONS OF PERSONNEL MANAGEMENT

How personnel are selected, supported, and evaluated depends largely on the philosophy of the business. If the recreation supplier expects to operate with an orientation of personal advice, then the ability to contribute to that image and atmosphere is central.

Recruitment Often the lower-level hiring in a recreation retail business is "off the street." Floor salespersons may have been customers, fellow participants in some recreation activities, or others who have sought such work. The seasonal nature of some business may allow for the hiring of students or others whose work hours can be adjusted to business needs. Only when the business grows to the point that specialized skilled personnel are required, such as for financial management, is there likely to be a need for a public recruitment effort. The longer-term needs of the business can be kept in mind during recruitment by recognizing that all those hired will not have opportunity for advancement. The store will need some employees who are willing to fill functional positions in stocking, maintenance, and selling without concern about career advancement. Balancing the needs of the store for functional maintenance and still obtaining staff who will work with enthusiasm and intelligence can be quite difficult.

Selection The manager should have a clear definition of what is needed in the job. In some cases, it is possible not only to interview but also try out the role in a contrived situation. More often, after minimum training the prospective employee is put on the job as a trainee with a stated period of learning and evaluation. During this period managers should be available to help and inform and also give a clear statement of the criteria for evaluation. Ideally, during and after the training and evaluation period the atmosphere is one of cooperation and openness rather than judgment. The trainee is encouraged to ask questions and to offer observations about the business and the style of operation.

Supervision Supervision is more than giving orders and assigning tasks.[2] It involves negotiation, communication, support, facilitation, clarification, motivation, direction, and affective sharing. It involves structuring the position so that the tasks can be accomplished and yield some reward on completion. Supervision is management as well as a relationship. Bringing together the organizational skill to develop a functionally integrated business system that get the jobs done *and* maximizes the satisfaction of workers is something of an art as well as a learned skill. Employees are taught, evaluated, assisted, and rewarded. They are also watched with some care because they can damage the atmosphere of the business, which depends on relationships for its existence. Finally, an employee should know what kinds of rewards are to be forthcoming in the event of superior performance.

CASE: PERSONAL SELLING AND THE STORE IMAGE

Jim had turned his knowledge of camping into a viable and satisfying business. The surprise had been the growth of the volume. Then the expansion into a winter line of skiwear had been a natural development from the initial lines. In fact, some of the same manufacturers and wholesalers were promoting jackets, winter boots, gloves, and other items as well as the tents, hiking boots, dried foods, and other equipment associated with camping in wilderness areas. Since Jim also engaged in Nordic skiing in the winter, he was able to continue the store image of personal knowledge and advice that went with the selling.

Then came two changes. The first was an overall growth in volume that required hiring three other floor salespersons as well as a part-time assistant to deal with stock, inventories, and storage. The second was competition. One of the discount stores on the edge of town had a new manager for their sporting goods and outdoor department. This manager used the national purchasing advantages of the chain to build up a fair selection of tents, jackets, outdoor gear, sleeping bags, and other merchandise in some of Jim's more general lines. And the discount prices were 20% to 40% lower!

In the early phase of the competition Jim didn't handle the situation well. When customers were bold enough to mention the prices at the discount mart, he impatiently told them that if they were willing to take their chances on inferior goods, they should go ahead. Finally one of the floor sales staff, a part-time student who was planning to leave at the end of the summer, confronted Jim with the fact that his attitude was compounding the problem rather than leading to a solution.

At a staff meeting, Jim's personnel helped him list their advantages:

- They provided expert advice as well as selected merchandise.
- They had a full range of goods needed, not just those available from the national supplier.
- They offered competing brands, not only a house label.
- They provided limited repair service in the store.

Yet the problem remained that business volume was down and especially in some big-ticket items such as tents, parkas, and down jackets being stocked by the discounter. Was the heart of the solution in sales as well as in a different marketing strategy?

First, the sales staff decided to be more aggressive in dealing with customers. Not only would they greet those who entered the store and offer help but they would take the initiative in pointing out the variety of merchandise. They offered alternatives by analyzing significant differences in ways that engaged the customers in a decision, suggesting complementary items, and stressing quality and reliability. They would also remind customers of their liberal in-store warranty and service policy.

Second, they would meet the price issue head-on by always having on the floor a number of sale items. The suppliers would be enlisted in a program of securing lines from the previous year at discounts. The displays would stress the brand names as well as the prices. There would always be available discounted merchandise, if limited in selection, as a symbol that all the discounts were not in the other store.

Third, they would develop a tryout program in which some kinds of equipment could be rented for a brief period and the rental applied to purchase of new goods. Their advertising and in-store sales approaches would stress that the customer would *know* the quality and value of the goods.

Fourth, Jim would spend some money redesigning and remodeling the front of the store. Its present closed facade would be opened up to become more inviting and to utilize the store's location on a main street of town. Some kind of sale banners would be employed to attract new customers who had assumed that the specialty store always be an expensive place to shop and perhaps only for experts in the recreation activity.

The key to meeting this challenge was responding to the suggestions of other personnel and then developing a plan that enlisted their skills and interest in personal selling. They had helped formulate the plan and were integral to its implementation. Further, the interest in the recreation for which the store was a supplier would be incorporated even more into the store promotion and image.

Some critics have written about the decline in personal selling. In the former sense of one clerk for every customer in the store attending to all wants and answering every question, the loss may be insignificant and even a relief. Many shoppers prefer to have time to examine and consider merchandise and to feel that they can enter and leave a store without being cornered for an immediate decision.

However, in the sense of providing information, alleviating doubts, suggesting new aspects of the selection and affirming the choice, retail selling remains important to a local business. Further, the store should be designed to provide a context for such selling. By clustering merchandise on the basis of activity, allowing for space in which salesperson and customers can meet and talk, and even recognizing the need to hold and manipulate some recreation equipment, a store can be laid out to facilitate personal selling. The agenda of selling is to identify customers, guide them to the product lines, and bring them into some relationship with the goods, often by encouraging them to try out an item, responding to questions and uncertainty with information and assurance, and meeting objections to a decision to purchase. It involves listening and empathizing, knowing when to suggest something else rather than push for a decision, and asking leading questions that engage the customer in an interchange that may lead to a sale. And in a local specialty business, goodwill may be more important than a sale.

SELLING AND SERVICE

There is more to sales than exchanging money for some good or service. Among the wider aspects of selling are the services that accompany the sale. Already emphasized is the sharing of knowledge and expertise about the goods and the associated recreation. Other services include the following:

Personal services such as some form of child care, storage of purchases, and availability of literature about the use of the goods, locales for recreation, and conditions of recreation environments.

Credit availability through in-store credit plans, bank credit systems, "plastic money"—the national credit card systems—and a variety of layaway plans. One problem is often the availability of enough cash to make the purchase. Whether or not the retailer chooses to share in the solution depends on a number of factors in the business. However, more and more the buyer will assume that some form of credit is available. Further, the cost of such credit is built into retail price structures so commonly that it is part of the competitive environment. Whether a merchant decides to pay the cost in delay, slowed cash flow, and writing off bad debts, or by paying the constant percentage of the bank card system depends on the reliability of the clientele and the customs of the community.

Service contracts and repair are one way that a local supplier can differentiate from the chain or comprehensive competitor. While any warranty is regulated by law, the provisions can be made clear enough that misunderstandings are minimized. The point is that the service facilities of the business are used to develop the store image of reliability as well as to enhance customer loyalty. In recreation the season may be all-important. Equipment is purchased for use during that particular time. A service policy that ensures a very brief turnaround on repairs or replacement may be the single greatest asset of a product-supplying firm. On the other hand, delays in servicing will diminish customer loyalty and decrease satisfaction in ways that do irreparable damage to the store image.

Other services include delivery, wrapping, adequate parking, space for customers to repair or alter goods purchased, and loan services in case of the temporary incapacitation of purchased equipment.

MANAGEMENT OF MERCHANDISE

The sales personnel stand between the customer and the merchandise. Even the best selling cannot substitute for the "real goods"—the merchandise offered and sold. The management of merchandise is a multifaceted process.[3] Just buying and handling merchandise involves the following:

Assigning responsibility for buying merchandise
Gathering information about customer demand
Determining merchandise sources
Evaluating products
Negotiating purchases
Concluding purchase agreements
Handling merchandise
Reordering
Reevaluating purchasing plan

In some cases buying will be done in cooperation with other firms through an agreement. Some stores arrange exclusive contracts with suppliers that grant the store some price advantages, shared advertising, use of brand name and symbols, or exclusive sales in the market area in return for specializing in products from that supplier. Some manufacturers or wholesalers offer extended terms for purchase so that merchandise may be in the store for sixty days or longer before payment is due.

CONSUMER DEMAND AND MERCHANDISE PLANNING

How is it possible to know what to order and in what quantities? A well-established retailer will have records from past seasons that show quantities, prices, sizes, and brand distributions. Trends over time as well as records of merchandise that had to be disposed of at end-of-season sales give information pertinent to revising orders from previous selling seasons. Further, suppliers usually have their own sales forecasts, sometimes based on market research. However, such forecasts are hardly disinterested and may not represent the particular markets of the retailer outlet.

Other sources of information are comments and responses from customers that have been reported by sales personnel, trade publications, key informants active in the related recreation activity, and competitors. Most retail managers keep track of the competition with personal visits to other stores. Competition involves not only price comparison but also being ready to meet the offering of new products and lines of merchandise.

Along with evaluating the potential markets for merchandise, the buyer must evaluate the products as well. Final choice is based on bringing into focus the target markets, the product lines, and the store image and orientation. In some stores price is a primary factor in choice while in others quality and style come first. In most cases the buyer attempts to provide within the limitations of space and purchasing power a range of merchandise to attract all the markets sought as customers. One problem in contemporary choice is the variety of sources of goods. A shoe or garment may look like ones ordered before but be manufactured thousands of miles away under quite different conditions. Brand name has less and less meaning for quality assurance in either workmanship or materials. As a result the purchasing temptation is to make price the primary factor in the decision since it seems often to be the only sure element. However, the reputation of the store is at risk with every purchasing decision.

Some merchandise is purchased directly from the manufacturer, who organizes shows, sends catalogs, and employs company representatives. Often the manufacturer will also provide shipping and credit. Full-service wholesalers buy the merchandise from the manufacturer and arrange shipping, storing, and often credit and promotion. Limited-service merchant wholesalers provide a line of products without the services. Many are primarily mail-order or even cash-and-carry distributors. There are also agents and brokers who arrange for purchases at a commission but do not take title to the goods themselves.

CASE: SEASONAL DIVERSIFICATION

A comprehensive recreation goods store usually has high and low seasons for selling but is not dependent on a single recreation activity with a segmented time for participation. Christmas selling is important as are the beginning of participation seasons, especially summer in four-season climates. However, there are always the winter seasons, purchases for use in other climates, and preparation for upcoming seasons. Further, the overlaps in participation seasons alleviate the peaks and valleys of sales volume. The problem is to order months in advance of the seasons in quantities that will meet the demand without overextending the line of credit or space for storage.

However, in a specialty store the season may be all-important. Further, most stores have to lease space for twelve months even though their sales are concentrated into three or four. The common remedy for this problem is diversification.

One store that found its diversification almost out of hand had begun with supplies for backpacking and remote-area camping. The interest of the two founders was in the packs themselves. One had designed a style for which the store became the test outlet. The problem was that both founders had other jobs. Therefore, they immediately had to hire part-time help for the store. This actually worked out quite well since they found a more than adequate supply of outdoor-oriented men and women who knew the activity and the equipment. In fact, the owner-salesperson group became a social entity with considerable off-season interaction as well as summer journey to the woods and mountains.

However, the employee situation presented a difficulty when business dropped off almost to nothing. In order to offer year-round employment new sales lines were developed. They included cross-country ski equipment for sale and rent, books and clothing for both kinds of skiing, and a general line of cold-weather sports attire. The business grew to the extent that a new location with three times the space had to be found. Except for one snowless and warm winter, the off-season business became as important in volume and profit production as the original season.

But such expansion came at some cost. One partner found the expanded management tasks too time-consuming and left the business to concentrate on his backpack design and manufacturing. Merchandise and personnel management became too demanding for part-time owners. Matters such as ordering diverse lines, selecting merchandise for season-end sales, expansion of the general apparel lines, Christmas sales, maintenance of equipment in the rental department, and so on, became too complex for simple cooperation. The financial integration of the operation required more than hiring a part-time bookkeeper. Dealing with credit from the bank as well as from suppliers was a monthly balancing act. Diversification had come at a high price in terms of management simplicity and style.

BETWEEN BUYING AND SELLING

The essence of a retail business is that it buys goods and then sells them. But what happens in between?

Once the merchandise is ordered, received, checked, and opened, a number of functions remain before the customer and sales personnel engage in their interchange. The merchandise must be checked against the shipping invoice and original order, prices marked, and displays must be set up, divided between the number on the floor and those in the back room, recorded for inventory control, and given some attractive sign calling the attention of customers to its location.

Further, records must be checked regularly, either personally or through a computerized inventory system, in order to reorder items and sizes in short supply. Finally, decisions are made at various points during the product selling season to mark prices down, change displays, advertise sales, and in other ways attempt to minimize the inventory that will have to be stored at the end of the selling season. Again, the seasonal nature of so much recreation makes this type of control and planning especially critical.

INNOVATION

The diversification of lines illustrated above, which rests on the experience and expertise of the staff, is one type of innovation. There are many others that may make a difference in a competitive retail environment.

Complementary product and service lines may be selected to take advantage of the initial attraction of market segments to the store. The key is knowing what kinds of recreation are most likely to be associated. Although there are no one-to-one relationships in which all participants in one activity also do another, there are common combinations of interest. Participants in music are often interested in other arts as well, so that a cooperative sales gallery for painters complements a store handling materials for musicians and dancers. In some communities, becoming a ticket outlet for arts events can be a key method for attracting a range of potential customers to the store's location.

For sports and outdoor recreation, shoes and clothing seem to be the classic complementary product lines. There is always the possibility of crossover not only in recreation participation but also in the use of warmups and other clothing from one activity to another. However, sportswear marketing is becoming increasingly activity-specific and specialized.

Specially identified locations in the store are a useful innovation. For example, there may be a "Novice Nook" for low-cost or used equipment best for those trying out an activity. A "Cellar" may be used for discounted items, related food goods, or do-it-yourself repairs that build customer loyalty.

Sometimes another noncompeting business may be willing to donate or rent display space. In graphic arts a changing display of paintings in a nearby restaurant or retail store can bring new trade to a specialty shop. Such arrangements have to be worked out very carefully but can be mutually beneficial in cost reduction and promotion for each party.

PRODUCT CYCLES

The concept of the product life cycle is important to any recreation business. It implies that almost any product will have an escalating period of sales during an introduction and growth period that is followed by a leveling stage of maturity and, finally, decline. For the retail merchant deciding on merchandising programs, orders, and promotions months in advance, the shape of the product cycle curves is of more than aesthetic interest. There are a number of possibilities:[4]

It is the task of the product representative to convince those who do the ordering for retail outlets that the new product will have a boom, seasonal, or plateau cycle. In order to move from the introductory period to one of growth, some program of promotion will be planned. However, without retail outlets the promotion will fail.

For the buyer, there are a number of criteria for ordering:

- Is the promotion likely to reach and be effective with the targeted market segments in the store's trade area?
- How large is the potential market segment? And will the sales pattern be for repeat sales or one-time purchases?
- Does the product tie into current recreation participation or does it require some alteration in investments of time, money, or other resources?
- Can the targeted market segment afford the product?
- What is the probable recreation satisfaction curve for the use of the prod-

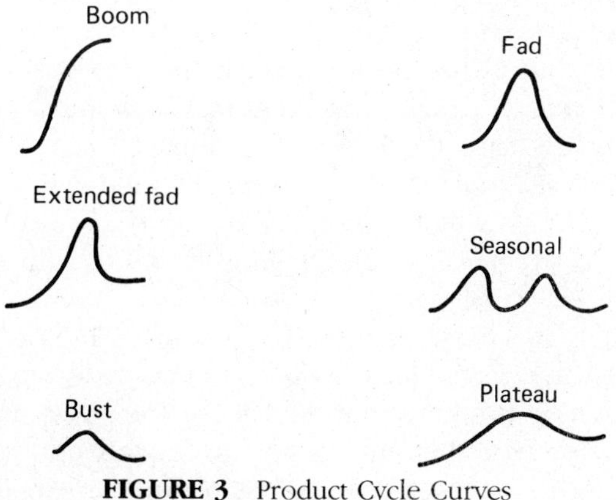

FIGURE 3 Product Cycle Curves

uct? Is it easily mastered so that boredom sets in quickly? Is it so difficult that frustration will be a common experience? Are there an escalating series of levels of mastery in its use?

- What are the social contexts for the product use? Is it likely to be taken up as a basis for joint activity by already-formed recreation groups such as school peer cohorts, household dyads, or organized programs?

Also, some protection on the "down side" is important to the business taking a risk in ordering a supply of a new product. The return policy of the supplier, extended credit for the retailer, and the stability of the supplier are significant matters for consideration. Recreation has fads and sometimes considerable profit can be made by catching the sales wave before it crests. On the other hand, quick saturation of a market may also leave a retail firm caught with an inventory that was stocked at premium prices and must be disposed of at considerable loss.

In recreation there is also the possibility of expanded markets. An activity with a currently restricted participation base may change. Some years ago a combination of expanded opportunities through public recreation programs and resources and some attention-getting media events broadened participation in tennis considerably. However, the social basis for that expansion had already been laid as the once elite sport had been introduced to schools and to the recreation programs of smaller towns and city parks. There had already been a demonstrated extension of interest in a horizontal trend. Similar growth was found in gymnastics, swimming, and skating after they were highlighted in Olympics coverage on television. However, in each case there was a predictable plateau cycle in which the difficulties and costs of the activity led to a decline after the maturity peak in participation.

ASSORTMENT STRATEGIES

How much inventory should a retail establishment carry and how should it be distributed? There are several strategies that may be selected or mixed.

A *wide and deep* strategy has the advantage of meeting most of the customer's expectation at the cost of a high investment in inventory. A *wide and shallow* strategy meets a broad market at lower cost but may disappoint customers with the limited variety. A *narrow and deep* assortment builds a specialized and loyal clientele but at the cost of limited traffic and markets. A *narrow and shallow* approach is least costly to the store but limits traffic with a weak image and limited loyalty.

Recreation supply businesses are often "narrow" in their assortment with a specific store image and a clientele who know the store and its offerings because of regular participation in the related recreation. They may build considerable customer loyalty. However, they are also highly dependent on a limited market segment and subject to adverse impacts of decreased participation or increased competition. On the other hand, a wide assortment weakens the store image and makes it difficult to provide expert product counsel on everything sold.

Inventory control may be related to a number of prior functions and conditions. The seasonality of the merchandise use will set a timetable for inventory decisions. Ordering, maintaining stock, markdowns and sales, remainder displays, off-season storage, and ordering for the following season are shaped by the seasonal curve of demand. The diversity of merchandise, traffic flows, complementarity of items, size and scale of the operation, and division of tasks in the store are other elements in determining the nature of inventory control. In a small shop the manager may personally check inventories several times a week during slow sales periods. In most outlets there will be a system of recordkeeping that enables the manager to identify stock depletion in ample time to reorder. In a large and complex operation all merchandise will be coded so that the electronic register at the point of sale feeds into an inventory program that prints out stocks at the end of each day and highlights items in short supply. The nature of inventory control depends on the complexity of the operation, but it is necessary in any retail store to minimize customer disappointment when the inventory does not meet the demand for standard items in a high-use period.

LAYOUT AND STYLE

Any retail area has shape as well as size. Just how it will be laid out depends on what is there as well as the merchandising objectives of the business. Designing the store layout begins with the market objectives of the store concept. The design and layout may emphasize the "star" merchandise by displaying it where it can be seen by those passing the store. In other cases the merchandise that attracts customers is placed so that customers pass displays of other items that may interest them. A common display format is to group complementary products so that persons coming to purchase or replace one item of equipment or apparel will be attracted by other goods used in the same kind of recreation.

A second and sometimes conflicting factor in store layout is the prevention of theft. Small merchandise, clothing that can be concealed, and items that require handling are especially subject to shoplifting. As a preventative, such merchandise may be displayed where it can best be watched and protected rather than where it might best attract sales from floor traffic.

When seasonality is a factor in a recreation business, the layout and display designs will usually change several times a year. Limited prime space makes it poor practice to place out-of-season merchandise in prime space where it only impedes passage and the attractive display of those goods likely to be the object of the store visit.

In general, the store layout and space plan should be functional. Layout reflects and announces the nature of the store, its image and style. Further, the design should work in terms of display of product lines, protection of merchandise, sales coverage, and sight lines from outside the store. It needs to work so that merchandise can be brought to the customer efficiently, purchasing can be completed without undue delay, and there is space to view, examine, and, when necessary, try the recreation goods. Further, the spatial relationship of sales and service areas should be such that the primary draw into the store is utilized to enhance interest in the other elements of the business.

CASE: MARKETING AND INTERIOR STYLE

The fundamental decisions had been made. The new store would feature sportswear and would lease about 20,000 square feet in the new White Oaks Shopping Mall. The sportswear decision was based on statistics demonstrating that this was the fastest-growing part of the clothing market and had wide year-round demand. The shopping center decision was partly a response to the attractive lease terms offered by the developer, who wanted to fill the new facility quickly, and partly a recognition that such malls tended to draw a disproportionate amount of trade away from older, more traditional retail areas.

Now the decision revolved around the store image and merchandising issues. Would the store go for the high end of the market by designing the floor use with spacious dressing rooms, full lighting, fancy fixtures, carpeting, and entry and wall display stands? Consistent with this choice would be merchandise of only name brands and a generally upper-end price structure.

The alternative was to stock a wide assortment with most of the inventory in slightly off-price brands and styles. The layout would be utilitarian with self-service, rows of racks with merchandise divided by price and size, indoor-outdoor carpet, plain dressing rooms, and a cheery but spartan decor.

There was also a third alternative, to carry only private-label goods manufactured to specifications. Merchandise would be marketed as exclusive with their special "look" and a guarantee of quality. The owners had been manufacturers' representatives for several years and had the knowledge and contacts to take such a step. However, they also recognized that it was a high-risk alternative.

What should be the criteria for decision?

First, they knew the community. The population of about 150,000 was in an agricultural area and would draw widely enough to add another 100,000 to the trade area. The mall would be, at least for a time, the premier shopping place for the area. The population was diversified, comprising a good percentage of executive and professional families, career singles, and well-paid workers and supervisors in electronics and agricultural industries. There were a state university branch in the central city and two private schools in nearby communities.

Second, their competition in the mall would be primarily from the sportswear department of a regional department store and a branch of the Sears chain. Also in the community were three sporting goods stores with limited apparel lines and two discount stores with uneven selections of low-priced sportswear. It seemed to the entrepreneurs that there were openings in the market structure for both a high-end approach and a comprehensive price-elastic concept.

Because of their experience with the merchandise, the owners decided to make the decision primarily one of merchandising. They were familiar with the upper-end approach and would be able to utilize their contacts with the distributors of American and European ready-to-wear brands and a sprinkling of designer labels. This approach would concentrate primarily on the market segments of younger women, both those active in recreational sports and those who wanted to display a sports self-presentation. This store image would utilize the top sports brands to legitimize what was actually a specialized young women's apparel store. They also recognized that more middle-aged women were cultivating such active images and might become a major market segment. The problems with this approach were uncertainty as to the size of the market segments, the high cost of decorating, and direct competition with the department store that would be in the featured location of the mall.

Investigating the cost of the fashionable decor, mostly costs that were not recoverable in case of failure, led them to think again about the second alternative. Its advantages were the low cost of setting up the interior, appealing to the widest markets with a full line of sportswear for men and women, and having more flexibility in pricing. However, it would be difficult to establish an appealing store image that took advantage of the mall location and its walk-around traffic. The layout would be much more subject to shoplifting. Further, the mall lease placed fixed costs high enough that the store could never compete with the discount operations in price. However, they could include lines of merchandise that attracted men and women shopping together, employed "perishables" such as shoes to increase store traffic, and still establish an image of value and variety as well as reasonable prices.

Or was there a fourth alternative, one that combined most of the advantages of the others without the inordinately high cost of the first? The owners were very conscious of the dangers of becoming "just another store" that might never build up a clientele of loyal customers who responded to the statement of a clear store image.

One weakness of the owners' background was also their strength. They knew the merchandise, how to get it, and a variety of methods of display and marketing; but they did not know the potential markets well. When an advisor pointed out to them that they had done no market research, they admitted that their knowledge in this area came entirely from seeing the clientele of other stores. Further, they had not investigated the recreation participation patterns of the community to try to understand how sportswear styles were related to recreation styles.

Operations management is not a separate and compartmentalized element of retail management. Rather, marketing and market research, concept and image, philosophy, and long-term aims are all part of how merchandise is selected, made available, and sold. Although there are certain basic functions of operating a retail business. All may be carried out in a variety of ways that not only get the job done but also reflect the overall nature of the business.

FINANCIAL MANAGEMENT

The same issue of consistency applies to financial management. The overall plan of the business determines how management of capital, pricing, credit policies, and accounting are carried out. Financial management is instrumental to the operation of the business. However, failure to manage finances adequately can undermine and eventually destroy even the most creatively conceived venture.

A FINANCIAL PLAN

A financial plan includes a number of elements:

- Capitalization
- Managing working capital
- Budgeting for merchandise
- Revenue and payments management
- Pricing
- Credit programs
- Accounting:
  - Mandated accounting
  - Accounting for management

All these are related to the aims of the business. Although any business must not only cover expenses over time and pay for investment capital, the short-term objectives differ for a business in its own cycle of initiating growth, maturity, and planning for the future. A low return on investment in the early phases may be expected. Later periods may stress profit and debt retirement. The point is that financial management is designed to measure the accomplishment of the current aims of the enterprise.

Capitalization Capitalization has been discussed in the previous chapter. As already indicated, the costs of opening a retail store may be quite high, and the most common cause of failure is reported to be financial, undercapitalization leading to a cutting back of expenses just when the store should be expanding. A financial plan should take into account all the costs of establishing a business, including furnishing and stocking the store, the cost of credit for merchandise, a period of low revenues as a clientele is built, and necessary income for the operators who have usually foregone other income to start the business.

In the next chapter there is the outline of a marketing plan that can be used to discuss capitalization with lending agencies. Such a plan integrates the concept of the business being proposed with capitalization requirements, anticipated revenue and expenses by selling seasons, targeted market segments in the market area, competition, and marketing strategies. The presentation should include an anticipated schedule for debt retirement, both interest and principle.

Some recreation businesses require relatively little capitalization. When established with a service orientation in inexpensive locations and relying on the expertise and experience of the principals, a business may require modest initial capitalization. On the other hand, retail businesses in competitive markets generally require a solid initial investment of capital. In many cases the local banks and other lending agencies are the first source. The federal Small Business Administration has underwritten loans to recreation-oriented businesses, especially in areas in need of economic development. Many communities have groups of investors seeking to place their capital in promising businesses. All these sources will insist on a well-constructed prospectus for the enterprise, demonstrated competence, target markets, legal safeguards for investors, and an assured commitment on the part of those making the proposal. Further, a realistic assessment of capital needs is more likely to attract support than a financial plan that does not support the concept and its development.

Initial investment can be minimized, however, with a number of strategies. Carefully selecting leased space that meets the needs of the business but is not in a choice high-rent location may be especially important for a business that will have a specialized and self-identified market based on current or anticipated recreation participation. Recreation themes, often with a rustic outdoor motif, can be used to decorate retail outlets without the purchase of expensive fixtures or the reconstruction of the interior space. Some suppliers will offer liberal credit and payment conditions to obtain a new account. In some cases enlistment of a cohort of activity devotees in the process of opening can cut costs and ensure their loyalty. Flexibility in plan and design as well as using the skills of interested parties may lower capital requirements and produce a store image superior to the chrome and glitter of the traditional new shop.

Managing Working Capital The financial management of a complex and growing firm involves too many technical aspects of capitalization, accounting, assessment and decision to summarize in a few paragraphs. However, some of the basic issues are central to visualizing the operation of a retail recreation business.

Long-term loans are usually secured with real property of some kind. A business may obtain twenty- to thirty-year loans to purchase or construct a building or other real estate. Intermediate-term loans are important in getting a business started, financing expansion, or developing a new image by remodeling. Fixed assets such as machinery, equipment, or fixtures are financed with loans of from one to ten years in repayment period. The servicing of both kinds of loans are then a part of the financial plan since regular repayment of principal and interest is usually necessary.

There are also a number of sources of short-term funds. Commercial banks may offer a line of credit to a firm that can demonstrate an adequate cash flow or net worth basis. The amount borrowed varies according to the current needs of the business. Such arrangements may be much better for the business than a series of commercial loans, even though interest and fees may be relatively high.

As already suggested, many suppliers of merchandise will offer short-term credit. Payment may be delayed for thirty, sixty, or ninety days, allowing for the generation of some revenue from the stock. One cost of relying on such distributor financing is that it requires foregoing any discounts available to stores that pay cash on delivery for merchandise.

Floor-plan financing involves using inventories as the collateral for loans. The unit value of the merchandise is the basis for the financing from the bank or other institution. This method includes an accounting of sales and repayment to the bank on a regular basis. Interest rates for such loans tend to be high. When interest rates go up, any short-term financing costs may prove to be a considerable burden for a store, especially one in a price-competitive market.

Cash flow management involves forecasting expenses for each salient period of the business year. The problem is to ensure that there will be adequate cash on hand to meet expenses when they come due. In a retail business, expenses and income seldom arrive simultaneously. For example, merchandise ordered in July for delivery by November 1 may call for payment October 20 in order to take advantage of the cash discount. However, the stock will not go on the floor until November 20, in time for Christmas buying. If that merchandise is purchased through a bank credit system, then it may be near the end of December before the revenue is available to the business. In the meantime, there are all the ongoing expenses of operation as well as added costs of holiday selling and promotion.

Effective cash flow management involves an analysis of the timing of cash receipts and disbursements over the business year. Maintaining excessive cash accounts is costly in foregone interest or reinvestment in the business. Depleted cash accounts may restrict the ability of the manager to enhance inventories at advantageous prices, meet competition, engage in promotion, reward productive employees, or just pay the fixed costs of doing business. And, again, short-term borrowing tends to be expensive.

A cash flow analysis begins by establishing the periods, usually on a monthly or weekly basis, for analysis. Expected income and expenses are inserted into the calendar periods. Sales are estimated on the basis of previous years and changes in the market demand. Both internal and external changes in the business situation are included in this forecasting. Sales revenues are calculated from the periodic estimates. When cash outflow for each period is also estimated, then the cash balance at the end of each period can be calculated. Even with a margin of error, the likely problem periods can be identified and the need for additional income in those periods anticipated. A failure to include the costs of such short-term financing in a business financial plan can lead to serious losses. In a business with highly seasonal sales, generating cash and avoiding high-interest credit may be the key to profitable operation.

In general, over a payment period there should be at least a one-to-one ratio in liguidity. *Liquidity* is calculated as the sum of cash plus marketable securities plus accounts receivable divided by current liabilities:[5]

$$\frac{\text{Cash} + \text{cashable securities} + \text{receivables}}{\text{Obligations due}}$$

A liquidity ratio of less than 1:1 is a warning that the firm cannot meet its obligations without borrowing or selling from its inventory.

The *current ratio* is defined as current assets divided by current liabilities. A general rule is that a retail store should have a current ratio of about 2:1. This allows for some loss in the value of inventories due to market changes or the failure to sell some stock and a loss in accounts receivable. Too high a ratio implies that cash is lying idle or that excessive inventories are being maintained. A business always needs some cushion to deal with the failure of other parties to meet obligations and to respond to changed conditions. Further, without a positive asset-to-liabilities ratio, the business has no recourse to loans without offering collateral outside the business as security.

CASE: CASH FLOW AND DAY-TO-DAY MANAGEMENT

A St. Louis sporting goods store was in its tenth year of operation. It had a good location with a reasonable lease. With an average markup of 40%, the managers had been able to charge their salaries to operating expenses and realize a profit on their investment. In the previous year they had produced the following income statement:

Net sales	208,000
Cost of goods	43,200
Gross margin	164,800
Operating expenses:	
Fixed expenses	41,600
Variable expenses	43,200
Total	84,800
Net profit for the year	60,000

One of the two owner-managers was interested in break-even analysis. To produce a break-even statement, they placed rent, depreciation, insurance, taxes, and basic staff salaries in the fixed-expense category. Other salaries, commissions, utilities, supplies, and maintenance were classified as variable. From this analysis they determined that the break-even point in sales would be $112,000. Thus, they were comfortably beyond the break-even line.

However, they wanted a more precise accounting by the day. Dividing by 52, they found that their weekly operating expenses were $1,632 and net weekly profit $748. To achieve this level they needed average daily sales of $666 with an average gross margin of $400, expenses of $272, and an average daily profit of $128.

When the one partner analyzed sales figures for the previous year, he found considerable discrepancies. Average daily sales were:

Monday	$ 500
Tuesday	$ 320
Wednesday	$ 280
Thursday	$ 800
Friday	$ 900
Saturday	$1200

By applying the 40% markup figure to each day, he discovered that the gross margin was less than the daily expenses of $272 for Monday, Tuesday, and Wednesday. He proposed to his partner that they consider a new set of store hours that would reflect the importance of the second half of the week. Further, he believed they should investigate the operations of other businesses in the market area to determine whether the hours now unprofitably open on Tuesday and Wednesday might not be better used by opening Sunday afternoon. His partner thought over the matter carefully before responding. Then he thanked his partner for his efforts but stated that there was too much missing from the analysis. For example, seasonal variation was not reflected by using averages in the analysis. Further, the number of customers who might be antagonized by variable hours might outweigh the costs of being open on unprofitable days.

Pricing Retail Merchandise The so-called keystone markup for retail goods is 50%. A general rule can begin with the likelihood that an item with a unit cost from the supplier of $1.00 will be priced at $1.50 in the store. To cover fixed and variable expenses and the costs of capitalization, such a pricing policy is not unusual. However, there are many factors that enter into a sophisticated pricing strategy.

The first is *price elasticity*. For some items buyers are quite sensitive to price changes. It may require business experience to measure such elasticity. However, some factors in recreation businesses are predictable. If the item is necessary for participation, then the price may be relatively inelastic in general. Golf balls, tennis balls, and shoes will be purchased somewhere. However, such items tend to be competitively priced. Equipment that is integral to the activity is most likely to be comparison-shopped and purchased where the price is lowest. Therefore, for the individual store such items may be extremely elastic in a competitive market. On the other hand, goods that are replacements or upgrades for participants are likely to be quite price-elastic, with purchase postponed until financial resources increase or prices are lowered. Another variable in price elasticity is the income level of the market. Price is a less salient factor in the buying decisions of high-income consumers.

Legislation, especially federal laws applied to businessses engaged in interstate trade, restricts pricing in several ways. For example, stores in a competitive trade area are not allowed to agree on prices, to conspire to fix prices. Some states have minimum-price laws to prevent pricing policies designed to drive competition out of the trade area. Manufacturers and wholesalers are prohibited from discriminating against smaller retailers. Unit pricing is required in some states so that the consumer can compare the costs of different-sized packages. Price advertising is regulated to require "truth" and the availability of goods advertised at a given price.

Suppliers are a factor in pricing due to the costs to the retailer of obtaining the merchandise. Some manufacturers guarantee prices and refund to the retailer the difference between actual selling price and the guaranteed price. More commonly, manufacturers resist having their products offered at prices that are seen to undermine their market image. A retail buyer may find suppliers unwilling to sell certain products without assurance that they will not be employed as advertised reduced-price leaders. Manufacturers also resist a retail store "selling against the brand" by using the known brand to bring customers to the department and then promoting a lower-price item on which the store gains a higher profit.

Competition remains a major factor in pricing. When the cunsumer has choices of substitute goods or alternative stores, pricing has to take such competition into account. In the recreation supply business, competition includes mail-order retail outlets, on- and off-site stores, and the pro shops at the recreation location. Just knowing the prices down the street may not be enough.

Retail Price Strategy Pricing involves a number of objectives. For example, a new store may want to use certain key items to demonstrate its "low-price" store image. A lower profit margin is accepted in order to attain longer-range objectives. At the other extreme, a new store may price some high-volume goods with a high markup in order to assure an adequate cash flow in the establishment period of the business. The overall aim of the store is the beginning of a pricing strategy and may override other considerations.

As an illustration of pricing strategy, we will take two items from the stock of a sporting goods retail store and follow the process:

The two items include one recreation necessity, running shoes, and one optional item, a name-brand line of warmup suits. In the store shoes have been a high-volume and high-profit line with the warmups being low-volume but also sold at a high markup. In the display warmups take considerable floor space while shoes are displayed only by a single-foot model on the wall and stored efficiently in the back room.

Price policy calls for a selection of the target market in the context of the store image and merchandise mix. The target markets for running shoes are two: those who engage in the activity regularly and those who just like to wear such shoes around. The first segment is relatively static in number, generally will pay what is necessary to obtain the model and brand they have found best, and are a repeat market. The second is mostly young, student age, and is both price- and brand-conscious. They often choose the least expensive model of the "best" brand. The chief target market for warmups is younger women, who wear such attire extensively both on and away from recreation locales. They are responsive to sales and prefer a wide selection for choice. The store image is one of quality with consistent pricing rather than wide fluctuations and constant promotions. However, sales are held twice a year in January and August. The store also attempts to have a comprehensive inventory.

Demand, cost, and competition are direct factors in pricing. In this case the competition for quality-brand shoes requires going to a different trade area, but low-price shoes are available from discount stores. Warmups are available in women's sportswear stores, but in limited quantities and selection. Cost to the retailer in these items is fixed and changes little except for occasional promotions by the various suppliers of warmups. Demand for the shoes is relatively constant, but demand for warmups changes with the season as well as being quite price-elastic.

Alternatives for pricing include several modes:[6]

Demand oriented pricing is an alternative to cost-oriented pricing. Cost-based pricing consists of adding a fixed markup to the wholesale cost of the item. Demand-based pricing adds psychological factors to the strategy. For example, the quality and prestige associated with certain brands of shoes allows for a higher markup without reducing demand. The key is estimating the level at which elasticity is encountered and consumer resistance to price reduces sales. How much is the Brand A label worth? Warmup brands and insignia are also valued by the target market, but this is a purchase that can usually be postponed. Therefore, price may lower demand by constricting the size of the market.

Cost-oriented pricing begins with the price to the retailer. The formula is simple:

$$\text{Retail markup percent} = \frac{\text{retail selling price} - \text{merchandise cost}}{\text{retail selling price}}$$

The costs of doing business are calculated and the profit from items needed in order to obtain an adequate investment return calculated. The retail markup approach calculates the percentage of the retail price that is above the wholesale cost. A second approach is based on the wholesale cost of the merchandise:

$$\text{Cost-based markup percent} = \frac{\text{retail selling price} - \text{merchandise cost}}{\text{merchandise cost}}$$

If, for example, the unit cost of the warmups were $12 per set, and a retail selling price of $20 was established, then retail markup would be 40% and the cost markup would be 67%. At least as a baseline for pricing, an overall calculation of the markup at cost required for operation is the beginning of the strategy. However, adjustments will include demand and other factors.

Further, each line of merchandise will have a sales history. The initial markup when the goods are first on the floor may be altered in time. Slow sales means that the stock takes up floor and display space for some time. That space is costly since there is an opportunity cost of lost revenue from goods *not* stocked and displayed during that period. Therefore, it is necessary to estimate such costs and take action that will minimize the opportunity cost of inventories that produce few sales. An initial cost-based markup may have to be adjusted in order to move slow inventories and increase the overall sales potential of the store. Some stores have automatic markdown periods for all merchandise. In a sporting goods enterprise, selective markdowns in price are more likely and are related to seasonal demand, costs of display and storage, likelihood of the items becoming superceded in the market by new styles and improved products, and the cash flow requirements of the business.

Competition-oriented pricing is based on the current prices for alternative goods and for the same merchandise at alternative suppliers. Competitive pricing may be below, at, or above the market.

Pricing below the market is common for retailers in low-cost locations, with few supplementary services, and who do not carry full lines of merchandise. Pricing at the market presumes that there are factors other than price that will attract buyers, namely, location, store loyalty, convenience, and brand availability. Pricing above the market presumes a high level of service, direction to the high end of the market, and offering of prestige brands.

Integration of strategies usually incorporates several of the approaches and factors. For example, the sporting goods retailer might develop prices for the two lines as follows: The running shoes can be priced at or even slightly above market because of the necessity of the item for participants and their brand loyalty. However, the low-end styles of name-brand shoes are more price-elastic for nonrunners. They are also most likely to be carried by competing, limited-inventory outlets who sell at or below market prices. Therefore, the pricing strategy might be to carry one style of the two prestige brands slightly below market with the alternative offering of less-prestigious brands at lower prices.

The strategy, then, is partly competitive and partly demand-oriented with a cost floor.

The warmups would seem to require more variable pricing. Price leaders can be displayed to attract interest in the inventories. The prestige labels are subject to demand pricing because of the value aura associated with their display. On the other hand, the opportunity cost of carrying the lines on the floor suggests that some below-market pricing is useful to move last season's styles and lines that have not sold well.

Pricing strategies are varied. *Odd-price* strategy is setting of prices at $4.95 or $19.50, rather than $5.00 or $20.00, to lessen the impact of the amount. *Leader pricing* involves promoting some items at a low markup to attract trade. *Multiple-unit pricing* gives a discount for buyers of larger quantities. *Price lining* begins with identification of preferred market segments and a selection of merchandise at price levels that are attractive to those segments. *Markdowns* are the reductions in price that occur at seasonal sales, special line or brand-specific sales, or the season-end clearance. Other systems of markdowns are based on the period the item has been on the floor. In this system each markdown is recorded on the tag so that the customer can see just how much is being saved from the initial full-markup price.

Retail Credit Programs Both consumer expectations and competition seem to force most retail outlets into some kind of credit extension. Although credit programs from "big-ticket" items can be revenue-producing if losses are limited and interest rates high, credit for most smaller retail stores is a "cost of doing business." The issue is how to develop a program that will minimize the cost and maximize the service.

A relatively new set of technologies has changed the credit programs of many firms. The electronic networks of finance now make possible an instantaneous debit of the purchaser's account and a crediting of the account of the retailer. Therefore, one of the costs of credit—delay—is alleviated. However, the firm will have to pay a percentage of the sales price for that service. In general, the increased services of credit have added to the costs of operation.

Some stores offer their own credit programs. These may be simple accounts due at the end of each month that allow the regular customer to delay payment. More often, a store will have a formal credit scheme that allows for extended-time payments but places the cost on the purchaser. Monthly interest on the unpaid balance is high enough to cover the costs of the system, usually with a margin to cover those debts that are never paid.

Most common are the various bank credit systems. The purchaser carries a card that allows for instant credit up to a certain amount. In these programs the consumer and merchant may share the direct cost through paying to the bank certain fees plus a small percentage of the purhcase price. For the merchant these plans allow for the extension of credit without the bookkeeping or risk of an in-store program. The percentage exacted on the purchase price by the bank gives the store a differential margin between cash and credit sales. However, in return for this loss of margin, the retailer has no "bad debts" and obtains cash quickly.

Some retailers offer a cash discount to equalize the price to the consumer who does not employ external credit. Others find that consumers are so accustomed to the system that they are ready to pay the fixed price without complaint.

Credit technologies have also had an impact on local retail markets by making it easier to order by mail. Consumers who are willing to entrust their credit card identification number to unknown and distant merchants can make quick and convenient orders of goods that might otherwise be purchased locally. Further, once the initial fees involved in obtaining credit cards are paid, the consumer may be more than willing to gain a return on the investment by using the card whenever it is convenient. Also, credit purchases produce a record that may be useful for tax return purposes.

Retail businesses that are at or near recreation sites attracting participants from a distance are especially dependent on such credit programs. Most purchases will employ credit cards, and a failure to offer the service is likely to lose considerable trade. The increased dependence on credit buying requires that pricing strategies include the costs of credit in retail prices.

CASE: HOW TO LOSE MONEY ON A 50% MARKUP

The combination of a winning personality and an established recreation reputation seemed unbeatable. So it came as a surprise to the former coach that at Christmas of his second year in business he did not have enough cash on hand to pay his bills.

When he asked a local business faculty member what might be the problem, he was directed to an accounting firm. He explained to the young accountant that he had done a business volume of over $200,000 during the past year. He had a consistent markup of 50% over the cost of goods. His promotion costs were minimal because of his local following and reputation. He had calculated his operating expenses at $3,000 a month including rent, utilities, salaries, and payments on his ten-year loan for fixtures and start-up costs of the business. That should have left a margin of $2,500 a month. How could he not have enough cash to pay salaries, especially during the high-volume Christmas season?

The accountant shocked the entrepreneur. He developed a balance sheet that demonstrated that the actual profit margin of the business was not the 50% markup or the 15% implied by the quick calculation of markup minus expenses. Rather, the business was losing money. The accountant pointed to the "10% down and 10% a month" credit policy as one factor. He also mentioned depreciation expenses, inventory costs, and cash flow as problems.

How is it possible that the store with such a volume might be losing money on a 50% markup?

RETAIL BUSINESS ACCOUNTING

In this introduction we will concentrate on what accounting contributes to the management of a retail business. How to do such accounting calls for a more intensive study of accounting methods and procedures.

There are two kinds of accounting for a retail business: The first is mandated. Tax law, corporation law, and other regulations require an accounting system. The second type of accounting is for management. Accounting is a tool of managing the business.

BASIC FINANCIAL RECORDS

Most retail businesses keep a record of daily transactions. This record includes merchandise purchased and sales. The old way was to have a set of ledgers in which the information was recorded in order of the transaction. Now such information is more likely to be computerized. An in-store terminal is used to type in information about merchandise in stock, location, date of purchase, price, and price changes. An inventory display or printout can yield daily or weekly accounting of items in stock, sizes, models, cost to the store, and current price. The software for such accounting is changing rapidly. The data storage and analysis programs can be on-site in a modern business computation system owned and operated by the store or off-site at a service installation connected to the store terminal by a phone line. Also, larger stores have programs tied into the checkout register, which "reads" the information pertaining to the items sold. Then that information is fed into the inventory program and no second transfer of data is necessary. A program can be employed that produces a daily or weekly list of items for which the inventory has reached a replacement level. The form of the report may even separate the items by supplier so that the report is printed on an order form.

Balance Sheet The basic accounting report is the balance sheet, which is designed to display the current financial condition of the business. It represents the following equation:

Assets = liabilities + owners' equity

Current assets include cash on hand, accounts receivable, inventories, and negotiable securities. The inventory value may change as prices fluctuate, so it may be valued at the lower of either cost or current market price. When an actual count of the items in inventory is possible, an assumption must be made about the designated cost to the store of goods bought at different prices. When a count is not possible, the inventory is assessed from records kept in each department or merchandise category. The methods of placing a value on inventories vary with the financial plan of the business and the kinds of records possible. However, inventories cannot be valued higher than actual cost or replacement.

A balance sheet for a local store might look something as follows:

Assets		December 31, 1985
Current assets		
Cash	5,500	
Accounts receivable	10,000	
Merchandise on hand	15,500	
		31,000.
Fixed assets		
Building, equipment, fixtures	46,000.	
		46,000.
Total assets		77,000.
Liabilities and Owners' Equity		
Current liabilities		
Accounts payable	7,100	
Long-term debt matured	2,000	
		9,100.
Long-term debt		
Note payable		36,000.
Total liabilities		45,100.
Owners' capital		
Smith 60%	19,140	
Jones 40%	12,760	
		31,900.
Total liabilities and equity		77,000.

Such a balance sheet appears quite neat but is only as valuable as the figures are accurate. Any business with public ownership will be audited each year. Almost any business will obtain accunting advice and assistance for tax reporting purposes. In this process the accounting firm takes steps to verify the values included in the balance sheet. The result is a general measure of the general financial condition of the business.

Income Statement An income statement provides a summary of income and expenses over a period of time and is usually prepared at least once a month. Trends in income, expenses, and profits are obtained by comparing monthly statements to those of preceding months and those of the same month in earlier years. Sales records are usually categorized by departments or types of merchandise. With computerized records, it is now possible to produce such statements much more often and to break down both expenses and income by brands, days of the week, for special promotion periods, and any other way that is designed into the program.

An income statement usually includes inventory figures as well as costs of rent, advertising, wages and salaries, payroll taxes and insurance, utilities, and other operating expenses. However, such a statement does not include such significant expense elements as long-term debt servicing and corporate taxes. It is oriented toward operations rather than overall financial condition. As such, it may be enhanced by adding to the records many kinds of allocated expenses and income. In a business with both retail sales and service components, it would be important to separate out the income and expenses of the two segments to measure their contribution to cash flow and profits. Particular lines of merchandise may be added to the basic inventory and require periodic measurement of contribution. Just knowing inventories and sales numbers is not enough. One aspect of a business may be costing more than it produces. Opportunity costs are incurred when space or staff are utilized for non productive elements of the business.

ISSUES OF RETAIL ACCOUNTING

Beyond the records necessary to operate the business, meet the requirements of taxing agencies and state incorporation or partnership law, and have a general statement of the business finances, what does a manager need to know? How can the operation of the business be improved with a well-designed accounting system? The answer, of course, depends on the nature of the business, its complexity and scope, and the degree to which the managers will incorporate financial information in their decision making. There are, however, a number of questions that can be at least partly answered through records analysis:

- Are the firm's cash receipts being protected with a system of transaction records that are checked against deposits and daily expenditures?
- Are all tax advantages of depreciation, investment tax credits, and payment schedules being exploited?
- Are all necessary tax payments being made accurately and on time, including payroll taxes, sales tax receipts, and other mandatory payments?
- Just what records are required by statute as well as by business practice? Does the accounting system make state reports relatively simple?
- Are there possible tax advantages to different methods of business organization, accounting, depreciation, inventory valuation, and borrowing? If so, what will the changes cost?
- If the business is growing, does the present accounting system anticipate the requirements of the future? What is the right time to investigate the

purchase of a minicomputer, time-sharing services, new business information systems, and sales transaction computerization at the time and point of sale?

CASE: THE HIGH COSTS OF DAILY OPERATION

It would seem that a simple business with little in the way of fixed expenses would be able to operate on a small margin of profit. At least that was the idea when Bill opened his motor repair shop in a Minnesota resort community between two popular fishing lakes and near a river intersection. All he would do was convert his garage into a shop, advertise in the Yellow Pages and recreation guides for the surrounding area, and leave fliers at the motor retail outlets where they did not want to be bothered with such repair business. He would promise 24-hour turnaround and operate on a cash basis. What could go wrong if he had enough business? If not, then he would lose little because there was little invested.

There were a few unexpected additions to the plan. First, he found that the 24-hr promise was complicated by parts supplies. So he had to borrow from the local bank for a parts inventory that seemed to grow with the business, from an initial $500 to a current stock valued at cost at over $6,000. The loan cost was over $100 a month. Telephone rates tripled for the business listing plus the directory fees. However, the biggest problem was his inability to enforce the cash payment practice with regular customers, especially local residents. Their style was to "run a tab," and they expected Bill to offer that option.

The crunch came when he was unable to make his house payments for two months in a row. Further, neighbors were beginning to hint that the traffic of trailered boats and the unsightliness of those left in the yard during repairs might cause them to protest to the county zoning authorities. Bill just didn't know whether or not the business could support the monthly rental of another location. Already the cash available seemed inadequate for business expenses and for his household as well.

He decided to invest in getting accounting advice. When the consultant examined the records, she made a number of discoveries. First, the accounts receivable had grown to a costly level. Bill had not calculated the cost of extending credit into his prices. So, the lag in income resulted in periods of negative cash flow. The cost of borrowing added an insupportable operating expense to the business. Second, the accountant found that Bill had not calculated into his price structure such items as income taxes, the cost of preparing reports, and preparing for later leasing of other space. Most important, he did not know how much margin over costs would be needed in the summer to pay fixed expenses in the winter.

The first task would be reconstruct the ledger records to develop a month-by-month cash flow estimate. From that, a new system of pricing and credit extension could put the operation on a sound financial footing.

A community of any size will have available a variety of financial and accounting services. It is not necessary for the entrepreneur to be an expert in accounting or computer programming. However, in order to develop a comprehensive financial and merchandising plan, the retail manager will need certain kinds of information. Decisions have to be made about staffing, ordering for next season and handling inventories from the last, the relative contribution of various merchandise lines and services, and the composition of the market. With available technologies it requires little additional time to specify brand information, period in stock, and other data that can be used for future planning. At the same time, financial records may be designed to answer the crucial questions about operation. It costs money to operate a business, and money costs money. Analysis of sources and timing of income as well as of expenses is basic to making a business work.

CHANGES IN THE RETAIL ENVIRONMENT

A retail business is not a self-contained entity. It exists in an environment of economic and social institutions that change. Further, a recreation business depends on one of the more volatile aspects of a community, recreation participation. To prosper, a retail recreation business will have to adapt to social, economic, and market changes. If possible, it is even better to anticipate those changes.

SOCIAL ENVIRONMENT CHANGE

Retail recreation businesses have found themselves in quite different market conditions from decade to decade and often from year to year.

One obvious example is the "energy crisis" of the 1970s. Early in the decade distribution shifts of fossil fuel products at the retail level brought about a rapid rise in prices of automobile fuel and, for brief periods, actual shortages. The impacts on recreation were both immediate and longer-term. First, vacation trips were postponed or canceled, weekend trips were limited to the miles in a single gas tank, and scehdules for recreation were adjusted to allow for obtaining fuel.

There were secondary impacts on the recreation-related industries. Sales on poor-mileage recreation vehicles fell off sharply, motorized recreation equipment orders declined, and alternative recreation activities that were closer to home and fuel-free began to increase. Political reaction in several states included possible restrictions on motorized recreation such as power boats and on residential heated swimming pools. As the shortage disappeared and the residual price increases began to level off, a second phase of adjustment began. Cost of fuel became more of a factor in recreation decisions, but not a prohibitive one. Rather, adjustments were made. RV trips were planned around staying longer in one place and driving less. Solar heating devices were installed at many home pools. And, to some extent, those who could simply absorbed the price increases. Nevertheless, there have been residual impacts on recreation participation and consequently on retail markets. At least some of the market increase for bicycles and perhaps for personal physical conditioning can be traced to that period of energy-supply change.

The energy-supply impacts also illustrate the usual pattern of response to a change in social conditions: First, there is a recognition of the change and often an immediate response to the usual mass media attention. Second, there are changes in behavior, often to a degree that is later seen as an overreaction. However, there are immediate impacts on retail markets.

Third, a period of adaptation or adjustment develops as the change is accepted, interpreted, and alternative behaviors tried. During this period, the adaptation is most likely to result in recreation patterns that are consistent with those prior to the change conditions. And, fourth, if the condition of change moves from crisis to a shift of degree in resource supplies, costs, or values, then longer-term adjustments back toward behaviors and values existing before the change are likely. The residual impacts of the change remain, but embedded in the overall value systems and investment patterns of the society.

What is indicated here for the retail merchant is that marketing strategies will be most effective if they anticipate the pattern of response. Failure to adjust marketing strategies to the immediate change may lead to business failure. Overreacting by dropping products or marketing plans entirely will abandon continuing markets and fail to meet the demand that remains during and after adaptation to the change. If some evident substitute for goods or services is at hand, one market strategy may be to exploit the overreaction by offering an enlarged inventory that is ordered only for a short period of supply. However, delicate calculation is required just to meet the peak and decline in demand. For most businesses, a conservative response is usually best.

Social condition changes can be anticipated to some extent. The more complex problem is to analyze how those changes will impact on the retail recreation markets. Again, a few examples will illustrate how changes may be so embedded in larger trends that the local merchant can take them into account.

The increasing markets for women's recreation supplies is related to changing roles and opportunities. As the majority of adult women are employed outside the home, their recreation patterns are becoming more like those of employed men. The need to get more satisfaction in less time has altered recreation scheduling and orientations. Employed women have more discretion over financial resources and somewhat more autonomy with which to seek self-expression and development. Further, women in daily social contact with others outside the home are more likely to be concerned about their appearance. And the growing proportion of single women has increased the desire for recreation pursuits other than the traditional "couple" activities for those who are married. The fundamental social change in women's roles and resources has opened both new and changed recreation markets.

The second demographic trend is the aging of the population. Much recreation supply in the past has been oriented toward children and youth, a shrinking market segment. On the other hand, there are many indications that both men and women of middle and later years now expect to remain relatively active in recreation participation. Further, the still-to-mature trends of retirement patterns will also have considerable impact on recreation demand. A retail supplier who does not adjust to such changes will not only miss new market possibilities but face loss in the traditional ones.

A third trend is based on the ongoing urbanization of the population. A higher and higher proportion of the population lives away from rural environments and opportunities. Further, the increasing cost of residential space suggests that external recreation resources may have growing use. If so, equipment and apparel markets will shift to meet the adaptation patterns.

There are many ways in which the local entrepreneur can be in touch with such shifts. The first is to study the population trends for the market area. This is especially easy if the area corresponds to a Standard Metropolitan Statistical Area (SMSA). The second method is to keep in contact with development interests in the area. Both housing and business development will affect the market composition and may open some entirely new target market segments.

The third method of tracking trends is to keep in touch with all the area and regional recreation resource providers. Knowing how the community public recreation programs are changing is crucial. Anticipating market changes if a new resource is opened in the region, whether it is a ski development, marina, or reservoir, can enable the retail merchant to be the first to promote an altered store image that is responsive to the participation changes that result from the change.

All this assumes, of course, that the retailer already knows the basis of the present recreation supply demand—the participation patterns of those in the market area and those who come for recreation purposes.

GENERAL ECONOMIC ENVIRONMENT CHANGES

Remember that recreation is price-elastic. Demand changes with economic resource changes. As a result the economic climate is a significant element in the viability of any recreation marketing plan.

In a society in which the chief source of income is employment wages and salaries, changes in that aspect of the economy will alter the fundamental market environment. There are market areas in which other sources of income predominate, such as retirement programs, government entitlement programs, or even investment income. However, the rise and fall of income in a market area related to industrial and service employment needs to be carefully monitored by any retail entrepreneur.

There are other aspects of the economic environment that affect retail markets. One is the so-called consumer confidence level that is a factor in decisions to take on long-term contracts for purchases, plan ahead for recreation-related commitments, and buy now rather than wait. Another is the cost of money. Any retail business that depends on borrowing for long- or short-term financing may find the cost of doing business drastically altered by changes in interest rates and the availability of loans. A business that extends credit to customers may discover that economic conditions impact both rates of repayment and decisions to take on consumer debt.

The community and regional infrastructure are also subject to change due to economic conditions. Any public service, such as transportation, that is supported by tax revenues will be affected by economic changes. This means that not only may the support of public programs for recreation be lowered in a period of economic recession, but basic support for the development and maintenance of roads, sewers, waste disposal, and so on may be lost as well. And transportation provisions are very important for access to many kinds of recreation resources. The bus system and snow removal may be more significant for recreation opportunity than specific programs or facilities.

A final variable in recreation markets is technology. Technological development may provide a new or enhanced recreation device or resource. However, at least as important for recreation-related retailing is general technological change. The invasion of so many aspects of institutional life, in the home and school as well as the factory and office, by electronic devices has impacts on all of life. It offers alternatives for entertainment and recreational activity, for problem solving and recordkeeping, for time-saving and time-investment, and for the development of new kinds of skills that may have recreational expression. Far more significant than the surge of interest in particular kinds of games or instruments is the impact on how people work, communicate, manage their lives, and approach challenges. The generations who are born into a miniaturized and computerized system may be as different from their parents as those born into the first automobile or television eras were from theirs. Technology is more than new products; it also is one factor in general change. While a market economic system may accentuate short-range change, the long-range effects are likely to be more lasting and profound.

MARKET ENVIRONMENT CHANGES

Of course, general social and economic changes already suggested are changes in the market environment as well. However, there are more specific market factors that are significant for analyzing markets and adapting to change.

The first market change is ecological. The market area for a retail store exists in space that has geographic shape. Changes in that shape are created by new highways and street patterns, different public transportation facilities, alterations in bodies of water or their tributaries, and the movement of people. Perhaps the most salient such change in most areas is related to private transportation and the use of the car for retail shopping. As the residential patterns of most communities have spread out from the old core districts, so retail shopping patterns have become more and more dependent on the car. Centralization of multiple retail outlets and adequate parking have been the basis of the shopping centers. The requirement for a block of land for development has placed them on the periphery of communities. One consequence has been to draw business investment away from central and neighborhood locations. As central retail districts decline at what often seems to be a geometric rate, location and relocation is a major issue for any retail merchant. In some cases it is possible for merchants to work together with investors and public sector planners to rescue or revive declining districts. The individual merchant may then be faced with a decision that combines community responsibility with judgments about the markets.

Related to this trend is the movement toward "superstores." The traditional image of retailing has been the single store, often in a row of stores on Main Street. Current retail development, on the other hand, is in clusters of smaller stores around one or more superstores. Space is leased rather than purchased. The mix of retail offerings and inventories may be regulated by the conditions of the lease. Direct competition is sometimes limited, at least for an initial period. And the superstore may compete with some aspects of almost every smaller store in the complex. In such situations there is usually differentiation of each store, a clear statement of store image, consistency between the operation and the stated image, and identification of highly segmented markets. It is necessary for the entrepreneur to understand just what is possible in such a business environment, what strategies may open certain markets, and how a plan can be evaluated and revised during the development of the business.

The third market change, one that every merchant hopes for, is growth. However, there is more to growth than a population increase. Growth is likely to be skewed toward certain household ages, sizes, education levels, income levels, and even recreation interests. Taking advantage of growth in the market area requires identifying the composition of market segments within the growth and an adjustment of strategies to meet the opportunities.

A fourth change is that of competition. Success often breeds competition. If one enterprise does well, another may be started, especially in a market area with increasing population or in a time of economic growth. The nature of the competition is one determining factor in the response. New competing enterprises may have quite different marketing strategies. The response decided on may be to stress differentiation, for example, quality rather than price. Or the response may be to suggest through promotional efforts that the old outlet is still the best. In some situations competition will almost inevitably capture some of the old market and necessitate a reanalysis of store content and marketing plan. However, in some cases competition may actually increase the total market and in time provide a complementary rather than competing business.

CASE: COMPETITION AND ADVERTISING

The established business with its general sporting goods line was closely attuned to the recreation resources of the region. A supply of outdoor forest recreation equipment was augmented by the owner's long involvement in hunting, fishing, camping, and canoeing. He knew his customers, the merchandise, and the opportunities for their use.

Now, after seventeen years, there was competition. A new store, part of a regional chain, had opened in a shopping mall on the edge of the industrial town. The new store advertised heavily in the sports pages of the local newspaper, stressing both price and assortment. Something was always "special." Fifteen-second spots on local television were used to announce the store to a wider clientele. Finally, the mall location attracted a large drive-in trade, which then became foot traffic in the mall. The owner of the older business was especially concerned about the loss of younger market segments who congregated in the mall on weekends.

He knew that he would have to launch an advertising campaign for the first time. The question was what kind of themes to stress in the ads and what media mix would be most cost-efficient for the market segments he hoped to retain.

The first decision was to identify the market segments that were most likely to remain loyal to the old store and location. The second was to decide what kinds of announcement, reminders, and promotions would be most likely to draw them to the older store. The third involved the advertising choices and design.

Should the older store have tried to compete in price or stressed the experience and service that only knowledge of the recreation and resources could provide? Should the younger market be let go or were there ways in which they could be persuaded to make the special trip to the old location? Were there special lines, particularly the forest recreation merchandise, that should be stressed even if some more general lines were abandoned? How could the decision have enhanced the profitability of the store?

What was happening to the population categories in the market area that provided the various market segments? Was the population in the industrial- and agricultural-based town aging with little growth among school-age segments? And just what had been the marketing strategies of the competition in other towns where they had opened stores?

A retailer is much more than someone who orders and arranges merchandise, talks to customers, handles the cash register, and counts the money at the end of the day. Retail management involves developing a marketing strategy. In the case of recreation retailing, the strategy is based on current and potential recreation participation and styles. The retail store is one recreation resource, a supplier of goods and services. During the life of a business there will be changes in the social, economic, and market environments. There will also be changes in products, technologies, recreation styles, and even in the buying priorities of potential consumers. A retailer who is "in the know" does not have to wait for problems, but may learn to anticipate change and respond to new possibilities.

SUMMARY OF ISSUES

Retail management tasks include buying and receiving merchandise, preparing the inventory for sale, customer relations, personnel management, handling money and credit, accounting, and planning.

Personnel management involves recognition, authority designation, evaluation, and supervision as well as recruitment and dismissal.

No aspect of retailing is exempt from control by law.

Recreation businesses tend to be labor-intensive and rely on the recreation expertise of staff in selling.

Credit and repairs are services expected from most retail enterprises.

Analysis of consumer demand and seasonal shifts is central to merchandise planning that incorporates innovation and diversification.

The product life cycle in recreation calls for planning that identifies market segments in relation to size, cost criteria, satisfaction curves, and social contexts of use.

Store layout may have to balance theft control and complementarity.

The general price elasticity of recreation markets leads to inclusion of demand factors, cost differentials, and competition in developing a marketing strategy.

The balance sheet and income statement are fundamental accounting forms. However, a variety of other techniques may provide considerable management information to the store owner.

Social changes in the retail environment include gender and age shifts as well as urbanization factors.

Market changes that can impact on a retail business include ecological shifts, superstores, market growth, and altered patterns of competition.

Consumer preferences and confidence change with new patterns of technological diffusion as well as overall economic conditions.

DISCUSSION QUESTIONS

1. If you were called in as an advisor to "Climbing the Wall," where would you begin the analysis?
2. How do laws regulating products and promotion protect the retail business?
3. How would you solve the defective shoe problem in the "Service and Return" case?
4. How can personnel management combine support and evaluation of employees?
5. What are the most challenging forms of competition for a retail recreation business? Are there highly competitive firms in your community? If so, how do they market against each other?
6. What are the characteristics of a good floor salesperson? What don't you like in sales approaches?
7. What are the advantages and disadvantages of staying small and simple as a business?
8. Give examples of recreation product life cycles. How could they have been predicted?
9. For which kinds of markets are "narrow and deep" strategies most effective?
10. How would you advise the owners of the "Marketing and Interior Style" case?
11. What factors were being overlooked by the first owner in the "Cash Flow and Day-to-Day Management" case?
12. Which pricing alternatives—demand-, cost-, or competition-oriented—seems most common in recreation retailing? Why?
13. What do you think was the problem with the store losing money on a 50% markup?
14. What types of advertising would be best for the store faced with new competition in the "Competition and Advertising" case? Try designing a sample ad.

EXERCISES

1. Document and analyze competition strategies of two or more competing stores.
2. In an interview, obtain the history of a store with special attention to crucial decisions, management problems, and plans for the future.

3. Develop a business prospectus for a retail recreation store that would attract investment capital.
4. Trace sales impacts produced by some factor external to recreation. How have businesses adjusted?
5. Outline a long-range marketing approach for a retail recreation business that will exploit the increased older population.

REFERENCES

1. Berman, Barry, and J. R. Evans. *Retail Management: A Strategic Approach,* pp. 253–255. New York: Macmillan, 1979.
2. Marquardt, Raymond A., J. R. Makens, and R. G. Roe. *Retail Management,* p. 346. Hinsdale, Ill.: Dryden Press, 1979.
3. Berman and Evans, 1979:291.
4. Ibid., p. 311.
5. Marquardt et al., 1979:388.
6. Berman and Evans, 1979:482–490.

6 COMMUNITY ACTIVITY CENTERS

ISSUES

How do activity centers differ from retail businesses?

What is the basis of an activity center concept?

How can markets for activity centers be identified and the resource differentiated from other opportunities?

What are the main factors in pricing for activity resources?

How can latent demand be measured?

What are useful sources of market data that do not require a primary research effort?

Is market research useful only when opening a new business?

Activity centers are labor-intensive, seasonal, skill-based, and involve special risks. How can management cope with these factors?

What are the particular financial management issues for activity centers?

What changes in the business environment are most likely to impact on such recreation businesses? How can new opportunities be anticipated?

Almost every community has some recreation businesses that offer participation opportunities. Some provide facilities for particular sports; others are oriented toward the arts, games, social activity, or some combination of activities. The key is participation. The business exists because the activity requires some kind of space or equipment that can be rented for use. Further, there is a demand for use beyond that provided through the public sector. These businesses are community activity centers.

Such businesses can be categorized according to the kind of activity they make possible:

Outdoor sports Golf, tennis, swimming, fishing, and shooting are some of the activities that may be the basis of a business.

Indoor games Electronic and mechanical games in arcades, card games, and a variety of gambling games (legal and illegal) are business offerings.

Physical fitness and development Fitness and exercise programs, development programs employing specialized equipment, and combinations with swimming or sports.

Arts Painting, ceramics, dance, music, theater, and other arts programs may include both instruction, equipment rental, and opportunity for exhibition of products.

Motorized activity Various kinds of motorized carts, small race cars, motorcycles, and winter sport vehicles may be rented and special space or track use offered by the day or hour.

Other outdoor activity Picnic grounds, horseback riding, gliders, flying, miniature airplanes, and a range of other outdoor activities often require special space and equipment.

Special activity A variety of opportunities for dancing, special parties, and meeting others at an activity-based event or program can be the basis of a business concept.

New technologies and marketing concepts keep the picture of such community activity-based businesses always changing. New combinations are developed that tie together compatible resources or appeal to the same groups of participants. Some of these businesses demonstrate a short product life cycle with a rapid growth and peak period followed by quick decline. Others build a stable market. We can be sure that each year or two will find some new "hot item" being promoted as the latest recreation opportunity. One aim of this chapter will be to help investors and managers distinguish between trends and fads.

Again, these community businesses are based on leisure participation away from the residence. Many kinds of recreation cannot take place—at least for most participants—in private space or with generally accessible equipment. Other kinds of recreation require some period of directed learning and coparticipants. Bringing together resources for skill acquisition, participation groups, special space, and equipment is considered worth a payment by some who could not engage in the activity *on that level* without the provisions. However, the basis of the business is the desire for participation. It is the leisure meaning of the activity to participants. The development and management of the business is directed toward providing the necessary resources for achieving desired outcomes if the business is to succeed. In brief, the components of the recreation experience are learning and doing. Business-provided resources may make the experience possible.

However, any business must complete a number of functions in order to become established and remain viable. These entrepreneurial functions vary in importance for different types of business as well as for different sizes and stages of development. This chapter is organized around certain entrepreneurial functions that are salient to local businesses offering resources for recreation activities. The examples given are intended to suggest issues common to such enterprises. Nevertheless, it is important to note that there are no procedures or strategies that apply to all community activity centers. Nor can the materials made available by related trade associations be more than suggestions. After all, each community situation and clientele is a bit different from all others and the skills and experience of each entrepreneur vary. And each advice giver has a point of view and frequently a purpose, namely, to promote a particular product or service. To develop and operate an activity center calls for continual analysis and flexibility as conditions change. The analysis that follows is intended to introduce significant issues, not present a blueprint for any particular business.

The chapter will include one theme case in each business function section. It is actually an amalgam of several racquet-sport businesses followed over a period of years. There will also be a number of "minicases" to illustrate issues or offer ideas that deviate from the main discussion.

THE CONCEPT

Any recreation business is based on some concept of what people want to do enough to pay for it. The simplest approach would seem to be to find out what people are doing now and then rent or sell what they need to do it. The problem with that approach is also simple: Within an access area, people are now doing those things for which there are already resources. To discover an unmet or latent demand, there has to be some basis for the presumption that new resources will facilitate new or increased participation. There are several possible analyses:

- Participation in other communities where resources are available may indicate a latent demand in a community where the resources are lacking. However, populations also differ and must be compared.
- Saturation of present opportunities as indicated by waiting periods, filled reservation schedules, or requests may demonstrate a market.

- For a new activity or resource, demonstration developments in similar areas may suggest that participation can follow the provision of the opportunity.

Note that in each case it is necessary to know about the population that is expected to provide the basis of the market. And just obtaining a profile of age distributions, income levels, and household compositions is only the beginning. Just as important as the basis for a concept is an understanding of how the proposed business will fit into the leisure patterns of such a population. Understanding not only what people are doing but *why* they are investing their resources of time, money, and energy as they do is necessary for developing a viable business concept.

Further, recreation businesses usually have one of two beginnings. Some begin with the interest of the entrepreneur in the activity for which the business will supply resources. Backpackers and campers are most likely to enter a business supplying tents and other gear. They utilize their knowledge and experience as well as perceive a possible market. Other recreation businesses begin when an investor or investment group is seeking an investment opportunity. An analysis of various possibilities in an area may lead to interest in a recreation business because it seems to offer the likelihood of a good return. In such a case, what may be lacking is an understanding of the activity and the nature of the latent demand.

CASE: THE TENNIS CLUB (1)

The tennis club, our ongoing activity-center case, was begun as an entrepreneurial scheme. At the outset a professional tennis player assembled a group of investors and presented a concept. Tennis was at that time, 1972, a sport with growing participation. However, for the most part in the Snowbelt regions it was confined to summer. Most tennis was played on public courts with a few outdoor private clubs being developed in high-income population centers.

The concept was simple—develop a chain of indoor tennis clubs to provide for those who would like to play all year. The plan for development included the following:

- Cost analyses of initial four-court facilities that could be expanded later. They were to be quite simple prefabricated structures that could be adapted for other uses in case of failure.
- Locations were also to be low-cost when possible, but accessible by car to population centers with current participation in tennis large enough so that only a small percentage playing off-season would provide a membership large enough to sustain the club. Locations

should also be zoned for business and be desirable for warehouses or light manufacturing.

- Communities should be studied and ranked so that new clubs would be opened in order of likelihood of success.
- Management would be by the parent corporation so that new managers could be trained in existing facilities and then moved to the new locations.

The concept, then, began with the experience and expertise of a participant in the activity. The argument for offering something new, however, was based on growing participation in the sport. Further, the business would complement already established resources and programs in the public sector. The hope was to "catch the wave" of participation growth and develop a stable constituency. From an investment perspective, the club would be able to set rates for an adequate profit margin because of a lack of competing businesses and would offer a "down side" alternative for the building use in case the tennis club failed. In a period of fast-rising real estate prices, that protection of the investment was a powerful argument.

The local tennis club that we will be following further is one of several begun in a three-state area by this investment group. However, at the time of the analysis, it is no longer managed by the parent company. The building has been leased to local managers who run the facility.

There are a number of other conceptual approaches to beginning a recreation business. Some are based on identifying a special market segment. Some stress the soundness or protection of investment capital. Others are a response to what is perceived as a significant trend.

For example, in the 1970s a relatively new sport had a dramatic increase in participation. Racquetball appeared to many as a golden opportunity for investment. The new facilities built in urban areas were a response to a perceived market that promised extensive growth. Some investment groups rushed in to head off possible competition. In the case of racquetball the resource had to create the market. Participation was to expand as facilities were built. The concept was essentially a faith in the new sport, almost a leap of faith.

Somewhat different was the concept behind the creation of a new dance studio. In a university town two dance teachers decided that there was a market for dance instruction outside the school and public offerings. There were already two "elite dancer" programs available as well as the group programs for beginners in the schools and in public recreation programs. However, dance as an attractive activity for those with some background but no professional aspirations seemed to be largely ignored. Especially unmet was the market segment of postschool women who were familiar with dance but not oriented toward sports. They were able to enjoy dance experiences while increasing physical competence and fitness. The groups were scheduled for employed and unemployed women, promoted as "fun and fitness" rather than having high skill thresholds, and taught in nontechnical modes.

The concept for a recreation business brings together some participation base with an identified market segment. In the case of the dance center preparation and past participation in dance were established. In the tennis club participation outdoors were also a known quantity. However, for the new racquet sport some estimate of the potential market had to be based on such items as expressed interest, school participation, and transfer from other racquet sports played outdoors and at semi private facilities at the YMCA and country club.

RETAIL STRATEGIES

It takes more than an idea to create a business. A *strategy* begins to formulate an approach to a business that can be evaluated and revised. Strategies link the various elements of the business into a coherent program. Elements in an initial strategy include the following:[1]

I. PHILOSOPHY OF A BUSINESS
- Reasons for enter the field
- A purpose for the business

II. OBJECTIVES
- Sales
- Profit
- Satisfaction of publics
- Image

III. STRATEGY
- Selection of a product or service category
- Identification of consumer characteristics and needs
- Overall strategy
  - Controllable components
  - Contingencies

IV. OPERATIONS
- Plan for operations
- The environment
  - Consumer
  - Business
  - Government
- Feedback and evaluation scheme
- Anticipated decision points

This strategy outline does not imply that every element of the business needs to be developed at the beginning. Rather, it is important to recognize that any number of contingencies cannot be anticipated. Further, a good business plan will include many means of feedback from customers, the community, and others in the business and service sectors as well as financial and management evaluation. The development of a business will also have certain critical points at which evaluation will become the basis for decisions. Insofar as is possible, these points should be anticipated so that the required information for evaluation is available. A good strategy minimizes the "Why didn't we . . .?" laments of business development.

PRODUCT DIFFERENTIATION

In a recreation business the product or service to be marketed is always in competition with other possible uses of time and resources. Except for a few devotees of an activity or locale, other activities, facilities, environments, and opportunities may be presumed by the potential client to provide similar or interesting experiences. Therefore, the business should include in the concept and strategy some means of differentiation.[2] The potential customers will be presented with an image that promises a different and better recreation experience.

The product may be demonstrably better for its purposes than others on the market. The service may enhance participation in some way by offering some facilitation that the clients cannot provide themselves. Or some combination of product and service enables customers to do something desirable easier, better, with less cost, more efficiently, or in a more satisfying way. Why is the commercial center worth the price, especially if there are also public resources that are less expensive? Does the activity center offer quality, innovation, social interaction, convenience in scheduling, easy introduction to the activity, a family setting, exclusivity, or low cost?

In the case of activity centers, the trade-off may be quite simple: price for access. At a higher price the client may have relatively easy access to the activity resource. The market sector can offer a quality environment with convenient access simply because the price excludes some potential participants. However, in most cases the business concept will stress quality or innovation more than simple access.

PRODUCT LIFE CYCLE

One common problem with recreation business concepts is the failure to distinguish a fad from a trend. Sometimes fueled by heavy promotional activity, a particular game, sport, or activity may demonstrate a dramatic increase in participation. Entrepreneurs seeking investment opportunities may say, "This is it! It's my chance to get into that dream situation, a rapid growth market."

However, the product-life-cycle concept is nearly universal. Almost every new activity or technology undergoes some period of growth followed by a peak or maturity and eventual decline.[3] There are many factors in being able to forecast the probable shape of the product life cycle. In a recreation business those include the size of the market segment that can afford the costs, the relationship of the activity or product to established recreation patterns, and the transience or stability of the participation aggregate.

The shape of the product cycle curve may vary significantly. Growth may be rapid, producing a very steep climb. Maturity may be long or short. The decline may be slow or rapid. More important, the decline often moves into a fifth stage, one of a plateau or stability. For example, the growth of tennis participation in the 1960s reached maturity and began a decline in the 1970s. However, a plateau of probable stability or even gradual "second growth" is now indicated. On the other hand, a heavily promoted product may have a rapid decline to almost total obsolescence.

In order to recognize probabilities for a product cycle in the growth and maturity stages, the analyst needs to understand the patterns of recreation and leisure participation in the society. If a market-provided resource—an activity center or a piece of equipment—fits into established patterns or trends, then the plateau is more likely to be a viable level of demand. In order to demonstrate this probability, the analyst needs to know:

- The relationship of participation to income, age, family life cycle, and other social factors
- Demographic trends in the market area population
- The likelihood of the development of competing substitute opportunities
- The satisfaction and disillusionment profiles of the activity or of similar activities
- Economic variables such as likely technological breakthroughs, lower-cost alternatives, and competing concepts

One example of such a product cycle has been that of racquetball businesses. In this case the shape of the curve was influenced by the facility costs. When the activity requires a costly initial investment for construction—especially a relatively inflexible one—the likelihood of the plateau period not remaining at a high enough level to support the considerable capital costs as well as operation expenses is increased. Alternatively, some activity centers have remained viable into the plateau period only because the facilities were purchased or constructed in a period of relatively low costs. Duplication at a later time would be quite impossible as participation levels shrink and the price elasticity of recreation takes its toll.

SUMMARY

It seems that a viable concept for a recreation business calls for more than identifying a "fun" activity. The first thought leads into a strategy. The strategy requires an analysis of both the business conditions and the recreation base of the business. In some of the cases that follow we will be able to illustrate how some of the important factors have affected activity centers for recreation.

THE MARKETING PLAN

The beginning of a marketing plan for any recreation business is an analysis of the community opportunity structure. Recreation is a multifaceted spectrum of activities. Some leisure is essentially resource-free, requiring little other than time or the presence of other people. Some leisure is highly resource-dependent, requiring special space, equipment, personnel, or environments. The willingness to pay for resources is based on some interest in or commitment to a resource-dependent activity or experience. Within a market area such resources may be abundant or scarce, accessible or restricted, costly or generally free. The marketing plan for a recreation business must take into account what else is there, the alternative opportunities available through both public and private sectors.

CASE: THE TENNIS CLUB (2)

The marketing plan for the tennis club was simple. The number of outdoor courts and their level of use during the spring, summer, and fall were observed. The size of the market area was estimated and the age and income characteristics ascertained. Key informants were interviewed, especially those in the retail sports business, to obtain opinions as to likely interest in an indoor facility. Finally, business experience in other communities was used to evaluate the latent demand in the market area. In general, all the information suggested that such a recreation resource should be used at or near capacity within a two-year inaugural period.

The participation factors in the marketing plan were current regular players in the population (an estimate) and seasonality. In the upper Midwest, the outdoor playing season was relatively reliable for about four months, problematic for three more, and generally forbidding for five. Therefore, the indoor facility would have four to five months of peak use and as much as four more of marginal usage.

The critical item in the marketing plan was price. How much would summer players who had been accustomed to paying little or nothing for court use be willing to pay for winter tennis? Was there some clear income demarcation that would define a market segment? Would year-round tennis be only for the higher-income "country club crowd" or could a price structure be developed that would attract a much wider clientele?

Since tennis participation was attracting a wide spectrum of income levels during the summer and sales of equipment and tennis togs indicated a willingness to invest in the sport, the marketing decision was made to try for the wider market. This meant keeping the initial investment low enough so that prices would not be forced too high. It also meant providing a facility that was cost-efficient rather than luxurious. The decision was reinforced by the presence in the community of a special market segment, university students who had an interest in the sport but generally limited incomes.

The main factors, then, were the composition and size of the market area population, the seasonality and current participation of the sport, and a decision to try for a wide market spectrum by controlling the investment costs and consequent price schedule.

Note that other types of marketing strategies could have been chosen. The tennis decision was based on the nature of current participation. But what about an activity in which current participation was minimal?

For a racquetball center the marketing plan was quite different. In one case the decision was made to seek a more limited clientele. The price element was assumed to be dealt with by the smaller size of the courts. When a relatively luxurious facility was built, the prices per hour were not much less than those at the local tennis club. Further, the center was located on the edge of a high-income residential growth area rather than in a lower-cost but less accessible industrial park. The market plan was oriented toward those with high incomes and those who anticipated reaching such income levels and were developing recreation styles appropriate to upper-middle-income affluence. It should also be noted that the marketing plan was developed in a time of general economic prosperity and optimism.

A dance center also developed a different marketing plan. It was to reach a special group, those not served adequately by public and professional programs. The name, orientation of program, scheduling, pricing, and advertising were all designed not to intimidate potential clients. Dance was marketed as recreation, a satisfying and enjoyable activity with outcomes of physical fitness and personal growth. Further, combining programs for mothers and children enabled the center to reach a significant synergistic market segment.

The market plan of the tennis club was based on current participation, that of the racquetball center on the presumed growth of participation due to the new opportunity, and the dance center on latent participation that had been inhibited by the nature of the community opportunity structure.

PRICE IN THE MARKET PLAN

Price isn't everything, but in recreation decisions it is usually a salient factor. A recreation business must have a market potential that is composed of more than interest in the activity; the market is for access to the activity *at a price*. Almost without exception, price increases reduce the market significantly unless income levels are increasing proportionately.

Price strategies involve more than adding some percentage to estimated costs. Among the factors are the following:

- Consumer factors
  - Price elasticity
  - Salience of price for each market segment
- Government factors
  - Fee levels of public resources
  - Price regulation
  - Prohibition of price discrimination
  - Requirement for pricing disclosure
- Supplier factors
  - Costs of necessary goods
  - Supplier regulation of prices through advertising and restrictions on discounting
  - Supplier price agreements
  - Loss of suppliers due to pricing policies
  - Price guarantees
  - Impact of supplier price increases
- Competition factors
  - Nature of competition
  - Pricing of competitive or substitute resources

In some highly competitive businesses there may be little latitude for pricing. Competition sets the maximum that can be charged for the product or service. In other circumstances pricing is related more to the importance of price to identified market segments. In most businesses there are basic costs of doing business that place a floor under prices.

Community activity centers usually have a number of pricing options.

- Price may be for access only, a *membership fee* for a period of time that entitles the member to full participation without further cost.
- *Membership fee plus* further fees for use of the resource or participation in particular programs.
- *Fixed use fees,* generally so much an hour for use of the facility.
- *Variable use fees* with a schedule of prices that are relatively low during times of low demand and higher during peak periods.

The form of the price structure is partly a marketing decision. The form that will maximize total income by maximizing participation rates per dollar of income depends partly on the discretionary income of the clientele. However, the nature of the program is also a factor. If there are several auxiliary services such as instruction, then additional fees are usually attached. If there is little variation in the use schedule, then variable fees may be a needless and annoying complication. If the need is for "up-front" income, then there may be a stress on membership rather than user fees. In general, flexibility will enlarge the potential market. However, flexibility may also be perceived as discrimination by those who see themselves as forced to pay the higher rates.

CREATING NEW MARKETS

The familiar model is that demand creates supply: When there is a market for a good or service, in time the market will transmit messages that increase the supply. But what about a new product or service? How can demand be transmitted when the potential users haven't experienced the satisfactions of the product? How is it possible to measure the potential market of something not now available?

In some cases the product or service is available in other market areas. The potential market in a different area is extrapolated from comparing the characteristics of the area populations and competing resources.

In other cases some similar or parallel service has been introduced. The possible response to another new concept is indicated by the previous market development. The obvious problem with this method is that in order for the new resource to be different enough to create a new market, it must also be significantly dissimilar to the comparison offering.

When a product or service is really new and different, the basis for analyzing the possible demand becomes something of a work of art rather than an exact science. What is required is a thorough understanding of the present recreation participation patterns of the populations. This means knowing not only what people do and about how often but also the patterns of social companionship, family life cycle and life-span influences, scheduling and timetable integration, current constraints and perceived opportunity limitations, and the various meanings and satisfactions attached to current activities and resource areas.

For example, one of the assumptions of the development of the indoor racquetball facility movement in the 1980s was that summer tennis players could and would transfer participation to the parallel new sport in the winter. It was seen as a space-efficient substitute. The market potential was in part based on the idea of *substitution* of one racquet sport for another. What was discovered over time was that such substitution was most likely among casual players who were not necessarily the most reliable market segment. Most tennis players who devoted themselves to the sport and expected high skill-acquisition and demonstrated competence outcomes preferred to stay with tennis in the winter, even at somewhat higher time and financial costs.

On the other hand, an activity that was complementary to current leisure patterns and would partially meet a perceived lack of opportunity might be proposed as a viable investment. For example, near an urban population center in the Northeast or West, a family skiing center could meet the latent demand for parents who want to introduce their children to a sport they enjoy and to engage in it as a family. However, the distant and expensive major ski areas to which they go on two or three weekends a year are not designed for children. Also, they may prefer to leave the children behind on such occasions. Therefore, the nearby and relatively tame resource actually creates a market for a type of skiing experience that did not exist without the resource.

ADVERTISING

The simplistic idea of the introduction of a new product or service has only two steps: getting the idea and advertising it. As already outlined, marketing is a much more complex design of elements than that. However, advertising is important. In some way, the potential market segments have to be informed about the opportunity. Advertising, accurately directed toward its chosen target, can announce and inform. However, it can seldom if ever create demand where the basis does not already exist.

During a period of operation a community recreation center will normally spend about 1–2% of its revenues on advertising. Such advertising is most often placed in the sports or arts sections of local newspapers. For a neighborhood center, fliers and brochures may be delivered house to house. Cooperation with public programs may permit some announcement of the business resource by having brochures available at or near public locations. When there is a particular target population, such as teens, spots on radio stations that program for that group may also be employed. Usually cost is a major factor in limiting such advertising.

However, for a new product or service it may be necessary to budget a larger amount for advertising. For example, a new dance center located in inexpensive quarters on a side street requires considerable media announcing to get attention and differentiate it from other programs. In the case of the family and nonprofessional program introduced earlier, much of that advertising can be done in ways that call for more investment of time than money. Fliers and brochures that are both attention-getting and explicit about the program can be distributed at a number of gatherings such as PTA meetings if approaches are made tactfully.

The advertising media mix is also significant. It is crucial to determine the aims of advertising for the type of business and the stage of the development. Most often, some expert advice is useful in determining the media mix as well as for design. A few examples suggest possibilities:

Bicycle shops The average ad budget is 1–2%, with major attention to the sports section of newspapers and less to fliers, Yellow Pages, direct mail, and cycling magazines.

Camera shops An average budget of 2–3% using direct mail, handouts, and the Yellow Pages. Cooperative advertising with manufacturers is placed in newspapers. Attention may be gained by donating services to community organizations.

Repair services A budget of 1½%, mostly in the Yellow Pages, with some use of signs on vehicles, direct mail, and "shopper" papers if available.

Tennis club Average of 1%, with announcement ads in the sports section of newspapers at the beginning of the season and brochures at the counters of summer tennis facilities when permitted. Cost-free word-of-mouth promotion by current clients is the central advertising medium.

Advertising alone cannot create a market. However, it may be essential in announcing the new opportunity to the previously identified market segments. Whenever possible, the current participation base for the new business should be contacted directly. This may be done through cooperation with complementary enterprises and programs. However, many will be hesitant to alienate other business interests perceived as competing with the new product or service.

OUTLINE OF A BUSINESS PLAN

In most cases securing financing from a lending institution such as a commercial bank will require the presentation of a viable marketing plan. Such institutions tend to be conservative in risking capital on new concepts. Further, even though recreation is increasingly recognized as a major part of contemporary business, it has the image of being high-risk for many investors.

A plan for a community activity center might contain all or most of the following elements.[4]

Activity Center Plan

I. THE CONCEPT

Product or service description
Relation to current resources

II. THE MARKET AREA

Description of population
Analysis of current recreation resources
Data on current recreation participation and trends

III. THE PROJECT

Full description of program, facilities, equipment, staffing, and scheduling
Project differentiation—analysis of relationships to current and planned public and private sector recreation opportunities
History of similar or parallel projects elsewhere

IV. MARKET POTENTIAL

Current participation base in the market area
Indications of potential growth
Competition

Market segmentation
Pricing factors
Promotion plan
Analysis of projected market growth

V. INVESTMENT

Cost of space
Cost of equipment
Personnel costs
Operating expenses—summary or pro forma statement
Taxation factors
Initial capitalization requirements
  Anticipated sources of capital
Start-up and five-year projections of financing needs
  Cash flow and break-even analysis
  Sources of income

VI. FORMATION

Form of business
Ownership and legal liability
Assets and loan securities

VII. THE FUTURE

Graphic presentation of projected participation and income
Timetable of beginning operations

VIII. PERSONNEL

Credentials and experience of principals in the project
Resumes of advisors and consultants

Such a plan has two primary uses. The first is to obtain funding from banks, individual investors, investment groups, and possible partners. Somewhat surprisingly, in most areas there is capital seeking investment opportunity. However, there is also competition for that capital, so that any project must be presented attractively and thoroughly.

The second use is for strategy development, organization, and scheduling. Whether or not a schematic network is developed that links project elements in a timetable format, there are some functions that have to precede others. A full and functional marketing plan will enable project organizers to avoid being caught midway in the project with some major requirement unattended. It will also help avoid the "unexpected" expenses that often arise in the development stages of a business.

OPTIONS FOR ORGANIZATION

There is no one "right" way to organize a community recreation center. (There may be some "wrong" ways, but they are usually the result of a lack of planning and skilled analysis.) However, a number of options are open to those who are planning such a recreation resource. Not as a complete list, but as a means of exciting the imagination, here are a few options that have been tried:

1. *The franchise* The advantages of a franchise operation should not be ignored. In some areas franchise businesses have several times the survival rate of independents. (But a franchise is no guarantee.) Assistance in obtaining financing, a tested marketing plan, name recognition and an image of stability, advice and discounts on equipment, cooperative advertising arrangements, and a head start on the "learning curve" of business operation are all advantages. Costs and a restriction of freedom to adapt to local conditions are among the disadvantages.

2. *Rentals* A center may keep initial costs low by renting or leasing everything possible. Most communities have some unused space that can be altered for an activity center. A dance studio can use many kinds of buildings, for example. Equipment can often be leased. Redecorating can be done by the future operators. A low initial investment makes possible considerable flexibility on pricing, cash flow, and later changes.

3. *Alternative uses* When it is necessary to purchase space—indoor or outdoor—keeping open options for alternative uses is good insurance. The most common example is the golf course in an area where housing expansion makes such land a good long-term investment. A building zoned for light industry with a minimum of fixed interior partitions is another way of keeping options open.

4. *Stability* In some cases a recreation business has already demonstrated considerable stability. However, management has not exploited many possible ways of increasing the market and augmenting income. The current balance sheet of such a business may be misleading and make the business a good prospect for investment with new management. One example is a small-town bowling alley with an established break-even clientele of evening leagues, but that has not sought new daytime markets or modernized its facilities.

5. *The tie-in* In some areas the developer of a new housing project—detached homes or condominiums—may be seeking some way to distinguish the development from others. Space for a special recreation center may be made available either at a low lease cost or even with some assistance in financing. If a recreation marketing plan can be presented that meets the demonstrated demand of the households targeted for the housing development, then the high cost of space and capital may be reduced in a cooperative arrangement. Such a business might be outdoor-oriented, such as a pool and tennis-court complex. It might also be indoor such as a health-and-fitness spa. In a housing complex designed for singles and childless households, adjoining space for social interaction may be made income-producing by selling snacks and beverages.

MINICASE: ETHNIC IMMERSION

Running a dance hall and bar in a Latin neighborhood of South Chicago has a number of requirements according to the owner-operator. One is "having friends," a set of supporters in the neighborhood. Another is willingness to work long and hard, to risk yourself as well as your capital. The business is based on the ethnic tradition of music and dance. Star attractions come from Mexico on the airlines that shuttle between Mexico City and Chicago. The owner sponsors local sport teams to gain recognition and neighborhood acceptance. With competition from several other establishments, becoming a meetingplace in the crowded urban environment is crucial. To do this calls for considerable risk taking and acceptance in the ethnic culture as well as management to create the right environment.

ADVERTISING AND RECRUITMENT

When a fitness-and-figure spa is part of a national chain, it benefits from national advertising on television and in women's magazines. Such advertising is aimed at cultural preoccupation with body shape and fitness. However, the program also recognizes that considerable recruitment is person to person. Therefore, any program participant who brings in a new member is given three months membership free.

MARKET RESEARCH

How do you know? That is the question that pervades all sorts of marketing plans. Concepts and dreams are enticing, but what is the evidence that they can be realized? One answer to such questions is found in market research.

The concept of market research may be quite forbidding, calling up the prospect of spending thousands of dollars to have some giant corporation reveal the secrets of consumption. As a matter of fact, the aims of market research are fairly simple: to find out who is now consuming the product or service of interest and whether there is any unmet demand. Further, most of the basic information is already available or easily obtainable.

The beginning of most local area market research is *observation*. In recreation the approach is likely to be participant observation. When interest in the recreation activity precedes investigation of the business possibilities, considerable information is known unsystematically about current participants, scheduling, seasonality, available opportunities, crowding and waiting, costs, equipment, and other such factors. Market research may begin by formulating in some systematic order the questions that need to be answered. Then information obtained by observation can be put in place and analyzed for completeness and probable accuracy and bias.

The second type of market research in a market area is usually seeking *key informants*. Current participants in related activities, those in supply businesses, and those managing public programs are all invaluable sources of insight. A variety of participants can give impressions of the quality and quantity of current resources. Established business suppliers can give evidence of the growth or decline of participation. For example, those who sell tennis, running, or dance shoes have one set of indications of growth or decline. The public recreation managers usually are well informed about use of their resources and programs as well as expressions of interest in new opportunities. The fourth kind of key informant is the operator of a similar business in another community.

The third type of market research is use of *secondary data*. Local public libraries usually have current census data on a community, especially if it is part of a Standard Metropolitan Statistical Area (SMSA). Also, in many cases the local chamber of commerce or newspaper will have developed considerable information about the local area in order to attract new business or industry and to secure national advertising. The trends in the population by age groupings, school populations, employment and income categories, household composition, and education level are all available. For example, someone considering the opening of a bar/cocktail lounge styled for white-collar singles would want to find out the size of such a market, the most common residential locations, and trends in household composition.

More general market data are often available from "the trade." Most business types have one or more trade associations and publications that gather information on yearly sales, number of businesses, sizes, and projections for the future. While the projections tend to be optimistic and should be evaluated critically, such information is extremely useful. In some cases the trade journals even have specific information about beginning a business.

Only after these three sources of market information have been fully exploited should the entrepreneur decide whether or not *primary research* is necessary. The assumption that some sort of on-site or household survey is always needed is, of course, quite wrong. In many situations market sizes and segments can be clearly delineated from observation, informants, and secondary data. Especially when the secondary data include information on participation trends by population aggregates, analysis may be a more accurate basis for decision than the questionable relationship between expressed interest and later participation. Current participation is still the best predictor of future participation.

Nevertheless, there are circumstances in which some primary research is valuable. For example, when the activity center is projecting use by some group now excluded from such a resource by price, membership, or distance, a survey of the target market segment may be essential to develop an estimate of potential interest and demand. Some of the methods for such research will be outlined. However, one warning is important. Social research expertise requires more than self-defined knowledge. Poorly designed research is worse than none at all because it is often misleading. In the design stage of market research, a small investment for competent counsel can save enormous waste and even fundamental decision error later. The problem, of course, is that self-anointed experts lurk in every business community, ready to snatch the money and trust of the unwary.

CASE: THE TENNIS CLUB (3)

In the early stages of a local tennis center, a relatively simple research plan was employed. First, the entrepreneurs were already in the business as well as in the sport. They had established similar facilities elsewhere. From their own experience they knew generally what kind of population and participation base was needed for a successful operation. In the case of a first-time business planner, such information can be obtained from those in the business elsewhere and from the trade associations and publications. A university town with a population of 100,000 and an additional 30,000 students exceeded those minimums comfortably. In a suburban area the composition of the population, distances to competing resources, population trends by age, sex, and income, and housing and transportation patterns would have to be analysed and mapped much more carefully.

Second, the current participation basis was not hard to ascertain. Both the public park and recreation departments and the campus recreation program had reasonably accurate estimates of current participation. At the time of this decision making, very few sporting goods outlets stocked tennis equipment. Their sales trends were also useful data.

Third, key informants in this case included several active tennis participants who were also part-time instructors, either privately or with the recreation programs. Their estimates, while limited to particular community segments and often geographical area, were indications of a participation base that was increasing in the late 1960s and early 1970s.

Fourth, the population (census) profile of the market area was compared to national statistics of participation. In the case of tennis, age and education level had been found to be key factors in participation. Estimates of the potential markets could be developed by comparing national or regional recreation data with the population analysis of the SMSA. Further, the area was in a growth period at that time with economic optimism high.

Fifth, an on-site survey might have been useful if the other decision criteria were at all marginal. Some indication of interest in an indoor center could have been obtained with a simple survey at a variety of sites and times during the spring, summer, and fall periods. Analysis would have required a weighting of the results according to demographic categories in order to project the results to the area population and to the likelihood of being winter participants at a viable price. Such a survey could also have provided information useful in designing and locating the facilities and developing the inaugeral program.

Finally, at a later time an internal questionnaire was used to provide information about changes and improvements of the facility and program. The issue after almost ten years of operation was one of upgrading the facilities. The original design had been quite basic, four courts, with two more added after five years, lockers, showers, a single sauna, and a waiting room with counter and a small pro shop. The quality of these amenities and the addition of others could make the center more of a "club," a comfortable place for relaxation and social gathering. A survey of current members was designed to measure the desire for improvements *at a price*. The result was that cost was more important to most members than a more elaborate environment and set of amenities.

A SECOND CASE: WHERE NO PARTICIPATION BASE IS ESTABLISHED

What about an enterprise for which there is no established base of current participation? In a community where the only resources for an activity are so scarce that complete saturation of available time by current users discourages new participants, how is it possible to estimate the potential demand? To what extent will increased opportunities create a new market that is not demonstrated by current activity? And how is it possible to find out?

In the case of an investment group seeking recreation-related business opportunities, the initial interest was in what appeared to be a growth sport requiring special facilities, racquetball. In 1978 a community with a SMSA population of 78,000 was selected as a possible site for a new business. The area had been growing, contained a large branch university in the state system and a solid economic base. The concept was for a health and racquetball center in a growing residential area with relatively high income. However, one commercial racquet center was already in existence as well as the quasi-public YMCA.

An interest survey was designed and administered in 21 target neighborhoods. The survey was intended to assess interest and current participation in racquetball and other racquet sports, interest in health and fitness activities and resources, and ability to afford participation in such a business center. The design allowed for comparison with participation figures from national surveys and also offered choices for types of programs and pricing plans.

Without going into details of the survey and its administration, several issues can be outlined:

1. *The adequacy of the sample* A carefully designed plan for reaching a representative sample of households in the targeted neighborhoods requires more than instructions on paper. Both incentives for canvassers—in this case college students—and continual monitoring of the operation are necessary. Further, the sampling plan for market research is different from a general social survey. The aim is to assess potential markets, not gain general community opinion.

2. *Comparison items* Standard demographic (census) items should be included so that the household composition of the sample can be compared by age, sex, size, income, education, and employment to the SMSA and other samples about which there is relevant information. Generally, some national trends on recreation are useful. However, they need to be compared to the market area and the surveyed population rather than imputed from national to local populations.

3. *Participation* Current recreation patterns may be more important than expressed "interest." After all, any new recreation participation and investment will have to fit into or replace current investments of resources. When a young parent indicates a desire to play a sport or engage in regular exercise, that desire may be inhibited, channeled, or scheduled by existing commitments and constraints. It costs nothing to say, "I would like to do that." Doing it, however, always has costs. Further, most adults seek a balance in their leisure so that anything new has to complement ongoing investments. There is seldom a vacant time slot and financial source just waiting for that new opportunity to be provided. The new center must compete for scarce resources, especially time.

4. *Product mix* The survey testing the market for a racquet and fitness center employed items that explored various options for the facility. The product mix of racquetball, other racquet sports, family activity including indoor and outdoor swimming, and types of fitness programs remained to be determined. However, once the building was designed, considerable flexibility was lost as walls were literally set in concrete. This survey discovered that the interest in fitness exceeded that in racquetball and that family activity was of considerable interest.

5. *The decision* Market research does not mandate any business decisions. However, when well designed and implemented, it can provide crucial information and analysis. In this case the decision was *not* to go ahead with the proposed center. Among the factors were the competing resources in a community small enough so that distance was not insuperable, the high initial investment, the lack of survey support for the prime activity of racquetball, and difficulties experienced by an established center in another location in the same state. Retrospective analysis suggests that the decision was a good one even though it went against considerable industry enthusiasm at the time.

6. *Design criteria* No standard-form survey is presented here because they present too many problems and a high likelihood of yielding misleading information. Further, design, execution, and analysis need to be integrated. The main criterion of a good survey is that it contributes missing information to the decision process for investment or operation. The business principals will seldom get a good survey when they cannot identify clearly what they need to know. Other criteria are related to representativeness of the sampling plan, consistency and lack of bias in the execution, clarity and simplicity of the survey format and instrument, a careful pretest, and a predetermination of how the findings can be analyzed. Details of methods can be found in a number of research publications.[5,6]

ASSUMPTIONS OF RECREATION MARKET RESEARCH

A new enterprise begins with the assumption that behavior can be changed. An addition to the stock of equipment, space, instruction, access to environments, and programs can induce people to do something different. Expansion of resources is based on some evidence that current participation is limited by a scarcity of opportunities.

The basis of such assumptions is knowledge about current leisure and recreation. It generally begins with some understanding of what has already been discovered in research. Specific market research, then, is comprehensive and useful only in the context of a bigger picture. That bigger picture is provided by the ongoing recreation research efforts of universities, government agencies, and private firms. A sound market plan for a business rests on the foundation of the following research base:

The Structure of Recreation Research

I. PARTICIPATION

By activity
By "families" of activities
By types of site and resource
By user groups
By participation styles

II. TRENDS—MEASURED CHANGES OVER TIME IN PARTICIPATION CATEGORIES

III. SATISFACTIONS

Types of satisfactions by activity, resource, social group, style, and life course variables
Trends in satisfactions and orientations

IV. OPPORTUNITIES

Public and private sector resources for activities
Location of resources and relative access
Use of resources

Out of an integration of such information a market-oriented analysis can be developed. Its aim is to identify unmet demand, the possibility of markets yet unrealized due to a lack of opportunity. A few suggestive examples related to activity centers may be illustrative:

- Changes in current recreation aims and investment suggest that those who are now in their thirties will probably be more active physically in 20 years than those in their fifties now.
- Increases in recreation participation by women with preschool children suggest the importance of child-care facilities at recreation centers.
- An increase in coeducational participation in a variety of sports and activities among students suggests that they may desire less sex segregation in programs in their postschool recreation.
- Satisfactions based on social interaction for programs with a sport, art, or fitness activity form imply that time and space for social gathering will be attractive elements in an activity center design.
- Research has found that some people interested in an activity, especially a sport or art, are inhibited in the beginning because they do not want their lack of skill to be on display before those who are adept. Therefore, beginning programs may need to be separated in time and space.
- Activities formerly closed to most women because of male-only opportunities present a growth opportunity for recreation business. Trend data may be more useful than actual current participation in selected activities.
- Such trends indicate that more men are engaging in arts activities and more women in sports—together. Such trends are most pronounced for those with higher-education experience.
- Time and energy costs in urban areas make the accessibility of recreation opportunities, public or business, critical in use patterns.

At the beginning of the chapter the issue of distinguishing trends from fads was mentioned. Market research cannot provide fully guaranteed answers to the question. However, research that takes into account the full "structure of recreation research" outlined above is more likely to come to an accurate conclusion. Single-issue analyses that look only at short-term sales figures, media attention, an unstable market segment such as younger adolescents, or regional manifestations of interest are likely to be deceptive. Research and analysis that includes participation, trends, meanings, and opportunities is more likely to provide the basis for a sound business decision.

ONGOING MARKET RESEARCH

Market research does not take place only once in the life of a business. There are a number of recurrent issues related to diversification, expansion, management, and changing market conditions that may call for research. One major difference in ongoing research is that there is now a clientele who may be studied. Further, an established business has many ways of building market research into its operations plan. A few examples again serve to illustrate the possibilities:

1. *Coded coupons* Coupons offering a discount on some product or service can be used to measure response to various advertising media. By coding the coupons the manager will know if they were from a particular newspaper, display site, or distributed in some other way. When the coupons are returned, it is also possible to ask one or two marketing questions, such as, "What is your primary interest in our program?", with a quick-code record on the coupon. If there is registration involved, then age, sex, residential location, and "business phone" will provide more information about new clients.

2. *Informants* Most activity centers operate informally enough that managers develop friendships with a number of regular clients. These clients can provide valuable information since they participate in or join many on-site conversations. While staff should be encouraged to exploit opportunities to obtain the opinions of clients, special informants can often gain different perspectives. The problems are those of bias. The most verbal may not represent the concerns of clients who keep their ideas and complaints to themselves. Further, some informants may be given undue weight because they are more persuasive or personable. One method of minimizing such bias is to have a simple form on which staff may record summaries of what they have heard as a part of their daily or weekly work-report sheets.

3. *In-house records* Considerable information about the flow of participation can be obtained from available records. For example, most activity centers have a daily schedule for facility use—room by room, court by court, or activity by activity. A summary of those records recorded each day over time can yield invaluable data: hours of peak use, age category and gender of users, and requests for services. Trends over time then become one basis for adjustment of fee structures, advertising decisions, expansion of facilities, scheduling, staffing, and promotional devices to induce categories of users to come at certain hours. Now that minicomputers are programmed for business records and computing services offer a variety of services, such trends can be fully analyzed by keeping the records in the computer memory. Such records analysis is a form of program "auditing" that parallels financial auditing.

4. *Experiments* Many aspects of a program or of pricing can be temporarily altered as an experiment to test new possibilities. For a month a facility can be opened an hour early at a reduced price. Special social incentives can be offered to groups, including a place to talk and enjoy free refreshments. In general, such experiments in marketing will be based on an analysis of the in-house records that indicate periods that are below a break-even level or spotlight some social aggregate with a rising or dropping participation rate. Just how the results of

such an experiment are to be recorded and used should be part of the program from the beginning.

The point of such ongoing market research is that most activity centers have available a number of sources of valuable information. However, unless that information is recorded regularly and analyzed systematically it becomes subject to argument and is used to reinforce the biases of the managers. Market research, formal or informal, is most useful when it tells us what we did not want to know, that is, when it challenges the common wisdom by which a business is being operated.

OPERATIONS MANAGEMENT

Community activity centers have a number of characteristics that affect how they will be run.

CENTERS ARE LABOR-INTENSIVE

Almost without exception recreation activity centers are labor-intensive. They employ a large number of people for the size of its clientele. As is the case with most services, a major part of the business consist of person-to-person assistance. In addition, providing instruction, dealing with financial transactions, and maintenance tend to require relatively large staffs.

In general, recreation businesses pay low wages to all except management. Those who deal with clients directly are often paid by the hour. In the case of instructors, some are on a salary-commission combination that varies with the number of students attracted. Further, the seasonal nature of many centers makes it difficult to secure trained staff who are available during peak periods and hours. For this reason many centers employ part-time staff, either students or "moonlighters" with another primary job. This makes loyalty and reliability major problems since the activity center is often secondary in priorities.

On the other hand, the experience of many such centers is that they have waiting lists of prospective staff. Further, much of the staff comes from the customer ranks. Participants in the program, interested in the sport, art, or activity, become the first pool for recruiting employees.

The selection of staff begins with the necessary skills. Activity centers require bookkeepers and janitors as well as desk clerks and program organizers. In smaller businesses there may be strange combinations of tasks, so that versatility is always of interest to the manager. Also, selection processes stress a demonstrated ability to get along with other people, greet and interact with them in a friendly manner, deal calmly with complaints, and in general contribute to an attractive atmosphere.

Such flexibility suggests that well-designed job analyses and organization charts are uncommon in such centers. Some of the most successful are informal, with considerable relaxed interaction among staff members and with managers. However, such a center does have a number of integrated tasks that must be done with some synchronization. A scheme of tasks, schedules, and responsibilities not only helps avoid crises but also can promote fairness in the distribution of tasks among staff.

Even in a small business certain elements of personnel management contribute to smooth and efficient operation. Further, staff are so important to a successful operation that all possible support should be available. Job specifications should be available in writing for new employees so they will know what is expected. Job descriptions for all personnel should be studied by employees so they know what to expect of others. A regular process of evaluation should be scheduled for each employee so that problems and antagonisms do not build up. In the recruitment process a manager will want to seek some variety to ensure that the image of the business is not skewed toward one age group, sex, ethnic group, or activity orientation (unless the target market is skewed also). Training should be well organized and evaluated by both the manager and the new employee so both are assured of competence. Finally, some clear avenue for advancement should be specified if such is available. And if not, that should be made clear at the beginning to avoid disruptive disappointment.

SEASONALITY

Recreation activity is often seasonal, not only due to climate changes but also in relation to school schedules and the traditional "seasons" of certain sports. Further, the seasonality varies from one part of the country to another. The high season for golf is summer in the North and winter in the South. Market segments change as people vacation in climates that support certain activities or even have dual residence to follow a climate and a specific recreation.

The community schedule is also a factor in seasonality. Any activity center that has a student clientele has to deal with peak periods of school activity, vacations, and often the details of school timetables for competing activities. The manager of a community activity center needs to know not only the compositions of the market but also the schedule commitments and preferences of each market segment. Such knowledge can be used to advantage if scheduling can stagger use periods and maximize total traffic.

On the other hand, seasonality often presents a major problem for a center. It requires, first, that all or most revenue be obtained in a limited period, perhaps as short as three months, even though the facility must be maintained and rents paid for twelve months. The financial practices of such a firm require careful use of income during the peak period so that cash flow does not completely stop during the low time.

Second, as already suggested, staffing is difficult for a seasonal business. If the high period is during school vacations and students can handle most tasks, then the seasonality may be an advantage. Recreation business can provide a major employment source for students, obtaining help for themselves and making a major contribution to the education process of the society.

UNEVEN USE

Unless user segments can be balanced in a way that spreads out use over the hours of operation and days of the week, a recreation center is likely to have periods of crowding and periods of almost total disuse. A golf course, for example, tends to be oversaturated on weekends in season and almost empty on Monday mornings.

In some cases slack periods can be used for needed maintenance. However, most recreation businesses will make some attempt to increase use during the low periods. For example:

- A dance center will offer programs with child care for preschoolers, a place to walk and have refreshment, and a more relaxed schedule *during* school hours.
- A golf course or racquetball center will not only have reduced rates during off-hours but will offer free instruction to beginners at those times early in the season.
- A bowling center will try to organize groups outside the usual weekday-evening league hours by giving groups a place to meet and reduced rates.
- An arts center will seek a summer clientele from the brothers and sisters of those engaged in sports programs by scheduling at complementary hours.

One common element in business failure for recreation centers has been an inability to cope with seasonality. The financial and management implications have to be part of the marketing and operations plan for the business or the drastic fluctuations in income will create loss periods that cannot be overcome at any viable price level during the high season.

A RECREATION ISSUE: SKILL

If people join in an activity center program that calls for the development of skill in the activity, then relative levels of performance become a major operations issue. One aspect of the relative-skill issue is fear of comparison. Whether the activity is exercise, dance, singing, writing, or gymnastics, those with a low or beginner skill level are seldom comfortable with those having highly developed skills. In most programs some separation of groups by skill is necessary.

Further, the exercise or enhancing of skills usually requires participation with or against others of an equal or higher competence. Those who are adept seldom learn if the instruction level is geared to beginners. When competition is part of the activity, skill gradation may need to be quite refined. In some sports as few as 5% of the total spectrum of participants at a center may be in a skill range that enables them to play or compete together.

The recreation basis of this issue is that of satisfaction. One of the major elements of meaning in arts or sport participation is the development of competence. To learn, experience growth, and demonstrate skill is integral to much regular recreation. If the program of the center does not promote such skill development, many participants will seek other opportunities.

The usual response to this issue is to provide a variety of formats and opportunities at the same facility. Variable scheduling means that regular participants may have to adjust their schedules to be at the center at the time selected for their skill level. The balancing and fine-tuning of schedules is critical to operation. Introduction of the skill-level variable into a timetable that already must take into account work and school schedules, family patterns, and seasonality calls for very careful listening to actual and potential clients.

CASE: THE TENNIS CLUB (4)

How do managers of an indoor club cope with seasonality and other scheduling variables?

One basic decision is whether or not to close entirely in the summer. One program's attempt to retain some loyalty and income during the summer was to complement the public recreation offerings in two ways. One was to offer low-cost lessons during the early morning and evening periods, when the indoor courts were relatively cool and when public courts might be crowded. Such an offering would depend heavily on the reputation and established loyalty developed during the indoor season with the instructor. The other offering was to provide a bad-weather option for regular players. At a modest fee members could have the indoor courts available for practice and matches on rainy or windy days. Careful accounting was implemented during an experimental summer to measure the cost-effectiveness of the off-season program.

More critical to the operation of the tennis center is scheduling the peak season of late fall to mid-spring. The heart of the business is "permanent court time" (PCT) in which members essentially lease a court for specified hours of certain days. That court is then reserved and rented for a specified period, in this case 16 or 18 weeks at a time. A slight price reduction is given for those who reserve at the end of the previous indoor season.

The remainder of the scheduling must then be constructed around these reservations. Variable pricing may be employed to try to concentrate PCT reservations in hours that interfere least with other programs. However, for the most part PCT regulars come first. Second, certain competitive programs have proved both popular and a good way to attract regular play. These leagues, categorized by type of play, skill level, sex, and other stylistic factors, are then scheduled at times that are likely to be attractive without interfering unnecessarily with the most popular periods such as 4:00 to 6:00 in the afternnons or 8:00 to 10:00 on weekday evenings. Reconciling the time availability of potential program participants with the center schedule is a major task at the beginning of each season. Further, the managers recognize that there are different styles of play and the format that appeals to someone who is highly competitive may turn off someone who aims are more in skill-development or social interaction.

Then there is the instruction aspect of the program. A variety of instruction formats—group and individual—at all levels of skill needs to be offered regularly. Further, special programs for children and youth can be scheduled at off-peak hours and build long-term loyalty for younger players and their parents.

Again, remember that recreation is price-elastic. While an activity center may depend on a core group whose commitment to the activity is high, most participants can be priced out of regular activity. The appeal of certain hours and programs is not unlimited. Prices can be placed at a level so high that a significant part of the potential market just doesn't consider the program at all.

The skill-level issue requires special handling. The principle is to offer as many different doorways and thresholds as possible within the schedule limitations. The *doorways* are opportunities at a variety of skill levels and times that may be presented as open and attractive. The *thresholds* are the excluding mechanisms that keep out those whose skill levels are too high or too low. For example, a set of doorways may be a range of doubles leagues in the evenings. The threshold device is to set a minimum skill level according to a standardized evaluation system, usually administered by professional staff. This minimizes the personal element of evaluation by coparticipants. Also, a center can institute a feedback mechanism in which the top finishers in one league are invited to move up and those at the bottom given the automatic option of moving to the next lower league.

This kind of scheduling involves many compromises. No group can have all the most convenient times without closing off many market segments that are necessary for the overall viability of the business. On the other hand, a careful analysis of the composition of the membership in relation to schedules, resources, and numbers in each category will often suggest how the scarce resource of "prime time" can best be allocated and off-peak hours made most attractive.

OTHER CASES

1. A racquetball and fitness center in an upper-income area of detached family homes added another dimension to its operation. The management found that the appeal of the sport was not adequate to keep use level at a profitable level. One remedy was to present the club as a family recreation center. Various programs, instruction, and leagues were designed to draw specific ages of younger players and a variety of gender and skill groupings of adults. The scheduling was designed to minimize interference with work and school schedules and yet maximize use. One problem was that the preferred time for the core membership group, younger men who played regularly, was after school but before 10:00 P.M.

2. A roller-skating center took a different approach by linking rink availability to the programming of community organizations. It is not surprising that a small-town skating rink would have a series of specials to attract skaters—ladies' night, tiny-tots hour, aerobics, after-school matinee, group rental nights, and even "cheap skate" night. Most of the profit comes from skate rental and concessions rather than admissions. The idea is to get people in. However, a persistent effort to entice community groups to have special nights culminated in a joint sponsorship by the rink and a local "religious" radio station for a series of evenings when only religious music was played for the skaters. The aim was to use the community organization structure of the area to gain a clientele who would otherwise avoid what they perceive as only a hangout for teens.

3. A bowling center had been a marginal business for years. While there was a solid core of business with leagues that used the facility every weekday evening, at too many other times the lanes were not used. Attempts to establish "housewives' leagues" and weekend programs met with only moderate success and were counter to the trend toward a high proportion of women being employed. The solution tried was to make the bowling alley more of a social center. Simple snacks, beverages, areas in which groups of various sizes could gather for conversation, and some electronic games were added. A storage area was carpeted and furnished with soft-seat groupings as well as traditional restaurant tables and chairs. Promotion was designed to change the image of the center from strictly bowling to a pleasant place for friends and family to gather, with the option of a common activity. In a community offering few such opportunities, the center began to draw more youth on Saturdays, women and retirees during the day, and families on weekends.

RISK MANAGEMENT

An activity center, even more than most retail recreation businesses, is subject to a number of risks that can threaten the life of the enterprise. Among them are the following:[7]

Property damage: to buildings, equipment, and inventories from fire, theft, and other events

Liability for employees: responsibility for health and safety during job-related activity requiring insurance protection, including workmen's compensation

Public liability: responsibility for personal injury or property damage on the premises of the business or related to any business activity

Shoplifting losses: a matter of increasing concern

Dishonest employees: access to cash or goods without a means of accounting creates opportunities for employee's theft

Losses from bad debts: a problem if the center has its own credit system

Illiquidity of assets: accounts receivable are a major problem for activity centers, often amounting to over a month's total receipts during the height of the season

Marketing risks: too much inventory, price changes, unexpected competition, weather problems in season, and high community unemployment can jeopardize any marketing plan

Other risks: death or health loss of key employees or managers, problems with property titles, changes in the labor market, loss of key suppliers of equipment due to business failure, changes in the capital supply situation such as rising interest rates, and other community business climate changes

Of course, an adequate insurance package is the first step in dealing with many of these risks. Long before a business is opened or responsibility assumed, satisfactory arrangements should be made for insurance coverage of possible property losses, public and employee liability, and other insurable losses. An activity center without a record of claims may be an insurance problem for a local agent. Some assistance may be obtained from trade associations in locating companies with experience with the specific type of operation. Also, the pricing of insurance should be explored carefully since variables such as the amount of loss excluded from payment ("deductable") may yield quite different rates. For an activity center with many employees and clients, insurance will be a major expense of doing business.

Other kinds of risk can be minimized by looking ahead. Careful design of the layout of the facility to control access and supervise any retailing area, a records system that keeps all cash accounted for in the process of the transaction, close attention to accounts receivable, and awareness of other businesses in the community are all ways of lowering risks. The central issue is negligence. In case of an injury that results in a legal suit, evidence that the business did not exercise reasonable precautions to avoid the injury will usually result in a judgment that could close the business.

In an activity center, employees are the first line of defense against liability losses. In their training and orientation program, employees who will be working directly with clients should be informed of possible dangers and alerted to signs of emerging problems. Protection against damage is a positive element of activity organization as well as a safeguard for the business itself.

SECONDARY ENTERPRISES

Almost all activity centers have some line of retailing along with the activity provisions. Among common secondary enterprises are the following:

1. *The pro shop* At the very least a center will need a way to supply equipment. The simplest method may be machine-dispensed balls, socks, and refreshments requiring no direct selling. More often, a pro shop will include basic apparel, activity equipment, and some auxiliary items. These items may be for sale or rent. The beginning of the shop is a supply of "I forgot" item such as socks, balls, and shoelaces. However, the demand for shoes and racquets, for example, is tempting due to their relatively high markup. Further, many suppliers will encourage adding lines of merchandise. Since an activity center always has someone "at the desk," a compact shop can add some income without incurring much expense. As a service to clients and a low-cost producer of revenue, it is almost inevitable.
2. *Food and drink* After or during many activities participants may want some refreshments. Again, vending machines are a way to provide simple food and beverage. However, such machines run out of items, "eat" coins without discharging goods, and require attention in other ways. The manager may decide that providing some appropriate refreshments will not only be a source of income but will also encourage clients to come more often, stay longer, meet friends, and spend more in the pro shop. Even the problems of obtaining licenses, inspection, maintenance, additional staff, assigning space, and obtaining equipment seem justified by the revenue potential. Just as important, such a provision may change the nature of the business by attracting a new and more varied clientele.

The bowling business described earlier is one example of enhancing the entire operation by adding food and beverages as attractions for those who do not come for the bowling alone. In the case of a fitness center, space may be at such a premium that the start-up costs are prohibitive. Even with strategies minimizing staffing and equipment costs, a secondary enterprise with the activity center can be a costly investment.

Of course, there are some kinds of activity centers where some sort of equipment shop and refreshments are almost universally expected. Business may be lost by the failure to include such provisions. A golf course without both would probably lose players as well as revenue. In Great Britain some kind of pub is generally part of any activity center because it is a general custom to gather for a pint after almost any activity.

The issue is to plan and manage such a secondary enterprise in a way that serves the main business in a cost-effective way. The nature of the users, their patterns of scheduling and of interaction, and customs surrounding the activity need to be taken into account. Most often there are ways to "test the water" by moving into the new offering slowly, with careful evaluation of results before any major investment is made.

A common rationale for such provisions is that they provide income for the business that may make the difference between a profitable and losing operation. They are a source of cash that may help in a business that has a high proportion of credit customers. Further, they are a convenience to the clients. On the other hand, they may require more space and attention from staff than the income warrants. The contribution of the secondary offerings to the business as a whole is difficult to assess. In some cases a minimal operation is run on a break-even basis because customers expect the services. In other cases, selling shoes at a $20 markup, coffee at a 10cent profit, beer at a 100% profit margin, and balls at cost will add up to a major part of the overall business revenue.

One method of providing the service with minimal risk is to lease space in the activity center to another business. A local delicatessen may be interested in operating a refreshment counter. A sporting goods store may provide inventory for the pro shop and share the proceeds. In some cases an employee may see the secondary business as a way of increasing income and take responsibility for it. The activity center then leases the space and provides auxiliary services for a fee or a percentage of the sales revenue. In this way the clients are served, with the activity center management still able to concentrate on the major recreation resource.

SOCIAL ELEMENTS

Already introduced are businesses with a social component built into the program. A dance center includes time and space for informal conversation before and after classes. A sports center has a place to sit and talk over the game off the court. A league program provides a way for newcomers to meet. A well-planned schedule offers opportunities for all family members to participate. A period for youth is coed in format. A Friday evening program encourages singles to participate by balancing the sex ratio of participants without requiring that people enroll in pairs. All these are part of a marketing plan to gain new segments for the business.

However, the operation of the business should also keep social aims and meanings in mind. Research on all forms of nonsolitary leisure has found that being with other people, the enjoyment of interaction, communication, beginning new relationships, strengthening ongoing ones, and expressing the meanings of social bonds in common activity are important factors.[8] But social interaction requires a context. It takes space for meeting and doing things together. It takes time in a program that is not crammed with instruction, physical activity, or something else every minute. It is not necessary to keep people busy in a recreation business, there should be time and space to allow for interaction and, even more, simple ways in which participants may learn the names of newcomers, occasionally sit down to talk, and discuss the common activity should be a part of the physical design and schedule of most centers. In fact, in some circumstances, if such space and time are not in the operations design, people will obstruct the program as they make their own opportunities for interaction.

SCARCITY OR COMPETITION?

From the business perspective the ideal situation is to offer a product or service for which there is an established demand in a market without competition. Some recreation centers have this luxury. They are "the only game in town." In some such cases almost any management will work. Those devoted to a particular skill will stay with almost any instruction program if there is no competition. Bowlers will come to the lanes despite the unpleasant manager or inefficient pin-setting. At least up to a point, in a condition of scarcity a recreation business need do little except avoid setting insuperable barriers in the way of clients.

However, these monopoly situations are becoming hard to find. Competition is usually there. At least in a metropolitan area, the advantage of being the closest center may be lost to competition with a superior program or lower prices. Travel time is traded for better experience or price. In other cases public resources are less convenient but do offer an alternative. Weekend times at a public golf course may be limited and often inconvenient, but they are an alternative if the private course raises prices or lowers quality.

Management of a recreation center needs to be quite aware of all forms of competition. The overall climate in which the business operates is one in which alternatives need to be perceived and their appeal measured for each market segment. The programs and resources at the business center have to be carefully differentiated from competing opportunities. Staff relations with clients, amenities, scheduling, instruction, participation programs and arrangements, and special elements can be presented in ways that indicate their superiority. Even at a somewhat higher price, the profit-seeking center can be perceived as "worth it" because the experience is superior.

CASE: NEW COMPETITION

In one community a racquet-sports center was being used to capacity 80% of the operating hours. Then the city's recreation department decided to convert an unused warehouse into tennis and racquetball courts. Due to the availability of the basic structure and land, their construction cost was low. User fees could be set above a break-even figure and still be below those of the established commercial center.

An immediate concern of the owners of the established center was that they would be driven out of business. Protests to the community board produced no result except an assurance that the new facilities would never be operated with a fee structure below cost. What could the management do to meet this new competition?

First, they analyzed their own market to estimate how many would be drawn by the lower prices and the different location. Second, they reanalyzed their customers in terms of the need for instruction, use of organized events and competitive programs, schedules, and commitment to regular reserved court times. The question was simply, What can we offer that is superior to the public facility? A second question was financial: How much business could the center afford to lose, and for how long, and still operate at a profit?

The program was revised to retain and enhance those market segments for which the commercial center could provide opportunities not available at the competing facility. New stress was laid on instruction, organized programs, the importance for busy persons of having a regular time reserved, and the significance of social relationships built up over time at the older center.

FINANCIAL MANAGEMENT

The earlier chapters have introduced many of the principles and techniques of financial management. However, some may be defined more sharply in the activity center application.

CASH AND CREDIT

At some periods in the year an activity center with seasonal high and low periods may have considerable cash available while at other periods the cash flow is strongly negative and meeting fixed obligations is a major problem. A financial plan that takes this situation into account is one that divides the year into "accounting seasons." Financial management for seasonality and for a steady state of revenues may be quite different. However, there are some factors that may alleviate the situation:

1. The period of high operating expenses will generally coincide with the period of high revenues. This is especially true if the pricing scheme includes user fees as well as memberships.
2. If the firm offers its services on some credit programs, then some of the income will lag behind the peak season. The difficulty may be that having a high accounts receivable level during the operating season may necessitate borrowing with interest and fees as well as the contingency of accounts that may never be paid.
3. A membership or membership-plus-fee price structure provides some financial cushion on which to center the peak operating season. This cushion plus extended payments on credit accounts can lengthen the income season far beyond the operating season.

The fundamental problem is that "money costs money." In order to be able to meet current expenses, some of which are fixed and year-round, a line of credit may be established at a financial institution. However, such credit, usually at interest rates considerably higher than prime rates, can add greatly to the cost of doing business. That cost must then be recovered in the financial plan with its price structure.

Credit may be a source of income if the business is able to extend terms and charge interest on the balance due. More often, credit losses due to defaults will exceed such income. A credit program should be worked out only after obtaining the counsel of financial advisors who can analyze the cash requirements and income probabilities.

CAPITAL SOURCES

As mentioned earlier, perhaps the most common problem of small businesses is undercapitalization. The investment source of capital is just not adequate for the needs of the business, especially in its inaugural stages. Even when incorporating methods of minimizing initial investment and risk, obtaining capital is almost always an issue.

The chapter on retail business suggests some sources of capital. Here we will only point out the dual nature of the problem of capital. The first, just outlined, is that of cash flow and seasonality. The second is that of basic or long-term financing. Building leases or construction, remodeling, equipment, initial advertising, retail stock, training of staff, and other initial expenses call for considerable "front-end" expenditures even in a service-oriented business. Licenses and insurance can seldom be bought on credit. Further, there are often discounts from suppliers for cash purchases.

A realistic financial plan for a business as well as a sound marketing plan is important in securing either investment capital or long-term loans. Such a financial plan will need to include a month-by-month anticipation of income and expenses, often keyed to high and low levels of expected business. Both the opportunity and the risk need to be spelled out in financial terms. Further, financial needs for which the business is not prepared can become especially costly when short-term borrowing comes at high costs.

ACCOUNTING AND MANAGEMENT

Accounting in a recreation business is more than just keeping a record of income and expenditures. It is an invaluable management tool that can help avoid many of the pitfalls of such firms. As already suggested, the seasonality and consequent uneven income of recreation businesses is one endemic problem. No pricing plan can entirely avoid this difficulty. Further, the peak periods are also ones in which a labor-intensive business has high operating expenses. How is it possible to know just how well a business is doing with such fluctuations?

Without going into the details of the accounting procedures, two modes of accounting can provide invaluable information on the state of the business.

Break-even Analysis Just what is the point at which a business begins to make money? Break-even accounting procedures calculate in advance the business volume required to break even and the profit margins above that point. The factors in one such formula are the following:[9]

$BEV = break-even volume at which the firm neither makes a profit or shows a loss

$FC = fixed costs over the period; includes rent, utilities, minimum labor, depreciation, insurance, debt servicing, etc.

%MC = percent merchandise costs of total sales volume; in an activity center a relatively low percent.

%VC = percent variable costs of total sales volume, including advertising, added labor costs, maintenance, short-term credit servicing, supplies, etc.

The break-even formula then is

$$\$BEV = \frac{\$FC}{(100\% - \%MC) - \%VC}$$

The major problem is calculating the variable costs in advance. For a stable business that has been in operation for several years such a calculation can be made with fair accuracy. For a new or changing operation estimates must be made month by month according to ranges of business volume. Since variable costs rise with increased business volume and income, levels at which additional staff, longer hours, and increased supplies and maintenance are required have to be estimated. Many centers can increase volume 50% without adding much expense except a larger supply bill. Those that are heavily program- and instruction-oriented will have increased labor costs unless owners draw a fixed salary and are working below maximum capacity.

An example for an activity center might be something like the following for a center with rented space and low fixed costs:

$$\$BEV = \frac{\$100{,}000}{(100\% - 20\%) - 30\%}$$

$$\$BEV = \$200{,}000$$

If the center has a seasonal operation in which there are three months of operation at 80% of capacity and three months at 50% of capacity, then a breakdown can be approximated month by month. It would mean that the business must do about 13% of its $200,000 volume in each slow month to break even, or $26,000 a month. In the same way the three peak months must do 20.5% of the volume, or something over $40,000 a month. These figures would allow a manager to know roughly whether the business was operating at a profit each month. Further calculations based on a month-by-month break-even graph would provide a quick estimate of the profit margin.

The pricing plan of the business would add another element to this formula. If memberships were to yield 70% of the revenue and a month-by-month proportional estimate made, then a very early calculation might be possible as to the probable profitability of the firm for that season. Such an estimate could be most valuable in determining operation policies for the season. If a loss of $25,000 were estimated by this method, then in most cases efforts would be made to reduce expenditures by that sum or more.

Ratio Analysis as a Management Tool Few businesses can exist for long, however valued their services by clients, without realizing a profit. Subsidies by owners or staff in the form of reduced income will seldom be carried on indefinitely. There are a number of accounting ratios that enable managers to assess the operating efficiency of a business, especially when utilized for several business periods.

For recreation activity centers, some of the most useful ratios would be the following:

1. *Fixed costs as a percentage of total sales* If fixed costs consume a high proportion of income year after year, then the viability of the business is threatened unless the assets are appreciating or the business is essentially self-operating.
2. *Labor costs as a percentage of total sales* A monthly accounting of labor costs is one way to keep tabs on the tendency of activity providers to add staff out of proportion to revenues.
3. *Operating expenses as a percentage of net sales* All operating expenses such as wages, supplies, maintenance, utilities, insurance, rent, taxes, bad debts, etc., divided by revenue minus discounting, returns, and refunds. A year-to-year comparison provides a measure of the flexibility of the firm as markets and programs change. A rising ratio can suggest that operating costs are taking a disproportionate amount of income even when volume is rising.
4. *Net income before income taxes as a percentage of net sales* Net income is operating profit minus the amount required to meet interest payments on debts. The ratio takes into account the impact of debt on the business and the ability of profit to deal with that cost.

The point is that the operation of a recreation business requires no less analysis because customers enjoy the activity. Smiles are satisfying to managers, but they don't pay the rent or satisfy the bankers and investors. Further, the variability of many recreation businesses calls for even more careful and timely analysis. The difference between profit and loss may well stem from a quick change in staffing or program strategy in mid-season. General impressions of customer satisfaction are no substitute for analyzing revenues and expenses and having accurate cash-flow accounting.

The key is knowing in advance what you need to know. What kinds of information will be useful or even essential for management? Both use and sales data are basic. Fixed and variable costs are also fundamental. However, for a recreation business, financial information is not enough.

CASE: THE TENNIS CLUB (5)

In order to provide a longitudinal analysis of market segments, sources of income, scheduling, and types of activity, the manager of the tennis club devised a computerized method of operational accounting.

The first question was the "need to know." The relevant questions were determined to be

Proportions of income from each market segment: youth, youth lessons, university student, adult male, adult female, and special group by membership and user-fee revenue.

Proportions of income by activity types: instruction, leagues, permanent court time, other court rental, groups and special events.

Proportions of income by schedule: days, periods of the day, weeks of the season, and "semesters."

To obtain this information the daily schedule form was coded with a user code distinguishing the market segments. Then the office computer was programmed according to day, hour, activity type, user category, and price for each activity or court use according to time. Coding the daily schedule by user category required about 20 minutes the following morning. A part-time staff member was interested enough in computers to take on the task of punching each day's data into memory. Then the program could be run weekly with the printouts compared to yield a record of just how much of the income was being produced by each element of the program. Further, the "problem periods of the day" and "problem days" could be quickly identified so that promotions and programs could be revised to attract revenue-producing business for those currently losing money or indicating a downward trend. However, after a year of such an analysis one of the managers was not convinced that she would not have known, in nonspecific terms, the essence of the analysis just by "eyeballing" the schedule records each week. The management issue became the value of increased accuracy and precision.

CASE: GAME LIFE

Another example of the same kind of analysis occurred in a game arcade. The active life of most electronic games had been estimated at about six months. With the exception of a few "stars," most games had a product life cycle of about six months, with the peak occurring in two months and the decline becoming more rapid about two months later. The games often ceased to be profitable after 4 to 8 months. However, what about that variability? At what point should a game be removed from the floor?

The manager devised a simple accounting system. The revenue from each game was recorded separately each day. Kept in a linear form, it took only minutes to see the trends of use. Further, when the space available was divided by the number of machines, then the revenue needed from each to cover expenses plus interest and profit was calculated. As any game began to drop toward that figure in weekly revenue, plans could be made for its timely replacement.

From this perspective financial management and operations management are not discrete functions. Further, the mode of operation and the accounting and records system are based on the market plan. As information is produced and analyzed, the market plan will be altered. Change is the essence of recreation businesses, especially those that provide resources for activity. Even though some advance commitments are involved, to some extent the decision to use an activity resource is made again and again. It is influenced by many factors that cannot be fully predicted by any market analysis. So the activity center has to be prepared to understand, respond to, and even exploit change.

DEALING WITH CHANGE

Change need not be a threat. In recreation many changes open new opportunities. However, a failure to respond to opportunities may mean lost revenue for a business, and may never be recognized if the business is operating successfully. On the other hand, setbacks often require a quick response in order to maintain the business. One such is the case called "New Competition," which called for careful market differentiation and revised programming. As suggested above, it is the business with a useful set of records and longitudinal analyses that is best prepared to cope with changing conditions.

BUSINESS SETBACKS

Some business problems are contingencies that cannot be anticipated. Some event of low probability such as a serious health problem of a key person can create a major problem. Other changes are stochastic, that is, they will usually occur three years out of ten, but no one can predict a specific occurrence. Some probabilistic conditions may be weather-related, such as a cold summer or snow-free winter. A third kind of change is nested in the general state of the economy. A recession may alter the employment and income structure to a market area to the extent that once profitable enterprises drop below the break-even level. Adaptation to such changes varies according to the situation and the general market position of the business.

However, there are some changes that require a marked response by the business. They are not temporary but alter the fundamental context of doing business. For example, a new highway that permanently reroutes traffic flow in a community or the opening of a new shopping complex that radically diverts the former shopping patterns may call for rethinking the advantages of a location. Communities change in geographical as well as demographic shape, and businesses may have to adapt in order to survive. A 20% reduction in student population at a high school or university may mean that certain recreation resources are oversupplied. The addition of a new recreation opportunity may call for a reorientation of program or facilities by an activity center. In some cases markets disappear because enthusiasm for a specific activity or resource wanes.

CASE 1: A DAY CAMP

For twenty years two teachers from the local school system had operated a summer business that had proven both interesting and profitable. They secured twenty acres of land, with access to a local lake, on a long-term lease about six miles from a population center. Beginning with their reputations in the community, they had built up a clientele of middle-class families who sought a healthy and developmental summer program for their children, but who did not believe they could afford expensive residential camping.

However, the number of campers was dwindling, from an average of 65 a week five years ago to 42 last season. While no systematic accounting had been instituted, the partners estimated that their own income after expenses had been reduced from almost $4,000 each to about $700 for the two months. Now they wondered what to do.

Trade journals had been reporting the downward trend for general summer camping. In their region almost half the residential camps had closed, and most of the others had sought specialized markets. Some families whose older children had been in their program all summer had not enrolled the younger boys due to their involvement in the growing number of organized sports programs. Vacations also seemed to be concentrated into the last August weeks after such programs had wound down. The former market for the day camp had been reduced. Was it time to negotiate a way out of the lease and close down?

The partners identified two alternatives to closing. The first was to specialize. They could attach themselves to the seeming sports boom by offering weeks of special emphasis—baseball, water sports, and even football and soccer in early August. However, that would involve the expense of hiring special coaches and securing equipment. The second was to move down in age and offer a general care program in the outdoor environment for young children with employed parents. This would require a higher staffing ratio and extra bus runs to meet the various employment schedules of parents. However, it was less costly than the sports emphasis.

CASE 2: AN ALTERED DEMAND CURVE

The problem seemed plain enough: Fewer people wanted to play racquetball enough to pay for it. The product life cycle had started down from the peak, and an activity center that had been moderately profitable at the peak was now losing money. Investors were complaining, and it was difficult to maintain the quality of the resource under the pressure to cut expenses.

At a meeting of investors the corporation president proposed two alternatives. The first was to declare bankruptcy as suggested by an attorney. The problem was that the facility had been designed for the single activity with concrete partitions dividing the space into courts. It was a quality resource, but rather inflexible. The second alternative was to try to diversify the operation and gain new markets. Some of the space could be used for fitness programs, weight training, and child care for participants. Other space could be adapted for a delicatessen and refreshment center that would encourage clients to stay and spend more rather than rush in and out for an hour of the one activity. The problems with this alternative were the cost of remodeling, limits posed by the immovable partitions, and the possibility of further losses to investors.

The willingness of owners and investors to compound the risk of capital and operating cost in the face of losses and change depends largely on their aims. In some cases the personal investment in an enterprise and the satisfaction obtained from its operation will outweigh the financial factors. In other cases, where the primary aim was investment return, the main element in the decision is to consolidate previous profit or cut potential losses. However, one principle is evident: A business designed for flexibility is more likely to adapt to change and remain viable than one locked into a single concept, narrow market, or fixed market plan. The business least able to adapt to change is the one with no plan at all.

ACTIVITY CENTERS IN THE FUTURE

A number of factors will impact on the future of activity centers. While no one can fully forecast just what will be the most attractive business opportunities in five, ten, or twenty years, there are a number of trends that should be taken into account.

Demographic Trends Changes in the composition of the population will be discussed more fully in chapter 15. However, some trends have special relevance for those who are developing plans for local activity-based recreation businesses.

- The population will continue to age. Markets for activity centers will grow at the upper end, those ages in which discretionary income tends to be higher and inclination to engage in physical activity lower. Programs that appeal to this later-life segment will need to lower thresholds of participation in terms of physical competence in order to reach this market segment who can afford the costs.
- The proportion of women who are employed will remain high. As a result, scheduling programs for women will have to impinge on the times that have traditionally been held for men. Partially offsetting this problem will be the likelihood of more flexible employment hours for many that will permit recreational engagements at times during the weekday. Businesses that are located near employment locations will be especially able to respond to this change. On the other hand, a center in a strictly suburban location, away from work locales, may be more affected by women's employment and have to deal with sharp peaks and valleys in scheduling demand each weekday.
- Market analysis will recognize cohort differences such as that the proportion of later-life adults engaging in physical activity or arts participation in the 1970s may be considerably smaller than in the 1990s.
- Such activity centers are local businesses, different from those in metropolitan hotel complexes of destination resorts. Therefore, economic and social changes in the market area—the community—are quite important to the business. Critical analysis of the economic structure of the area and of the likely future of the types of firms providing major employment is part of any look at future markets.

Life-style Changes Whether or not the product life cycle of the resurgence of interest in health and physical fitness will show a sharp or moderate decline from its peak, there is the high likelihood of a plateau that will support a range of both public and commercial programs and resources. In the same way, even though interest in a particular arts form may peak and decline, the high education level of the population indicates a continued growth in lifelong interest in the arts. Particular expressions of concern for self-development and expression will rise and fall in popularity, but the general attitude that it is both right and healthy to engage in self-development activity is not likely to disappear.

There are, of course, economic factors in life-style changes. Relative affluence, at least in the sense of having resources above and beyond a survival level, is related to self-development investments. Activity center businesses are not likely to thrive in a period of prolonged economic crisis. With this limitation, certain life-style shifts seem significant for activity centers:

- A more profound concern for health, including physical and emotional fitness as well as environmental conditions. Some investment in health is justified as preventing higher cost later.
- There is evidence of a trend toward different life definitions. Women claim greater independence and the right to determine their own lives. Men and women believe that there is more to life than providing for the next generation, even their own children. Such attitudes may create new markets for resources that make possible a variety of expressive and developmental activities.
- More of the population will be single, either as a transition between relationships or as a chosen state, than was the case in the 1950–70 period. While the familial base of much leisure will continue important for most adults, providers will find larger and more diverse markets in the adult population at every age.
- Life-styles may more and more be characterized by diversity. As a result it will be unnecessarily limiting for those who formulate market plans to assume that most people are like themselves or their friends. In fact, the new markets may well be those unrecognized without some exploratory market research.
- While most leisure in the past has taken place in or around the place of residence, there may be some shift toward away-from-home opportunities. This will be caused by the increase in housing costs and the decreased amount of at-home space available to many households.

Technological Change Activity centers are often a response to technological innovation. New developments in sports technique, conditioning equipment, games for arcades or other commercial gathering places, transportation, and the media may create new businesses or reorient older ones.

For example, developments in electronics are having a number of impacts in the 1980s:

- New methods of banking utilizing electronic communications and instantaneous records retrieval are altering the means of payment, accounting, and inventory records for local businesses.
- A variety of games, training devices, feedback mechanisms for arts instruction, and analytical devices for physical activity are being employed at high and low skill levels.
- The possibilities of cable TV for in-home leisure choice and for interactive communication are still in early stages.
- Quick feedback for business operations is available both in-house and through a number of types of services.

Perhaps the most central issue in relation to technological change is the at-home and away-from-home issue. Analyzing strategies for any activity center that draws people away from home will have to incorporate the likelihood of technologies that enable participants to have a similar experience at home without the costs of travel. A sound long-term basis for an activity center includes a requirement for facilities or interaction that is not possible at home.

Risk Minimization A number of ways of decreasing the risks of activity center businesses have already been introduced. These include leasing space rather than buying (unless real estate appreciation is part of the investment package), designing space for flexibility and avoiding fixed and immovable partitions and equipment when possible, and a reflexive management style that is always looking for possibilities of change in the business.

Other ways of lowering risk, especially in the early stages of a business include the following:

- Emphasis on secondary locations such as buildings in older strip locations, abandoned supermarkets and stores, and buildings that have been empty long enough that the owners are ready to make an attractive offer.
- Seeking markets in smaller communities where initial costs are much lower.
- Using inexpensive construction materials. An innovative designer can often create a striking space with exposed weight-bearing beams, concrete blocks, and colors that do not hide the functions of the space.
- Lowering the down-side risk by including some plans for alternative use of space and equipment in case of a decision to move or close.
- Incorporating some price flexibility in the market plan and the business capitalization so that price-elastic market segments can be attracted, especially in off-hours of operation.

In general, there would seem to be a wide spectrum of possible outlets for entrepreneurial investment in local recreation centers that can identify viable markets and provide an experience that cannot easily be duplicated elsewhere. An assessment of both the recreation resources available, leisure patterns, and the business potential can suggest many opportunities.

SUMMARY OF ISSUES

Activity center businesses rent a resource rather than sell a product. Therefore, investment opportunities and costs usually require considerable front-end capital.

The basis of an activity center concept answers the question, What do people do enough to pay for? A related question is always, Why?

Retail strategies involve selection of target markets, product differentiation, access and quality trade-offs in pricing, and assessment of the life cycle of the activity base.

Market segment identification is based on participation and takes account of alternatives as well as size and financial resources.

To secure capital a full marketing plan may be necessary. It should include options such as space rental, alternative uses, stability of markets, and tie-ins.

Factors in pricing are related to consumer resources, supplier costs, and competition.

Latent demand stifled by lack of opportunity may be released by the provision of a new activity facility.

Observation, key informants, secondary data, and trade information usually precede primary research in market analysis.

Valid market surveys are designed toward decision criteria with present behavior as a central element.

In a labor-intensive center both flexibility and a scheme of tasks, schedules, and responsibilities are important to personnel management.

Activity centers have the special factors of uneven cash flow, seasonality, scheduling and staffing, risk management, and skill-based usage.

The development of skill and gradations of competence call for both doorways and thresholds in programming.

Secondary retailing in equipment and refreshments poses space and staff costs as well as income opportunities.

The social dimension of recreation activity requires planning for physical space as well as programmatic facilitation.

Cash flow, credit costs, "accounting seasons," and periodic analysis can be aided with various forms of ratio and break-even analysis.

The future of activity center businesses will be influenced by new technologies for at-home and away-from-home resources, demographic trends, and life-style shifts toward health and self-development concerns.

The risks in such business ventures may be minimized through inclusion of alternatives in the initial plan.

DISCUSSION QUESTIONS

1. What is the best measure of the possible market for an activity for which there is now no provision in a community?
2. Which is more important for success in managing an activity center, experience in the activity or in business? Why?
3. What kinds of information would be most important to guide decisions during the first year of operating a center?
4. Analyzing current activity growth patterns, which seem to be fads? Why?
5. Propose a "variable use fee" schedule for an activity center that will maximize total income by expanding the user groups.
6. What are some of the advantages of a membership-fee pricing plan?
7. Contrast high-end and low-end marketing strategies for an activity center. Using a specific example, how would each determine location, provisions, pricing, investment, and management?
8. Try to identify latent demand for a recreation activity now limited by lack of opportunity that could be supplied by a business.
9. Give examples of how activity centers cope with seasonality and scheduling peaks and valleys.
10. In what kinds of centers will refreshment provisions contribute most to the business?
11. How can a racquet center meet the price competition of the "New Competition" case?
12. How would you test different possibilities for the racquetball center that is now losing money in the case called "An Altered Demand Curve"?
13. Is there an adequate market for a women's center in a community of 100,000? Why or why not? If so, what might its program be like?

EXERCISES

1. List the variety of recreation activity businesses in your community.
2. Outline an investment prospectus for a new activity center, including location and market estimate.
3. Design a brochure announcing a new business activity center. What should be featured?
4. Design a survey for measuring the market for a new center, including a sampling plan and key variables. Try to keep the cost down.
5. Borrow copies of the schedule sheets of an activity center for a week and analyze their content to provide management information.
6. Develop a "need to know" records analysis program for an activity center.
7. Develop a concept for an activity center of the year 2000.

REFERENCES

1. Berman, Barry, and J. R. Evans. *Retail Management: A Strategic Approach,* p. 506. New York: Macmillan, 1979.
2. Marquardt, Raymond A., J. C. Makens, and R. G. Roe. *Retail Management,* 2nd ed., p. 40. Hinsdale, Ill.: Dryden Press, 1979.
3. Berman and Evans, 1979:309.
4. Hosmer, Larue T., A. C. Cooper, and K. H. Vesper. *The Entrepreneurial Function,* p. 309f. Englewood Cliffs: Prentice-Hall, 1977.
5. Dillman, Donald. *Mail and Telephone Surveys: The Total Design Method.* New York: Wiley, 1978.
6. Churchill, Gilbert A. *Marketing Research: Methodological Foundations,* 2nd ed. Hindsale, Ill.: The Dryden Press, 1979.
7. Steinhold, Dan, B. A. Deitzer, and K. A. Shilliff. *Small Business Management: Cases and Essays,* p. 40. Columbus, Ohio: Grid, 1975.
8. Kelly, John R. *Leisure Identities and Interactions.* London: George Allen and Unwin, 1983.
9. Marquardt, Makens, and Roe, 1979:299.

7 RECREATION TRAVEL

ISSUES

What is the scope of recreational travel?

What are the variables distinguishing those who travel?

How do travel styles point to market segments for recreation businesses?

How does the resource base affect travel decisions? How are weather and infrastructure fundamental tourism resources?

Why do people travel?

What typologies of travel and vacation styles are most useful in identifying travel-related markets?

Are Veblen effects and Engel curves descriptive of current tourism?

What are common life-course changes in recreational travel?

What are implications of the price elasticity of tourism?

How are time and discretionary income the basic resources for recreation travel? Why?

How does the ecology of recreation shape recreational travel decisions? How do time, distance, cost, experience, and resource factors enter into trade-offs and decisions?

Travel for recreation purposes, often called tourism, is more than merely going from one place to another to play. Tourism is recreation on the move, engaging in activity away from home in which the travel is at least part of the satisfaction sought. Like other leisure, recreation travel combines a number of motivations and satisfactions. Nevertheless, fundamental to tourism is the premise that people like to travel, to get away and to go somewhere.

Our discussion of tourism will be divided into three chapters, this one on travel, the next on direct services that support recreation travel, and the third on destinations. However, the separation is largely a matter of convenience. Getting to a destination on a vacation trip is often more than getting there. The trip is an inclusive experience of anticipation and planning, travel, special destinations, and recollection.

More than any other form of leisure, tourism requires a complex and manifold set of support services. For this reason many kinds of recreation businesses are in some way travel-related. Businesses may arrange for the transportation, lodging, and even meals en route or at the destination. Other businesses either rent or sell kinds of equipment for the journey or for activities at the destination. The overall set of provisions combines business resources at the place of origin, along the way, and at the destination.

THE NATURE OF RECREATION TRAVEL

Over 128 million people in the United States took at least one trip lasting ten days or more in 1981. Over 20 million visited another country. Despite the growth of air travel, 83% of all trips were taken by car.[1] The one-to-two-week auto trip is still the standard American vacation. In fact, marketing other forms of travel is usually in some sense selling the advantages of the alternative over the group trip by car.

There are many kinds of leisure travel. Among the most common are:

- The multipurpose vacation trip combining destinations.
- The multipurpose local trip: to the shopping center, to deliver an item to a friend and pause for a chat, and pick up the kids at the pool.
- The business trip that includes leisure opportunities and associations over the weekend or during the evening.
- The weekend trip to a recreation destination.
- The weekend trip to visit family or friends.
- The day trip to a recreation destination.
- The day trip to visit family or friends.
- The day trip primarily for the drive itself.
- Local trips to recreation sites or programs.

- Local trips to prepare for leisure: to purchase or repair equipment, make arrangements for a later trip, or take lessons or engage in conditioning for a later trip.
- The trip to a second home or shared recreation site.

However, any list is misleading because of the mixture of purposes and motivations for so many trips. Further, the car is more than a means of transportation. Its styles and shapes, equipment and symbols, as well as the sense of power and movement it provides are signs of social identity and a means to freedom. With the automobile the individual can make a decision and effectuate a result, control power and speeds, demonstrate social status in multiple locations, and actually do something that seems to provide an alternative to so many of the limitations of life.

Most recreation-related travel does not require direct support services. The means of transportation is the multipurpose car. Destinations are familiar and nearby. Meals away from home are taken at facilities that combine local and transient trade. Plans and arrangements are simple and made within the household decision modes. Therefore, only recreation travel that is at least over one night and of more than local distance requires the support of special business. For the most part, recreation travel businesses serve trips that encompass at least a weekend and range up to extended travel for vacations or even an entire season. There are a number of statistical indications that such trips provide a number of major markets.

THE SCOPE OF TRAVEL: INDICATORS

Three kinds of indicators suggest the scope of travel in general and recreation travel in particular. They are revenues, participation, and industry growth.

Travel Revenues Travel is a major segment of American business. In 22 states in 1974 travel business receipts were over one billion dollars. In California travel-supported businesses are estimated to have produced almost 400,000 jobs.[2] In three states, Hawaii, Florida, and Nevada, tourism is the largest industry. And there has been considerable growth in tourism in the last decade. According to the U.S. Travel Data Center, in 1981 travel industry receipts totaled $179 billion—$80 billion for transportation, $26.5 billion for lodging, $45 billion for food services, and $15.2 billion for recreation and entertainment.[3] There are a variety of estimates of the jobs produced. However, one estimate is that in 1976 travel generated about 3.8 million jobs directly and another 2 million indirectly. Even allowing for a margin of error and some industry self-enhancement, the totals indicate that travel is a major segment of the American economy.

International travel alone is a significant business sector. In 1978 tourism receipts from international visitors to the United States were estimated at $7.5

billion, with 35% of the spending coming from Canada, 24% from Mexico, and 41% from other countries.[4]

Air travel has been the fastest-growing segment of the industry, especially since the introduction of jet aircraft. In the United States, Civil Aeronautics Board figures show yearly growth in passenger revenues of from 3% to 20% a year between 1966 and 1975.

Total revenues for domestic air travel in the United States were:

$3,534,000,000 in 1966

$6,209,500,000 in 1970

$9,926,000,000 in 1975

Even adjusting for inflation, the totals suggest that air travel has been a growth industry. Further, in 1975 over half of that domestic travel was estimated to be recreational rather than business, with the mix varying from 20% to 80% according to the destination and season.[5] Travel is affected by the state of the economy. During periods of recession both business and pleasure are cut back, with significant consequences for the load factors and revenues of airlines. Since 1980 deregulation of airlines has had severe impacts on fares, schedules, load factors, and corporate strategies. As a consequence statistics for the industry are changing considerably during the current decade.

Travel Participation General statistics for travel are also subject to change due to economic conditions as well as to the marketing strategies of commercial carriers. Nevertheless, a few figures suggest the scope of domestic and international travel.

In 1978 there were some 20 million arrivals in the United States from other countries, with Canada being the origin of 64%. The same year there were 23.5 million departures from the United States, with 35% going to countries other than Canada or Mexico.[6]

Domestic air travel increased from about 5 billion passenger miles in 1947 to over 20 billion in 1955, over 80 billion in 1967, and 200 billion in 1981. Rail travel, on the other hand, fell from about 33 billion passenger miles in 1950 to less than 20 billion by 1967, and less than 5 billion in 1981. Bus travel remained relatively steady at about 20 to 25 billion miles per year.[7] It was not until 1956 that air travel surpassed rail, but air passenger mileage has totaled over four times that of rail travel since the mid-1960s. This increase is dramatic when we realize that even by 1970 half the population had never traveled by air.

However, the car remains the primary means of transportation. The Transportation Association of America reported that in 1981 travel in the United States was divided as follows:[8]

Automobile	83%
Air	13%
Rail & bus	3%

Such figures vary by region and locale. One estimate is that 95% of travel miles in California are by car. On the other hand, in a concentrated urban area 40% of the households may not own a car. Overall, over a trillion passenger miles are said to have been covered by car in 1977. The federal interstate highway system has over 40,000 miles of roads that carry 20% of the total traffic.

Elements of Travel-related Business Again, a few numbers will suggest some of the scope of travel-based businesses:[9]

- Campgrounds: There are about 17,000 campgrounds in the United States and Canada of which 8,000 are privately owned.
- In 1979 some 6 million recreation vehicles (RVs) were on the roads. RVs include travel trailers, campers on pickups, and motor homes. Most were used for at least one two-week vacation trip and up to ten weekend trips.
- There are 45,000 hotels in the United States which in 1978 had a total of two million rooms. Total revenues in 1978 were about $16 billion. Location, design, and marketing differences indicate that some hotels are primarily convention centers, some business-oriented, and some primarily aimed at the recreational traveler. One strategy for urban hotels is to provide special incentives for nonbusiness stays on weekends.
- Tour wholesalers did a $5 billion business in 1975 by providing travel packages for over 5 million tour travelers.[10] Tour packages are more common in Europe, with major firms providing integrated travel, lodging, and entertainment arrangements. In West Germany, for example, 90% of such bookings were made by only two companies.
- Second homes include cabins, condominiums, and in-place mobile homes. Condominium resort communities have been planned by the hundreds in North America alone.
- In the ten years before 1975, 26 new cruise ships were put into service. There are over 25,000 cruise-ship beds on the Caribbean alone.
- The number of appointed travel agencies doubled from 6,600 to 12,240 between 1966 and 1976. Median dollar volume of business rose from $700,000 in 1970 to $900,000 in 1976. However, the total sales revenues increased from $5 billion to almost $15 billion.[11]

Such totals are only the beginning. Not included in any of the totals are the revenues of businesses that depend on travel for a major share of their sales, including all those that service the automobile. Travel and tourism are the basis for a wide spectrum of employment opportunities in the public and private sectors of the economy. Among the types of firms and agencies are the following:

Lodging—hotels and motels

Recreation—camping, boating, flying, travel parks, destination amusement centers, etc.

Transportation—ground and air; sales and rental
Tour agencies
Food services
Destination housing and development
Second homes
Services—fuel, food, clothing, equipment, etc.
Market research and trade associations
Government agencies for tourism
Public destination management

All this is oriented primarily toward North America and other developed areas. However, tourism is of crucial importance to the economies of many less-developed nations. Any possibility of maintaining viability in the world markets requires the contribution of "hard" currency brought in by tourism. Mexico is only the closest example of a major nation that depends on tourist receipts to plan toward a viable balance of payments with other nations.

WHO ARE THE TRAVELERS?

The simplest answer to this question is fundamental to more sophisticated answers. Those who travel, especially for pleasure, are those who can afford it. There are other factors in travel, but discretionary income is primary. Every study of tourism, especially travel overseas, demonstrates a direct and dramatic positive correlation between income and travel. Further, the style of travel is also income-related. High-income people not only take more trips, but they spend more along the way.

In 1975 about 16 million families in the United States had incomes of $20,000 or more. Members of these households are the major market for recreation travel services. However, households of more moderate means also travel, usually by car and not to expensive destination resorts. Middle-income families do take vacation and weekend trips. They go by car, often visit relatives or friends, camp or stay in budget motels, and eat along the way in fast-food franchises. A single trip may combine some recreation such as fishing, sightseeing, and camping with visiting. By saving, planning, and using credit cards, they may also take a major trip to an especially attractive destination once every five years or so. They are quite a different travel market from the high-income households who were found by airline research to travel overseas.[12]

Income	Transatlantic Trip Rate
Under $5,000	4 per 1,000 families
$5,000–9,999	9 per 1,000 families

$10,000–14,999	20 per 1,000 families
$15,000–19,999	47 per 1,000 families
$20,000–24,999	108 per 1,000 families
$25,000–49,999	253 per 1,000 families
Over $50,000	753 per 1,000 families

In brief, almost everyone with a very high income goes to Europe each year while few with incomes under $20,000 give such a trip serious consideration. Of course, there are other factors. However, identification of likelihood to travel and style of travel begin with income. Income may not determine *what* we do as leisure, but the cost of travel makes income the primary factor in *where* we do it.

Granted this basic factor, what are other elements in travel participation?

Age Young adults are a major travel-oriented group. However, the 40–55 age group is also prone to recreation travel and early-retirement adults are a significant travel market. In general, Americans seem to be more likely to travel for pleasure as each generation moves into adulthood. More and more, travel is an expectation of life styles.

Family life cycle Young, single adults are more likely to engage in commercial travel than those who are married. Further, young parents, with the constraints of child rearing and values geared toward the establishment of a family, are more likely to stay near home for their leisure. Young parents who are striving to build the basis for a work career are also more likely to invest time in work-oriented activity. However, as children become older and eventually leave home, the parents become better able to travel. Older adults who combine freedom from parenting with adequate incomes often choose to do the traveling that they have postponed. However, we should be careful not to assume that those who are 25–30 now will, thirty years from now, travel at the same rates as those currently 55–60. Rather, most indications are that leisure travel is more an expectation for each cohort entering the life cycle.

Education In modern society, education is highly correlated to income. Nevertheless, the interests and values developed in higher education are another factor in propensity to travel. Students in higher education, without high incomes, also tend to travel widely if inexpensively. The interests in other places and cultures that are fostered through education are combined with a greater confidence in coping with different environments and people.

Time Too much attention has been given to the presumed reduction in average weekly employment hours. The long-term decreasing trend has leveled off in the past decade, partly due to the shift in employment from industrial production to services.[13] However, the significant time factor in recreation travel is not the average time spent at work but the blocks of time available. Travel requires more than coming home from a job an hour earlier; it requires the "long weekend," the vacation, or the ability to control schedules of work and family. Trends in allocating such blocks of time are not clear. More and more people are employed in services—retailing and health care, for example—that call for varied schedules and some weekends on the job. On the other hand, many corporations are experimenting with greater flexibility in work schedules. Also, the increase in women's employment may complicate the ability of a family to free a common period for travel while adding to the financial resources for travel. In general, however, those with the greatest discretion over their schedules are most likely to be able to travel. These include students and the retired as well as the single and those at higher levels of employment.

Demographic trends The population of the United States is aging. There will be a higher proportion as well as a greater number of retirement-age people. Families are smaller and the child-rearing phase of the life course compressed into a shorter period. Most women, including mothers, will be employed outside the home. Marriages are increasingly unstable, producing a higher proportion of the adult population in some stage of transition, in or out of a marriage, and at all ages. The travel characteristics of particular age groups may become more varied as income, family context, work situations, and life-styles and orientations become more differentiated. The decrease in the young adult population and increase in those approaching and entering retirement will impact on travel markets in the coming decades.

Income and other factors are the basis for the *resources* for leisure travel. Travel requires money and time and is directed by interest. However, there is another important aspect of travel: *style.* In order to understand who travels, we need to know more than income and age characteristics. We need to know about the styles of travel of various groups in the society.

TRAVEL STYLES

Most industry studies of travelers deal with only a segment of the overall spectrum, that segment who fly overseas (when the research is sponsored by an international airline) or those who are clients of a national travel agency. For example, American Express did a study of their own clients and produced the following profile:[14]

> The American Express traveler is about 50 with a college degree, and income in the upper 10 percent ($25,000 or over), married, and more likely male than female. About half are professionals or executives. Most travel at least once a year to domestic vacation areas such as Florida or California and less often to the Caribbean or Europe. About 80 percent go on package tours. Many own second homes or vacation condominiums, usually near water. They seek water sport facilities, golf and tennis opportunities, shopping, entertainment, and scenery as well as the chance to relax in a different environment. When travelling, they seek historical and cultural enrichment as well as natural beauty. Air fare prices are a factor in decisions about when and where to travel.

The profile seems to be of the "standard-brand affluent tourist." But that is only one of many styles of leisure travel. Already outlined is the family who travels by car, taking advantage of many cost-reducing modes of overnight accommodation and eating. The travel industry tends to focus on the traveler who spends the most money through industry channels, travel agents, airlines, tour packagers, resort operators, and hotel/motel providers. However, quite successful businesses have been developed that service the en route needs of budget travelers as well as special-interest groups.

- Club Med has identified a young adult group, employed with discretionary income and freedom from child rearing, who want a different culture, considerable peer interaction, and usually warmth and water.
- Business campgrounds meet the needs of RV travelers who use the interstate highways to get to natural-resource destinations.
- Urban hotels have developed weekend programs for adults who want to change from suburban or apartment living to the urban environment of restaurants, nightclubs, theaters, and shopping.
- River-running outfitters have discovered that guided trips through canyons and rapids in safe rafts attract not only the young and adventurous but also older men and women who want to enjoy a different environment and have, at least once, a different experience.
- Tour wholesalers recognize that many international travelers want free time to explore the new locales as well as predetermined costs and basic travel and lodging for the trip.

The styles and motivations for travel are as varied as the life-styles and values of those within a modern complex culture. Resources and opportunities, interests and capabilities, past satisfactions and future anticipation all vary so that providing travel-related services is an endless set of possibilities. Developing a viable business is as likely to mean identifying an obscure market segment as attempting to compete for an obvious one.

RESOURCES AND OPPORTUNITIES

Tourism is more than a business. The resources that make leisure travel possible and attractive involve everything from sewage disposal to guide services. One basic distinction among these resources is between infrastructure and superstructure.

Infrastructure includes all the forms of construction that make integrated life possible in an organized society: transportation projects, such as roads, parking, railway lines, and airport runways, as well as sewage disposal, power and water utilities, and other basic built items. Infrastructure usually also includes the basic institutional structures that operate the constructed items.

Superstructure consists of the built items such as terminals, hotels, restaurants, shopping facilities, and the institutional organization to operate them. The focus of business is generally on the superstructure. Superstructure is more likely in the private sector and in a capitalist or mixed economic system to be provided by profit-seeking firms. However, a breakdown in the infrastructure will bring everything to a halt. Especially in recreation businesses such as resorts, the condition of the regional and local infrastructure is essential to the operation of the business. The public and private sectors are highly interdependent rather than separate or in competition.

Further, tourism frequently is dependent on resources that are *common ground,* available to the general population. Tourism businesses on the Oregon coast depend on public access to the beaches, which have been declared common ground. Much recreation travel is to areas that have access to water resources that are common, open for use to those who want to swim or boat on them. Considerable vacation travel is directed toward the scenic vistas that are available to everyone who travels the public roadway or who flies over. In most countries many of those special resources are held by the state as common ground, with at least regulated access given to visitors in some equitable manner.

Therefore, recreation travel is highly dependent on public action that provides the infrastructure and ensures access and use of common ground for recreation. The access networks of airways, waterways, and highways is essential for travel. A political system that ensures freedom of movement as well as an integrated system of transportation and utilities is a prerequisite of tourism.

As a consequence it is often necessary for those who are developing travel services, recreation businesses, and destination resorts to become involved in the political decisions of the local, regional, and federal governments. The planning of a new set of recreation resources can seldom be carried out without considerable interaction between the public and private sectors. This is especially true in relatively undeveloped regions where the economic, social, and environmental impacts of tourism may be most critical. Planning for growth in the superstructure of an area, to provide resources for travelers, requires coordinated development of the infrastructure. Failure to provide for the social viability of residents and the environmental protection of the ecological system will lead to a deterioration and possible destruction of what has made the area attractive in the first place.

Travel-related recreation businesses do not exist in a state of social, economic, or environmental segregation. Rather, they must plan in ways that take into account the resources for leisure travelers as well as the markets who might be attracted to the resources. A drive along the shorelines of many beach areas or lakes where crowding has led to deterioration and a once lovely area has become a recreational slum is a vivid reminder that recreation business can destroy the resource that once gave it life.

Weather: a Fundamental Resource One final introductory note on tourism business is so obvious that it is frequently overlooked. It is, of course, weather. So much recreation travel is dependent on weather than an otherwise viable business can be destroyed by weather conditions in a few years or less. The first peril of ski-based businesses, for example, is two or more consecutive seasons without snow. At the very least, any ski-based business must be capitalized to cope with one season without snow in some areas or a season in which too much snow blocks access in others.

Weather is a fundamental factor in recreation travel and in planning a travel-related business. A few examples will illustrate the point:

- The states most dependent on tourism income, Florida, Hawaii, and Nevada, are warm-weather areas that attract the "snowbirds" fleeing cold climates. However, unseasonable cold can produce millions of dollars of cancellations in a few days.
- Destination resorts with a central activity that is weather-dependent, such as skiing, golf, or sailboating, must charge enough in good weather to pay for the cancellations caused by bad weather or provide alternative opportunities that are not closed by thaws, rain, or whatever prevents the primary activity.
- Seasonality is a major fact of most tourism planning. What do freshwater fishing resorts do in the winter? Can their trails be made accessible for Nordic skiing? What do the resort hotels do in the off-season, close or adapt? And remember that the off-season is almost entirely dictated by climate.

There are two interrelated elements: The first is climate, the conditions of seasonality of an area. The second is weather, the day-to-day changes in temperature, precipitation, and winds that are part of the recreational environment. Some resource-based recreation calls for adapting to weather changes as part of the experience—wilderness hiking or competitive sailing, for example—but most resource-drawn tourism is based on climate and highly affected by weather. The marketing of recreation travel support requires inclusion of a variable that is, at least in part, out of control. Both the resource of climate and the variable of weather are elements in the development of recreation business.

TRAVEL AND TOURISM MARKETS

If leisure is understood primarily as an experience, then recreation travel is going to an environment that is expected to facilitate the experience. To begin with, different environments are most likely to make possible different experiences. Those who seek excitement and those who seek rest and relaxation would tend to go to different places. Further, people engage in leisure travel in different ways and with varied aims. Identifying both the aims and the people is the purpose of market research.

Why do people choose to travel? Recognize that the costs of travel are high. Not only is travel generally the most expensive form of recreation, but there are other costs as well. Think of all the people sitting in traffic jams and trying to get back into the city on Sunday evening after a weekend trip. Remember the lost baggage, sleepless nights in strange hotels, lost reservations in strange cities, plans spoiled by weather, and just getting lost? Home may be familiar and contain all sorts of tasks, but travel is not an unmitigated joy either.

No two trips are alike, but all may be analyzed with some basic elements:[15]

1. For a trip there are the anticipations, the experience of the trip itself, and the recollections. All three elements are part of the benefits.
2. The trip experience is made up of at least four elements: satisfactions intrinsic to traveling, companionship, the benefits associated with the destinations, and educational factors. These elements are combined in different proportions to make up the total experience. For one trip just getting away may predominate. For another the special environment of the destination—a special performance of a play or a quiet beach—is central. Sometimes it doesn't matter where we are as long as we are with certain people. In almost any new setting we may have the satisfaction of exploration and learning.

These elements have a nearly infinite number of combinations and intensities. Styles of leisure travel differ. Some people return to familiar locales year after year; others never go to the same place twice. Some go with their families; others want to get away. Recreation dimensions within a travel experience may include relaxation and activity, familiarity and novelty, dependence and autonomy, and order and disorder. One analysis suggests that the tourist is seeking to renew a relation to the history and meaning of the social world rather than seeking the novel.[16]

STYLES OF TRAVEL

The Boeing Company developed one set of tourism styles with four types:[17]

"Suzie" is an 18- to 25-year-old office worker who seeks fun and the possibility of romance on a trip that is protected from danger or social embarrassment.

"Rose" is also a white-collar worker, 30 to 45, probably divorced and with older children. She seeks the excitement and learning of foreign travel but is concerned about comfort and the let-down after the trip.

"Empty nesters," couples with grown children, are going through a transition and may want a new experience. They are not put off by the idea of an organized tour and seek destinations of cultural and historic interest.

"Private wheels" are the blue-collar workers who prefer to travel in their own cars or RVs and who are not seen as a market for organized tourism by air.

The aim of market research is to identify viable markets for particular sponsors. As a consequence, styles of travel unlikely to enlarge their market are ignored or rejected. However, those who travel in their own wheels are just the market sought by the private campground industry.

Further, almost all the typologies obscure the differences among those identified as a type. For example, there is the distinction between vacationers, who seek relaxation, and travelers, who seek excitement. Up to a point it is true that the comfort of familiarity and the learning of novelty seem incompatible. But what about those who return to their usual lakeside resort each summer and yet travel to Europe without the children in the spring? What about those who go new places, but always with the "plastic bubble" of the organized tour and even with a group that has traveled together before? What about the pilot who flies a light plane across the mountains to spend a weekend relaxing in the home of friends or family?

VEBLEN EFFECTS AND ENGEL CURVES

One motivation for travel often suggested in historical literature about the "grand tour" and other such travel is that of social status. Thorsten Veblen proposed that in his era, the 1880s and 1890s, there was a "leisure class" who purchased the identifying symbols of their affluence with conspicuous waste.[18] They took expensive trips so they could report on the exotic cost. They purchased to demonstrate luxury rather than use. Some suggest that social status is still one element of tourism. Further, as once exotic and expensive destinations become more common, they tend to lose the high-status clientele. The budget tour and motel drive out the luxury market.

Engel curves represent the "preferred superior goods" that take a higher percentage of total expenditure when discretionary incomes rise. For example, leisure travel is so valued—a preferred good—that the rate of purchase increases more rapidly than the income itself. That is, as incomes rise, travel purchases increase even faster. The implications are that tourism will increase more rapidly than average income levels in an affluent economy, and that a rising gross national product will lead to a disproportionate increase in travel markets.[19] The issue of the extent to which travel is a good preferred over, for example, housing at various income levels has not been well tested.

VACATION LIFE-STYLES

One of the less biased studies of vacation styles employs a method known as psychographics to identify general styles of vacation orientations.[20] The study was based on mail questionnaires in urban areas of the Southeast and Great Lakes states. Measures of activities, interests, and opinions (AIOs) were factor analyzed to produce groups of vacation orientations. Both the method and the results are of value for understanding styles of travel and nontravel. Five styles of vacationers were identified:

1. *Budget travelers* Almost 28% of the sample were interested in travel, but always at a price. They are often campers and seek educational gains in their travel. They tend to be middle-income adults with some college education. They are least likely to use credit for travel. Their occupations are often managerial, and they may have begun families earlier than the rest of the sample.
2. *Adventurers* Those who seek excitement and are willing to pay for it comprise 24% of the sample. They like to relate accounts of the challenge and uniqueness of their trips. They are younger, have higher incomes, and are financially optimistic. More sophisticated in their social life, they are least home-oriented, most nontraditional in role expectations, and not involved in community organizations, even cultural ones. They want to "get out and go."
3. *Homebodies* Twenty percent are distinctive in the travel they do not do. They have no travel plans even though they may have enjoyed some vacation travel in the past. Neither camping nor educational tours interest them. They are more withdrawn socially and concentrate their lives on home activities and resources. They are the oldest group, least optimistic financially despite relatively high current incomes, and least interested in the world outside their own households.
4. *Vacationers* This smaller set, 7% of the sample, are the opposite of the homebodies. They like to travel, are constantly making plans and changing them, leave home on weekends more frequently, and talk about vacations a lot. They would like to travel first-class, even on credit. They tend to be quite active socially even though their incomes and education levels are the lowest of the five styles.
5. *Moderates* Over 20% like to travel, but within limits. They are low in inclinations to camp or engage in sports. They are middle-level in income and education and without definitive characteristics in relation to vacations. Vacation travel is just one interest among many. In this analysis, they are the residual category with travel orientations difficult to define as a reachable market.

In general, the variety of travel styles reflects the variety in life-styles within the culture. Most adults cannot be easily and dramatically identified by their commitment to one form of leisure. They are more likely to seek a balance in associations, environments, and satisfactions.[21] This balance is based on a common core of engagement in relatively accessible activities with regular associations, family, and friends. People watch television, read, listen to music, talk and walk, and go out to eat together. Beyond such familiar activity they choose a set of activities that fit their interests and values. Travel takes a place within that overall scheme of leisure and life. For some it is a dominant form of leisure. For most it is one interest among many and restricted by the high costs of time and money. Nevertheless, there are different styles of travel that require different support services and marketing approaches.

MARKET SEGMENTATION

The total tourist market has been divided into three segments:[22]

1. *Holiday tourists* Generally considered to be highly sensitive to seasonality and price, the holiday tourist may be attracted by low off-season prices and packages that assure a cost ceiling. The holiday tourist tends to go to well-known resort areas, including cities as well as winter "fun in the sun" locales.
2. *Business tourists* Demand is not seasonal, price-elastic, or easily altered by marketing. Business visits tend to be to population centers and of short duration. However, convention and business meetings can be influenced by amenities, entertainment opportunities, and personal benefits that are paid for out of the business expense account. Holiday and business markets for transportation and lodging are clearly separated but may be highly complementary in scheduling, with peaks in demand for one paralleling valleys for the other.
3. *Common-interest tourists* These tourists are those visiting friends and relatives, seeking educational gains, and traveling to destinations with something to offer the individual or group. Absolute price is important and may rule out trips entirely. Convenience and cost tend to be more important than special amenities or attractions.

There are many other ways of segmenting the tourism market. For the most part they are related to a particular type of travel, set of resources, or region. For example, one state tourism agency, that in Massachusetts, found five types of leisure visitors to the state:[23]

- *Frequent visitors* are usually older people visiting relatives and who use few travel-related services.
- *Sightseers* tend also to be 50 and over. They do not come great distances, but employ services for food, lodging, and car in their driving to areas of scenic interest.
- *Sport and relaxation* seekers, often young and single, value a climate permitting outdoor activity, the quality of resources and accommodations, and opportunities for relaxation as well as skiing and water sports. They usually are price-conscious, with limited incomes and often quite specific aims for their trip. (It is possible that further segmentation might distinguish younger sports participants from older travelers who use the outdoor environment more as a place to get away and relax.)
- *Young nature buffs* are the youngest set, generally single, who travel no more than a day's drive, watch every penny, and seek quality outdoor environments. They have high education levels and low incomes. Many are

still students. However, in the evenings they may also seek congenial locales in which to gather for eating and drinking.

- *A representative subgroup* is a residual category of those who take one-day trips for a variety of purposes including sightseeing, business, visiting, entertainment, or getting to school. They use general support services, probably in ways that are related to the purpose of the trip.

Note that there seem to be two types of market segmentation. One is related to a form of transportation, usually air, and stresses destination, distance, price, and timetable. The second is regional and usually concentrates on those who travel by car and use resources and services that are reached by private transportation. Market segmentation is not a general exercise but is specific to the sponsor—the firm producing a product or service or an agency concerned about the economy of a particular city or region.

A more general and yet useful approach to market segmentation focuses on salient characteristics of the sample. For example, styles of travel vary according to place in the family cycle. Further, the kinds of services and accommodations desired also vary according to the composition and aims of the travel group. Leisure orientations as well as resources and constraints vary through the life course.[24,25] Therefore, the importance and modes of recreation travel are significantly affected by role changes and transitions. For example:

- Those who are not married usually hope to travel to environments where they will have opportunities for social interaction with age peers.
- Two-career couples may have discretionary income but are limited by the necessity of coordinating two work schedules as well as the aims of establishing and advancing work careers. Time tends to be the scarce resource.
- Parents of preschool children most often travel, when they travel at all, in ways that utilize space and services for small children. Unless they leave the children behind for a special trip by air, they most often vacation by car, with distances regulated each day by child-care logistics. However, they also value the opportunities to use the trip as a nurturing and companionship experience for the family.
- As children move through the school years, their schedules become a greater determinative factor in travel decisions. Not only the school year but also summer activities may limit the vacation trip to late summer. Again, the orientation of travel tends to be quite familial, with destinations chosen that facilitate common actiity and interaction.
- Postlaunching adults, whose children live away from home, have a new schedule freedom and often greater financial resources. Travel may be redirected toward the kind of trips that were neither possible nor preferred in the more familial periods. Air travel, urban destinations, historical and cultural attractions, and nonfamilial group travel are often of

interest. In a period when the present may be valued because an end is recognized, the possibility of investment in present and postponed experiences may increase the likelihood of more cost-intensive tourism. Also, services sought can be chosen more for convenience and comfort than for price.

- Throughout the life course there are the possibilities of a break in the family life cycle. Death or divorce may end any marriage at any time. Therefore, the market for those undergoing a transition in or out of a marriage and family context is increasing. Singles come in all ages now. Both the hopes and fears of those who make their travel plans alone need to be taken into consideration in providing services.

The aims of market segmentation are more than just developing a basis for advertising. What is marketed is a product or, in the case of tourism, a set of products that together make up a service. Integration of the advertising and the organization of the services requires knowing not only the interests but also the needs of those targeted for the services. Further, marketing calls for continual evaluation of the service. Personal recommendation is always important in retaining and enlarging demand for travel services. Also, travel is a recurring purchase for most people. Providing a reliable quality service is the only way to build up a clientele that returns year after year.

PRICE ELASTICITY

Recreation travel is not a necessity. It can be postponed, substituted, or foregone altogether. Only the highest-income portion of the market will not consider price as a factor in travel decisions. Price elasticity has several implications for travel service marketing.

First, travel services are interdependent. A price increase or decrease in one part of the overall set of services will impact on all others. A change in transportation costs is especially critical. Gas prices for auto travel or air fares are basic to trip costs. Drastic changes require adjustment in other costs for most travelers; and one change may be to reduce or eliminate the trip altogether. Opportunity costs may become too high and leisure at home or in the community will be seen as an attractive substitute.

Second, travel services may become highly competitive in pricing. When price is a major factor in decision making, there is usually the possibility of seeking a lower price from competing providers. Travel businesses have to be quite conscious of such competition and prepare to respond.

Third, out of the spectrum of leisure possibilities there are always substitutes. Not only may a household or individual choose a different travel experience at a lower cost, but leisure without the cost of travel is generally possible. Most leisure experiences can be obtained in a variety of locations. Travel is, by its very nature, a selection among alternatives. As a result it is highly subject to pricing factors that alter the demand.

TRANSPORTATION AND SPACE

Leisure involves space, a place for activity. The most commonly used leisure space is the residence. Further, time and space are interrelated in that it may require time to gain access to necessary space. As a consequence, leisure decisions may be mentally categorized in terms of time/distance costs. Some leisure resources—the television or a book—are immediately at hand. Some require a short walk. Others require starting a car or waiting for a bus. The kinds of leisure opportunities that require travel services are those with high time/distance costs. They are those that need a block of time for participation, usually a weekend or vacation period.

Think of the opportunities that are opened simply by a "long" weekend. For example, a 200-mile range of camping and outdoor resources is made available for use by just one additional day, three instead of two. On a two-day weekend, a trip of 2 to 3 hours leaves little on-site time after the trip and setting up camp before it is time to begin packing. Adding one full day means that up to four hours can be spent traveling, with one full day and two half-days remaining for on-site recreation.

AN ECOLOGY OF RECREATION

An ecology of recreation begins in the metropolitan area where most people live.[26] The key is transportation. Private transportation has become a presupposition of recreation resource management. As the city has spread out to become a network of subcities and suburbs linked by roadways and superhighways, recreation providers think in terms of auto transportation in defining their market areas. However, metropolitan diffusion has led to a number of problems for recreation:

- The concentration of people in the inner city places those least likely to have reliable private transportation farthest from most outdoor resources.
- Filling land with incremental development increases the time and travel costs for trips to beaches, parks, museums, concert halls, theaters, and homes of friends and family. The residence, yard, garden, shopping center, and television may be substituted for the forest hike or live performance.
- Access to many leisure opportunities becomes more and more unequal due to distance. Entrance fees may be the smallest part of the price of many kinds of resource-based recreation, public or private.
- The distance of the city's downtown concert halls, museums, theaters, entertainment offerings, and restaurants from the higher-income families

in the suburbs poses problems for gaining regular support for such offerings.

- The clustering of shopping out of the neighborhood and in drive-in shopping centers removes much of the natural fabric of interaction from the neighborhood. As a consequence, leisure may become more and more private. Away-from-home leisure becomes a special event, planned well in advance to cope with the various costs. The logistics of arranging synchronized family timetables makes recreation travel a feat of management.
- Commuting to and from work in the metropolis may require so much time and energy that little remains of either at the day's end. This concentrates travel-related leisure, even 30 minutes from home, into weekend and vacation time slots.

LEISURE ACCESS IN AMERICA

Opportunities are one factor in shaping recreation participation. Choices are made within the realm of the possible. They begin with a tacit assumption that there is a range of possible activities. The financial, time, or skill costs of some rule them out of consideration. Other possibilities require extraordinary resources such as a minimum block of time or special equipment. Other resources are close at hand with costs already paid. Therefore, leisure access has a resource base that is, in part, ecological. The space factor is one important element. When space resources require overcoming the barrier of distance, then that costly element, travel, is introduced into the opportunity scheme.

The Northeast contains 75% of the population of the United States while the West has 75% of the federal recreation land and only 18% of the population. There is no way of equalizing access to Glacier National Park or the Grand Canyon. More important, the abundant campgrounds of the Pacific Northwest are just not a viable opportunity for those who have to compete for a bare little "pad" in Maryland. On the other hand, Lincoln Center for the Performing Arts or Walt Disney World are outside the travel radius of most people, too. To some extent people seeking recreation resources have to adapt their interests and plans to the climate, natural and cultural resources, and ecological environment that exists where they are. They can adapt some resources and enrich others. They can learn new skills and develop new interests. However, the geography of leisure resources remains a central element in the opportunity structure of leisure choices.

That means that marketing travel resources and services begin where people are. The "nearby geography" of leisure choices begins in the residence and the immediately available environment. It expands out in gradations that might be characterized as follows:

1. Private home and yard or immediate common ground.
2. Neighborhood amenities usually within a 5- to 10-minute walk, especially for children.
3. The community—accessible by public transportation or private car, preferably 15 minutes or less in travel time.
4. The larger community—within an hour's drive.
5. The area—accessible by car in a day's round trip but requiring planning to clear the block of time.
6. The region—accessible by car on overnight trips on weekends or vacations.
7. Domestic destinations—reserved for major blocks of time.
8. International destinations or tours—high in time and financial costs.

Those who provide recreation travel services need to identify the types of resources that stimulate each kind of trip and the kinds of commercial resources such trips require. In the next chapter we will examine such services at the point of origin and en route. In subsequent chapters the focus will be on destinations. However, it is important to keep in mind that recreation opportunities include all eight kinds of environments. Further, at least the latter five call for various kinds of support services and take place only after a decision to invest a measure of time has occurred.

SUMMARY OF ISSUES

About half of all travel is recreation-related.

Despite the increase in air travel, 85–90% of trips are by car.

The first factor distinguishing recreation travelers is income. However, interests developed in education, family life cycle, and age are also significant indices of types of travel.

Since travel requires blocks of time, control over time is more important than average employment hours in travel opportunities.

People travel for reasons intrinsic to the travel experience as well as those related to companionship, the destination, and educational aims.

Combinations of personal resources and orientations produce a variety of travel styles. Such styles—budget, adventure, vacation, moderate, home-based and others—are one way to identify market segments for recreation businesses.

Markets are also segmented in terms of resources such as time and discretionary income, social factors such as household composition, and access factors such as geographical location and travel costs.

The price elasticity of tourism makes decisions subject to income changes and alternative opportunities.

Travel is one way of coping with inequalities of access to recreation resources due to time and distance costs. Recreation travel, then, involves calculations of alternatives and trade-offs between costs and anticipated experiences.

DISCUSSION QUESTIONS

1. Why are most vacation trips by car? Is this likely to change? Why?
2. Are more people of middle and lower incomes likely to engage in recreation travel in the next decade? Why or why not?
3. How will the greater number of retirement-age travelers affect travel styles and businesses?
4. Profile as many styles of recreation travel as possible. What are the major factors in shaping each style?
5. How do recreation travelers adapt to weather changes? How can providers adapt in business-enhancing ways?
6. How do Veblen effects increase markets for recreation business? Give specific example.
7. In analyzing the Engel curve for recreation travel, is there evidence that travel is a preferred good more than other types of leisure investments?
8. What is the most useful type of market segmentation for destination resorts? For travel agencies? For tour wholesalers?
9. Why is travel so price-elastic? What are the business implications of elasticity?

PROJECTS

1. Develop a tour program that is different from the usual packages and that meets the travel interests of a viable market segment. Construct a newspaper ad to announce the tour.
2. Which of the psychographics-based vacation styles is most likely to provide a market for recreation business? Outline a business proposal based on that style.

REFERENCES

1. U.S. Travel Data Center, Washington, D.C.
2. Lundberg, Donald E. *The Tourist Business,* 4th edition, p. 2. Boston: CBI Publishing, 1980.

3. U.S. Travel Data Center, Washington, D.C.
4. Proceedings, 1978 Travel Outlook Forum, U.S. Travel Data Center, Washington, D.C.
5. Lundberg, 1980:139.
6. Lundberg, 1980:3.
7. Lundberg, 1980:47.
8. Annual Report, Transportation Association of America, Washington, D.C., 1982.
9. Various industry sources.
10. Touche Ross and Co., 1975, p. 253. In *Tourism Marketing and Management Issues,* D. Hawkins, E. Shafer, and J. Roverstad, eds. Washington, D.C.: George Washington University, 1980.
11. Harris Biennial Study. *Travel Weekly* 36(33):1, April 28, 1977.
12. Lundberg, 1980:282.
13. Kelly, John R. *Leisure,* chapter 6. Englewood Cliffs, N.J.: Prentice-Hall, 1982.
14. Goodrich, J. N. Benefit Segmentation of U.S. International Travelers," p. 134. In Hawkins et al., 1980.
15. Kelly, 1982:305–6.
16. McCannell, Dean. *The Tourist: A New Theory of the Leisure Class.* New York: Schocken, 1976.
17. Boeing Company, 1976, in Lundberg, 1980:279.
18. Veblen, Thorsten. *A Theory of the Leisure Class.* New York: Macmillan Company, 1899.
19. Lundberg, 1980:291.
20. Perreault, W. D., D. Darden, and W. Darden. "A Psychographic Classification of Vacation Life Styles." *Journal of Leisure Research* 1977:208–224.
21. Kelly, John R. *Leisure Identities and Interactions.* London: George Allen and Unwin, 1983.
22. Burkart, Arthur J., and S. Medlik. *Tourism,* 2nd edition. London: Heinemann, 1981.
23. Calantone, R., C. Schewe, and C. Allen. "Targeting Specific Advertising Messages at Tourist Segments," p. 154. In Hawkins et al., 1980.
24. Rapoport, Rhona, and Robert N. Rapoport. *Leisure and the Family Life Cycle.* London: Routledge and Kegan Paul, 1975.
25. Kelly, 1983.
26. Kelly, 1980, Chapter 14.

8 TRAVEL SERVICES

ISSUES

What are the recreation components of travel services?

How do point-of-origin and en route travel services differ?

What are the services offered by a travel agency?

What are the main problems in operating a travel agency?

How is the travel agency business changing?

How is an advertising campaign designed?

What are the elements in tour operation?

How do types of tours differ in relation to target markets?

What do hotels, motels, and campgrounds offer as recreation?

How are recreation and marketing related for en route lodging providers?

What is needed for people to engage in recreation away from home? First, they need a means of transportation. Second, they need various kinds of support for the travel itself, beginning with transportation arrangements and continuing throughout the trip. Third, they need recreation resources where they are going. In this chapter we will examine both the travel support and recreation resources that begin at the point of origin and continue through the journey. The following chapter will deal with destinations.

From the previous chapter we will assume several central elements of the analysis. First, our attention will be given to recreation travel that is primarily for the leisure experiences anticipated on the way or at the destination. Second, although most recreation-related travel is local, we will be focusing on travel that requires blocks of time and takes the participants out of immediate range of their residential resources.

Third, there are many different types of travel. Recreation businesses find their main travel-related markets among holiday travelers, those who are away from home at least one night for recreational purposes. However, as introduced in the preceding chapter, there are many market segments among those holiday travelers. They may be divided by income and expenditure styles, by family life cycle and social orientations, or by general sets of values and life-styles that shape leisure travel.

Fourth, there are many kinds of travel support that are provided by the business sector. Rather than attempt to be exhaustive, we will concentrate on those directly related to the recreational experiences of travel. Assumed to be complementary are all sorts of public infrastructure provisions, general travel services by public and private sectors, and many kinds of business that are vital for the trip to be made at all. We will not, therefore, deal with auto service stations, fast-food franchises, or the actual provision of transportation.

This chapter is divided into two sections: recreation travel services at the point of origin and those utilized en route.

POINT-OF-ORIGIN SERVICES

In the chapter on retail businesses we will introduce many kinds of recreation business whose markets are, at least in part, dependent on recreation travel. For example, a shop in Chicago that stocks Alpine ski equipment and apparel certainly is supplying a market that is dependent on weekend and week-long trips to the slopes. A fitness center is in part preparing customers for activities that will require travel to a beach or mountain. Retail suppliers of outdoor equipment, boats, recreation vehicles, and countless other goods are meeting a travel-dependent demand. However, in this chapter we will focus on more direct travel services. At the point of origin, the main recreation entrepreneur is the travel agent.

THE TRAVEL AGENCY

Just what are the services of the travel agent for the recreation traveler?

First, the travel agent arranges transportation. A major part of such business is making airline reservations and selling tickets for business travel. In the typical multiservice travel agency, the commissions from such sales provide the core income around which the operation can be planned. As a consequence, regular business travelers must be provided with a satisfying level of service. However, except for specialized agencies in urban financial districts, business ticketing alone is not adequate to support the enterprise. Recreational travel arrangements are an essential part of the whole operation.

The airlines pay commissions to the travel agent for retailing tickets. These commissions vary according to the nature of the flight—domestic or international, for example—and the classification of the ticket from first-class to special discount fares. In the 1980s deregulation of the industry in the United States has produced rapid changes in regular fares, schedules, special-incentive fares, and other promotions and restrictions. Even with modern computer terminals tied into a national system, keeping up with the changes has made the agent's task quite complex. Therefore, it is impossible to provide current commission information.

In general, commissions have varied from 5% to 12% of the fare. Estimates for the 1976–77 period indicate that travel agents handle about 50% of the total domestic airline passenger sales and up to 85% of international sales. The domestic share has increased from 30% in 1965.[1] Increased complications of scheduling and ticketing have probably increased the domestic percentage by near 65% in the 1980s. Travel agents handle a relatively small part of rail and bus sales, about 14% for AMTRAK in 1976. However, this proportion, too, has been increasing each year.

What does the agent do for this commission? The agent usually has leased one of the major airline computer systems with current information on schedules and fares, connections, and seat availability. With the terminal on-line, the agent can respond to an "I want to go to Los Angeles Wednesday morning" request with a rundown of flights, fares, and reservation status. Once a decision is made, the agent can write the ticket and sell it for cash or credit. Through the system a local agent can book seats on flights beginning thousands of miles away on any date months in advance. All this is at no direct cost to the traveler.

Second, the travel agent retails a variety of tour packages. A significant share of the recreational business of the local agent is selling at retail the tour package organized and offered by various wholesalers. Many firms, large and small, organize such tours at a variety of levels and prices. Some are deluxe and complete; others provide only transportation and lodging. Some are unique and offer an experience related to a special event; others repeat the same package with departures several times a week.

It is the task of the agent to listen to the interests of a customer and fit those interests with the array of tours offered. In most cases the agent has had some experience with the wholesalers and the quality of their services. For the most common destinations a variety of travel styles and levels of accommodations and services can be offered to the client. Once a decision is made the agent books the tour, makes the financial arrangements, and receives a commission.

Many travel agents themselves also engage in tour organizing. Either independently or in cooperation with some local organization or entrepreneur, they make the arrangements for a special tour with a local point of origin. In many cases local individuals will develop a following and receive free or discounted travel in return for promoting and/or leading the group tour. Tour providers range from the smallest once-a-year bus-trip organizer to the mammoth conglomerates such as American Express who retail their thousands of tours through tens of thousands of agents. In 1975 they provided transportation and ground services for over 5 million leisure travelers.

Third, the travel agent also provides a number of auxiliary services. Among these are selling traveler's checks, helping with passport documents, and in some cases even arranging for credit to help finance a trip. These services may be sold directly in contrast to the basic commission structure of the agent's income. For the most part the travel agent is selling services that will be provided by others. In this arrangement the agent is held responsible by the client for any number of contingencies largely outside local control.

A main attraction of the travel agency is also a major problem. Since the agent does not have to develop the product, initial investment in the business may be small in comparison to the potential for gross return. On the other hand, the agent is continually in the position of selling services that may not be delivered as promised. Planes may be grounded, schedules changed, tour operators fail, individual managers or guides prove incompetent, hotels change management styles and room quality, and so on. Nor can the agent predict the weather or guarantee congenial travel companions.

Travel Agency Organization In 1841 the British firm of Thomas Cook and Son organized their first tour, a train trip to a temperance meeting, and Henry Wells arranged his first shipment of gold for the firm that became first Wells Fargo and then American Express. Thomas Cook invented the hotel coupon in 1867 and American Express invented the traveler's check in 1891. Arranging for the travel of other people, especially leisure travel, is not a new business.

The role of the travel agent, in distinction from the tour operator, is retailing. The service is convenience and expertise. What seems like a simple function has become both complex and necessary to the entire industry. Further, it has become so financially successful that the traditional agencies are having to face the competition of multiservice firms such as banks, department stores, and mail-order houses.

Licensing The travel agent must be appointed by the various air traffic conferences in order to do business. The International Air Transport Association (IATA) and the U.S. Air Traffic Conference (ATC) along with the various rail and ship conferences have requirements for obtaining a license. They include having a viable place of business, at least one staff member with certified experience in the travel business, a performance and surety bond, a yearly fee, and agreement to certain standards of business operation. The business must keep current records of transactions. In the United States, a travel agent office of the Civil Aeronautics Board handles complaints and can remove an agency from its approved list.

Further, the industry has a number of trade associations. The American Society of Travel Agents (ASTA) has over fifteen thousand members representing some seven thousand agencies that do approximately 80% of the sales. Continuing education in the field is offered by airlines and shipping lines as well as trade organizations. Major tour operators also have incentive tours designed to familiarize agents with the destinations and services.

Legislation has now been passed that allows a variety of firms to function as travel agents. The competition of the convenience of buying tickets at a bank branch or shopping-center department store will call for new marketing strategies from the traditional travel agencies.

One function of the IATA has been to fix international fares. However, many nonmembers have set their own discounted prices and weakened the position of any fare-setting organization. At present, the price elasticity of international travel is being continually tested by a variety of airlines offering simple service at reduced prices.

Commissions The agent is a broker between the consumer and the producer. The product is transportation or a set of travel services in some sort of combination. That is, the agent is the local retailer for the transportation provider, the destination or en route hotel, and the tour organizer. Income is from the commissions on sales and ancillary services. Commission income may be augmented by return on the short-term investment of money deposited by customers and from prepayments. Some agents also sell their own tours.

Costs of doing business A travel agency is labor-intensive. As much as 60% of the costs of doing business are in the salaries and wages of staff.[2] The nearly universal adoption of computerized reservation systems has allowed some agents to reduce staff. However, clients now expect immediate confirmations and are less willing to wait for arrangements to be finalized. The introduction of microprocessors into businesses will have a further impact on local accounting and recordkeeping in some agencies. The amount of time required for each transaction may be reduced. However, the level of expectation of the customer will rise at the same time.

One breakdown of costs for a local agent is as follows:[3]

Salaries	60%
Rent, light, heat	7%
Telephones, cables, etc.	7%
Depreciation, financing	3%
Advertising, promotion	4%
Travel	3%
Other expenses	16%

This does not include borrowing costs to cover accounts receivable, a major element of business accounts. Also, these proportions would be quite different for agencies with heavy financing and capitalization costs or doing considerable advertising in a highly competitive market. Further, the lease of computer capabilities changes ongoing costs by allowing for a significant reduction in personnel while adding on equipment expense.

Training and Job Descriptions Most training for travel agency employment is on the job. However, several airlines offer more formal training. TWA, Eastern, and American have been leaders in this field. There is also training available in the operation of computerized reservation systems. When an agency adopts a new system, on-site trainers from the airline assist the agent with familiarizing himself with its intricacies.

In a larger agency the manager has responsibilities for selecting and supervising personnel, policy decisions about marketing and finance, and product choices about tour lines, auxiliary services, and affiliations. The floor personnel—"travel counselors"—carry on the day-to-day interaction with clients and make reservations, advise on trip planning, and assist clients in other necessary preparations for a journey. Some agencies will also hire specialized personnel to do after-hours ticketing, advertising and promotion, or accounting. In small agencies one or two people may do it all.

If a person were to specialize in the recreation travel aspects of a travel agency with a total staff of five, what would be the main components of the job? First, a recreation travel specialist would identify the special markets in the area. Such markets would be segmented in a number of ways:

By season and destination: for example, winter travel to the South from cold-weather states.

By preferred mode of travel: independent, escorted tours, unescorted tours, or in some point-of-origin affiliation group tour.

By income and likely spending range.

By travel style: familial, single, couple, recreation-seeking, tourism-oriented, and others suggested in the previous chapter.

Second, the size of the markets would be estimated and some selected for promotion. Third, a promotion plan would be developed in consultation with the manager, tour wholesaler, and airline advisors. While such a plan would include elements such as price, convenience, and general attractiveness of destinations, its special orientation would be toward leisure. What kind of leisure satisfactions are paramount for the targeted groups? Which travel offerings are most directed toward those orientations?

Finally, if advertising is part of the promotion plan, how can the potential satisfaction of those leisure aims best be communicated?

TRAVEL MARKETING AND ADVERTISING

As introduced in chapter 3, the famous "four P's" of marketing are product, place, price, and promotion. The *product* of the travel agency is the brokerage of a service linking the prospective traveler to desired services for transportation and support. In a business sense the product of recreation travel is the trip. However, the leisure trip is much more than a folder full of tickets, vouchers, and schedules. It is an experience, anticipated, planned for, gone through day by day, and then evaluated and remembered. The travel arrangers are able to provide a context for the experience. However, the provisions are only instrumental; the experience is the end.

The *place,* or places, of tourism is crucial. Altogether, the trip encompasses a number of places, en route and at the destinations. Further, problems with one place, perhaps a hotel, can depreciate the values experienced in the larger setting, say, Paris or the fjords of Norway. So the place in which the product is experienced is actually a bundle of places, related by geography and by the logistics of the trip. Often one element of the overall "place" is the focus of promotion and advertising. Nevertheless, not only the general environment of the destination but also many other aspects of place are outside the control of the travel agent. Place is actually a range of possibilities that the traveler may employ and to which the traveler must adapt.

Price has been found to be an important element in recreational travel decisions. The price elasticity of leisure travel suggests that most decisions are made with price ceilings or some sort of "benefit per $100" calculation in mind. One function of the travel broker is to present a range of prices as well as a clear picture of what is gained and lost at various price levels. Transportation is especially subject to price calculations by the prospective traveler since money not spent on getting there may be used for entertainment, shopping, or some special unanticipated experience. This element of price has been approached by many tour arrangers by offering a range of accommodations at destinations. Airlines set their tour fare and then add on hotel packages ranked by price and presumed quality of accommodation. For most clients travel decisions may balance hoped-for experiences and price. There are always substitutes for the leisure of tourism when the price is too high.

Promotion may be carried out in many ways. Some travel agents concentrate on developing a wide set of associations in a community. Some seek to become known for special aspects of the service-domestic tours, international expertise, or lowest fares. Some work extensively through organizations in the community to develop group business and draw those who have not traveled into the market. Some concentrate on a particular clientele—students in a university town, business travel in the central city, or tours for later-life adults.

In communities where there is a competition and a variety of market segments, some advertising is usually one part of the overall promotion plan. Before going on to an outline of advertising approaches for recreation travel, it may be useful to review the various market segmentation approaches introduced in the preceding chapter. Advertising is only one part of an overall promotion strategy and is not likely to be cost-effective unless the markets are clearly identified and located.

An Introduction to Travel Advertising An advertising scheme can be divided into eight parts:

- Identifying the target market
- Defining the product
- Choosing professional assistance
- Selecting the media
- Constructing the message
- Designing the format
- Integrating the campaign
- Evaluating the results

Identifying the Target Market In a case based on the operations of a travel agency in an industrial city with a population of 160,000, a decision is made to attempt to increase the recreational, or "pleasure", market. The agency competes with five others in the city and has traditionally had a 50–50 mix of business and recreational travel receipts. An important part of the recreational travel market has been organizational and "incentive" tours to traditional vacation locales such as Hawaii and Florida. Incentive tours for the sales programs of various industries have grown in dollar volume about in proportion to the business growth in the region.

How is a market segment chosen?

First, such a segment must have the ability to pay, to make a travel decision, and to be attracted to the product. Further, some sort of package tour offers the most return on time invested for the agency.[4] How is an underdeveloped market for tour packages to be discovered?

The market mix for the agency should be analyzed first, and then the established markets of competing firms. Finally, insofar as is possible, past successes and failures by all local firms should be analyzed.

One market segment identified as meeting the primary criteria would be two-income post-launching adults. In this community the retirement-age market had been thoroughly exploited with special tours, organizational promotions, and various forms of advertising. However, an analysis of demographic trends revealed that adults between the ages of 40 and 55 were a growing population category, over 60% of the married women in that age group were employed, and that mean incomes were the highest of any age cohort. By income, family life cycle, and discretionary time criteria, mid-life adults should be a prime market. Further, developmental psychology literature has identified this age group as one seeking to find new meaning in life and ready to make changes.[5,6]

Furthering identification of the target population would require investigation of their travel styles and orientations. The psychographic study of vacation styles categorized adults as budget travelers, adventurers, homebodies, vacationers, and moderates.[7] From the profiles in the previous chapter it would be possible to select two of these categories—the budget travelers and the moderates, who together made up 48% of the total sample. Budget travelers seek clear gains from their travel, including learning and personal growth. The level of accommodations is less important than maximizing the experience at a minimum price. The moderates choose to travel out of a number of vacation alternatives. They are midlevel in income and education but without clear aims for travel. In general, these two stylistic categories will be price-conscious, seek more than pleasure and escape from a trip, and yet not be highly adventurous. Further, with two work schedules to consider, employed couples will be concerned about time as a scarce resource and may be willing to pay a bit more to conserve it.

Defining the Product Where would such people most want to go, and when? What product should be offered? If the city is in a climate area with a long winter, then the most common destinations are Florida and the Pacific Southwest, followed by Hawaii, continental Europe, Great Britain, and the Caribbean. Further, this age segment is likely to reserve some summer vacation time for family gatherings, often in locales with a history of vacation recreation. Therefore, the product selected might be a tour to a warm winter-vacation locale in a time- and cost-efficient format.

A review of competing offerings might reveal that there already was a quite intensive exploitation of destinations in Florida and the Caribbean, with a wide variety of tour formats, prices, and schedules. Further, the likelihood seemed high that people with good incomes in their fifties would already have tried the Eastern destinations, and even developed preferences for particular resorts. Therefore, the product choice pointed westward. In an attempt to provide something different and appealing, a tour was developed that included a sample of San Francisco along with two locations in Hawaii. With time and cost in mind, the first decision was to gain maximum vacation time with no more than one full week away from employment. The tour would leave at 2:00 P.M. on a Friday afternoon and take advantage of time zones to offer dinner and either a play or evening free in San Francisco. The Saturday flight to Honolulu also arrives in time for dinner before early retirement. The Hawaiian part of the vacation would allow for only two days on Oahu and almost five in a beach resort area of one of the less crowded islands. In both locations three levels of accommodations and price would be offered. The return on Sunday would allow for an individual decision to go to work Monday morning or take a day to rest from the trip.

The product, then, would feature the following: three destinations with cultural opportunities as well as a break from winter, maximum use of time, low air fares on the group rate, flexible pricing for the two main destinations in Hawaii, and a combination of arranged events in San Francisco and around Honolulu with open time in a resort area with beaches, hiking trails, tennis, golf, and shopping. Further, the preset price would be inclusive enough to allow for rather exact budgeting.

Choosing Professional Assistance Now that the target market and product are selected and defined, the issue is communication. How can the market segment be informed of the opportunity? In some cases someone on the travel agency staff may have enough experience in advertising so that the extra expense of employing an advertising consultant or agent can be avoided. However, at least until such experience is developed, such assistance is usually needed. Therefore, in this case the issues are those of criteria for selection and the information the advertising consultant will require.

Travel advertising is not exactly like advertising for a supermarket or a furniture store. The appeal is an experience, one that must simultaneously be different from what can be obtained at home and yet one with which the traveler can cope. Further, the tour package must promise more than the traveler can arrange alone. The persuasion of advertising is emotional as well as intellectual. It appeals to what a person would like to be as well as to calculations of time efficiency, cost savings, mental and physical benefits, and activity.

An advertising agency can be chosen with consideration of most of the following factors:

Cost Agencies receive income from the media as commissions on the ads they place. They also charge fees for services. A full understanding of costs should be negotiated.

Experience Past work in recreation/travel-related business *may* be useful. However, many will not take an account if they already work with a competitor.

Size An agency should have a staff large enough to do the work *on time*. A small travel account can get lost in a large firm. Most important, an agreement should be reached as to just who will handle the account and do the work.

Style Get samples of past work so that compatibility in style and approach can be assessed.

To perform his or her job, the advertising consultant will need to know just how the market segment is defined, the details on the product, and price. Also, an advertising budget needs to be worked out in advance so that media can be selected and balanced.

Selecting the Media Assuming that the existence and reputation of the travel agency are established in the community, the advertising can concentrate on the particular campaign. However, for a relatively new business there is always the need to advertise the institution—the agency—as well. Building a community reputation is basic to business growth. The manager needs to decide the extent to which the campaign promotes the agency as well as the particular tour.

Consumer advertising employs many media: direct mail, local newspapers, and local radio and television. Further, in some cases a local travel agency may combine with the resources of a tour wholesaler or air carrier to promote a travel package of some sort. Such cooperative advertising is especially common in major point-of-origin market areas.

For a local point-of-origin product aimed at a local market, the choice of media is more limited. An advertising agency will be able to specify the nature of the readership of every local newspaper and the audience of each radio and TV station. Times, ad sizes and location, and other options have different costs. The advertising decision is always one of reaching the largest part of the market segment at the lowest cost.

Newspapers The newspaper ad is often most effective because it allows the reader to return for more information and can employ visual representation of the destinations. Copy can be changed easily and scheduled precisely. Photographs and art are available from airlines and the tourist bureaus of destinations. The critical question is the extent to which the market segment uses the media. In the case of the established adults of age 40 to 55, a local newspaper, especially on weekends, is often a good choice for such a purpose.

Direct mail Most people do open their "junk" mail and can be attracted to a product in which they have an interest. A direct-mail organization can usually prepare mailings for some approximation of the target market—for example, home owners in a community. A mailing can include more information than any other form of advertising and provide for direct action such as a return card. However, it can also be quite expensive, especially if the sales target is only fifty people for a single tour.

Radio Frequently useful for calling attention to something new, radio is limited in its lack of visual image. On the other hand, the large number of radio stations with varied programs allows the advertiser to select in terms of style and taste at minimum cost. For the market segment selected, news programs listened to on the way to and from work or music background stations may be best. Also, repetition of the name of the travel agency is valuable institutional promotion for likely markets.

Television Television has the advantage of the widest general audience and the disadvantage of high cost. Color pictures of destinations are probably most appealing. However, the cost for such advertising calls for a large potential market unless the particular tour promotion is combined with institutional recognition objectives.

Out-of-home media Outdoor advertising such as billboards, bus signs, and taxi posters can be quite cost-effective and are often overlooked. The limitations of brevity and lack of flexibility make them more useful for institutional than product-specific advertising.

Any business should also be aware of the potential value of such media as the Yellow Pages, point-of-purchase materials such as leaflets made available to those taking other trips, and a variety of community sponsorships. Overall, a business should strive for a media mix based on their objectives and markets.

In the case of this particular tour the advertising agency advised selected radio spots, Sunday travel-section newspaper ads during the period when decisions were most likely, and institutional advertising with signs in the local airport buses.

Constructing the Message Developing the message for the selected media begins with research. Copywriters must understand every detail of the product as well as specifying the market segment. Attention-getting phrases and ideas are essential. One set of principles includes the following suggestions:[8]

Spotlight unique differences
Facts are better than generalities
Have a "big idea"—a differentiating highlight
Use long copy when useful
Alleviate anxiety about going to a strange place
Try provocative new ideas
Go first-class—the ad should demonstrate quality
Employ news potential—feature any announcement that is really news
Bargains are still a feature
Coupons can be the feature of the ad
The entire ad can be a coupon
Caption photographs; people do read them

The word *free* gets attention

Advertise one product in each ad

Other elements of constructing the message are more related to the target market. What kinds of outcomes and experience will they seek? What problems are they likely to anticipate? What will be the main decision criteria? To go or not to go and whether or not to select this particular package. One way of developing relevant and appealing copy is to do some informal research by talking to a number of people in the market segment about the tour. Using other associations to test ideas and approaches can considerably reduce the advertising budget.

Each medium has different requirements for style and format. However, directness, clarity, attractive format, and a vivid appeal are always important. For recreational travel, the attention-getting lead is most likely to be oriented toward the desired experience. It is important to remember that the customer is buying an anticipated pleasurable experience, not a durable good to utilize for ten years.

Designing the Format In one form of another, an ad consists of a headline, illustration, copy, and a signature. The ad needs to attract and hold attention, present an appealing image, tell the story, and clearly identify the provider. Principles of design are too complex to present here and usually require skilled preparation. However, the manager should at least be involved to the extent of being sure that the format meets certain criteria:

The format should call attention to the main appeal of the product. The format should not conflict with the nature of the product. For example, a cluttered and crowded format does not connote relaxation and pleasure.

The format should have grace and appeal and, for the corresponding tour, even a touch of elegance.

The format should suggest some cultural congruity with the life-styles and communication modes of the market segment.

Type styles, illustrations, photographs, color, and all the characteristics of the medium should be exploited in the design. Designing advertising is directed toward producing a response among a designated category of people. Nevertheless, there is art to design. The travel agent should be critical of the design as well as supportive of the designer.

Integrating the Campaign Integration is partly a matter of selecting media mix and style. It also involves timing. For a winter tour the advertising schedule works back from the tour itself to the decision closing, probable decision period, and the time of announcement. Materials for the campaign need to be prepared according to that schedule. Advertising consultants who cannot provide services according to that schedule are of little value no matter how creative or otherwise skillful.

Further, there may be intermediate goals set for the campaign. The announcement advertising should stimulate a certain number of inquiries by a given date. If not, the campaign may need to be changed or the entire project abandoned. A promotion campaign is a long step-by-step process. It needs to be planned with both a calendar and a clearly specific set of objectives.

From the first product development and marketing strategy sessions to the closure of enrollment in the tour, each item of advertising should have objectives that are integrated with the entire campaign. And the campaign has to ration the expenditures so that one element does not become so costly that no others can be done effectively.

Evaluating the Results Of course, whether or not the tour attracts enough travelers to cover all costs and make a profit is the final evaluation. However, there are other important elements of evaluation:

- Did the campaign raise the perceived institutional stature of the agency?
- Were intermediate goals met for inquiries, consultations on details, deposits, final commitments, and actual participation?
- Did those who bought the product respond to the advertising? If so, which elements of the campaigns were most persuasive for them? Informal interviewing can be of great value in planning the next such promotion.
- Was the promotion cost-effective when all the staff time is added to direct costs in the accounting?

TOUR OPERATORS

The tour business is made up of four parts. First there is the operator/wholesaler, who develops the tour itinerary and services, assigns a price, and distributes promotional material. Second is the retailer, usually a local travel agent, who is the broker between the tour operator and the customer. Third come the actual "hands-on" tour managers, who take the developed arrangements and are there to make sure they work. They are managers of people, recreation leaders who use the travel resources as a basis for a leisure experience for travelers. Fourth are the local providers, who rent their resources and services to the tour operator.

The Inclusive Tour The inclusive tour consists of transportation, lodging, and usually some other services. The single price covers these provisions. In many cases an air carrier and tour operator combine to develop the package. Some are to a single destination, for example, to a set of condominium apartments in Hawaii or the Caribbean. Once at the destination, the travelers are on their own until they return. At the other extreme are tours in which every meal, sightseeing bus, local transportation, and entertainment item are included. In such an inclusive group tour the tour manager or guide is always present to make sure that the group stays on schedule and that all amenities are provided.

Inclusive tours may be by scheduled airlines with discount fares, through block booking on regular carriers, or on a charter. The main purpose of the inclusive tour is to relieve the traveler of the burden and anxiety of having to make such arrangements. Also, the tour operator may be able to secure lower rates on transportation and lodging. The cooperation of hotel businesses and airlines with major tour providers allows for a reliable and standardized product. The major tour wholesalers usually offer a spectrum of tours, from the highly organized group with every day scheduled to the package that provides only transportation and lodging and even flexible travel with several nights open in or near the destination. Prices are in a range according to the luxury of the accommodations and the completeness of the services.

Marketing for such tours also varies. A mass-market tour operator may stress the appeal of the destinations and the reliability of arrangements in an attempt to attract the widest possible market. Brochures usually offer several price levels and many different dates of departure and return. On the other hand, some tours are directed toward quite narrow markets. These may stress a particular cultural event, such as a Bach festival at Salzburg, Austria, or a particular religious celebration for adherents of a certain tradition. There are tours that are developed around a recreational activity such as skiing or mountain climbing. There are even "adventure" tours that promise the hardship of the Antarctic or a cross-ocean sailing ordeal.

Tours are usually recreational in their appeal, as in the following:

- A fall bus tour of retirement adults through New England to see the foliage. The three marketing emphases are the group social experience, low cost, and trouble-free way of enjoying the fall colors.
- A rock-climbing expedition to Alaska for experienced—and generally young—climbers only. The marketing highlight is an adventure opportunity that would be difficult for just one or two climbers to arrange.
- Recreation destinations commonly feature particular outdoor activities such as skiing, sailing, or a major sports event as the central attraction. In some cases tour operators sell their product because of the difficulties in making reservations during seasons of high demand. However, price is also usually a major marketing element.
- The more traditional tour consists of the inclusive group trip to a number of destinations with a combination of organized sightseeing and free time at each locale. The fear of many less-experienced travelers of arriving in a strange environment, often without speaking the language, and being unable to cope is allayed by the inclusive tour. Seeing interesting places from the security of a tour has a wide appeal.

The point is that the tour is much more than a set of arrangements and schedules. It requires planning for particular orientations toward travel. In tour management, marketing and carrying out the operations involve market segmentation that identifies the kind of experience and support sought by the traveler and then plans the trip to facilitate such outcomes. The best leadership during the trip cannot overcome the problems that result when the retailer sells the wrong package to the customers.

Types of Tours At the point of origin the retailer is responsible for guiding the client to the right product. When the traveler comes as an individual, couple, family, or other small group, interests and styles can be assessed and appropriate packages suggested. However, there are other kinds of tour affinities. For example, an incentive tour may be offered by a firm to sales personnel who achieve a designated quota for the year. Or members of a trade organization may form a tour group. In either case it is likely that different styles of travel will be represented in the group. In such a case some flexibility within the schedule and level of service may be necessary.

As with most all forms of leisure, tourism is characterized by variety. Organized group travel may be based on freedom from schedule and a low price at one end of the spectrum and on "total care" at the other. Group travel is to some extent a social experience as well as one that depends on the different destination environments. As a consequence, "who" is as important as "where" in travel planning.

The Cruise: A Special Case In recent years, the ocean cruise has become a more popular form of vacation travel. New ships have been built and older ones refurbished and even cut apart and lengthened for the cruise trade. The ship is more than a means of transportation; it is a floating resort, a cross between a destination and a means of travel, where recreation environments and lodging are combined. Further, along with the ports of call the ship is the recreation environment for the period of passage.

A cruise certainly offers the experience of "getting away" to a different environment. Further, the cruise brings people together in a locale so restricted in size that a highly social environment is created. On the ship people expect to meet others in restaurants and at poolside, in organized activities and in the bars, while dancing and gambling, exercising and lounging, sightseeing and shopping.

With the trend toward shorter cruises there is more effort to get people socially involved quickly. The usual cruise lasts only a week. One "fun ship" offering includes eight meals and snacks a day, a "welcome-aboard" party, a singles get-acquainted cocktail party, a captain's cocktail party, a farewell dinner, a full gambling casino, two nightclub shows a night, and a variety of activities. Most weeks include three ports as well as the cruising. Prices vary depending on accommodations. Considerable stress is on the opportunities for shopping on shore as well as on the social opportunities on the ship.

The cruise ship is designed to appeal to particular market segments. Brochures include pictures of older couples as well as young pairs who have already attained both a relationship and a tan. Entertainment with ethnic flavors is mixed with shows similar to those found in any city. The mix is the possibility of new experiences in an environment that both protects and facilitates social opportunity. There is considerable stress on consumption, much of which is not included in the basic package of room, meals, and air fare.

The organized recreation programs aboard ship are oriented toward social facilitation. Some cruises are organized around single interests such as bridge, photography, backgammon, or archeology. However, much more common are the open cruises that require the recreation staff to provide to those on board a variety of opportunities for meeting and ongoing interactions. For the most part the recreational program serves as a setting for social interaction rather than as an end in itself.

Worldwide there are some 140 cruise ships in operation.[9] About 75 sail from the United States. However, shipboard cruising is also popular in the Soviet Union as well as in Western Europe. The pressure on peak periods such as Christmas vacation allows the operators to add a surcharge to prices in those times.

There are also domestic cruises, mostly on the rivers of the world. In Europe barges have been refitted for recreational tours. Riverboats, either refurbished or built for tourism, ply the great rivers such as the Rhine and the Mississippi. Being aboard a boat seems to have a special appeal, combining travel and seeing new locales with a protected setting for relaxation and social experiences.

Activity Tours Activity tours are also recreation-oriented but focus on a particular activity at a single locale. Some specialize in snorkeling or diving in tropical waters. Some feature skiing instruction and opportunities at a number of slopes and runs. Some involve training and self-directed sailing in boats chartered from marinas in Florida, California, or the Great Lakes. Some, such as the ski-resort packages, offer the sport by day and a set of social opportunities and entertainments at night. Some combine instruction with the opportunity to ski, sail, or engage in the sport independently.

In many cases the entrepreneur uses the capital of others to make up the total package. For example, lodging at the resort may be provided in condominium units or the charter sailboats owned by individuals who make them available to the charter organizer. In this way the apartment or boat can be depreciated and expenses deducted from tax obligations because the item is used primarily in a business.

In all such tours or cruises, the entrepreneur is bringing together resources and services in ways that enable the client to obtain a resource-based experience that might otherwise not be generally available at all. Providers of transportation, lodging, recreation equipment and locales, and support services have access to markets that would otherwise be untouched. Conversely, the vacationer has access to facilities and resources that would have remained open only to devotees of the activity and to those wealthy enough to purchase the resources for private use. Travel, then, becomes a part of the overall experience as well as a necessary means of getting somewhere.

CASE: TRAVEL, LODGING, AND RECREATION

In 1982 James E. Durbin, president of the Marriott hotel chain, spoke to the Travel and Tourism Association about changes in the hotel/motel industry in the next decade. Since costs of providing accommodations have risen—the construction and furnishing cost of a hotel room is six times what it was in 1960—prices have had to rise as well. Nevertheless, the Marriott group is projecting 50 new hotels in the near future. Along with such expansion will come changes in management tools. The computer will be employed for reservation systems, room management, and guest accounting as well as payroll accounting. However, changes in the market would seem to have more impact on management than these new instruments.

For example, the size of the industry is expected to increase. In 1980 total expenditures in the United States for lodging, airline tickets, and food and beverages exceeded spending for national defense. Although growth is related to overall economic growth, the scope of the travel-accommodation-entertainment complex is both vast and multidimensional.

Further, the nature of the market has been undergoing change. More women are rising to levels of business and government employment in which they do considerable travel. The design of accommodations and services, previously aimed at the male business traveler, will require different amenities if women are to be satisfied with provisions. In the 1980s women who engage in work-related travel during the week will also be making decisions about family and recreational travel during holiday periods.

During the same period there will be a 40% increase in the size of the 35–44 age group, a segment of the population that has generally done 50% more travel than any of the others. At the same time the somewhat older adults who have launched their children will be seeking travel-related experiences that do not include activities and concerns for children. Some vacation travel will be by "working couples" who have high expectations for the convenience and quality of accommodations but also seek travel experiences that differ from business travel and want a trouble-free environment away from home. In many cases the convenience expectations from business travel will be carried over into recreational travel.

Indications are that there will be a number of special markets:

- Family travel for adults who want to bring their children along but do not want to have to care for them 24 hours a day.
- Working-couple travel for adults who either wish to leave child care behind or whose children are now grown and out of the residence.
- Business and recreational travel for employed women.
- Weekend travel by those who can cut free from work by late Friday afternoon. Some businesses that cater to work-related travel during the week may be able to reorient their offerings to capture some of the special weekend market. But what, along with convenience, do those weekending adults want in their away-from-home experience? What kinds of combinations of activity and relaxation will attract travelers to a leisure locale?

And then there is the international market. In 1981, for the first time, travel to the United States brought in more money than was spent by American travelers abroad. Visitors to the United States now number more than 20 million each year. However, such visitors, many of whom do not speak English, require a different set of support services from the domestic tourist. Responsiveness to this new market calls for more than advertising in foreign periodicals. What modes of accommodation, entertainment, and sightseeing are preferred by those from the various cultures feeding into North American tourism-related industries?

EN ROUTE TRAVEL SERVICES

There are, of course, many kinds of en route travel services that have no direct recreation components. They may be necessary for the vacation or weekend trip and may depend on pleasure travel markets for income. However, they serve recreational travelers as they serve all others, by pumping gas, serving hamburgers, or offering a room with a bed and shower.

However, some providers of overnight accommodations have developed recreational aspects to their provisions. They recognize that "getting there" is at least part of the fun of many trips. Further, they seek to enlarge their own markets by gaining weekend trade and by turning "pass through" areas into "pause" areas. They offer more than their basic service.

HOTEL-MOTEL RECREATION

Like the rest of travel-related businesses, the hotel-motel industry is characterized by diversity. In urban centers we find the massive hotels that cater primarily to the corporate and convention trade. Their prices are high and the entertainment concentrated on evening fare of eating, drinking, and associated nightclub-style shows. However, an increasing number have added exercise and fitness facilities to their indoor pools.

Other hotel styles reflect their locations and clientele. Some smaller urban hotels are also business- and convention-oriented but priced and located to take the overflow and price-conscious trade from the majors. A few hotels seek a luxury clientele and feature full service with unusually well-appointed rooms. Their high prices ensure a selection of guests. However, in smaller cities the remaining hotels attempt to attract a general group of travelers who have some reasons for staying downtown rather than in a fringe motel. Most often they are business-oriented and furnish transportation from the airport.

Motels also offer a variety of styles and prices. Luxury motels are most likely to be found near major airports, in high-cost urban locations, and near major recreation attractions. At the other end of the spectrum are the budget motel chains with fixed prices and relatively simple appointments. They tend to be built and located to extract a maximum return on investment within ten years. In between are a full spectrum of sizes, styles, and price ranges. Almost lost from view are the older "Mom and Pop" motels located along highways and city entrances that have been bypassed by new interstate highways and exits.

From a recreation business perspective, there have been a number of developments in which the leisure potential of travel lodgings has been exploited. These are based on much more exact market segmentation than was common in the first wave of motel expansion in the 1950–70 period. In earlier days recreation was limited to outdoor pools. In fact, to lower overhead costs these pools were sometimes filled in by operators who simply sold adequate rooms at a price.

Among the current attempts to make even the one-night stop more of a recreation experience are the following:

- Reporting in the national directories of motel chains the availability, on-site or nearby, of golf, swimming, tennis, indoor racquet courts, fitness centers, fishing, boating, and visitor attractions of interest. The aim is to appeal to those who plan a trip with the hope of finding some recreation experiences in the late afternoons and evenings along the way.
- The refitting of urban hotels with a more elaborate set of recreation facilities than the formerly obscure swimming pool. Saunas, exercise centers, and whirlpools are common along with discount passes to nearby racquet clubs and health centers.
- A variety of programs to fill rooms on weekends may have leisure appeals. Urban hotels offer dinner-drink-room packages for couples who want to enjoy the urban environment and get away from home for one or two nights. Hotels and motels take children free to attract families on weekends. They also develop recreation-oriented packages that include passes

or discounted tickets to plays, museums, special exhibitions, concerts, dining at well-known restaurants, and other attractions.

- There are a growing number of convention centers located 30 minutes to 2 hours from airports but outside the city. They combine lodging and meeting rooms for business gatherings with golf courses, beaches, other sports, and evening entertainment. From the business perspective, the attraction is an environment where people stay together rather than disperse around the city. To attract smaller conventions, recreation is offered to those in residence. Often such a convention center is combined with a country club that would have many of the facilities anyway. Such urban fringe hotels also offer weekend packages for those who might drive in from around the region for a leisure weekend.

These are only a few examples of how travel lodging and recreation resources have been combined. They are recognition that travel itself may be a leisure experience. At least, destination and lodging may be chosen for recreation amenities even when the main aim of the stay is business or en route lodging. One hope is to change the "pass-through" to a "pause," that is, to lengthen the stay. A second aim is to utilize facilities at low seasons or weekdays. Recreation is employed in marketing efforts to widen what might be strictly an en route or business stopover. Further, there is a recognition that some travelers seek leisure opportunities along the way. They want to do more than sit and look.

Motel Recreation Offerings Some motels are now being designed around recreation resources. Even though they are located near airports, along interstate highways, or on the edge of cities, they are designed to attract travelers who will spend some time at the motel. They hope to extend stays beyond a single night by providing alternative opportunities for participation and relaxation.

When there is a special resource nearby, the motel can exploit it to attract and retain visitors. Travelers do become tired on a trip. Families traveling with children may be ready to break a car trip for a day to rest and relax if there is something attractive to do. Combining a second-night discount on room rates with information about the nearby lake, folk museum, reconstruction pioneer village, mine, or river trip may encourage longer stays. When the motel itself has facilities for the children, the likelihood is further increased.

How can such recreation stopovers be facilitated? The starting point is a clear delineation of just who the travelers are—size of families, ages of children, mode of transportation, styles of recreation—as a family and individually along with their spending capacities. Then, on-site equipment and opportunities can be combined with access to a nearby attraction to provide recreation packages. The motel is marketing en route recreation, not just a room for a night.

One example is the "Holidome" of the Holiday Inn motel chain. The Holidome is a response to the recreation needs of travelers when outdoor opportunities are cut off by climate.

CASE: HOLIDAY LODGING AND INDOOR RECREATION

The Holiday Inn chain was begun in 1952 to provide comfortable travel lodging for families at a reasonable price. Early inns had outdoor swimming pools and free ice as their main recreation amenities. Inns may be company-owned or operated on a franchise basis. In 1982 there were 1750 motels and hotels with over 300,000 guest rooms in all states and 53 countries. In 1981 Holiday Inns sold 72 million room nights and were opening a new hotel each week. Some 96% of all U.S. travelers have stayed in a Holiday Inn.

The chain recognizes the recreation segment of their trade by publishing a *Sports Hotel* guide that lists the availability of golf, outdoor tennis, indoor courts, and driving ranges for over 500 inns. For years there were indoor swimming pools at a number of inns in the north-central United States. In 1972 the pool concept was expanded to provide a wider set of indoor recreation opportunities. In 1982 some 192 Holiday Inns had Holidomes with indoor swimming, sauna or whirlpools, free game areas, and a dining/snack/drinking area. The company suggests that an investment in a Holidome be undertaken only when the rest of the motel is well developed and in good condition. The criteria for adding a Holidome are location, property size, existing amenity levels, and present and projected markets.

The initial aim was to enlarge the weekend market, especially for families. When rooms open onto the recreation area, parents can watch their children from the room. Play areas for small children, games for older children (now electronic), putting greens, exercise areas, a pool, and even paddle-game space might be provided. Usually one staff member is assigned responsibility for supervision and equipment.

In Decatur, Illinois, the largest Holidome includes three restaurants with French outdoor café motifs, a banquet hall, miniature golf, badminton or "nerf" tennis, and an exercise room. The facility serves regional conventions and meetings, business travelers, and weekend family trade. The manager works with the community to integrate the facility into its organizational and cultural life.

The Holidome is a response to the desire of many travelers to combine lodging and leisure. However, it is also a designed response to the multiple markets that may be attracted to such an indoor amenity. The space is for recreation, but not just one kind. Further, it can be adapted to adults at a convention or trade meeting, families with small children, or en route travelers who have been sitting in a car all day and find indoor exercise attractive. Further, it can help keep guests in the Holiday Inn for their food and drink when a fuller range of leisure resources is available.

EN ROUTE CAMPGROUNDS

Many campgrounds consist of little more than designated spaces for tents or travelers, a building with toilets and showers, and fireplaces for cooking. They are generally family-run and situated on land that was originally acquired for agriculture or an investment. Few amenities are added. The campground, once approved by local zoning authorities, is designed to bring in some marginal income as well as change the tax status of the land. Such campgrounds go in and out of existence so quickly that many are never listed in any directory or guidebook.

At the other extreme are the new "semidestination campgrounds" with full facilities for travel vehicles, including water, electricity, and sewage drains at each campsite as well as buildings with showers, toilets, meeting rooms, laundry facilities, and camp stores. Such campgrounds also have swimming pools, playgrounds for children, and other recreation resources. They serve travelers who stay for a period of time as well as the one-night stopovers.

The property values of the smaller campgrounds may be less than $500,000 including the limited amenities. However, those that are most successful as businesses have several of the following characteristics:

Location They are within two hours' driving time of a major population center, near a major vacation route or travel intersection, or close to some vacation destination attraction.

Environment An attractive environment is more than parking spaces. Campsites shaded by trees, near water, separated from other sites, and with a pleasant ambience are favored over those with no attraction except price.

Size Enough spaces to support a full set of amenities.

Marketing Some means is needed to inform travelers of the availability of the campground and what is offered to market segments. The facilities desired by couples traveling in elaborate, self-contained mobile homes are different from families carrying tents or pulling camping trailers. Certain travel routes attract different types of camping travelers. Further, competing campgrounds may specialize in ways that leave parts of the total demand unmet.

The major change in en route campground provisions is toward offering a fuller set of on-site recreation opportunities. Some campgrounds are not located and designed for en route camping at all. They have elaborate on-site facilities and are usually located near public recreation resources such as beaches, rivers, or lakes. Some are climate-based and designed for those fleeing cold winters in their motor homes. A new approach has been campground associations that offer membership programs. They market destination campgrounds with the spaces sold like condominiums. A national time-sharing program allows owner-members to use campsites at locations other than where they own space by paying a user fee lower than the outright rental. Further, they have access to campgrounds at attractive locations that would otherwise be closed to them. Such membership campgrounds are the upper end of the recreation camping market.

However, less elaborate campgrounds are also moving toward more on-site recreation offerings. The market segment targeted is usually the family travel group. Camping for cost-saving reasons as well as for the experience, families may be attracted by opportunities for children's recreation after an early-afternoon nap. In some cases family campers may remain at a campground for several nights if the on-site and nearby resources are found to be satisfying. Also, some campgrounds within two or four hours' drive of a city design their grounds to attract weekend family campers as well as those on their way somewhere else.

The Kampgrounds of America franchise group is one that offers its members a number of ways of enlarging their markets through a variety of lodging and recreation arrangements.

CASE: FRANCHISED CAMPING—THE SECOND MARKET

Altogether there are about 8,000 campgrounds in the United States, of which over half—close to 5,000—are publicly owned by federal, state, and local governments. They include campgrounds at the great national parks, hike-in locations in national forests, and a variety of destination and wayside provisions.

There are also thousands of business campgrounds. Most are locally owned and operated, often by landholders who are trying to gain some revenue from land already owned. Hundreds go in and out of existence every few years. However, about 1,000 of these campgrounds are franchise operations with a name-recognition symbol and some set of national standards and operating procedures.

Of these, the largest franchising group is the Kampgrounds of America (KOA). In 1980 the KOA system included 804 campgrounds in the United States and Canada. The system was begun in Billings, Montana, in 1960 to provide en route campsites for those traveling to national parks and other premier destinations. More recently KOA has become part of the international business scene with a Hong Kong investor becoming the principal shareholder and the company financial operations coordinated with an international holding company.

KOA estimates in the 1970s were that they captured about 2% of the camping market, all the nights spent camping by individuals or groups. Most KOA clients are transients who stay only one or two nights. The basic fee for two persons, which varies somewhat by location and hookup mode, is about one-third of a budget motel price. For that fee the camper is provided water, electricity, sewer hookups, a camping site, access to showers and other conveniences, a store, and some recreation facilities. Some campgrounds are located near recreation sites such as lakes and beaches. However, most locations are near population centers and along vacation-route highways. The marketing strategy from the beginning has been to promote KOA as assuring convenience and comfort. The major market has been those who travel with camping trailers, truck campers, or mobile-home vehicles.

The financial arrangements for the franchise in 1981 included a $10,000 initial franchise fee, a $10,000 "completion fee" before opening, a $300 yearly fee, and regular remission of 8% of camping fees. In return the campground operator is provided with management advice, national advertising, use of the KOA symbol, discounted sources of supplies and equipment, and access to new products, equipment, and marketing schemes. While some operators, especially those who are well established and in high-traffic locations, have withdrawn from the program, there has been a relatively high degree of stability.

The company has attempted some diversification. The first was into the highly competitive camping truck and trailer business in an unsuccessful venture. More recently KOA has acquired a national "instant printing" franchising firm with headquarters in California. They have also expanded somewhat into equipment leasing, consulting on industrial camping facilities, and international franchising of campgrounds.

A Harvard Business School case study in 1974 pointed to some changes in management and strategy during the early seventies. The period of rapid expansion of the number of franchises was considered over. Now the stress was to be on enhancing the quality of the experience for campers at the established locations. Responding to the increasing costs of operating the kinds of camping rigs that had provided a major share of the KOA clientele, local operators were being urged to consider tenting areas as well as preerected tent and cabin villages for those traveling in smaller cars. KOA believed they could compete successfully with the budget motels because they provided on-site outdoor recreation space and did not have the start-up costs of building a new motel with land acquisition at a high premium.

In general, the shift in strategy has been to continue the original aims of providing en route camping convenience, including a reservation system at a reasonable price, but more and more to become providers of recreation opportunities. The campgrounds themselves were being located at destinations with some available outdoor recreation facilities. Further, the campgrounds were providing more on-site opportunities, especially for children. Further, the possibility of a changing market was being anticipated by adding provisions for camping by those traveling in more fuel-efficient vehicles. Long-range plans call for placement of campgrounds in locations that are less energy-sensitive by being closer to population centers rather than at 200-mile intervals along routes to Yellowstone and the Grand Canyon. KOA has not only identified a viable market in its original format but is attempting to reorient to meet the changes in travel and recreation style for that market.

SUMMARY OF ISSUES

Providing part of the total recreational experience of travel is a marketing aim of point-of-origin and en route travel service businesses.

Point-of-origin travel services are enablers of travel as they market their resources, expertise, and convenience.

Travel agencies offer the client transportation, tours, and a number of ancillary services. Generally, their income is from commissions on sales from the airlines, tour wholesalers, and other providers.

Travel agencies are labor-intensive, with the added problem of selling services that may not be provided as promised.

Marketing recreation travel requires identification of target markets by travel styles as well as size and financial resources.

The eight steps of constructing an advertising campaign begin with market selection and developing a related product. Advertising strategies may be based on promoting the business as well as a particular offering.

Tours combine the work of the operator/wholesalers, retailer, hands-on managers, and local providers.

The variety of types of tours range from the inclusive and fully managed to the open and flexible. Each type appeals to different market segments.

Cruises are a special kind of tour combining transportation and destination in a recreation-oriented package with consumer and social aims.

Activity tours are increasing for those who seek a particular locale for a special activity.

Hotels, motels, and campgrounds are developing a variety of recreation-based facilities and programs to diversify and enlarge their markets.

Recreation-based marketing includes directories that list accessible recreation resources, on-site facilities and programs, and a variety of opportunities to appeal to families traveling together.

Location is crucial for en route travel services.

DISCUSSION QUESTIONS

1. How can a travel agency present its services in ways that gain and retain recreation travel markets?
2. What are the most significant travel agency markets in your community? Do agencies specialize or try to serve all market segments?
3. Why is cost so important in recreation travel marketing? Should price always be featured in advertising? Why or why not?
4. Are there leisure travel market segments often overlooked by travel agents? How can they be served by alternative approaches?
5. What are the special appeals of a cruise ship? Are there common impediments to the realization of anticipations?
6. How are hotels and motels adapting to the recreation elements in travel?
7. Would you invest in a motel or campground as the best business opprotunity for the next decade? How does location make a difference?

PROJECTS

1. Develop a marketing plan for a recreation travel promotion for an agency in your area. Specify target markets carefully by demographics and leisure styles.
2. Use the class as an idea-generating conference to plan an advertising campaign for a selected recreation tour.
3. Outline a hotel plan that takes into account the leisure aims of all traveling groups.
4. Develop a business plan for an en route travel business service that employs recreation appeal to maximize potential markets.

REFERENCES

1. Hawkins, Donald E., E. Shafer, and J. Rovelstad, eds. *Tourism Marketing and Management Issues,* Washington, D.C.; George Washington University, p. 262. 1980.
2. Burkart, Arthur, J., and S. Medlik. *Tourism,* 2nd ed., p. 172. 1981.
3. Universal Association of Travel Agent's Associations. In Burkart and Medlik, 1981.
4. Reilly, Robert T. *Travel and Tourism Marketing Techniques.* Wheaton, Ill.: Merton House, 1980.

5. Levinson, Daniel. *The Seasons of a Man's Life.* New York: A. A. Knopf, Inc., 1978.
6. Kelly, John, R. *Leisure Interactions and Identities.* London: George Allen and Unwin, 1983.
7. Perreault, W. D., D. K. Darden, and W. R. Darden. "A Psychographic Classification of Vacation Styles." *Journal of Leisure Research* 1977:208–224.
8. Ogilvy and Mather, in Reilly, 1980:69.
9. Chubb, Michael, and H. Chubb. *One Third of Our Time?,* p. 398. New York: Wiley, 1981.

9 DESTINATION ATTRACTIONS AND RESORTS

ISSUES

What are the economic impacts of tourism on the host area?

What are the components of modern comprehensive theme parks?

How are theme park markets segmented and programmed?

Do comprehensive parks face special problems?

How do resorts depend on the resources and infrastructure of their political and social environments?

How does marketing differ for theme and variety destination resorts?

Why are destination resorts both labor- and capital-intensive?

How can the investment risks of resort development be shared and reduced?

What are the special business opportunities in destination areas with recreational appeal?

From the previous chapters the analysis of recreation travel has identified a number of significant dimensions:

- Travel is recreation that includes anticipation, en route experiences, destinations, and recollection.
- Resources for recreation travel are both direct and indirect, with a host of secondary services underlying the provisions of recreation, lodging, travel, entertainment, and food.
- Recreation travel is more than just getting somewhere or getting away. Most often, travel as leisure involves getting away with others to one or more attractive destinations along a route with additional anticipated benefits.

Recreation travel, then, involves both the compounding of experiences and a network of resources. More and more, the most common leisure trip, the vacation, is expected to yield satisfaction along the way as well as on arrival. Recreation experiences are sought along the highway and at the hotel or campground as well as at the destination resort or resource.

Nevertheless, destinations are central to the planning of a recreation journey. The destination is usually selected first, with the route planned to maximize the total experience. Sometimes the destination is people, a community where family or friends reside and who are visited with some consistency. In such a case there may be additional incentive to find recreation enjoyment along the way. Often, however, the destination is a leisure attraction of some sort—a natural environment, special resources, entertainment park, special program, historical site, or resort. The focus of this chapter will be on destination recreation, especially the entertainment centers and resorts that are likely to be seen as worth a special trip.

ECONOMIC DEVELOPMENT

The economic impacts of tourism development are twofold. First, there are costs to the destination area for infrastructure improvements. Roads, health, sanitation, police, fire protection, and other services must be provided for the additional population, both temporary and resident. Such costs may be quite high in some areas and disruptive in those that have in the past had rural types of services. Tourism may create a peculiar kind of urbanization with pronounced peaks of usage and with income earned and taxed elsewhere. Taxation policies have to be developed that finance the needed services and meet the often considerable front-end costs for adding the capital costs of highways, schools, hospitals, sewage treatment, and other facilities needed if resort development is extensive.

Second, there are the economic contributions to an area. Recreation travelers spend money, often considerable amounts, that has been earned elsewhere. Tourism is an industry that may bring in income, create jobs, and add to the tax base without requiring commensurate investment in services such as schools or programs for the elderly. If tourism generated $7 billion for the economy of Florida in 1979, then it has created jobs by the thousands.[1] There is a multiplier effect in which not only those dollars spent by tourists but also those spent out of income generated by tourism are added to the economy. For example, if a tourist stays in a resort hotel, 20% to 40% of the bill will go to hotel employees who usually spend most of the income in the local area. This multiplier effect has been estimated to vary from about $1 to as much as $2.50 for each $1 spent by the tourist. In an area such as the state of Hawaii, those dollars comprise most of the regional economy.

But the income is not distributed evenly. Who benefits most from tourism revenues? First, there are the land and real estate development interests. The big money (and sometimes big losses) go to the entrepreneurs who put together the land packages and develop the areas for resale to those who will provide the services and live in the area. Land developers and sometimes land owners benefit first.

Second, contractors who build facilities and financial enterprises that provide capital in various forms benefit from the development. Third, the providers of other services and those who find employment in tourism-related businesses and services will benefit. However, in some recreation resort areas, there is considerable "leakage" of income.[2] In an area where food, furniture, building materials, and special equipment has to be imported from outside, as little as 25% of the tourist expenditure may remain in the area. Further, during the period of high construction efforts, temporary workers imported from outside the region may impact on services heavily and yet spend a high proportion of their income back in their residential communities.

In order to calculate the direct and multiplier effects of recreation destination spending on the economy of an area, a number of questions have to be answered:

How is the tourist dollar spent? Are purchased and rented goods and services produced locally or imported from outside?

How much of the tourism-related employment is local and how much imported? How much is year-round and how much is seasonal?

Is return on capital investment remaining in the area or being returned to corporate investors elsewhere?

What kinds of public services are required by temporary residents, both tourists and those employed to build or operate the recreation resources?

What economic development possibilities are lost due to the development of other kinds of industry and other uses of the natural resources?

How much real estate is not on the tax rolls because it is reserved by a public agency for recreation use by nonresidents? The environment that attracts recreation travel may be excluded from taxation by public ownership and management.

However, the economic impacts of recreation development are impressive, despite the costs. Donald Lundberg[3] summarizes a number of such estimates that indicate its significance. The U.S. Department of Commerce reported that in 1980 dollars a 300-room hotel with 60% occupancy and an average room rate of $24 will generate income equal to an industrial plant with a $6 million payroll. In Hawaii the tourist dollar was calculated to be spent as follows:

Lodging	32.3%
Food and beverage	27.2%
Transportation	11.7%
Clothing	9.3%
Gifts and souvenirs	9.7%
Entertainment	4.8%
Other	5.0%

In 1977 group tour visitors spent an average of $60 a day. Further, in national economies in which obtaining "hard" currency such as American dollars or German marks is a critical need, tourist expenditures are a major contribution to the support of the local currency in international exchange. All in all, the economic impacts of recreation destination development are considerable and complex. The condition of the regional economy may be a major factor in public agency decisions to facilitate and support or to discharge and inhibit recreation development.

RECREATION DESTINATIONS AND RESOURCES

The attractiveness of a recreation destination depends on the resources that are available to visitors. These resources may be those of the natural environment, the climate, historical sites, and cultural events. Or they may be opportunities especially planned and developed for recreation visitors. The various types of recreation destinations are related to the types of resources as well as the kinds of visitors attracted.

Natural and built environments Destinations that exist because of their proximity to a natural resource may be oriented almost entirely to the recreational use of that environment. Entire communities exist because of the development of mountainsides for downhill skiing or the summer use of an ocean beach. Complex sets of provisions including hotels with thousands of beds are built adjacent to the recreation environment. However, at the other extreme, recreation travel resources may also be provided in the midst of cities where all the resources are constructed. Perhaps the most common combination is that of built resources that augment the natural resource. For example, in some ocean-side communities with a warm winter climate, the beach itself is some distance from most of those who come to the area for recreation purposes. The ocean and climate are the initial reasons for the location but are only part of the total destination attraction.

Day visits and residential communities Again, there is a full spectrum of destination provisions. There are amusement parks that are designed for single-day visits alone. Most often they are placed near other destination attractions such as those near Orlando, Florida, or near metropolitan centers. At the other extreme are the recreation communities that presuppose stays of at least a week and that also provide for year-round residents who have central recreation interests. In between are the destination resorts, such as Walt Disney World, that are designed to offer a wide range of activities and opportunities for both families and different age groups for periods of from three days to two weeks.

Special activity and multiple provisions Some resorts are focused on a single activity. They exist because of beach use, tennis, golf, skiing, fishing, or river rafting. Those who choose that destination come for the activity and whatever social interaction surrounds it. On the other hand, destination developments are increasingly tending to be comprehensive, to offer a variety of recreation opportunities in one place. Especially when planners recognize that many come to destination areas in preformed groups, usually families, with a range of ages and interests, the more comprehensive approach widens the potential market. A primary group with members who cannot ski or who burn easily on the beach can still be accommodated with recreation possibilities. Even when single-activity packages are featured, such as six days of prepaid golf with two hours of lessons, there are alternate opportunities for companions who prefer other activities.

Age-graded and comprehensive Some amusement parks or resorts are developed almost entirely for one segment of the market—families with young children, teens, postschool singles and pre-parental couples, or later-life adults. While a few limit entry by age, many expect 80% or 90% of their revenue to come from one age segment. On the other hand, more often provisions and programs are varied to offer comprehensive opportunities. A major resort hotel does not want to eliminate any potential market segments arbitrarily. Teens who come with parents may want most of their time with other teens. A major resort can organize some separate activities and space that will enlarge the market 20%. The key is to recognize that some activities are age-differentiated, usually more in style than in the form of the activity itself. For some destinations, the ideal is a resource such as a large beach that can accommodate different modes of use at the same time. On the other hand, a comprehensive destination may have to plan programs carefully and with a recognition of age-cohort differences in order to minimize conflict in recreation settings.

Attraction style Some separation of types of recreation visitors is produced by the variety of attractions. A destination area may be known for a particular kind of recreation—Las Vegas for gambling and popular entertainment, colonial Williamsburg for restoration and history, Vail for Alpine skiing, or Lake of the Ozarks for fishing and waterskiing. Those who choose the area separate themselves from those with different recreation aims and styles. Only the destinations with multiple attractions and styles have to face the problems of conflicting aims and behaviors by groups with different leisure intentions.

Of course, most of the major destinations combine more than one of these dimensions. They tend to combine natural and built recreation environments, have visitors who come for different periods of time, draw many ages, and offer multiple opportunities for participation and entertainment. As a result, they have relatively wide markets that are determined more by income and geography than other factors. Further, they seek to project an image that is widely attractive rather than narrowed on a single mode of participation in a single activity.

DESTINATIONS AND RECREATION BUSINESS

In the sense of providing a context for some leisure experiences, almost all travel destinations have some recreation components. Even a hotel that caters primarily to business trade, an urban concert hall, or a restaurant does recreation-related business. However, in this chapter we will concentrate on businesses for which recreation participation is a recognized factor in planning and in producing revenue. Organized amenities or programs for participation will be the criterion for inclusion in this introduction to destination businesses.

The recreation participation component is largely absent in businesses that directly, for example, offer food and lodging at a historical site. However, in recent years the desire to enlarge markets has caused motel/hotel businesses at sites such as Williamsburg to offer tennis instruction and golf/swimming packages as well as access to the historic area. What had been planned first as lodging for the historic area became first convention providers and then recreation package purveyors.

In other cases, however, the urban hotel offers little except lodging in the midst of the attractions of the city. The shop sells to anyone, of course, with tourist business being only one segment of the market. Even though such provisions are part of the total set of recreation travel provisions and services, they are not businesses with a manifest recreation component. Here we will be examining the recreation, marketing, and planning elements in destination businesses that have recreation-based strategies and images.

Further, even though gambling and highly developed entertainment complexes are surely recreation and are a context for recreation experiences, they have rather different orientations from participant recreation. The resort hotel industry is massive and complex. Here we will focus on the recreation dimensions of the industry without any attempt to encompass all aspects. Further, en route services have been outlined in the previous chapter. One-stop attractions such as "Alligatorland" or "Wombat World" that are used as a lure into a roadside restaurant and novelty shop will not be included. In chapter 10 we will study those recreation businesses that are primarily complements to natural resources for outdoor recreation. The focus here will be on destination recreation businesses that offer participation experiences as all or part of their strategy. Recreation participation is integral to the business, whether it is all or only a part of the total surprise.

This narrowing, however, should not blind us to the diverse and comprehensive nature of business provisions in a destination area. While all businesses are not recreation providers, the interrelationship of various kinds of enterprises makes up a web in which each makes some contribution to the whole, or in time it will fail. Developing a destination recreation business requires being aware of the complementarity of the public resources and other business provisions in the recreation environment.

CASE: INTEGRATED INDUSTRIES

What does it take to go skiing? From the perspective of the skier the requirements may seem simple: a snow-covered hill, some way to get to the top of the hill, and skis on which to slide down. That is, of course, for Alpine, or downhill, skiing. For Nordic, or cross-country or trail, skiing, all it takes is skis, poles, and some snow.

Of course, that's too simple. What about boots that fit, refreshments, transportation to the snow, and some overnight accommodations? What about access to the hill, some care given to the area, and lifts and/or tows? In fact, at the more established ski resort, there is quite a combination of services:

The ski area itself, with lift tickets, parking areas, and concessions.

Direct equipment services for boots, skis, repairs, instruction, and so on.

On-site food and drink.

A variety of auxiliary services from safety and accident services to snowmaking machines and parking-lot plows.

However, that is only the beginning. At a major ski resort town, hundreds of businesses seek to sell or rent to visitors:

- Restaurants, cocktail lounges, bars, fast-food shops, and a variety of retailers serving those who stay in self-contained units.
- Entertainment businesses from movies to game arcades and nightclubs to concert halls.

- Lodges that augment their accommodations with health clubs, indoor tennis and swimming, eating and drinking, group entertainment, day care for children, and retail shops for reading material, sundries, clothes, and even ski equipment.
- All the ski instruction offered at various levels and prices.
- Large combination stores, specialty shops that often include designer clothing and international stocks of jewelry and other gifts, one-person repair shops, and any number of retailing firms that combine the interests of particular owner-managers.
- Transportation businesses that sell and rent cars, 4-wheel drives, snowmobiles, bicycles, airplanes, and cartop ski carriers.
- A variety of packagers who put together travel, lodging, ski access, equipment, and entertainment in combination deals, especially attractive to first-time visitors.
- The businesses that sell, rent, manage, and care for houses, condominiums, and other residential facilities.
- Builders, financial institutions, and entrepreneurs who are at work planning and providing for expansion.
- And don't forget the orthopedic surgeons and helicopter rescue crews that keep busy when the slopes are crowded.

The point is that the business infrastructure surrounding the hill and the snow may become both complex and highly integrated. Travel provisions not only complement other providers but also each other. The travel agents at the point of origin are complemented by the destination rental agency who has a supply of snow-competent vehicles available. The banks at the point of origin complement with their credit card programs and loans the businesses at the destination. Further, many major purchases of equipment are made in Chicago for use in Aspen or Chamonix.

There is also the public-private complementarity. In North America many of the ski provisions are on public land that is leased to private sector firms. Further, skiers arrive on public roads, land at public airports, and require a variety of public services and protections when they are at the resort. For example, in some areas ski resort operators provide financial support for avalanche patrols that are organized by the Forest Service.

The markets for skiing-related goods and services are far from monolithic. Both instruction and equipment are closely related to the level of skill of the skier. As skill levels rise, it is often necessary to change equipment. Further, experts often want to *appear* competent as well as *be* competent. They become renewable markets for clothing and supplementary gadgets as well as more sophisticated skis, boots, and poles.

Then there are the styles of equipment and apparel that symbolize income levels or orientation as well as skill level. Since skiers tend to be relatively affluent as well as young, they often seek to identify themselves in the ski area by their clothes, their cars, and equipment that announces cost as well as preference. Engagement in the multifaceted life of the ski resort is seen to require the right labels and styles as well as equipment that works on the hill. As a consequence retailing in such a consumption-intensive environment may stress symbolism rather than utility.

Finally, there is also the laboratory, where product development never stops. For example, the bottom surfaces of the skis have been changed almost annually to enhance certain skiing qualities as well as convenience. Technology is presumed to lower the time and effort that is required to raise skill levels. The introduction of fiberglass transformed the skis themselves. But the variety of boots, gloves, headgear, and bindings changes every season to produce new markets for the latest models. Technological innovation is combined with style and identity-oriented promotion to keep the demand high season after season.

The point is that the businesses based on sliding down a snow-covered hill on skis are not only varied but also integrated into a complex service system in which the introduction of one new product or service will create a complementary demand for others.

ENTERTAINMENT PARKS

Entertainment parks are designed to offer a set of experiences through constructed facilities. The most common are rides such as roller coasters and other "thrill" designs that produce sensations of speed, vertigo, and excitement. However, most amusement parks also include a variety of exhibitions, fun houses with different themes, entertainment, food and drink, and opportunities for dancing and other activities. In one sense they begin with the relatively small mobile "carnival" in local shopping-center parking lots and expand to the Six Flags, Disney World, and Tivoli parks. Some charge one admission fee that admits the visitor to all attractions while others lease space to separate entrepreneurs who charge by the ride.

In all there are estimated to be between 300 and 400 such entertainment parks in North America.[4] The traditional parks such as Coney Island in New York have had much the same format for almost a century. However, the newer development has been the *theme park,* of which the California Disneyland is the archetype.

HISTORY OF ENTERTAINMENT PARKS

The first amusement parks were built on the fringes of major cities in the late 1800s. They consisted of rides such as roller coasters, Ferris wheels, and a variety of spin and twirl designs. Also included were various exhibits and shows, participation booths for throwing and shooting for prizes, and several ways in which to eat and drink. For the most part they were located on or at the end of streetcar or electric-car rail lines, and some were built by the transportation companies. On the waterfront of Brooklyn, Coney Island, with its long history of success, failure, fire, and competition, still draws thousands on summer days. Other such parks have now closed, the victims of more sophisticated entertainment, economic recessions, and changing demographic patterns.

The lure of the water led to the construction of a number of piers extending into the ocean or lake from urban or resort seashores. The piers were especially popular in Great Britain, where close to 100 were built before 1960. Almost half still exist in various states of repair and use. Some extended as much as 400 to 800 meters from the shore and provided space for restaurants, dance halls, theaters and concert arenas, food and drink stands, game arcades, and a variety of special events. Damage by storms and the high cost of upkeep in exposed locations has led to a deterioration of most piers and the removal of many as dangers, eyesores, or both. However, the high cost of urban space suggests that many may survive or be redeveloped.

In 1955 Disneyland opened in California and led the way into a new concept for entertainment parks. Developed around the five theme areas leading off Main Street and trading heavily on the loyalty and familiarity of the Disney film characters, the facility set a new standard for organization, cleanliness, crowd management, security, and family entertainment as well as for cost. By 1978 there were 18 "superparks" that attracted over 2 million customers a year.[5] In 1983 Disney interests cooperated in opening a Disneyland in Tokyo just after opening a major addition to their Florida attraction, Walt Disney World. Other theme parks, however, experienced difficult economic times. The future of such parks as viable investments in the overall recreation spectrum is far from certain. Those doing best are either accessible to major population centers, which can supply repeat business, or at a major destination resort area. The escalating cost of such enterprises is one aspect of the problem, with a major ride now costing in excess of $3 million not including land and operating costs. That means that the ride must net a profit of almost a half million dollars a year just to yield an investment return in an established park. Depreciation and the product life cycle add to the revenue requirements in the early years of operation.

RECREATION AT THE PARK

The recreation provisions at major amusement parks are structured; that is, they offer a particular experience with a set sequence. The participant gets on or in, moves through space in a regular sequence, and comes out at the end having experienced the same motion, sights, and sounds that everyone else has had. While some rides such as bumper cars offer a degree of control, the variation in experience is minimal. When you enter the "haunted house," the arrows and directions are quite specific as to direction and the traffic flow tends to determine the speed of movement. Even the twisting slide or the parachute drop offer little variation except for positioning the body or the choice of going alone or holding on to someone else. While arcades offer interactive games, in general the amusement park is a place in which the attractions provide a prestructured experience. They are not games with uncertain outcomes or environments in which the participant develops a processual social experience.

However, few come to such parks alone. Almost all entrants come in groups. Teens may prefer to come with age peers. Some adult social organizations come together as an excursion. Groups of children may be brought by adults. For the major destination parks, the most common group is the family, the unit with at least two generations and an age range of twenty years or more. As a result, the interaction is central to the experience. Recreation in entertainment parks is not just going on the rides. It is going on the rides, walking and looking, eating and drinking, and generally experiencing the environment *together*. It is a social occasion in a special environment. The magic castles, super whirlygigs, electronic shooting galleries, and "world's highest/steepest/fastest/longest thrill ride" are not only individual excitement but also an episode meant to be shared. The expressive elements consist not only of vertigo on the way down or apprehension on the way up but also of the anticipation, sharing, and recollection of doing it with one or more intimates or friends. As with so much other recreation, the park is a context for leisure in which the social dimension is at least as important as the provisions of the recreation place.

Planning such a destination park in ways that attract customers once and bring them back again requires an awareness of the components of the total experience. One kind of ride or facility may be designed to engage only one age group. Others may be oriented toward the multigeneration family group. Some rides are for children escorted by parents whose aim is to please the child. Others may be multidimensional and provide enjoyment for both children and parents. Some amenities may be set a bit apart and offer a secure place for teens to meet, and to be rounded up later if they came with a family group. And always there are the auxiliary enterprises that provide refreshments, souvenirs, and other sundries that may be sold to people in a pleasure-seeking mood. Park design is more than getting a variety of rides into a given space; it calls for recognizing the recreation orientations of the various market segments that may be attracted to the park. It means designing not only for the episodes of entertainment and participation but also for traffic patterns that minimize conflict and allow for both movement and the gathering of groups.

COMPREHENSIVE DESTINATION PARKS

There is considerable diversity in destination amusement parks. However, they all seek to provide a variety of experiences to a full range of users. They do more than offer one special ride or show. Unlike "Birdland," they combine entertainment and participation in multiple attractions for all or most age ranges. Further, they seek to hold the visitor for at least a full day, so the overall experience combines special events with eating, drinking, talking, watching, and interacting with companions.

Walt Disney World The most comprehensive destination amusement center is the complex developed by the Disney corporation near Orlando, Florida. The WED division, which conceived and designed the recreation center, have set both styles and standards for the industry. They have been successful to the extent that most of their promotion is in conjunction with travel and tourism interests who want to have their offerings associated with Walt Disney World (WDW). WDW is a destination itself on a scale with the nation's capital and the premier natural wonders. It has become the magnet attracting around it an incredible system of hotels, motels, secondary amusement parks, and travel and tourism services. Within the park itself image-conscious companies bid for the opportunity to sell their goods on Main Street in the Magic Kingdom or around the lagoon of the World Showcase. They are ready to pay for the privilege of being there under the conditions imposed by the WED design for the park.

Who comes to WDW? In a sense, everyone. However, there are certain market segments for whom the attraction is designed. In 1981 some 12.5 million visitors passed through the gates. They paid about $15 each per day, depending on the type of ticket and length of stay. That, of course, was only the beginning. The streets containing shops as well as food and drink purveyors did business to raise the visitors' per capita expenditure 50% to 150%. Some visitors come in tour groups, especially older adults and children's groups from the area and at vacation time. Some come in peer groups, such as the college students who descend on Florida during spring break. However, the most common visitors are families. They include children under twelve and seek some experiences that they can enjoy together. Much of the pleasure of the parents comes from that of the children. In many cases the trip is one that has been planned for over a year and has involved some saving to cover costs. Many families plan to return to WDW about every three to five years. The most common states of origin are Ohio, Illinois, Pennsylvania, and others in the Northeast and Midwest, as well as Ontario in Canada. The marketing and planning from the very beginning of Disneyland and WDW has been family-oriented. As with Disney films, the intent has been to produce entertainment that can be enjoyed on several levels.

The major change in this approach came in 1982 with the opening of the Epcot Future World and the World Showcase. Epcot Center is about four miles from the Magic Kingdom, which was opened in 1971. It is expected to add eight million a year to the current twelve million annual visitors. The total investment for Epcot Center will be about $1 billion in the first stage. Total investment in WDW was $1.7 billion by 1983. The Experimental Prototype Community of Tomorrow (EPCOT) was first envisioned by Walt Disney as a real community in which technologies to deal with urban problems would be demonstrated in attractive ways that utilized the Disney communications know-how. After Disney's death the concept was altered to the extent that more emphasis was placed on demonstrations by corporations of their technological developments and less on a demonstration community. As opened in 1982, Epcot Center has two foci, the World Showcase, situated around a lagoon with mock streets of various national sites and cultures, and Future World, a collection of technological displays by corporations. While there is considerable Disney showmanship to interest younger visitors, the general level of presentation seems to be higher than that of the Magic Kingdom. There is less for the small child and more for teens and adults.

The marketing emphasis is on destination travel, for which WDW can be *the* destination. Along with the Magic Kingdom and Epcot Center, there are 2,500 acres of hotels, resorts, campgrounds, beaches, golf courses, and other recreation. The three Disney hotels have eighteen hundred guest rooms and are augmented by thousands more on and off the WDW grounds. There is a shopping village to supplement the shops in the amusement areas. All are connected by buses, monorail, ferryboats, and other conveyances.

Seasonality is a factor, with crowds averaging 15,000 to 25,000 a day during the low seasons of January and early fall, but reaching peaks of 60,000 to 70,000 a day from Christmas to New Year's Day and over 50,000 a day around Easter weekend. The record was 123,000 on December 28, 1982. Entertainment includes 400 one-day outside performing groups as well as the eleven hundred regular WDW entertainers. In 1983 about 70 young performers and representatives from other countries were at work in the World Showcase. However, employment at WDW means a readiness to work within the Disney system. To prepare new employees and those already employed, there ia an on-site "Disney University" as a training center.

The organizational structure of this vast enterprise includes departments of foods, wardrobe, marketing, publicity, casting, training, "wonders" program, operations, merchandise, entertainment, resorts, finance, photography, show development, sales, guest relations, central reservations, golf, tennis, management for each resort, accounting, personnel, as well as various kinds of maintenance and construction. The central planning is done at WED in Glendale, California. Further, the corporate structure, based in Burbank, California, is interlocked with the Florida enterprise and has considerable movement back and forth across the country. About 20,000 persons are employed full-time on the Florida site, with an additional 3,000 or so hired in the summer. The impact on the central Florida economy made by WDW alone, without all the satellite businesses is tremendous.

The history of the park, from Walt Disney's idea of an entertainment center for families to the risk and development of Disneyland, is now legend. The land limitations in California and the secret accumulation of 28,000 acres near Orlando, the draining of swampland and planning of WDW, and the subsequent success add their own fantastic layers to the tradition. Now another billion dollars has been invested with an assurance that Disney enterprises can set the trends for American entertainment.

But what can we learn about destination recreation from the facts as well as the legend? First, imagination and quality seem to be essential ingredients of success. Second, front-end investment and planning are indispensible. Third, "Middle America" is a very large recreation market, even if the resource requires considerable expense and travel. Fourth, a site that can be operated the year around permits greater permanent investment in construction and land. Fifth, there is no substitute for corporate image. The Disney image made possible a unique undertaking. Sixth, the world will come to a destination that promises enough, especially for the family, and that delivers enough to maintain its reputation. Seventh, most people want to be secure and comfortable in their recreation environment rather than threatened by people or conditions that seem a danger to health or safety. Eighth, people are willing to put up with crowds, costs, waiting in line, and travel fatigue for what promises to be a special experience of recreation.

The Theme Park There are a number of theme parks that share characteristics. The Six Flags chain probably best exemplifies the genre. This "superpark" chain generally locates its enterprises on the edge of major metropolitan areas near one or more interstate highways. They offer both thrill and nostalgia rides, child- and adult-oriented entertainment on stage and walk-around shows, and a variety of amenities for sitting, climbing, sliding, and other postures. There are many kinds of fast foods and souvenirs. Half the revenue may come from inside expenditures and half from entrance fees. A Six Flags park will have a featured thrill ride, with a new one added often enough to bring back visitors who have "done everything."

The key for marketing such theme parks is attention to the various segments of potential users:

- The first market segment is the day-visit family group with young children. This is primarily a weekend market and is attracted by rides that can be shared as well as auxiliary services for food and drink. Safety and security are also important elements for families that will return several times a season.
- The second market segment is the children's peer group. Usually brought by adult coordinators, such groups often come during the weekdays. Since they help fill a slack time, they usually receive group discounts. The security of a system that provides excitement with safety is important to those who make the decisions, the adult leaders.
- The evening market changes radically. The teens and young adults who are

attracted for the evening may take some of the thrill rides. However, they also come for entertainment at stage shows, dancing, eating, and being in an environment with others of similar age-group interests.

Special events are employed to attract local repeat trade. For the daytime there are various exhibitions from folk dancing to skydiving. For the evenings there are "name" entertainers and even the touring companies of musical shows. The events are used in advertising to encourage coming at the proximate time, not to postpone the decision to spend another day or evening at the theme park. The importance of regional business is reflected in much of this marketing.

- However, the tourist market is also significant. The major theme park is one attraction that may draw visitors from a distance of up to a day's drive. Therefore, some advertising is planned for the larger market area, especially population centers within 400 to 500 miles. In many cases such advertising is in a joint effort with a city tourist bureau, other destination attractions, and tour organizers at the point of origin. Here the family business is the central market segment, but there is also interest in teens old enough to travel in independent groups.
- Finally, there is the pass-through market. Recognizing that most vacation travel is by car, billboards, brochures in motels, and other forms of attention-getting advertising are designed to get the travel group to detour to the theme park, stop there for the day, or include it as part of a vacation plan.

The promotion is often directed toward the enjoyment of the varied environment. "Experience and excitement!" is one theme that summarizes what the theme park has to offer. The theme park offers an environment designed to produce an experience of entertainment, physical and sensory excitement, and a change from the usual. For the most part it is a one-day-at-a-time context. Further, it is intended to be a social experience shared with others whose companionship is enjoyed. It is "culture, cuisine, and camaraderie" broadly defined.

There are a number of factors in planning and operating such a recreation business: First is seasonality. The Disney enterprises are in year-round warm climates. Many theme parks in the North are open all week for only 16 to 18 weeks and for weekends another 12 weeks. The considerable investment, over $100 million for a Six Flags park, must be paid for in that limited period. A theme park such as Six Flags will do 70% of its business in three summer months. As a consequence 85% of employment is for the summer only.

Second is market segmentation scheduling. Weekdays, weekends, and evenings attract different kinds of patronage. The aim is to design so that there is maximum appeal to multiple segments and to schedule for minimum conflict among groups with different leisure styles and aims.

Third is the product life cycle. A new park that is well promoted will almost certainly have considerable first-time business. However, the park itself and its feature rides and entertainment have a limited life cycle in which the period of decline may come as early as the third or fourth year. Therefore, the operators are always planning programs that are unique, events that are attention-getting, and the addition of rides and amenities that will draw visitors back. They strive for a balanced offering familiar enough to draw those who enjoyed previous visits and new enough to interest those who feel they have "done" the park. Further, some have speculated that the theme park as a concept has a life cycle of its own, that the wave of enthusiasm that followed the Disney successes has begun to wane, and that only the best-designed and -located parks will be commercial successes in the coming decades.

Other Comprehensive Parks There are many other styles of theme parks. For example, at "Old Chicago" the rides and entertainment were combined with a shopping complex. For a cost of almost $50 million, the intent was to provide entertainment for those who also came to shop and for some members of a group that might split up for part of the visit. The park had major rides including the requisite roller coaster, a supervised play area for children, a number of local historical exhibits, weekend dances for teens, special events, and a theater with a variety of shows scheduled. However, sustaining repeat markets proved a major problem and led to bankruptcy.

Theme parks are found in all parts of North America and also in Europe. However, the trend is to locate them in destination areas where the local and tourist markets can be combined. The key concept is saturation. How many trips to a theme park, however varied its program, saturates the interest of the visitor? And how many parks saturate the continuing market for such experiences? One important element in the analysis is the continual bringing of new households into the life cycle at each point of interest. Even though families are smaller, there are always new children, new families seeking recreation, and new teens with their somewhat different tastes in music and dance. Even in a decline or plateau product cycle period, every year brings new cohorts of customers for parks that are well designed, maintained, and located.

SINGLE-THEME PARKS

Most of the more than 350 parks are not "superparks" even though many involve investment in land, buildings, and amenities in the millions of dollars. Others are also pieced together with minimum investment and are designed to interest the recreation traveler for no more than a half hour on the way to somewhere else. Such parks are part of destination complexes. They do not attract tourists to their offerings as destinations but seek to attract those who are coming to the area for some other reason or find themselves with time on their hands while traveling. Many of the larger single-theme parks also seek to draw customers from the region even though recognizing that the potential for repeat business is less than for the comprehensive parks. There are many types of single-theme attractions:

Satellite parks cluster around those that serve as magnets for recreation travelers. The classic example is the countless set of offerings around Orlando, Florida. Not only are there larger theme parks such as Circus World and Florida Marine World but there are also the one-stop offerings of alligators, snakes, baseball memorabilia and hitting/pitching machines, Native American exhibits, Spanish cultural artifacts, swampland, and wax museums. They provide variety for those who have been drawn by the magnet of WDW. In much the same fashion major arteries leading to other magnets tend to have some single-stop and single-theme parks.

Urban parks are those that seek to create an image that will draw a continual trade from a major population center. Near New York or Los Angeles, for example, there will be a wild animal safari, a West World, sealife exhibit, or entertainment park. When there are millions of people within 20 miles, the potential for business is considerable.

Historical-cultural parks are found in almost any area that attracts recreation travel. In some cases, they are carefully designed or reconstructed villages, forts, theaters, churches, schools, or other buildings of significance. The most elaborate, such as Colonial Williamsburg, are not profit-seeking businesses. However, many less developed sites do seek to attract both local and tourist trade into a location in which entry fees and on-site sales are business-oriented. Such "parks" range from the most carefully restored and presented to unbelievable historical parodies that are promoted as giving a glimpse of the past.

Highway parks are those that employ billboards and other advertising to stop the en route traveler. Some use the single-theme attraction to get customers into a souvenir store, and others rely on entry fees for revenue. In either case they promote their offerings as exotic, exciting, and able to be experienced in a brief stop.

Central-theme parks are those that have created an image based on a single attraction ad then expanded their offerings. For example, Cypress Gardens, a few miles from Orlando, is probably best known for its waterski show. However, it also offers a number of theme gardens, an aviary, aquarium, rides, boat rental, tours, food stands, and a set of auxiliary shops. The waterskiing exhibition is the central theme that provides the major draw. However, the park provides a number of modes of entertainment and retail shops along with the main theme.

These are only the types of parks associated with destinations, recreation travel that is oriented toward experiences of enjoyment, social interaction, learning, and excitement. There are also the traveling shows beginning with the two Ringling Brothers and Barnum and Bailey circus units, extending to ice shows, musicals, pageants, and exhibitions, and including the most ordinary small-town carnival. There are also the entertainment cities such as Las Vegas and Atlantic City, with their special forms of participation. And, finally, there are the resorts, to which we now turn our attention.

THEME RESORTS

Comprehensive resorts provide the resource itself. They are the beachfront complexes or the ski resort with runs on owned or leased property. *Complementary* resorts are near resources that are also available to others. They are adjacent to the mountain or water, the theater or historic site. They provide everything except the primary recreation resource that has drawn their clientele.

However, both comprehensive and complementary resorts are based on participation in recreation that requires the special environment. Most people cannot live on the beach or at the foot of a mountain all the time. The ecology of employment as well as the scarcity of such environments dictate that immediate access is to be a special occasion for most people. They have to travel to the resource, take accommodations that facilitate access or entry to the environment, and schedule both the necessary travel and the activity participation. What distinguishes such resorts is the goal of participatory recreation of the trip.

COMPREHENSIVE RESORTS

The comprehensive resort does it all. On-site are not only the food, lodging, equipment, instruction, and auxiliary provisions but also the primary resource itself. The business is able to provide opportunities and control access to at least part of the recreation resource. Both support services and the resource itself are part of the package.

The scale may vary widely. From a complex ski or beach resort with hundreds of rooms and control of an entire hillside or mile of beach to the five cabins alongside a mountain lake with fishing boats for rent at the dock, the comprehensive resort presents all the recreation visitor needs to engage in the activity. The critical factor is location. The resort is in an environment that is restricted by distance, ownership, or cost to those who participate in its offerings.

CASE: MAKING THE RESOURCE

In Scottsdale, Wisconsin, the primary differentiating factor has been the distance to the Milwaukee-Chicago-Gary urban spread. The problem was that there was no mountain there as a ski resource. So a hill was constructed from the excavations for the hotel and artificial lake. The hill, although not large, was designed for a variety of downhill-skiing styles. Further, the marginal snow conditions were compensated for with a drainage system for melting snow runoff, and artificial snow-making equipment. Skiing time on weekends was extended with lighting. The design was intended to augment the major ski resources of the more distant resorts in Colorado and elsewhere. The more limited resource was built and operated for the nearby population as part of an entire ski season experience. Attention to preparation for a major ski trip and skill acquisition complemented the reduction of travel costs to utilize the constructed resource. However, those using the resource still yielded the full range of income for the business through lodging, food and drink, equipment, and user-free expenditures.

CASE: PROGRAM EXPANSION AND IMAGINATION

Much farther from the population centers is the ski resort of Telemark in northern Wisconsin. Telemark may be unique in both the vision of its management and the attention to special events that it sponsors. The complex consists of a lodge with two hundred rooms. It passed the critical break-even point of 45% occupancy in 1979. The peak winter months had a 70% to 80% occupancy in that year. Special low rates for weekday packages, corporate and association meetings and conventions, and special events all make up part of the market for lodging.

The story of how the resort developed to this point in remote northern Wisconsin is long and complex. It began when Tony Wise got his MBA and returned to his home area to buy a 550-acre hill in 1947 for $750. That humble beginning has developed into the spectacular lodge, a 70,000-square-foot sports and convention center with four indoor tennis courts, town houses, 1600 acres of land with 93 kilometers of ski trails, the downhill slopes with two lifts, 21,000 square feet of banquet and ballroom area, a bar, restaurant, coffee shop, cafeteria, skating rink, indoor and outdoor pools, a theater, and a few shops. The history also includes a major fire that destroyed the base lodge, the development of a corporation structure, an attempted takeover, bankruptcy and financial reorganization, a federal loan, and a major shift in recreation markets. Analysis of Telemark as a recreation business would be an entire course in itself. However, there are a few elements that are especially instructive in understanding the comprehensive theme resort.

Telemark's developer and guiding genius describes himself as an entrepreneur. By this he means that he has consistently taken risks in the development of his business, with his own investment at the heart of the risk. His vision has constantly outrun his financial resources, so that the enterprise has been continually in debt.

Flexibility has been the hallmark of the development. Although begun as a downhill ski resort, by the time the lodge was completed in 1972 Wise had already recognized the limitations of that activity base. The resource for Alpine skiing was mediocre at best and at considerable distance from the primary Midwest population centers. Wisconsin just could not compete with jet travel to the Rocky Mountain slopes. However, the almost unknown activity of Nordic, or cross-country, skiing was another matter. The wooded hills in the Hayward area were ideal for this activity. The problem was that there weren't enough participants. Nonetheless, the transition to this recreation base was begun.

Promotion of Nordic skiing required attention-getting events. Telemark became the home base for the "American Birkebeiner" race that evolved from an event with less than 100 skiers to its present draw of over 3,000. The first American World Cup event was arranged, sponsored, organized, and subsidized. Now some 60 miles of trails are laid out, groomed, and patrolled, including a special World Cup course. During a single winter Telemark now hosts at least five special Nordic events, an Alpine open downhill race, two cultural festivals, and Nordic events every weekend. There are events for the young and for "Master" skiers over the age of thirty.

Promotional literature pictures the multiplicity of amenities, activities, and guests who may enjoy Telemark. There are the winter offerings with two types of skiing, dancing, swimming, tennis, dining, shows, drinking, family and couple interaction, skiing in solitude and skiing in a mass event with thousands, relaxation, and strenuous exercise. In the summer there are also golf, tennis, and the swimming pools.

Telemark in one sense broke all the rules. Its location was selected out of sentiment rather than a geographical market analysis. Its initial development did not take account of the superior competing resources or the development of air travel that made a 1,000-mile trip often more convenient than a 300-mile journey to a rural area. The costs of development consistently outraced the established revenue sources. The desire to do things well, especially in architecture, came at a price. And, most flagrant of all, the participation base for the second major activity, Nordic skiing, had to be developed. The activity needed to be promoted and Telemark had to be established as a major resource for doing it.

Out of the story to date, what is learned? First, as with WDW, quality will attract recreation travel and revenue. Second, a market can be created, especially by multifaceted combinations of promotion, education, and resource development. The freedom and experimental elements of leisure can be utilized to gain new participants in an activity. However, it takes time as well as effort.

Third, there is considerable risk in such an enterprise. Imagination has to be coupled with an unflagging entrepreneurial spirit.

Fourth, a destination theme resort will have to identify its potential markets carefully, cultivate them as well as contact them, and develop an image that in time carries some of its own momentum. Partly by using the special events, Telemark has come to be known as a kind of mecca for Nordic skiers. That did not occur by accident or through some unique set of natural resources. It was *developed* in the fullest sense of the term.

CASE: TWO SEASONS AND DUAL MARKETS

Big Sky was the dream of a retiring TV news anchorman, Chet Huntley, who wanted to return to Montana. After his death it has become an example of the expansion of an inaugural concept. Big Sky was envisioned as a deluxe dude ranch with its location near Yellowstone Park as an added magnet. The summer season would be filled with the usual ranch recreation revolving around horseback riding. In the fall there was hunting in the area.

However, Big Sky has now developed into a major winter resort. The emphasis has been on Alpine skiing with a number of slopes at the resort. There are four chair lifts and one gondola lift that together form a network of access to 24 slopes ranging from easy to quite demanding. Along with the slopes, equipment shops, instruction program, and ski patrol, there is a mall with shops, restaurants, and cocktail lounges, a rustic bar, and a variety of Western-style entertainments. Lodging includes room in the lodge and several styles of condominiums.

The problem for a resort such as Big Sky is distance. It is an hour's drive from a Montana airport that most people have never heard of. While the Bitterroot Mountains and Yellowstone Park surround the lovely valley south of Bozeman, it just isn't a place one stops at on the way to anywhere. The location raises the cost, requires a special decision to go to that particular place, and cannot expect spinoff business from other destinations nearby. The distance raises both the cost of travel and the threshold of decision. Those interested cannot look in while staying at a resort nearby, as in the case with ski resorts in the Colorado Rockies or Utah. Nevertheless, with the addition of Nordic skiing, Big Sky has diversified in ways that give it a year-round appeal for a wide spectrum of recreation seekers, if they can afford the special costs. In order to succeed they must provide a quality experience that yields repeat business and word-of-mouth recommendations among the affluent circles, develop at a rate commensurate with the growth of clientele, and always be ready to offer amenities and resources that widen the appeal to those who do not engage in the central activity of the season. Of course, there are condominiums for sale that provide both capital for further development and a built-in clientele. Also, the cost of the location comes with a benefit, protection from overcrowding for those who have become disenchanted with the high-season lines at Vail or Sun Valley. High-end marketing in recreation is frequently based on separation from resources that have become too popular and too accessible.

Market Research and Planning Comprehensive resorts require large amounts of front-end capital for development. Land acquisition, initial construction for lodging and amenities, resource access and preparation, and staff development all come at a high cost before the first recreation visitors appear. Further, a strategy that seeks to be comprehensive rather than rely on external services may maximize revenue in the long run but is investment-intensive in the beginning. There are a number of important elements in the initial planning:

1. Access to and control of the basic recreation resource. If the natural resource cannot be owned, then both access and the long-term quality must be assured. This may involve zoning, long-term leasing, or outright purchase. In any case, it must come first.
2. The infrastructure must be feasible. It takes roads, airports, sewage disposal, water supply, power, and fire and police protection in order to operate a full-service resort. The costs in some areas are far beyond the capabilities of the local government to provide. In many cases it is necessary for the developer to provide the capital and the planning in order to assure an adequate infrastructure.
3. The overall ecology of the area is important. Environmental protection that does not permit degradation of the natural environment and at the same time facilitates the recreation development needed for the resort is critical to the future of the business. While the developer is concerned about access to recreation resources, amenities that come at the expense of the environment, which was the initial attraction to the location, are counterproductive. The developer needs to work carefully with authorities who cooperate in a long-range plan that both conserves the resources and enhances an appreciative use of them. For example, a littered beach, no matter how wide, becomes a source of discontent and discourages return renters and possible purchasers of housing units.
4. A plan of development that keeps capital requirements, facility management, real estate sales, promotion, and the recreation opportunities in synchronization calls for a well-formulated timetable and usually for some experience. The frequency of bankruptcies in resort development testifies to the difficulty of achieving this measured and sequential synchronization.
5. One essential of the development plan is good market research that identifies the potential markets for the recreation resource, locates them geographically and demographically, and provides the basis for promotional efforts that announce the development and attract interest at a rate

that can be accommodated. The marketing plan is more than having a product and advertising it. Recreation business development is based on the interests, skills, investment, schedules, and competing opportunities of people who are seeking new or enhanced experiences.

6. Attention to promoting the image of the resort, important as it is, is no substitute for a well-planned and well-managed recreation program. Such a program needs to take into account the various interest levels, skill levels, and satisfaction profiles of those who become the guests of the resort. The satisfaction will come from participation, not from facilities and resources alone. One example of this attention is found at an Arizona guest ranch. At this resort the three main activities are horseback riding, golf, and tennis. It is further assumed that most guests will spend some time in or around the pool. However, not only are there programs to introduce each of the main activities but there is a special program designed for "nonsports partners" whose interests in equines, racquets, and tees is minimal or less. Further, each sport and nonsport orientation has a separate set of rates that incorporates the resources required for participation but does not require nonsport partners to pay for something they do not intend to use. In this case marketing and recreation programming are integrated in the overall image promotion and management plan.

COMPLEMENTARY RESORTS

The complementary resorts differ only in that the major recreation resource is off-site. The management of the resort then becomes more supportive and facilitating than providing. The resort must maintain services that enable the visitor to utilize the resource. Whether the resource is a beach, lake, mountainside, restored village, theater, music pavilion, or some combination, the complementary resort maintains access for guests, provides transportation as necessary, rents needed equipment, and is prepared to offer the support services that enhance the recreation experience. The resort becomes a base for activity rather than its provider. Its services are auxiliary to the attraction.

However, the complement may include recreation provisions. For example, a motel complex fifteen miles from Disney World offers free use of a tennis club next door, matches and lessons, and a large pool for the tired and footsore visitors. Further, they arrange for small meetings and conventions that can combine the tennis, pool, and WDW excursions with a set of meeting rooms, lodging, meals, and two locales for liquid refreshment.

A resort alongside the Lake of the Ozarks in Missouri gives access to the lake for fishing and waterskiing. There are cottages, rooms in the lodge, restaurant, and bar. However, the lake is the attraction, so the resort rents fishing boats, guides, canoes, paddleboats, power boats, houseboats, and so on. Boat rentals run from $16 per day for a 14-foot boat with a small motor to $55 per day for a bass boat with an 85-horsepower motor. The season requires that most revenue be produced between Memorial Day and Labor Day, but off-season rates are available to entice business at low season.

Operation of a complementary resort is less complex than of a comprehensive program. However, it is dependent on a resource that cannot be fully controlled. This resource may become polluted, crowded, or otherwise degraded without the resort developer being able to prevent the damage. The greatest protection is having the external resource managed under strict law, as with a national park, or under some sort of zoning regulation that prevents serious degradation. In such a case the business manager will work closely with government agencies to protect, improve, and enhance the long-term attractiveness of the recreation resource.

Again, marketing research may reveal that the overall demand for the resort may be increased if there are alternative recreation opportunities for members of groups who do not fancy the primary recreation activity. In a family everyone may not like to fish, waterski, sun on the beach, or trek into the forest. Attention to alternative opportunities may vastly increase the attraction to families or other groups with diverse leisure orientations who must decide on a location that is most attractive to as many of the group as possible.

VARIETY RESORTS

The second main type of resorts are those that offer a range of resources and activities. They seek to attract visitors for at least a week at a time and cater to diverse and multiple recreation interests. Such resorts are both capital- and labor-intensive. They require considerable investment and employ large numbers of people to construct, maintain, operate, and service the multiple amenities and recreation opportunities. Luxury resorts may employ as many as 1.5 persons per guest. More often the employee/guest ratio is less than 1:1. Resorts are labor-intensive because of the variety of services expected. However, the largest number of jobs are related to maintenance rather than program. One person may clean 12 to 15 rooms in a hotel per day during the same period that another will be lifeguard and supervisor at the pool.

INVESTMENT ISSUES

The fundamental principle for understanding most comprehensive variety resorts is that it is real estate that drives the investment plan. A single resort may operate entirely on a rental basis with the ownership vested in an individual, partnership, or corporation. In such a resort all revenue must be gained from those who visit and pay for accommodations and services. However, in many cases the resort includes some kind of units that can be purchased. Telemark has plans for selling lots for building and for condominium development. Big Sky already has clusters of condominums that are included in the rental program when not occupied by their owner. In major resort hotels on Hilton Head Island or Longboat Key, real estate offices offer a range of condominiums and other types of real estate to the visitor. With costs of land and construction escalating, a major investment return often requires a significant real estate component in the overall strategy.

For the resort alone, an investment plan is an integral part of putting together a financial package. Lending institutions usually require an independent market study and investment plan. It may require a complex computer program to integrate all the elements in such an analysis. For example, a plan includes:

- All the tax factors—real estate, income, corporation, excise, and others—over the period of return on the investment.
- The various sources of revenue from the resort including visitors, auxiliary services, real estate sales, and space rental.
- Costs of maintaining necessary capital—a line of credit for operations, major debt servicing and retirement, and contingency funding.
- All sales costs, including promotion, on-site sales, and representation at point-of-origin cases.
- Operations costs anticipated in relation to the growth of the resort and increase in visitors.
- Construction costs, including the necessary payments for land acquisition, infrastructure, and recreation resource access and care.

The factors in the market analysis are much the same as with other recreation businesses. The central question is the visitor market potential for the resort. In order to estimate this market, a number of variables have to be included in the equation:

- Participation rates and interest for the targeted market areas in the primary recreation experiences to be offered.
- Population characteristics in the major and secondary market areas.
- Transportation costs and convenience.
- Competing resources both in the resort area and in alternative destinations.
- Special attractions for the planned resort and area.
- Occupancy rates and recreation resources utilization in competing resorts in the area and at alternative locations.
- Sales trends for recreation-oriented real estate in areas similar in quality, price range, and resources.

- A balance between the target size of the resort offering, the scope of the market, and the ability of the resources in the area to absorb and service the recreation market without deterioration.

Such factors are integrated into a plan with a schedule. The plan moves from market and financial analysis, resort concept, preliminary design, and environmental planning through program development, financing, working plans, construction, and refinement of facilities to initial sales efforts, promotion, and step-by-step inauguration of program. The critical issue is to integrate all these elements into a timetable that not only brings the resort on-line and ready for operation, but synchronizes financing and marketing with the on-site development.

At the center of the development program is the basic recreation concept. Just what are the key resources for leisure that will be provided? How will they be developed? Who will be expected to be attracted to them? What will be the styles of participation? And what will be the projected image of the resort? That is, how it will be seen as special and different by prospective guests and investors? Will it feature a resource, program, location, or price? How quickly can its drawing power be expected to yield a break-even occupancy?

Major Resort Hotels Large resort hotels, usually part of a major chain, are amazingly similar. They generally have at least 200 guest rooms, some with water views. Available on-site are beach access, indoor and outdoor swimming pools, a health and fitness center, restaurants and bars, shops, convention facilities, and a hospitality service that arranges for excursions and other recreation. Either on-site or nearby are tennis courts, golf courses, and often some kind of marina. In the area there will be other resources for eating, drinking, entertainment, and shopping. In most cases the main hotel restaurant or lounge will feature some kind of evening entertainment. In season the pool will be a meeting area at which it is possible to be served food and beverages. The hospitality service will arrange transportation, tours, court or tee time at off-site facilities, instruction in sports, child care in the room or at a daytime facility, car rental, and access to any other recreation resources of the area.

How do so many such resort hotels keep an occupancy rate that produces a profit, especially in the locations where there is keen competition? First, they offer a full package of secure lodging and recreation. Everything is available or arranged. Going from one opportunity to another is convenient and easy. Relaxation is paramount.

Second, they provide enough variety so that groups with members who do not all want to do the same thing at the same time can be accommodated. This is especially important for business or professional associations and family groups.

Third, they offer a standard of quality that takes most of the uncertainty out of the experience. With the expectation that most visitors will stay three days to a week, they can control almost all the environment except the weather. The prices are high enough to exclude most whose leisure or life-styles that might be disruptive to guests. At such a resort hotel one knows what to expect.

Fourth, they are located in the midst of one or more attractive recreation resources. The beach, entertainment, and other attractions are right there to be utilized with an ease impossible in most residential locations. Fifth, they market not only the recreation-oriented location but also programs and events that enable guests to enter the leisure environments easily. Such programs offer both segregated activities for group members who want to do different things and group-oriented settings for those who prefer to stay together. Ease of entry is combined with variety so that a guest can choose among a number of options for any part of the day or evening.

The marketing, program design, and operations are developed for a number of market segments. There is the family unit with young children and an income adequate to afford the special opportunities to be both together and separate. There are the business and professional groups who combine meetings with recreation. There are the postchild-rearing couples who seek a change, convenience, and joint activity. For the most part such resort hotels do not find major markets among the retired, singles, or young couples.

CASE: THE DISNEY-DESIGNED OUTDOOR COMPLEMENT

As various modes of camping became more and more popular, the Walt Disney World planners realized that to provide a complete set of opportunities, they needed to respond to that mode of family travel and vacationing. After examining a number of camping developments, both public and private, they designed Fort Wilderness. It is not an inexpensive place to camp. However, for families of four or more, it lowers the cost of staying right at the destination. Even more important, it is a variety comprehensive resort with easy access to the Magic Kingdom and Epcot Center. There are beaches, slides, game areas, boat rentals, and a variety of sites for teens and preteens to play apart from their parents, for parents with younger children, and for any who want to enjoy the outdoor activities. The destination attractions are nearby but may be taken in at a more relaxed rate and with the interspersion of other kinds of recreation by a group camping for the week. Fort Wilderness is the clearest expression of the WDW desire to be a complete recreation destination. It is designed to provide a Disney package of rather traditional recreation activities—beaching, boating, swimming, camping, and social interaction. It helped when a layer of sand was discovered under the swampy mud at the site, but Disney ingenuity and investment would have found another way. The target market is clear, families with children who have already invested in some form of camping equipment or vehicle. However, for those who have not, there are camping trailers for rent.

CASE: DESIGNING FOR EXPERIENCE

What can one more barrier island recreation destination do to project an image of being different and especially desirable? The Kiawah Island Company faced this question, partly because they were in a highly competitive market with numerous alternative destinations and resorts. Their answer is a recreation-oriented one.[6]

They designed a recreation experience, one that could be visualized, promoted, and have wide appeal. It was based on a number of factors in the recreation aim of visitors to such a beach resort. First, it was indigenous, a reflection of the culture of the region. Second, it fostered social interaction. Third, it could be pictured and packaged as a special attraction. Fourth, it was environmentally sound. Fifth, it could be managed as either a separate and extra-cost item or part of a package, but would not be accessible to those in the resort who do not pay for it. Sixth, it could add income to the resort.

The program was their Pig and Oyster Roast. Located on a point a mile from the main resort, it embodied some of the food culture of the Carolina lowlands and the seashore. The group participation activity was designed carefully for site, menu, funky transportation, music, dancing and entertainment, service, costume, and script. Capable of serving 50 to 400 people at one time, the roast has become an "event." It happens on time and with a standard schedule so that all needs for personnel, food and drink, transportation, cleanup, and entertainment are totally predictable. Guests reserve and pay in advance for everything but the cash bar. The setup anticipates the exact number who have reserved.

As a result the resort managers believe that their design has done what they wanted. It turns a profit because of the standardization of supplies and personnel needs. It is different and adds to the image of the resort. It differentiates Kiawah from the other destinations along the Carolina-Georgia barrier island coast. Perhaps most important, the design is toward an experience. It is more than a seashore cookout. It is a total event through which the participants are led at a pace they can handle and enjoy, different and yet not threatening. It blends with the environment and yet is highly social and interactive. Finally, it excludes few who might be attracted to the resort; it is an inclusive recreation program.

CASE: CLUB MED—THE TOTAL RECREATION RESORT

The market segmentation was the starting point. Club Med was begun in France to provide a new kind of destination resort for young adults who wanted physical activity, a simple environment, participation resources, peer social interaction possibilities, and a fixed price. Club Med (short for

Club Mediterranee) began in 1950 with tenting holidays at Mediterranean coast locations and has expanded to over 80 villages around the world. The emphasis is still on fixed prices, group activity, sports, an outdoor-oriented environment, and a kind of simplicity. The original beach-and-sun orientation has been expanded to include snow and skis. The tents have become cottages and more traditional hotels. The destinations sound more like the travel agent's checklist of where to go in season. However, Club Med's recreation dimensions are not like any other concept or variety resort. Here are some special elements:

- At Club Med no one carries money. A necklace of beads are exchanged one by one for services and special equipment and the total is added to the final bill.
- While there is a regular and ongoing schedule of events, no one has to participate.
- Each resort has one or more special recreation resources and activity programs, such as windsurfing, skiing, tennis, or some combination. Each has entertainment and multiple options for any hour of the day or evening. However, there is always choice and variety.
- The local culture is part of the experience, but filtered through the set-apart location and regular staff.
- The assumption is that young adults usually come to such a destination in order to be together or to get together. This does not mean that liaisons are fostered or managed, but the social interaction is the atmosphere as well as the program.
- The markets have been expanded so that Club Med now attracts older visitors as well as prechild-rearing young adults. There are couples with children, couples whose children are grown, those who want access to instruction and participation in the featured activities, and any who seek such an interaction context. Program provisions for children are featured at some of the locations.
- The European fixed-price approach has proved appealing to many. Meals, wine, activities, equipment, and entertainment are all part of the lodging package so that the costs can be anticipated and budgeted with considerable accuracy. Also, group air travel rates are arranged from major population centers to their most popular destinations. Club Med visits can be arranged directly or through travel agents.

One special market has been recognized and met by the organization. It is the employed adult who wants a break, a change in environment and social climate in the midst of a work period. Club Med programs and packages are designed for the person who can leave the job for a week, afford a reasonable recreation experience, and return on schedule but without the time to do much in the way of planning and scheduling. From airport to return Club Med has done the arranging. However, the destination is not a regimented tour group but an open and varied leisure environment. Further, the concept begins with the understanding that most valued leisure is activity *with* others.

Dimensions of the appeal, then, are

Climate and natural resources

Activity selection: windsurfing, swimming, snorkeling, scuba diving, waterskiing, sailing, aerobics, volleyball, tennis, archery, riding, crafts, computer games, and so on.

Cuisine: Food in abundance and combining local cuisines and fresh food with wine, desserts, and snacks.

Evening entertainment: Shows, dancing, and participation.

Off-site sightseeing

A social interaction style that is inclusive and including

The inclusive price

The combination has produced a large and growing destination resort system around the world. At the heart of the success if the identification of the market segment most inclined to engage in recreation travel to a destination, the employed young adult. Further, the concept meets the social, environmental, and activity orientations of that market. Perhaps the greatest surprise has been that there are others outside that segment with similar and compatible orientations.

ELEMENTS IN DESTINATION RESORT OPERATION

From the cases and general discussion, a number of factors have emerged.

1. The high investment cost of a comprehensive destination resort requires not only solid financing but also clearly identified sources of revenue.
2. The significance of location. A destination area that is recognized for certain attractive recreation resources is crucial. The exception in which the development creates a new destination area is rare and risky.
3. The stress on participation in recreation. Program does not mean regimentation. However, such resorts offer convenient entry to and engagement with the resource-based activities. The image of the resort should be a facilitating one.
4. Clear price policies that are responsive to the market segments and that maximize revenue over the longest possible season of use.

5. Understanding that the product being sold is a recreation experience that is unattainable in the residential environment. This experience involves resources, activity, and a social context. Program planning, then, combines an indentification of who the participants will be and their styles of recreation as well as the development of the opportunities.
6. Comprehensive destination resorts provide a variety of opportunities in recognition that all those who come together do not always have just the same interests, skills, and anticipated satisfactions.
7. The marketing and promotional departments need to be in communication with those planning and managing facilities and programs so that those attracted are not disappointed, that what has been promised is in place and available. This is especially important during the earlier stages of development.

A comprehensive resort provides most of the recreation resources on-site. A complementary resort is located to provide access to a major resource that is attractive but not owned or controlled by the business. Such a resource may be a national park or a set of built environments such as the Las Vegas Strip. In any case, the resort is planned to offer recreation and services that complement rather than replace the off-site opportunity. The program is not intended to be all-inclusive, but involves facilitating use of the external attraction.

CASE: MANY WAYS OF ENJOYING THE OUTDOORS

The area around Jackson Hole, Wyoming, and the Grand Teton Mountains is striking in its beauty and outdoor opportunities. There are many ways in which recreation businesses complement the public land resource.

At the high end of the spectrum is the "Rockresorts" lodge that was designed to be a model of leisure amenities coupled with environmental planning. Nestled in the forest on the rocky hillside with view of the jagged mountains, the natural materials blend into the setting and yet are an architectural statement of some grace. Within the resort are the services and recreation amenities that provide a full base for enjoyment of the spectacular setting. The location south of Yellowstone National Park and surrounded by National Forest, with the ski developments of Jackson Hole nearby, is the primary attraction. The lodge complements the recreation environment rather than attempts to be a self-enclosed facility.

However, the prices at the modern lodge do not appeal to all those who would engage in resource-based outdoor recreation in the area. There are Alpine skiers, Nordic skiers, and hikers in the winter and those who fish, hike, hunt, backpack, and drive in the summer. The range of accommodations begins with simple lodging and a map of the area for those who will find their own way and extends to other lodges that offer a complete package of transportation and access to the various off-site resources. Some have their own stable and guides for riding into the forest and even camping overnight in the mountains. Some have fishing boats and equipment for rent. Some arrange flights over the mountains for sight-seeing, ski instruction, or snowshoeing tours. Some have heated pools. Some offer all meals and entertainment; others provide a local directory of such services. And the prices may vary as widely as the facilities.

Choices are partly based on price. One hundred dollars per night per person does not attract everyone, especially in an area to which travel is expensive. Some choices are dictated by availability as the preferred resorts fill up for high-season weeks. However, there are also different tastes. Some recreation travelers prefer as much privacy as possible and seek quiet and separation from the daytime recreation crowds. Some seek just the opposite: a gang that will party into the night and be open to all who would like to join. Some concentrate on a particular activity and choose the resort with the best location, access, or facilities for that participation. Some are coming for the first time and allow a travel agent to make reservations at the lodge with a reservation network affiliation. In any case, the fundamental appeal is Jackson Hole and the Tetons. The resort plans and program are designed to enable guests to utilize the environment for the varieties of recreation possible there. Unlike the all-inclusive and comprehensive resort, they make accessible the surrounding opportunities rather than attempt to provide everything themselves.

CASE: COMPREHENSIVE BUT NOT EXCLUSIVE

A quite different kind of resort would be exemplified by a massive hotel such as the MGM Grand in Las Vegas. With a strategy that places the hotel in the middle of the gambling and entertainment "strip" with its rows of recreation-oriented construction, the hotel also can be considered self-contained. Although most visitors go to other hotel-casinos as well, at least for the dinner and evening shows, the Grand can occupy a weekend's time right on site. There is a casino over a half mile long, a two-thousand-seat fronton where jai alai is watched and wagered on, a shopping center with over 40 stores, a nightclub seating almost 2,000 people, seven restaurants, two movie theaters, tennis courts, bowling, swimming pools, sunning decks, health centers, a child-care and entertainment facility plus outdoor amenities such as a small lake and a campground.

The hotel has everything necessary for a variety of visiting groups. Convention business is always sought and provided for. Those middle-years couples who fly in for the entertainment have access to the hotel's offerings as well as transportation and reservations services for other shows. And even those who bring children can join them at the pool or leave them at the care facility. Las Vegas is a recreation environment that offers and promotes activities that are not available at all in many places, are less lavish in others, and illegal in many. The environment encourages behavior that might not be acceptable back home. Therefore, the hotel not only provides a variety of activities and opportunities but a social and economic climate that is free from constraint, except for the constraint of cost. In fact, even money is defined as just one more instrument for enjoyment.

In this context it is important to see the resort—comprehensive or complementary—as a destination that is different from the point of origin in several ways. It offers leisure resources that may be different. It may offer climate, access to opportunities, convenience, and freedom from home responsibilities and schedules. It is an escape *to* a recreation environment. However, the programs and opportunities are only part of the appeal. The resort is also a legitimating atmosphere. It is a social climate where one is encouraged to ignore many routine elements of the daily round and to engage in pleasure-seeking behavior. The social climate of the resort is important in providing a permissive and legitimizing environment. Once the decision is made to come, the expressive, relaxing, developmental, social, and experimental orientations of leisure are not only accepted by encouraged.

BUSINESS ASPECTS OF RECREATION PROPERTY

Earlier it was suggested that in many cases it is real estate that drives the destination recreation department. That is not always true, of course. Some destination resorts are wholly owned by investment interests or the operators. They are run on a rental basis with all the recreation resources and services made available on a temporary basis for a fee. The fee may be segmented for each activity or service or it may be inclusive. The inclusive fee is becoming more popular as resorts market packages for lodging, some meals, access to the activity resource, and often instruction in related skills. There are usually auxiliary opportunities such as health centers, pools, and evening programs open to all visitors.

However, the costs of land acquisition and construction are formidable for most destinations. Land in an urban center, on the beach, or prepared for a sport such as golf generally comes at a high price. Costs of building have increased rapidly since 1950. Sharing the investment risk and regaining capital quickly is often not possible on a rental fee basis. As a result, a number of strategies have been employed.

The simplest real estate strategy is to set aside land for purchase by those who will construct their own residences on the lots. In this way the division of the land parcel can be leveraged by selling in smaller units. Land purchased for

$5,000 an acre can be sold at multiples of up to 40 when divided into two to ten lots per acre. Even after the infrastructure is constructed, common ground prepared, and amenities added, the profit margin can be considerable. We will discuss this aspect of "recreation communities" in chapter 12.

More common is the development of condominiums at recreation destinations. These provided individual ownership of a resident that is not on privately owned land. The design may be for attached town houses, multiple-unit buildings, or some combination. For recreation residence the condominium is a method of ownership that relieves the owner of caretaking responsibilities. Exterior maintenance, utilities, protection, and management of the unit available for rental are all provided by the development company. As a result condominiums are often purchased as rental properties by those who do not occupy them, for tax shelters by those who intend to use them only briefly and rent them at other times, and as long-term investment in areas where prices are likely to increase. For the developer they maximize the number of units that are placed in a given space, ensure control over the overall design and quality of maintenance, and yield an early return on investment. Further, the developer then has available a supply of rental units without the capital costs to recover.

A more recent version of such recreation ownership is called *time-sharing.* In this scheme the year is divided into weekly units that are then sold to individual purchasers. There are several variations. In some the specified weeks are purchased and prices vary according to the recreational desirability of the period. In others the schedule changes each year so that all owners have access to the prime periods at some time over a cycle of years. While some time-sharing is by lease, more popular is the arrangement by which the purchaser actually holds title to the property for the period specified. This program has been enhanced by services that provide exchange possibilities. For example, a two-week period at Acapulco can be exchanged for one in Hawaii in a unit of approximately equal size. Such services charge a membership fee and an exchange fee. However, they give a flexibility to condominium time-sharing that makes it more attractive to some who are not sure they want to go back to the same place every year.

From a business perspective time-sharing has the major drawback of high sales costs. A unit has to be sold over and over to fill the 50 open weeks. A management organization has to be in place. Also, in destinations where there is a low season it may be difficult to sell units for those weeks even at a considerably reduced price. The advantage, however, is striking. A condominium that may otherwise sell for $100,000 will time-share for a total of $300,000 to $400,000. Further, the marketing element is significant. Those who make a first commitment to a development through time-sharing may in time become buyers of more time in the program for other units. Some instability in time-sharing businesses, especially during recession periods, has raised doubts in the minds of some prospective purchasers. However, the programs are expanding as a way in which those who have enjoyed a particular destination area can protect themselves against the likelihood of rising costs in the future.

Another method of lowering the investment costs for resort development and increasing revenues is by leasing space for service providers. Just as public recreation providers lease space at their sites for marina operation, food concessions, equipment rental, guide services, rafting, and other services, so the business provider can plan for external operation of some services. A food business may lease space in which to develop a restaurant. The decoration, equipment, promotion, operation, and entertainment are planned in conjunction with the resort developer but paid for by the lessee. The lease specifies some conditions of design and operation so that the overall aims of the developer will be fulfilled. The lease is for a long enough period that the operator can afford the investment in decor and fixtures. Overall, the developer has a service that is necessary for the resort strategy and a regular rent without front-end costs other than constructing the empty space or the problems of management.

The same kind of arrangement can be made for any number of recreation or auxiliary provisions. A golf course or tennis facility may be managed by an organization with special interests or experience in the field. The personal service shops may be independently owned and operated. The comprehensive resort developers are not required to design and manage every aspect of the overall provision. They can specialize in those areas they understand or believe will be most profitable for them.

One difficulty with the lease strategy, however, can be serious. It may become a problem if the leasing operators do not conform to the standards and philosophy of the resort. Only when design, styles of service, and even prices have to be approved by the developer can there be some assurance of maintaining quality. The terms of a lease agreement need to be carefully negotiated. Even more, the aims and modes of operation of the developer and leasing company need to be compatible.

A major logistical problem for both destination resorts and their potential clients is reservations. In order to plan a recreation trip one must be assured of a destination. Further, not only having lodging but being in a desirable accommodation is imperative if the aims of the trip are to be accomplished. Nor can every point-of-origin travel agent know everything necessary about every possible destination. Therefore, resorts that are not part of one of the major hotel chains have increasingly entered into cooperative reservation systems. Toll-free phone systems, regional promotion programs, specifications of prices for types of accommodations and recreation resources, and assurance of payment can be arranged through the system using some form of national credit. One call or visit can assure a travel group that has never been there before that they will have a type of lodging, recreation opportunities, and price level long before they pack to leave.

As will be introduced in chapter 12, recreation destinations now may combine accommodation of short-term recreation visits with various forms of property ownership, part-time residence, and full-time residence including retirement. There are recreation-oriented residential communities such as Sea Pines on

Hilton Head Island or other developments in Florida or California that are at the same time destination magnets. Intricacies of planning and marketing such destinations will be outlined.

DESTINATION AREAS

Briefly, the concept of a *destination area* that has as its drawing power some special resource should also be introduced. The distinction from recreation-providing resorts is that the destination is the setting, the location, rather than the resort. Most often, the overall provision of lodging, food, entertainment, and activity is offered by a number of independent businesses rather than one comprehensive enterprise.

THE CITY AS A RECREATION DESTINATION

The city of Boston is illustrative. Not only does it contain a series of historical sites and buildings that can be visited but many of them are on a historic "walking trail" that begins in the center of the city. Further, the redevelopment of the waterfront area around Faneuil Hall with the restoration of the market into shops, restaurants, pubs, and other attractions has been combined with marinas, residential condominiums, and visitor accommodations. The city itself is a destination for recreation travel. The various public and market provisions together offer a series of experiences as a destination. In parallel ways many other cities around the world have the same kinds of magnet attraction for visitors.

Tourism or recreation travel depends on the availability of a large number of related facilities, amenities, and services. While there is some area planning involved in such provisions, to a large extent they are offered by entrepreneurs who identify a potential market and move to meet it with a business. When one such business is successful, it is usually followed by others that engage in direct competition or seek to offer a somewhat differentiated product or service. The market sector is the major provider around the public resources.

What is involved in such destination recreation-oriented businesses? First, the entrepreneur has to know who is coming. In Boston travelers who engage in some use of the facilities include business travelers, their companions, families seeking historical immersion, younger adults who enjoy the urban ambience, and various tour groups. These mix with locals who enjoy the same environment and utilize the same business provisions. These market segments are seeking particular kinds of experiences and will employ market services to enhance those experiences. However, what is sought by the urban-style young couple on Saturday may be rather different from the family of four who walk the trail in search of old buildings and ships.

Second, the variety of businesses needs to be complementary to both the magnet resources and to each other. A business concept should involve a careful study of not only who is coming and what they do but also of what is already available. In some cases current provisions are overcrowded. In others the locations are too concentrated while the participation is dispersed. Sometimes one new resource or business opens up possible markets for another enterprise. Especially as areas are redeveloped or restored, a set of services at the new site and along the way from other sites is needed.

A third factor is the range of visit lengths. A number of services that are superfluous for those in the city for only one to three days become attractive for those staying a week. Some investigation of the patterns from the main providers of accommodations may reveal a pattern unrecognized by current businesses. For example, if a boat trip to offshore islands takes at least half a day, it may not be attractive to those in town for less than three days, but it might have a market among those who stay five days or more.

Fourth, many visitors who are not familiar with an area enjoy some type of packaged experiences. The traditional bus tours provide such an introduction. However, there may be travel groups who want something more, perhaps a deeper introduction to history given by a well-prepared instructor, a sample of nightlife, a family-oriented visit to Plimoth Plantation or Cape Cod, or a special set of services for children that includes a history tour on their level.

The point is that there are numerous opportunities for imaginative providers of recreation experiences in the destination city. However, it takes a thorough knowledge of both the environment and of the range of visitors to develop a viable business concept and plan.

THE EVENT AS A RESOURCE

Many travelers are drawn to a particular destination for a specific event. In some cases the event is an ancient ritual that now attracts interest, such as some of the castle parades in Great Britain. In others the event may be developed to add to the economic base of the city. In Stratford, Ontario the name association with Shakespeare's Stratford led to the planning of a theater festival in an area that was losing some of its industrial economy.

Another type of event as destination attraction has been the cultural festival. Some are in rural areas and last for only a week or a weekend. Others are seasonal. Some are connected with a historical event that is in some way reconstituted or dramatized for a period each season. Others are more ethnic and based on displaying the history or culture of some group located in the area such as a Native American tribe or a European religious community.

Whether the event is historical, cultural, or artistic, there are two types of business that may be developed to support the event and the tourism it attracts. The first is the set of support services for lodging transportation, food and drink, and secondary support. They are not much different from the en route services described in chapter 8.

The second type of business provides complementary recreation opportunities. Again, there are a number of rather simple questions that raise the issue of the types of recreation business that might be possible:

- Who is coming and in what kinds of groups? There may be those who would prefer other kinds of recreation from the primary event. Among them, of course, are the children who come in the car with parents drawn by a festival, theater, or historical drama.
- How long do they stay? Are there other recreation resources in the area that can be utilized to offer a diversity of experiences at the same location? Often travel groups seek some change from the primary activity or attraction if they stay more than a day or two.
- What kinds of recreation experiences are not being provided by the primary event? For example, many like to maintain physical activity even when attending a music festival. Are there opportunities for a business that facilitates such activity by providing locales, access, transportation, scheduling, instruction, or some other program?
- Are there facilities for a variety of recreation travel styles? Just as Disney identified the camping market, other areas may not have recognized the variety of travel styles, groups, orientations, and desired amenities drawn by any special event. In many cases the organizers of the central attraction will be quite willing to provide information on visitors, help with a complementary opportunity that may enhance their own markets, and even cooperate in promotion of the new enterprise.

Destinations as Recreation Resources People do travel as recreation. While some of the meaning of the trip is in the travel itself and some depends on the traveling companions, the destination is central to decisions to allocate time and money to the total experience.

For some destinations the meaning is centered on the various provisions for recreation activity. In some way participation is enhanced by the resources found at the destination. For other destinations the environment is central to the experience. Recreation is one dimension of engagement with the environment, whether it is the built environment of a city or the natural environment of a national park.

In either case there is a range of recreation businesses that serve and support the recreation aims of the travelers. Some businesses provide only one item in the entire complex of provisions. Others seek to provide the entire context for the period at the location. Some are oriented toward the sale or rental of equipment or facilities. Others are directed toward more personal services such as guiding, instructing, or arranging for participation. However, in most destinations recreation businesses either support the enjoyment of the central resource or develop the resources that are *the* context of the leisure destination. Business is an integral part of the set of provisions for which the destination itself is the basic recreation resource.

SUMMARY OF ISSUES

Economic impacts on an area hosting tourism include both costs and contributions. Those firms involved in development tend to benefit most as well as assume the greatest risks.

The complex complementarity of business provisions at a recreation travel destination affords a number of entrepreneurial opportunities.

Disney World is the prototype comprehensive entertainment park demonstrating the elements of front-end investment, quality, image, and the strength of the "Middle American" market.

Comprehensive theme parks have to cope with the factors of seasonality, scheduling for designated market segments, and product life cycles leading to saturation.

Theme destination resorts are linked to a particular activity or resource. Planning includes market research on access, infrastructure costs, ecological factors, target markets, capital costs, and possibilities of new markets created by new resources and promotion.

Variety resorts may be real-estate driven in their investment plans, but they are still labor-intensive in their recreation and amenity offerings.

Multiple market concepts call for carefully integrated schedules and programs in comprehensive destination resorts.

Some resorts have developed images and offerings for particular market segments.

Dependence on off-site recreation resources requires planning and cooperation with those who manage the external resources.

Condominiums and time-sharing are two methods of sharing the investment risk and burden at destination resorts.

Destination areas such as cities are the context for a wide variety of recreation-providing businesses that complement the in-place opportunities for particular tourist market segments.

DISCUSSION QUESTIONS

1. Is resort development more likely to benefit or damage the destination areas? How? Who tends to benefit most? Least?
2. Outline and rank markets for some specific destination businesses.
3. Give example of complementary business provisions in a destination community without which the overall set of provisions would be significantly reduced.
4. What are the best ways to gain experience in destination recreation?

5. How can the social elements of destination visiting be used to develop viable business strategies? Give examples.
6. What market segments are most often repeat visitors at theme parks? Why?
7. What kinds of recreation resources are attractive and scarce enough to be destination magnets?
8. In estimating potential variety resort markets, are demographic or geographical factors more important?
9. What would a North American Club Med program and image include? Are there new market segments for such inclusive provisions?
10. Try to identify urban visitors with recreation interests unmet by traditional provisions. Be specific to a city and types of visitors.

PROJECTS

1. Develop a plan for a low-investment destination business that depends on recreation for its market.
2. Carefully observe what people actually do at an amusement park. Who are they with? How much time is spent on rides? Does the clientele change during the day and evening?
3. Formulate a market research strategy for the assessment of the business potential of a new destination resort.
4. Outline a plan for a comprehensive destination resort that builds on a unique resource or recreation program.

REFERENCES

1. Lundberg, Donald A. *The Tourist Business,* 4th ed., p. 158f. Boston: CBI Publishing, 1980.
2. Ibid., p. 157.
3. Ibid., p. 164.
4. Chubb, Michael, and Holly Chubb. *One Third of our Time?,* p. 377. New York: Wiley, 1981.
5. Ibid., p. 379.
6. Glick, Myles, and Bill McKenzie. "The Use of Infrastructure to Orchestrate a Large Group Experience and Maximize Profits," pp. 59–66. In D. E. Hawkins, E. Shafer, and J. Rorelstad, eds., *Tourism Marketing and Management Issues.* Washington, D.C.: George Washington University, 1980.

10 OUTDOOR RECREATION COMPLEMENTS

ISSUES

What are the special characteristics of businesses that complement publically managed outdoor recreation resources?

Are there special factors to consider in the formation of an outdoor-recreation complement business?

How does the resource base for recreation shape the nature of the business?

What are environmental factors in the analysis of markets for a complementary business?

How is an enabling approach applied to such businesses?

How do the types of complementary businesses differ in operations?

What are the significant resource-related elements in operating an outdoor-recreation-based business?

How can the "right size" for a business be assessed?

When is cooperation between a complementary business and public management most likely to break down?

Over 260 million acres of federal land are available for recreation use. States provide another 42 million acres, and local government bodies about 10 million acres. This land includes forests, lakes, rivers, mountains, deserts, beaches, trails, prairies, and other terrains. Of this about half is forest, 9% wilderness, 10% fish and game preserves, and 6% parks and other designated recreation areas.[1] Federal land in the coastal and mountain West, not including Alaska, make up about 75% of all this area.

On these public lands and waters people hike, fish, hunt, climb, sail, canoe, tube, race, run, play games, ski, camp, drive, soar, and enjoy innumerable other kinds of activity. In some locations the government agency managing the resource offers access, safety protection, facilities, prepared resources such as ski slopes and harbors, and other improvements that make recreation participation possible. At other places the agency does nothing except permit use for recreation. In either case there may be much more support needed for most people to use the land and water for recreation. They may need equipment services, protection, knowledge, associations, food, shelter, or transportation.

Outdoor recreation complements are those businesses that facilitate or make possible recreation activity at special outdoor resources. They provide a place to get a boat into the water and keep it safe. They offer guide services to the back country complete with equipment that would be expensive and impractical to purchase for infrequent use. They fly fishing groups to hidden lakes and teach novices how to canoe in the wilderness. They teach safety on climbing a sheer rock face and for soaring and gliding from the cliff above. They repair equipment at the site and even maintain the resource itself.

Public recreation providers in most areas make no attempt to offer all the facilities and resources necessary for the recreation use of the land and water. They depend on market sources for many enabling goods and services. In this chapter we will be introducing the businesses that are directly dependent on the natural resources. They in turn complement the point-of-origin businesses. The entire provision scheme includes public and market suppliers on all scales and levels. Outdoor recreation complements, however, are different in that they are directly dependent on a particular natural resource—a specific river, shore, body of water, forest, or mountain.

Some resource-complementary businesses are at the site of the recreation resource. A marina is at the harbor area of a lake, reservoir, river, or other body of water. The guide service and fishing boat rental business is on the lake or river. The ski rental is at the slope. The canoe rental is on the river and the rafting expedition organizer is located in the town on the river just above the canyon.

Of course, there are also land and water areas that provide resources for more than one kind of recreation. Forests may be the environment of many different kinds of camping and hiking as well as nature study, wilderness survival schools, and hunting. A reservoir will be used for power boating, waterskiing, sailing, swimming, fishing, canoeing, family picnics, regattas, and amphibious flying, and sometimes all at one time. Businesses at the site may respond to the multiple uses by offering for sale and rent items from several of the activities. Or there may be specialization in which different businesses have their own activity-specific clienteles. Also, there are general businesses that sell food and drink without regard to the activities.

In some cases the recreation participation may be spread out over a considerable area. A major body of water may have a dozen or even a hundred usable access points, especially for light craft such as canoes. A forest may be entered from most of its perimeter, with legal car parking being the main constraint. Or there may be many lakes, forests, shores, or rivers in a geographical area that can be reached easily from some concentration of people. Then the complementary businesses may be located in the population center rather than on-site. They may provide many of the same services, equipment rental and sales, instruction, and group experiences. However, it is more efficient to be in the regional center rather than depend on the more limited market of a particular resource.

However, in this chapter we are not dealing with every kind of business related to outdoor recreation resources. In other chapters there are analyses of resorts, retail businesses in point-of-origin communities, travel support such as lodging and en route camping, and businesses in residential areas. Here the focus is on those businesses that buy or lease locations that directly serve outdoor resource sites and that are dependent on recreational use of those sites. They provide activity support for or at the resource. They exist because there are markets for goods and services at the outdoor recreation resource. They complement the resource, public or market sector, by enabling or facilitating its use for recreation activity.

There are many examples, some quite specific to the location. Among the most common are marinas for boating, guide and rental services for backcountry entry, schools for activities such as rock climbing or sailing, and multiactivity complexes at public or private watersides. More esoteric are the hang-gliding schools at the dunes, the river-running service for adult and family groups, survival experiences in backcountry, and winter camping stores at the entry to a mountain park. It is difficult to draw a clear line between the board-sailing business in town that offers instruction at two nearby lakes and the urban boat business with sales aimed at a general population rather than a particular resource. However, in the following analysis we will concentrate on the business complementarity with the outdoor resource and activities that require that kind of support.

The analysis will be structured according to business functions rather than the types of resources. While there are important differences in operating an urban-fringe marina and a national-forest white-water rafting business, the same functions have to be accomplished if the business is to do well. In the cases we will be able to illustrate differences as well as similarities in function.

As already introduced, government bodies manage enormous areas of land and water that are available for recreation. The National Park Service in 1978 administered some 300 units: 37 national parks, 81 national monuments, 108 historic units, 29 shoreline areas, 4 river segments, 5 parkways, and 2 preserves, as well as the National Capital park system.[2] Over 17 million overnight stays were registered in those units in 1976.[3] The Forest Service of the Department of Agriculture in 1980 managed over 200 million acres of forest, grassland, and desert for multiple use including recreation. The Bureau of Land Management was responsible for 400 million acres with over 50 million visitor days in 1975. The Army Corps of Engineers with its reservoir, river, and harbor provisions, and the Bureau of Reclamation with its western water projects, the Fish and Wildlife Service, and other federal agencies along with the park and forest services record hundreds of millions of visits each year. And many recreation uses of public resources are not recorded.

What do people do in these outdoor settings? In the 1977 Outdoor Recreation Survey[4] it was found that during the year some 56% of the national sample had gone fishing, 30% camped in developed areas, 28% went hiking or backpacking, 26% drove off-road vehicles or motorcycles, 21% camped in primitive areas, 19% went hunting, 16% used rivers for boating or other river running, 16% waterskied, 15% sailed, 11% snowmobiled, 7% engaged in downhill skiing, and 2% went trail skiing. This does not include the use of public lands by the 69% who went driving for pleasure, the 46% who swam outdoors at beaches and in rivers, the 34% who engaged in boating other than sailing, and so on. Analyses of such participation reveals that there are vast existing markets for various support services. Further, increases in participation in such activities as cross-country skiing, more widespread competence in swimming and other basic skills, and the greater proportion of the population introduced to such interests through educational associations suggest that markets are likely to grow in the future.

The business marketing question is simply, What is necessary for such recreation participation that may be scarce, inaccessible, or not available through nonmarket sources? Subquestions include: What are the limitations to participation that may be alleviated through some business provision? How can participation be increased through marketing? Are there complementary products and services that together form a viable base for a business? And, What are the best locations for such businesses?

THE FORMATION FUNCTION: CONCEPTS

To begin with, a viable business requires an idea. In order to develop the fundamental concept for an outdoor recreation complement business, both the resource base and the activity patterns have to be analyzed.

THE RESOURCE BASE

The nature, size, and location of the recreation resources shape participation. The differences in boating between a Newport harbor and off the dock in a Kansas reservoir influence the type and size of boat, style and costs of equipment, length of the outing, secondary activities, size of the party, and likelihood of some sort of competitive event. Sailing in a small lake or one of the Great Lakes makes quite a difference. Paddling a quiet stream and running Colorado white water are quite different experiences and require quite different skills and equipment.

Consequently, the business concept begins with the resource. What is there now? What can be developed or enhanced? What kinds of recreation activity are now available? Are there limitations that might be the basis for a profit-making business? Is the resource saturated or is there the potential of expanded use and markets?

Any recreation resource has one or more prime uses and a set of secondary uses. For example, a particular beach may be excellent for swimming but too narrow for extensive sunning. Behind the beach there may be excellent picnic sites in the trees or only a few partially shaded tables in the dirt and scrub. Parking may be adequate or require a hike along a dusty road. There may be opportunities for hiking in a rain forest or the beach may be bounded by private land and closed off by fences. To analyze the business possibilities at a resource requires a careful assessment of what can be done there. Among the dimensions of the analysis are the following:

Size Not only the acreage of the resource but also its recreational carrying capacity are significant. Just how many participants can be accommodated without a perception of crowding or actual activity interference? The possibilities for expansion can also be investigated.

Resource adaptibility What kinds of activities are possible at the site? To what extent are they complementary, likely to be engaged in by the same visitors?

Quality Is the resource of superior quality in general attractiveness as well as an activity base? This is especially important if there are competing sites with similar access for the user population.

Availability Is the resource public or private? Would a complementary business necessitate buying or leasing space on the site or near it? What would be the likely terms of purchase or lease? If the site is public, would there be restrictions on the business use that would affect development?

The point is just that the potential for an outdoor recreation complement business is not infinite. What can be done is always tied directly to the resource, its current use and potential, and the limitations that are endemic to the site. Activities can be added, participation increased, and amenities added, but the basic resource, be it a body of water or land, cannot be altered at will.

THE PARTICIPATION POTENTIAL

The target markets for a complementary business consist of those who use or might use the resource. They are involved at some level in the activities based there or could be if certain constraints were removed. They have reasonable access to the site for regular or periodic use. They may engage in similar recreation elsewhere or at some rate of frequency at the place of interest. Or they may be part of a population segment that is a demonstrated market elsewhere but have not developed the interest or investment in the market area.

An analysis of the participation potential would include these factors:

Current use Who is now using the resource? How many? How often? In what groups? With what patterns of activity? And at what costs?

Current resource constraints Just what are the factors limiting use? If they are inherent in the resource, then the business potential may be small. However, if they can be mitigated through some change in access, amenities, or design, then the participation patterns could be enhanced.

Market area analysis Figures are available on the participation of various population aggregates in recreation activities. While there are important regional differences related to developed interests as well as resources and climate, a profile of unrealized potential for the population with access to the location can be developed. For example, a lack of trails, boat facilities, or rental equipment may make current participation in Nordic skiing, sailing, or rafting far below the averages for similar market segments elsewhere. The possibility of basing a business concept on inhibited participation is more risky than meeting an evident current need but may also have greater possibilities for long-term growth.

Location The time cost of travel is critical for recreation participation. Therefore, the time-distance travel costs to the resource from the probable markets are fundamental to estimating the business possibilities.

Participation costs In the case of some activities, the money costs of participation may be quite limiting. If equipment required for engagement in the activity limits purchase to high-end markets, then the market segment study has to be especially focused on income and discretionary spending patterns.

What can the business offer to recreation participation? In some cases a complementary business may just provide on-site goods or services now available only at a distance. In other cases the resource itself may become more usable because of the business additions to its natural base. While the business possibilities cannot outrun the potential of the resource, they can alter current uses. The concept development should involve more than just present users.

BUSINESS REQUIREMENTS

An initial question for any business concept is centered on capital. What will be the capital requirements for the business? Can the concept be tested without high front-end investment in real estate, buildings, equipment, or personnel? The investment requirements have to be weighed against the possibilities of the resource and participation.

Other issues for an outdoor recreation complement firm are those of permanence, access, conditions of doing business, and expertise necessary. Does the site offer a location that can be purchased or leased for a long enough term to justify the capital investment? Is access guaranteed or may it be altered by some action of a legislative or regulatory body? Does doing business at the site involve special permits or licenses? Will there be limitations on size of facilities, products rented or sold, or clientele with access? Will there be regular inspections and the possibility of closure without adequate process of law? What will the managers have to know about the resource, activities, equipment and supplies, and skill and safety factors? Do those developing the concept have the expertise to anticipate requirements and provide what will be necessary to operate the business? If not, what will such expertise cost in learning or personnel?

Developing the foundation concept for a business of this kind requires something more than examining the market and competition for a particular retail outlet. The interrelationship of the natural resource, developed amenities and facilities, access, and users calls for an analysis of both the resource and its recreation use. The resource provides the base and exercises limitations on what may be possible. The participants, currently adapting to resource availability and quality, have to be studied as both current and potential markets for the business offerings. And both resource and users provide the potential for a business as they come together in recreation participation that depends on the particular outdoor environment.

CASE: STARTING WITH SCARCITY

In a midwestern state that has quite limited water recreation resources in all but its northern section, a natural lake was used by the local population for boating, fishing, and swimming. Its size and surroundings were not enough to draw from a wide area, even though there were several mid-sized industrial towns within 60 miles. The concept was based on resource scarcity and observation of weekend summer recreation.

One entire side of the lake was farmland and included a small peninsula that extended almost like a pier several hundred feet into the otherwise round body of water. Purchasing that section of the farm, the developer began modestly but with a plan of expansion. The target market was precisely defined, family groups that wanted to be outdoors for summer day and weekend trips. The difficulty of finding swimming and beach environments in the area was evident. So the developer began with enough sand to make a functional beach on the peninsula. Immediately added were refreshment stands, necessary amenities for showers and changing, and picnic sites close enough to the beach so that children could be watched by parents. A lifeguard and cleanup program was in place at the opening. In general, "The Beach" was a pleasant place for families to spend a day outdoors.

The response was so great that expansion took place almost immediately. Campsites, a restaurant, various game locations, boat rental, group areas, and a convenience store were operating within three years. The development stopped only when the capacity of the site was exhausted. The concept together with the scarcity in the area had combined to produce a recreation business that exceeded even the greatest dreams of the owner. Further, the use patterns were quite stable because children wanted to return often, and "The Beach" became an available resort for those without the income or time to travel to Lake Michigan or Myrtle Beach.

MARKET ANALYSIS

Outdoor recreation, with its dependence on site-specific resources and climate, requires some rather special market analysis. The specification of markets for a complementary business, as introduced in the previous section, involves an interplay of three complex variables: the potential attraction and use of the resource, the present and potential participation in resource-based activities by those in the market areas, and the impact of business development on the use of the site.

OUTDOOR RECREATION COMPONENTS

What are the special elements in outdoor resource-based recreation? The combinations of aims and satisfactions in different activities and settings can vary considerably. Snowmobiling and trail skiing have different perceived outcomes even when done in the same forest. The intentions of a group of teens coming to a beach together may have little in common with those of the family with preschool children. Nevertheless, there are some elements of such recreation that in one form or another are common to the type.

1. *Dependence on the environment* The nature and quality of the environment has consequences for the experience. Whether the beach is clean or dirty, crowded or sparsely used, wide or narrow, rocky or sandy, and with a shallow bottom or rapid drop-off in the water have impacts on what can be done there and on the mode of behavior. The same is true of forests, rivers, and mountainsides. The quality of the resource has enough of an effect on the quality of the experience that alternatives may be sought. From a market perspective, recreation resources are always in competition with different environments and activities as well as with the same kind of opportunities in different locations.

2. *Dependence on climate and weather* "Outdoors" means some exposure to weather conditions. Rain can ruin the picnic. Calm can end the sailing regatta.

A storm can make hang gliding or rock climbing too hazardous. Further, the general climate of a region shapes how a particular resource can be used. Especially location by latitude generally defines the length of summer and winter seasons. The market for a recreation resource is bounded by the climate as to season length, and the weather impacts on each possible use day within the season.

3. *The resource is an activity context* What do people do when they get to the resource on a day of acceptable weather? In some cases they may do many different things. At "The Beach" they swim, sun, talk, flirt, play games, engage in sports, eat, drink, walk, camp, sail, fish, canoe, waterski, cook out, read, tend children, avoid children, seek escape, go to a movie, and make love. In other cases they may do only one thing. At a cliff face with no camping or overnight provisions they climb or, more likely, they organize, climb, instruct, talk, snack, make plans, and tend equipment. But the climbing is the focus of all the rest. The point is that from a recreation market perspective the resource has to be understood as a context in which people act, usually in groups.

4. *Distance* Few recreation participants live right at the site of such activity. They come from somewhere, usually near where they work. Most often they come from a population center. The distance is part of the cost of participation, both in time and money. That means that there is generally some calculation, however informal, of costs and alternatives. The resource has to be nearer, more attractive, less costly, more facilitating, socially interesting, or in some way a combination of dimensions superior to going elsewhere or not going anywhere. This also means that there are always opportunity costs, the benefits given up to use that particular resource.

5. *A hierarchy of market segmentation* Some users have a very high degree of commitment to a particular resource-based recreation activity. They must sail, climb, ski, backpack, etc., somehow and somewhere. For them, the resource competes only with other resources in quality and access. At the other end of the spectrum are the users who *may* come to the site *if* all conditions are favorable and nothing else comes up. Usually something else does. In between are the market segments that have varying degrees of commitment to the site and the activity as well as to other sites and activities. In terms of increasing market shares, they are the prime targets. Further, they are differentiated by location, financial resources, schedules, household composition, and recreation styles.

THE MARKET SEGMENTATION STRUCTURE

Still operating on a high level of generalization, what is the structure of identifying markets for an outdoor resource-based recreation business?

A. The Resource

Location

Carrying capacity for activities

Relative quality as an activity environment in relation to alternatives for the same activity or set of activities

Climate conditions: average of days of ideal, viable, limiting, and prohibitive weather in the season

Development potential: possibilities for change

Access control: ownership and management

Cost structures

B. Recreation Use

Activities possible

Numbers of participants in those activities in the designated market areas

Participation trends in those activities

Social patterns: kinds of groups participating at such sites

Participation styles: combinations of activities, orientations, levels of management

Activity completeness: one activity tends to fill all time on one site or is one among many to fill the user day

Constraints to participation: resource abundance or scarcity in the market areas

Relative costs: relation of use of this activity environment to other recreation environments for same and different activities

C. Business opportunities

Place of the business in total environment: Is it necessary, facilitating, or peripheral? Is there competition, direct or secondary?

Place of the business in the activity: Does the business provide the environment, equipment, support facilities, accommodations, backup supplies, secondary logistical services, optional enhancement, or unrelated services or goods?

Competition: on-site, en route, or at the point of origin? directly competitive or providing substitutes?

Image: Can the business create an image that ties it directly to the anticipated satisfaction of using the activity environment?

Mode of provision: sale or rental, personal or product provision, repeated or occasional, fundamental or secondary to other suppliers?

Pricing: relation of pricing policies to the discretionary income of market segments and to competitive goods and services

One basic question is whether or not the participants can engage in satisfying recreation in this or other available environments without the business? That is, does the business provide services that are necessary or only supplementary? When equipment rental, food sales, or instruction is simply a convenience rather than a necessity, then the cost-benefit calculations of some market segments will come out negative. They will go to the more crowded public site, bring old equipment, and pack a lunch.

A second basic question is relative scarcity. Is this "the only game in town" or are there a number of alternatives? And further, will success at developing markets tend to spur the inauguration of competing resources and businesses?

Third, how are decisions made? A study of winter recreation in Wisconsin demonstrated that most plans are made up to three months in advance.[5] When a trip, reservations, and timetable commitments are involved, then even a weekend event may be planned with some care. Alternative sites, costs, and environments may be considered by those who are committed through an activity to engage in such planning. On the other hand, some day use of recreation resources may be relatively situational, depending on weather and available companions on the day of decision. The nature of a business and a scheme of marketing has to take into account how decisions are made.

Fourth, what are the current constraints to participation for each market segment? For families the main constraint to weekend travel in the summer may be time, but winter adds the hassles of packing for children. For students the main constraint may be cost. For some attractive activities the skill requirements are the primary inhibition. For others, such as waterskiing, the cost of equipment is the first block. The issue is the extent to which a business can remove those constraints at a price that is viable for the identified market segments. This is an *enabling* approach to recreation business. The aim of the business is to enable participation by providing goods or services now otherwise unavailable to significant market segments. In order for this approach to be successful, the size of inhibited markets has to be carefully estimated.

CASE: THE COMPLEX MARKET FOR BOATS

The boat market can be crosscut in several different ways:

1. Type of boat: sailboat, powerboat, fishing boat, deck or pontoon boat, canoe, cabin cruiser, rowboat/dinghy, inflatable, special rafts and designs, homebuilts, and, of course, yachts
2. Use: racing (lake, offshore, etc.), waterskiing, fishing (deep sea, river, lake, trolling, etc.), auxiliary to another boat, family outings, cruising from port to port, weekends and vacation abroad, learning, and various combinations of uses
3. Size: from 5-foot inflatable dinghies to very long yachts

4. Cost: from $25 to $250,000
5. Quality: includes lines that stress the "most boat for the money" to the "cost is no object" exclusives
6. Accessories: radios, navigation electronics, comfort items, galleys, TV, stereos, radar, sonar, trailers, furnishings, extra sails, motors, fishing accessories, pumps, potties, safety equipment, etc.
7. Sales, service, rental, instruction, storage, and other functions

All these dimensions make it difficult to profile a typical dealer. Further, the on-site business usually combines a number of functions as well as sales lines. The average dealer carries five lines of boats and often several types. In 1982 the two major sources of income for marinas were repairs, service, and maintenance; and fuel sales, berths, storage, and other services. In order, the next revenue-producing areas of business were hardware, accessories, clothing, and supplies sales; new boat sales; used equipment; new motors; and other equipment.[6]

However, the percentages vary for the type and location of dealers. Rentals may be a major source at some locations and insignificant at others. In general, more of the income comes from services to boaters and less from sales than might be expected. The marina operator is in the enabling business first of all. Equipment sales and boat service are continuing elements of the business. Further, boat sales are highly competitive with buyers shopping over wide areas for the best prices and the "right" model of the boat sought. The marina is right there and in a less competitive position for ongoing trade and services. Further, the accessories market and the continual need for services tend to be less sensitive to economic cycles and changes.

For the marina operator the key is having a clearly defined picture of the local market. The kinds of boating practiced, the income levels of market segments, and the services needed all yield a profile of the operation. For example, a marina used heavily by weekend boaters who cannot trailer their boats will emphasize storage and repairs. On the other hand, a business next to a launching ramp for bass boats may stress equipment sales and service and other lines that enhance the fishing use of the resource. High-end sailing marinas may emphasize "mast-up storage" and berths for keel boats as well as designer sports apparel. A river-pool operation can find a growing market in the deckboat trade of family groups that want to spend time together on the water in relative comfort. The point is that marina operation can be quite varied and complex. However, few operations will try to do everything. The specialization is related to the resource and the kind of boaters drawn to its environment.

CASE: DESTINATION CAMPING

Destination camping businesses are different from en route camps in more than their locations. The en route camp draws a major part of its market from those traveling to a destination with some sort of special camping rig aboard or in tow. Destination camping is, for the most part, family camping. Further, while camping at public sites is often the only way to stay overnight at a desired location, the business-sector campground is seldom in a unique access position. There are usually alternative opportunities—public campgrounds, competing private facilities, motels and cabin businesses, and alternative locations.

What can the destination campground offer to maximize its markets? First, there is price. A high proportion of those choosing to camp as groups want to save money. The first rule of marketing is to offer as much as possible at a price that is measurably below other kinds of accommodations in the area. Since it is almost impossible to operate at price levels below those in public campgrounds, the business campground is often in a position of taking the overflow.

However, there are ways of utilizing such a position to increase return trade. One of the most effective is to offer certain kinds of activity resources that are not found in the public area. For example, since most camping groups consist of families with children, a well-designed play area away from the campsite in which younger children can safely meet and knock around is attractive to children and parents alike. Or a business campground may cater to the high-end older campers with great attention to the quality and accessibility of amenities such as showers, laundry areas, meeting rooms, and a convenience store. The question is the extent to which a private destination campground can provide extra amenities and still retain its price advantage over more elaborate accommodations. The greatest single asset of the destination campground is usually immediate access to the major recreation resource. Location is all-important.

CASE: MARKETING AN AREA

In many areas marketing may be cooperative as well as competitive. Recognizing that most destination-oriented vacation and weekend trips are planned in advance, one Wisconsin county engages in the winter distribution of an area vacation guide. The cover shows winter skiing and summer canoeing on a lake colored by a reflected sunset. The cover description is "Over 1300 lakes, trout streams, and forests." The remainder of the 48-page color booklet consists of illustrated advertising from over 100 businesses. Most are resorts on one of the lakes that place the visitor right at the resource and offer accommodations, meals, and a selection of activity opportunities. Beaches, playgrounds, boat rentals, waterskiing, and fishing are most common in the summer, and snowmobiling and skiing in the winter.

The businesses are highly competitive. In their advertising they try to emphasize the features that differentiate their offerings. However, the managers recognize that what they have to sell is the outdoor recreation environment. They offer ways to be in the environment and to use it. First of all, they have to reach markets hundreds of miles away and attract them to the area. They advertise a variety of levels of comfort and amenities *in that special environment.*

They also have to be aware of who is likely to come and what they will do there. The emphasis on fishing has to be balanced by recreation opportunities for vacation groups, usually families. According to the 1980 Wisconsin Camper Survey,[7] the most common activity is swimming, followed, in order, by walking, hiking, boating, and then fishing. Marketing an area with lake and forest recreation resources begins with knowing the target markets and what they seek from a trip that involves advance planning and a commitment of time and money.

Part of the secret to marketing outdoor recreation complements is an awareness that most resource use is not monothematic. People talk about a fishing trip, a camping expedition, or a sailing weekend. If the activity label were all that were involved, then the business supplier could concentrate in providing for that one activity. However, there are two added dimensions to most such resource use: First, others often come along who are less committed to the named activity. Marketing strategies may attempt to attract their interest and provide for their recreation in ways that create the likelihood of returns. Second, even those primarily engaged in the central activity usually spend some time in various social interaction activities and also secondary recreation. They not only eat and drink but they may seek other activity. Business opportunities may be created by an analysis of *who* is coming to the resource and of the actual time use of all in the groups.

TYPES OF OPERATIONS

The three main types of outdoor resource-based recreation and complements are retail sales and service, activity provisions, and environment bases. Each has parallels in businesses in residential communities, especially the retail and activity businesses. However, there are some differences in strategies and management related to the kind of resource environment.

RETAIL SALES AND SERVICES

Far and away the most common kind of complementary businesses are the on-site retail sales and service operations. For example, in 1980 the following sales were recorded for sailboats:[8]

	Units	*Retail Value*
Nonpowered boats	69,000	$181,677,000
Auxiliary-powered boats, 30 feet and under	1,100	32,230,000
Auxiliary-powered boats, over 30 feet	3,000	209,500,000

Further, the accessories markets add about as much to the retail business revenues. All sorts of equipment to add to the boat or to replace old items constitute a major part of most on-site businesses. Finally, there is the necessary and expected service of those products that are sold and of those that have been purchased elsewhere but are being used at that location. Some service trade is transient and some local. In any case, the product and service mix requires a complex set of operations when so many different goods and services are offered.

How does the resource-located retailer differ from the community retail store? First, the on-site retailer is dependent on the participation season. For the most part, there are no customers in the off-season unless there is a year-round location as part of the business. Second, sales are more related to participation. An inventory is usually tied more closely to what is actually used in the activity, be it fishing or waterskiing. Third, the store stock is for that particular use area rather than for the activity in general. Resources draw users who find that environment in some way superior to others for the way they engage in the activities. The retailer has to know *how* people engage in the activities and what is required in those modes of participation. Fourth, service is almost always at the heart of the business. When equipment is necessary for participation and people are already there in order to do the activity, an equipment failure is often a major setback. Prompt service, an adequate parts supply, and repair skills are essential to developing customer loyalty. Time is of the essence when a failure blocks engagement in which there is already the investment of time and money to be there.

In a community retail store the main lines of merchandise are the core of the business. The concept emphasizes sales, assortment, and often price. For the complementary business, support items and service may be more significant than the main product lines. It is always desirable to sell a boat, new skis, or a trailer. However, more likely the on-site business will sell a new propeller for the outboard, bindings for the old skis, or bearings for the trailer's seized wheels. As a consequence the approach and concept of the business not only stresses such support items but also has to receive an adequate profit from them. Interpreting the price structure of a business open on site for only five months of the year is often a difficult task when the customer complains that he could get it "at home" for 30% less.

A survey of marinas in Kentucky found that there are two basic types of such businesses. The first is a "resort" with a wide range of goods and services. There are facilities for the boater as well as for the boat. Considerable recreation time is spent out of the boat. The second image is that of the "boatyard" where the attention is given to the servicing and storage of the boats. In some cases the boatyard is not at the water site but at the place where the boats are stored.[9]

In the state of Kentucky alone, there are about 120 commercial marinas with some 16,000 moorage spaces, of which 44% are covered slips. The average marina has 135 moorage spaces and an occupancy rate of 91%. About 40% of the boats moored are 30 feet or longer in length. And the average cost of a marina was over $300,000 in 1979. Despite the heavy investment in moorage and docking facilities, moorage income accounted for only 30% of the gross revenues. The picture is of a business that is quite investment-intensive. In order to provide the services that draw the various kinds of retail trade, the marina operator has to invest in considerable water and land space, space that is usually expensive. It is no wonder that such businesses depend on households with considerable discretionary income to make up their markets.

However, an enabling approach can offer different business opportunities. For example, many water-based activities require equipment that is quite costly. This is true even of an activity such as sailboarding which is in turn less equipment-intensive than sailing larger boats. There are two problems with equipment costs. First, there is the inhibition of purchasing a $1,000 piece of equipment when you don't know whether or not the activity will be satisfying. Second, $1,000 may be just too much money to tie up in equipment for an activity that can be used only occasionally during a limited season. Therefore, rental businesses offer the activity to a wider set of users and potential buyers. They expand the market with a revenue-producing business concept. In some cases dealers even rent sailboats that belong to clients who visit the site only periodically. The dealer may sell the sailboard for $1,000 and receive the profit on the sale. When the board is rented, the dealer can receive $30 of the $40 per-day fee. In return the owner receives $10 a day for use and also avoids a storage fee. From a recreation perspective the rental service opens the possibility of beginning and continuing the activity to many who could not afford the initial purchase. In the long run the business also benefits by building potential sales markets. In the short term the business that has an instruction program may obtain revenue from instruction fees as well as the rental and sales.

Rentals are an important sector of recreation complement retailing. Transportation equipment, activity equipment, special clothing, tools and other repair items, and secondary amusement such as games may all be rented. Even an activity such as backpacking now supports many rental businesses as the equipment has become increasingly specialized and costly.

Selling is as important a part of the business on-site as elsewhere. It consists first of having what the recreation participants need for their use of the natural environment. However, it also means anticipating what might increase their enjoyment of the experience and being ready to offer appropriate goods and services. In general, recreation-related selling emphasizes the "cooperative" approach in which the salesperson and client engage in mutual problem solving. The end is to maximize the recreation experience. The customer who has entered the place of business seeking some item or service may be led to consider other possibilities that would enhance the excursion. In order to augment the original sale the businessperson has to take the time to become familiar with the background and aims of the customer. The adversary relationship of some selling should be avoided as the salesperson identifies with the aims and interests of the customer.

ACTIVITY PROVISIONS

A second type of complementary business actually provides the participation opportunity. The business sets up the canoe trip or the backpacking expedition. The only way of gaining a particular white-water experience may be through the businesses that have permits to use the river or access points. There is an increase in such business concepts and strategies as the variety of outdoor recreation activities increases. Such businesses are based on a series of factors in recreation participation:

1. *Cost* For some activities, particular items of equipment are required that are not cost-efficient for household ownership. A sailboat that is in a location where it will be used only for one or two weeks a year is uneconomical for all but a very few owners. The special rafts required for traversing a particular white-water river are too bulky to transport as well as expensive. Further, in some cases they are adapted for that particular set of conditions. On the other hand, public agencies are not likely to provide such equipment for the upper-income markets at locations distant from population centers.
2. *Skill* Other outdoor complements are based on the skills required for participation. Coping with strenuous conditions, learning to handle special equipment, and other such skills have to be taught. There is no innate ability to handle ropes on a cliff face, the lines on an ocean-going sailboat, or the controls of an ultralight aircraft. Again, such expensive activities are seldom introduced in public programs. Some sort of business enterprise is the usual skill-acquisition medium.
3. *Resource access* Although the ocean, a northern lake, or a major river may be public, gaining access may call for some sort of business facilitation.

Businesses often offer the only way to rent a boat on Lake Superior, hire a wilderness canoeing rig in Canada, fly into a remote fishing lake, get onto a wild river, or get up a mountain in order to ski down. In many locations the resource or the user population may be limited in ways that preclude more than one or two businesses developing viable user markets. As a consequence, *the* ski tow, canoe rental, or outfitting center for a particular resource is a single complementary business. The business is the primary way of using the outdoor recreation resource.

There are many examples of such businesses

Backpacking Experience Three requirements for a successful wilderness backpacking experience are locale selection, proper equipment, and a viable group. A beginner may be intrigued by the kinds of outcomes such activity yields, but lack knowledge and experience. Therefore, a basis for an auxiliary business is to augment a point-of-origin retail operation with several planned expeditions each year. The retailer with considerable experience selects an interesting locale, rents whatever equipment had not already been purchased, and forms a small group. The aim from the business perspective is to introduce new customers to the skills necessary to get started in an activity. The organized trips are a way of expanding the market for retail sales. However, in time the scheduling, managing, and leading of the trips may become the major job assignment of a staff member.

Rediscovering the Rivers A generation or two ago rivers were an important recreation resource in many parts of the country. They offered banks from which to fish and on which to picnic. They were often the basis for the rental of rowboats and canoes for quiet paddling by couples and small groups; and there were also the old riverboats that catered to weekend excursions and parties. There is still the general boating use, especially where the rivers are wide and deep enough to form expanses for maneuvering. There are still the various forms of fly-fishing on a Montana mountain stream to bottomfishing in the Mississippi mud. And there are a few excursion boats on major rivers. However, the new activity is river-running where the water flows fast and various impediments add to the excitement. To shoot the rapids in a special canoe, kayak, or raft rather than portage around has become a source of excitement as well as social gathering.

In some cases, the long and dangerous stretches of fast river can be entered only at certain points and require elaborate outfitting and experience. In those situations, one or more companies may be issued permits to carry passengers or organize groups. Other white water is more accessible, so that the business providers complement the resource with equipment rental, instruction, and retrieval services. The 200-mile stretch of the Colorado River running through the Grand Canyon is only the most famous of such resources. Shooting the rapids has become a recognized sport around the world with refinements in equipment and skills that depend on businesses for availability.

Also growing in participation are various kinds of rafting/tubing/floating in less exciting but more accessible rivers. Businesses are being developed at a variety of put-in locations alongside rivers that draw thousands who want to be in or on the water in warm weather. The businesses complement the resource in ways that are more oriented to refreshment, equipment provision, and transportation than to high levels of skill or challenge.

Winter in the Flatlands What do outdoor-oriented people do in the winter when they do not live in areas blessed with mountains? Some have the money to travel. Some stay inside and wait for summer. But more and more are finding ways to get outside. A study of winter resource-based recreation in Wisconsin[10] offered a number of insights into such activities. A few camp in the snow. Some hike and snowshoe. But more common are those who take to the woods and fields on snowmobiles and those who are engaged in cross-country skiing. Studies of participants in the two activities indicate a number of differences in their orientation to both the activity and to the resources. Those differences are acute enough so that some business concepts depend on protecting ski environments from snowmobilers.

However, the two types of winter outdoor enthusiasts have a number of things in common. First, they are attracted by the quality of the trails and environment. Second, they have made enough of an investment in equipment and plans that they will seek out the best opportunities. And, third, they tend to come in social groupings.

Business may be based on the provision of the basic resource itself when access to a trail network is owned or controlled. More often the business supports the resource use through offering instruction, equipment supply and repair, and a context for the social aspects of the activity. Snowmobilers often go from one warm gatheringplace to another. Nordic skiers are more likely to seek warmth, refreshment, and a place for interaction at or near their trail access point. Those who come with age peers and those who arrive as families may want somewhat different social opportunities. A variety of businesses may be responsive to different segments of the participant market in the same location. More commonly for the skiers, the trails are a necessary resource for the practice of the activity. Therefore, a business that can offer access to the resource may also gain considerable revenue from various support services.

Activity-provision businesses seldom can provide the only resource for participation available. However, the key to this approach is to identify an attractive activity or set of activities that are inhibited in *that market area* by resource limitations.

CASE: COMBINING FINANCE AND RECREATION INTO A BUSINESS

The market is not an enormous one, but it can be profitable. First, the purchase of a used 32-foot sailboat for $50,000 is a major purchase decision for even those high incomes. Second, when that boat can be transported only at considerable cost and inconvenience, its use is limited largely to one base and one climate. Therefore, sailing in the Gulf of Mexico in the winter and in one of the Great Lakes in the summer in the same boat is precluded. Third, smaller boats that might be more movable by trailer do not provide the comfort, stability, and safety for offshore sailing required by this market segment. Fourth, upper-income households are always interested in the tax implications of financial decisions. After-tax costs for those in high tax brackets may mean that items are purchased and maintained with dollars that cost less than 50 cents. Fifth, most people do not want to commit all their available time to a single activity or environment.

The business concept is simple. Over one hundred larger sailboats are handled in a charter business with two locations, one at a harbor near a Great Lakes area of great sailing appeal due to its islands and the other at a popular Florida center on the Gulf. At least that was the beginning. Owners of boats or those interested in such a purchase could place their boat at one of the two locations. By sailing it no more than two weeks themselves, they would be able to show depreciation and upkeep as business expenses. Interest on any loan was also deductible. In the plan boat owners would still have their own boat with priority on the time they wanted, a major tax write-off, access to boats in the other location for reverse-season sailing, and assurance that their boat was being cared for during all those weeks they did not see it.

The simple business concept developed into something more complex. In time the demand was so great that two more locations were added. The corporation now operates marinas in three states, has a major brokerage business selling new and used craft, conducts sailing schools, organizes special 3-, 5-, and 8-day vacation packages, and has resorts at two marina sites. Special discounts are offered in the off-seasons and boats are also available for day rental. Of course, selling, maintaining, and repairing all the equipment on such boats is also a major part of the business.

The tax advantages to such up-market clientele who then provide the equivalent of close to $5 million in capital for the business is a special aspect of this business. In that sense it is similar to condominium management in resort areas. However, it is also an enabling approach. The kind of sailing that would otherwise be limited to very wealthy owners is opened to a new market, those with adequate discretionary income to afford the $1,000-a-week charter but not the capital and upkeep costs of ownership. The constraint of ownership costs is reduced both for the owners who join the charter organization and for those who prefer the flexibility of rental. Further, the charter management center spins off a number of other revenue-producing business elements.

ENVIRONMENT BASE BUSINESSES

A third kind of business is the provision of a base of operations for the recreation use of an outdoor resource. Included are a number of the most familiar businesses such as campgrounds and activity-oriented resorts. These have been discussed previously in the chapter on destination. However, there are some resource-related aspects of such businesses that may be emphasized here.

As already outlined, the quality of the resource is the basis for such a business. In recreation decision contexts in which there are alternatives, an activity-based business is in a competitive climate. There are other places to go and other activities. Second, access to the resource is crucial. It is not arbitrary that "beachfront" usually means a marked price increase over "beach access." It is for this reason that both Alpine and Nordic ski-resort businesses usually include lift or trail tickets as part of the vacation package. Third, such a business needs to be conceived with an understanding of what goes into the total set of provisions in order to achieve the participation satisfactions anticipated. Recreation experiences tend to be more complex than the labels of "skiing," "sailing," or "fishing" suggest.

Location, then, is all-important. One problem is that land with prime access to the water, mountain, or other resource may be either public and unavailable for purchase or under ownership with investment aims and a high asking price for any sale. Any calculation concerning land purchases must balance the factors of access to a quality resource with projected rate of return on the investment. The most desirable location may be priced out of its business potential. It requires the combination of proximity to a major population center and/or a recreation resource of extraordinary quality with a limited potential of access to justify high levels of investment. This is why the owners of many marinas, resorts, and other such businesses maintain that they could not start such a business today at current real estate costs.

The other side of the issue is the development of markets. For example, the costs of a major boat marina adjacent to a city may be prohibitive. Waterfront property at thousands of dollars a front foot—or more—cannot be repaid at interest by even a high-end operation. However, there may be opportunities that do not require such a real estate investment. One would be the growth of board sailing. Near Chicago one business has expanded since 1980 by exploiting public resources. The business has three levels of instruction courses that include the use of sailboards, dry-land simulation, wet suits in colder weather, safety equipment, and everything else necessary for training. The cost is kept low enough so that relatively few who might be interested are ruled out. Even the full ten-hour course is less then $100. Further, those who complete this course become new markets for rentals and sales. The business is the base of the activity introduction and participation but does not have the heavy investment costs associated with boats or resorts. The concept combines a relatively new activity with a major population base having large numbers in the market segment of youths of moderate means.

CASE: A TRADITIONAL ACTIVITY BASE

Actually, there are hundreds of "Elk Lake Wilderness Canoe Trip" businesses. They have been a major means of entry into backcountry canoeing and fishing areas for decades. Their seasons are limited. They must attract first-time clients who have never seen the exact location. And they have to supply, at least for some visitors, almost everything needed except clothing.

One such business is located in northern Minnesota and takes its clients into the Canadian lake country. They are an *outfitting post* with rental of canoes, gear, tents, sleeping bags, packs, and utensils. Special food supplies and bug repellent are sold. They offer guide services in which an experienced leader will take a group. They will provide a "catered" trip in which meals are a part of the package and a variety of menus can be selected in advance. Or the outfitter will rent just the equipment needed by the party, who bring some of their own equipment and supplies.

In the beginning the main activity was fishing. Therefore, the fishing season was *the* time in which all the investment in equipment had to be recovered. However, in recent decades wilderness canoeing itself has taken over as the primary resource use. The season is extended considerably—although it is still relatively brief—and the composition of the parties has changed. Now more family groups come together, and the former all-male expedition is less common. The importance of the planned vacation orientation has also meant that many women are attracted to the activity, with the understanding that meals will be provided.

The change to family markets has also led to an expansion of the base operation. Now there is a lodge with a restaurant and a set of cabins. This not only serves as a base for striking out into the wilderness but also as a first-time or tryout experience for some who are not sure they are prepared to take off into the wilderness for a week or longer.

Environment base businesses may offer chiefly a place from which to use the outdoor resource. Often campgrounds are placed to provide entry into the forest or access to the water at a reasonable overnight cost. Others provide a full set of services that together enable people to participate in resource-based recreation. In either case there is an essential complementarity between the business and the resource. The base needs to be designed and marketed for the kinds of people who use that resource. The markets need to be carefully identified and segmented so that what may be a considerable investment is not misdirected.

An approach to all activity- and base-providing recreation businesses that often opens new markets is the lease and rental arrangement. A major limiting factor in much resource-based recreation is the cost of owning equipment and/or facilities that can be used only periodically. Just as important, many people hesitate to make an investment in such items before they are sure that the activity and environment will provide outcomes they want to incorporate into their regular leisure patterns. Therefore, rentals, leases, leasebacks, and other such business approaches may have greater growth potential than those that depend on retail purchases, especially when costs are high and the development of new skills and tastes are necessary to test the outcomes of the activity.

BUSINESS OPERATIONS

Again, we do not want to repeat the material on operations and management from previous chapters. The functions of management for any retail business are applicable to outdoor complement firms. Here we will introduce only a few issues of special relevance.

RESOURCE DEPENDENCE

The central difference between outdoor complements and other businesses is their direct dependence on the specific recreation resource. For example, when Lake Michigan underwent a cycle of invasion by lampreys and the destruction of the fishing resource, any number of businesses failed or moved. Only after the countering alewives were in turn checked by the introduction of coho salmon did the return of lake trout signal the renewal of the lost resource.

A resource complement recreation business cannot exist without the resource to which it is tied. Every management policy, access change, public pricing policy, use regulation, and improvement or degradation of the resource will impact on the business. In some cases the business can be reoriented to meet and even take advantages of changes. In other cases the survival of the business may mean engagement in political and social action.

When the recreation resource is in the public domain, the first stance of the business operator should be one of cooperation. In both day-to-day management and in planning for the future the business and resource managers should cooperate. In order to do this the essential complementarity of the two sectors needs to be recognized and understood. The mission of the public sector manager is to protect and enhance the resource in ways that enable current use by the public without endangering its long-term viability and quality. The aim of the business provider is to offer goods and services that maximize the satisfaction of those who use the resource for recreation. Anything that damages the resource is counter to the public interest and a danger for the business.

This has a number of implications for the business operation:

- Equipment in the inventory for sale or rent should be selected for its compatibility with the environment. For example, high-powered boats and motors endanger certain kinds of fragile shorelines and marshlands. A marina or fishing base business should promote kinds of boating appropriate to the environment.
- Information about the resource, regulations concerning its use, and recommendations for its preservation may be distributed through the business. The business can serve as a contact point for users so that the resource managers come to rely on the business to transmit important information to resource users.
- In turn, the business interests should be represented on any kind of planning committee for the resource. Public managers who do not include the business perspectives in their consultation about management policies are risking ignorance and even conflict that is both costly and unnecessary.
- An especially critical factor is access to the recreation resource. This includes such items as parking, equipment launching and storage, location of access, regulation of entries, and safety provisions. Again, the business and the public manager may be able to cooperate in ways that are mutually beneficial. For example, a common problem for the management of outdoor recreation resources is entry outside designated access points that are damaging to the environment and prevent the application of safety precautions such as registration and checkout. The business personnel can act to minimize such entries in their role as recreation advisors. In turn, the public managers may consult with the complementary business as they plan new or revised access points.

The point is that the complementarity between public and market sectors becomes especially acute for the resource-dependent business. While the public providers are unlikely to become outfitters and retailers, they require such provisions if the resources are to be utilized for safe and satisfying recreation. Business aims and interests ought not to be in conflict with public welfare, at least in the long run.

Mutual support and cooperation between the two sectors may involve the business operator in various kinds of voluntary organizations and political activity. Resource managers, especially those concerned with recreation, are involved in struggles for scarce resources in personnel and budget, in adjusting regulations to their particular resource and missions, and dealing with the communication problems of any large organization. The business interests can be invaluable in using the democratic political processes and instrumentalities to assist the public manager in developing support for policies of mutual benefit. Sometimes this may be done through national or regional organizations or trade associations. Just as often there are more local government entities—county boards and national forest chiefs—who may need to be lobbied, educated, and persuaded.

ONGOING OPERATIONS ISSUES

While all the management functions already introduced are of significance, there are special issues related to outdoor recreation complements.

First, such businesses range in size but tend to be small or moderate in scope. For the smaller businesses, often located far from the centers of wholesale distributions, obtaining supplies and inventory may be a problem. Location can escalate wholesale prices. Now in a number of recreation businesses, purchasing syndicates have been formed that combine the buying power of large numbers of businesses. The usual scheme is for member businesses to pay a one-time membership fee and a yearly fee. In return they may receive discounts of 15% to 35% on common items for their inventories. Further, the united buying power is organized in such a way that the distribution potential of the syndicate is sought by firms with new or improved products. The small retail business may be in the forefront of product introduction rather than far behind the urban chain.

Second, the common seasonality of such businesses calls for a well-constructed month-by-month accounting system. Break-even analysis, cash flow forecasts, and other accounting procedures may be of critical importance if the in-season profit margins are to sustain the business for the full year. Add to the regular seasonality the dependence on the specifics of weather as well as the framework of climate and the problems escalate. Can the business weather a wet and cold summer or a dry and warm winter? The overall financial position of the business may be subjected to extraordinary stresses. When the primary reason for entering the business was to live in the recreation environment and be engaged in related activity, then the likelihood of interest in rigorous accounting and financial analysis is not high. As a result the survival rate of such businesses often depends on conditions that are no longer possible—ownership of land, location, buildings, and equipment that were bought prior to inflation and with a replacement cost ten times or more the original investment. Today, in a recreation business climate that is likely to become increasingly competitive, careful financial management is crucial to success.

Third, personnel are also a critical area for such businesses. Like many other types of recreation business, the outdoor complement tends to be quite service-oriented and personnel-intensive. The relationship between staff and customers may make the difference between repeat business and customers who choose to do their business and recreation elsewhere the next season. Securing staff who are adept in customer relationships and knowledgeable in the recreation-related line of goods and services is difficult enough. Retaining such staff season after season, especially if the business does not operate the year around, may be even harder. As a result the full participation of the owner-operators of the business in training, supervising, supporting, and helping other personnel is necessary in businesses that require considerable in-season employment. In some situations student help can offer a partial solution but poses the problems of transience and commitment when career opportunities are absent.

CASE: COMPETITION AS PROMOTION

Most waterskiers are vacation participants or "weekend warriors" for whom the activity is a summer enthusiasm. Most often they were introduced to the sport by friends, learned some basic skills, and then found opportunities to continue. Those who become regulars and are the major market for skis, equipment, and the costly boats capable of towing have made a commitment to the combined benefits of the water environment, skill development in a strenuous activity, and social interaction. They usually gain information by being around other skiers at the businesses where they obtain necessary service and equipment. Much of the exchange is informal and in response to questions about varieties of skis, boats, and locales for participation.

However, the position of a dealer is different. In an area in New England where several reservoirs and rivers offer places for waterskiing, there are many dealers both on-site and in the cities. Competition is keen for customers. How can a business be recognized as a superior source of goods and services?

In marketing there are always the elements of price and product. However, one dealer decided to emphasize promotion. Because of his experience as a competitive boat racer and judge, he was able to offer logistical support for a number of competitions. Providing drivers and standardized ski boats—one primary and one backup—gained access to the contest site and the right to place the business insignia on the tow boats. Also, some display was usually possible. Since most of the spectators at the ski tournaments are amateur skiers, this allows the shop to be established as a "special" resource for skiers. It is associated with high-level skills, expertise, and support of the sport.

Providing the service to clubs that sponsor competitions is one way of engaging in promotion that distinguishes the store from its competition. It can become a place to go when advice is needed on equipment upgrading and improvement of skills. The image of the store is tied visibly to the aims of an important segment of the market, those who want to improve their skills demonstrably. The store is also associated with the prestige of demonstrations of skill in the activity.

CASE: POSITIONING

A ski shop at the slopes had no direct competition for years. The shop was the only place to arrange for instruction, get repairs, or buy or rent equipment within 35 miles of the state forest ski area. Then two changes occurred. In two of the towns that were major sources of weekend skiers for the resource new ski supply shops opened. Second, another ski area opened in the same forest but two miles away and entered from a different highway. Now there were two places to ski as well as point-of-origin competition for equipment sales and care.

One strategy would be simply to accept the losses and tailor the business to the remainder of the market that would continue to need on-site services. The problem with this was that it not only meant a cutback in business volume, with consequences for the building lease and inventory, but also might start a trend toward decreasing trade that would in turn reduce what the firm could offer.

Another strategy was to engage in the marketing tactic called positioning. Just what were the advantages of the business, its location, history, clientele, personnel, and opportunities? Were there particular market segments that could be reached if the business were to develop an image that would be especially appealing to those consumers? In this case the analysis began with the resource. The slopes in the second area were less steep and more likely to attract beginners and groups with several levels of skill. Therefore, the business began a program of advertising, promotion, and services that would appeal to those with a higher skill level. The market position sought was that of a special supplier and gatheringplace for the "real" skiers who come to test and develop their skills in the most challenging environment. The next question was just how to announce this new position to the right market segments. What might such repositioning mean for store layout, personnel selection, repair and instruction services, and retail inventories?

BUSINESS GROWTH

The aim of most businesses is to grow. There is the assumption that growth will lead to greater efficiencies of scale, higher profits, and more sharing of responsibilities among staff. However, growth may not come automatically just by staying in business. Growth usually involves some planning for development of opportunities.

How can the managers of a business plan for growth? There are the initial factors of organizing the business in a form that allows for growth and diversification. Further, the structures, records, decision-making processes, financing, and tax position should be planned with the possibility of expansion. The intention is not to close off possible avenues prematurely.

On the other hand, some recreation businesses are not more profitable for the owner, more satisfying to operate, or more efficient when they become larger. The aims and philosophy of the owners may not be to create a company with complex financing, structure, and operations. A small business that specializes, is in contact with a viable market segment, is well located for both trade and for the life-style of the owner, and allows for concentration on the product or service the owners know best may be highly efficient and satisfying to operate. However, such a philosophy has to contend with the real world of business, a world in which various forms of competition may threaten the specialist. Or, with an outdoor recreation complement, some alteration in the recreation resource may require changes in a previously viable business. Any business has to be prepared for change.

What is the optimum size for a recreation-related business? Of course, it depends on the aims of the owners, market area, type of goods and services provided, participation trends in related activities, and several geographical factors. What works in Kansas City may be inappropriate in Westchester County and impossible in Miami. What does seem to be evident is that larger is not always better. Here are questions that can be asked in the process of considering expansion:

- Will enlargement or diversification of the business reach larger markets in the area? Is there a measurable demand?
- Is capital available for expansion? What will necessary borrowing do to the costs of doing business?
- How much of the expansion cost is irretrievable? Will the change call for investment in equipment, facilities, real estate, training, or other preparation that cannot be disposed of in case the markets do not develop?
- What will be the personnel requirements? Are staff with the skills and experience required available in the area or will expansion involve costly training or relocation?
- What will be the management requirements of growth? Are the present managers competent to handle the enlarged and more complex responsibilities or will new management be necessary?
- What will be the impacts of growth on the lives of the principals in the business? Will life-styles, primary relationships, and other commitments be curtailed in ways that may create dissatisfaction?
- Will growth alter the style and aims of the business to the extent that some of the current issues may be jeopardized?

In general, it cannot be presumed that bigger is always better. The flexibility and personal style of modest size may be much more compatible with a service-oriented recreation business than expansion and diversification. Efficiency is measured by customer and worker satisfaction as well as by how many widgets are sold per week or how many canoes can be routed through a chain of lakes per month. Efficiency may be measured by the extent to which the aims of the business are achieved, by quality as well as quantity. Just as natural resources are to be managed for the long term, so a resource-based business may be oriented toward providing its service well over the working lifetime of its owners. Growth should be evaluated in terms of a life satisfaction "bottom line" as well as an accounting balance. Then the organizational and financial questions can be analyzed and decisions made.

CASE: CALCULATED EXPANSION

The rental costs of the marina location required growth. Increases in taxes and land costs had led the landlord to raise the lease price. Now the manager had to find some way of increasing revenue or give up either the business or the location.

An analysis of possibilities yielded a number of limitations. There was no space for more storage or mooring. The boat sales market seemed about saturated, with replacement sales level over several years. Competition had limited the proportion of the regional boating market that would be attracted to this particular site and business.

However, an examination of financial records revealed two possible sources of increased revenue in the same place and space. One was the growth of the rental business, especially for younger or beginning power boaters. The problem with expanding this part of the business was that it is space-intensive. It requires mooring, storing, and launching more boats. The second growth trend had been in accessories and especially electronics. Boat owners who did not plan to change boats seemed to be buying equipment for the craft they owned. Whatever the reason—safety, novelty, enhancement of the experience, or just being "gadget-happy"—the sale of electronic equipment for radio communication, direction and navigation, and fish location had been a growth area in sales.

From this analysis the decision was made to stock more electronics and expand the repair facilities. Trade representatives were contacted, other dealers questioned, and a repair expert who was willing to relocate hired. Two lines of products were selected and arrangements made with the distributors. Sales personnel attended workshops introducing the product lines. The repair shop was renovated. And from other dealers it was found that electronics were most often sold in "packages." These combinations of integrated items would perform their functions best when linked to compatible equipment. Most electronics sales were made in $5,000 packages of functionally integrated systems. The markup on such goods is high, the warranty and repair business consistent, and the market among boat owners renewable by the introduction of innovative products. In this case growth was necessary. Emphasizing a new line allowed for business growth without changing the location or space requirements for doing business.

PUBLIC SECTOR AND BUSINESS COMPLEMENTARITY

The general complementarity of public recreation and the market sector is a theme that has been repeated throughout this book. It is demonstrated most clearly in the outdoor resource-based recreation complement. The business often cannot exist without the public resource. On the other hand, considerable use of resources justifying their public retention and management depends on business provisions.

The first rule of engaging in such business, then, is cooperation. As already suggested, the business and resource management interests are in long-term compatability more often than not. Cooperation and communication about short-term operations can be carried out in a framework that presumes that each needs the other. For example, while some kind of access restriction or vehicle use may impact on a business that depends on getting people and canoes to backcountry lakes and rivers, a reasonable application of the restrictions will permit the businesses to operate in an environment that will continue to be a richer wilderness experience for the clients. In some cases the conflict may be between, on the one hand, local residents who have come to define the resource as theirs to do with as they wish and, on the other, the public and business managers who seek to preserve some special qualities of the environment.

But what about the basic aims of public welfare and private gain? Is there some inherent conflict that underlies even the most amicable relationship? For example, public recreation programs are based on a principle of equity that ensures some unbiased right of access and even favors those with the most restricted opportunities. Business management, on the other hand, is aimed at profit for the investors in that business. While a long view may seek less immediate profit in the pursuit of business stability, the aim of producing a return on investment and opportunity costs remains.

A second basis of public resource management is the conservation of the resource. The business, on the other hand, seeks to maximize access to the resource in order to increase markets for its products and services. The more backpackers, rafters, or swimmers come, the more the business will prosper. Management practices that limit the use of a resource also limit markets. How, for example, is a marina operator to respond to a regulation that limits motor size and boat speeds in an estuarial bay in order to stop damage to the marsh plants that protect the land, absorb tidal flow, and are the home of countless creatures?

In some situations it is possible to negotiate for variety. One lake may be managed for maximum recreation use with several campgrounds on its shores, zones for all kinds of boating, and leases for businesses that provide entertainment to campers and other water users. It may be an "urbanized" recreation area. A nearby lake, usually the one more protected in location, may be managed for "purity." Campgrounds are set back from the water and campsites limited in number, vehicle access is restricted, powerboats are prohibited, and other management practices aimed toward preserving the quality of the environment for appreciative use. But what about unique resources in locations where there is only one such river, lake, or mountainside?

The problem is the condition of scarcity. In the Pacific Northwest there may be the luxury of abundance of resources; in Virginia or Ohio there may be more potential users than resources; yet the quality of resources and long-term conservation are issues there, too. In those conditions reconciliation of legitimate aims is not simple. Users and the businesses that provide for them have rights. However, some uses create irretrievable impacts on the environment and alter the quality of future use.

The obvious fact that outdoor recreation does require a resource base and the implication that the quality of the resource will be a factor in the recreation experience do not lead to a solution of the dilemma. Probably most "solutions" will be compromises and have to be developed for the specific situation rather than as general rules. If this is so, then communication and cooperation between the market and public sector managers and decision makers are all the more important. In that cooperation business interests that develop concepts and plans that exploit public resources for the few at the eventual cost of the resource itself are neither socially responsible nor follow sound business policy.

SUMMARY OF ISSUES

There are many business opportunities that enable recreation participation using public resources. They include both on-site and population-center firms.

Formation of a complementary business begins with an analysis of what is required for recreation at the resources, factors limiting participation, and how marketing may increase participation.

The business concept includes evaluation of the resource, its size, accessibility, quality, travel and participation costs, and both primary and secondary uses.

Market analysis incorporates environmental factors of climate and ecology as well as user segments ordered in a hierarchy of commitment.

An enabling approach to the business concept may increase markets by facilitating participation.

Retail sales and service businesses concentrate on use-related products, with service as an essential ingredient in marketing.

Activity providers offer cost reductions, special skills, and access to a resource in ways that increase the efficiency of equipment use and resource maintenance as well as capital investment.

Access to the resource is the primary factor in environment-base enterprises. Facilitation offerings such as rental and leasing may open lower-end markets.

Resource dependence calls for cooperation with public managers as well as coping with all the problems associated with seasonality.

Appropriate scale is more than a continual attempt to grow. Growth has impacts on owner/managers as well as on the requirements for management and capital.

Equity in access and long-term conservation are most likely to conflict with short-term business aims in a condition of scarcity.

DISCUSSION QUESTIONS

1. How many specific kinds of outdoor recreation resource complement businesses are there? Can a list be exhaustive?
2. In what ways may complementary business provisions increase use of a resource for recreation? Give examples.
3. What are the critical factors in analyzing whether an outdoor resource can support a business complement?
4. Take a case in your area and apply the market analysis questions under "Participation Potential" to it. How can inhibited participation be estimated?
5. How do on-site and point-of-origin businesses compete? What are the advantages of each?
6. How is expertise in the resource-based recreation important to operating an on-site business?
7. Why are up-market resource complements so attractive? Are there ways to alleviate the investment problems of high-cost locations?
8. What are the relative merits of locating near a population center with its competitive climate and at a more remote resource location?

9. What are common conflicts between public resource and business managers? How can they be reconciled?
10. Give examples of how the limitations of seasonality can be minimized.
11. How can promotion be more cost-effective than advertising? Give examples.
12. When may bigger not be better?

PROJECTS

1. Use the "Market Segmentation Structure" outline to analyze an accessible outdoor complement business.
2. Develop a case study of a resource complement recreation business.

REFERENCES

1. Chubb, Michael and H. R. Chubb. *One Third of our Time?,* p. 417. New York: Wiley, 1981.
2. Ibid., p. 514.
3. Kelly, John R. *Leisure,* pp. 400–402. Englewood Cliffs, NJ: Prentice-Hall, 1982.
4. Ibid., p. 407.
5. Cooper, R. B., P. S. Sadowske, and M. D. Kantor. *Wisconsin Winter Recreation Study.* Madison: Recreation Resources Center, 1979.
6. *Boating Industry,* May 1983:53f.
7. Cooper, R. B., R. Novak, and K. A. Henderson. *1980 Wisconsin Camper Survey.* Madison: Recreation Resources Center, University of Wisconsin—Extension, 1980.
8. *Boating Industry,* May 1983.
9. Kreag, G. M. *1979 Business Information Analysis of the Kentucky Marina Industry.* Princeton, Ken.: Research and Education Center, University of Kentucky, 1980.
10. Cooper et al., 1980.

11 RECREATION PRODUCTS

ISSUES

What is the relationship of product development to recreation participation?

What are the differences between inventions and innovations? Between innovations and improvements? Which has the greatest market potential?

What are the common sources of new products?

Why are the eight stages of product development sequential rather than concurrent?

How are new product concepts based on recreation participation?

What are major criteria for evaluating a new product idea?

What are the major business factors in new product development?

What market elements are crucial in each stage of the development of new recreation products?

Why do most new products fail to attain profitable markets?

Are new recreation services developed in much the same way as new products?

Retail stores, community activity facilities, travel-related services and resources, and outdoor recreation opportunities are all part of the entire recreation business spectrum. Each of these segments provides some selection of resources for recreation participation. And each utilizes in their offerings a variety of things that are produced for recreation use. This chapter will introduce the development and marketing of those "things," recreation-oriented products.

TYPES OF RECREATION PRODUCTS

No list of all those "things" is possible. They range from special-length shoelaces to $500,000 ocean yachts, from socks to surfboards, and from caps to computers. Here we can examine the process by which products are developed and brought to the market, but the elements of discovery, process of design, and criteria of profitability differ for each item. The cases in this chapter are illustrative, but of issues and processes rather than being precise instructions for launching any specific product. Just a classification of types of products indicates why product development will vary widely in aims and methods.

Types of Recreation Products

Type	*Example*
Sports	User equipment: racquets, clubs, balls, etc.
	User apparel, shoes, etc.
	Facility items: surfaces, goals, etc.
	Instructional equipment: from batting cages to fishing lines
	Special facilities: artificial ski slopes, half-size tennis, softball, training apparatus, etc.
Services	Environmental care for grass, surfaces, amenities, etc.
	Safety equipment
	Storage lockers, etc.
	Food preparation equipment
	Maintenance equipment and products
Arts	Instruments and equipment
	Facility design and maintenance
	Amenities
	Auxiliary services and products such as tickets, refreshment dispensers, etc.
	Recording equipment
Technology based	Fiberglass, epoxy, or other products requiring a materials expertise

	Computer products for management, fitness measurement, or the activity itself
	Plastic parts, products, and other items requiring molding technologies
	Other electronics
Hobby based	Tools for material shaping, cutting, fastening, etc.
	Storage for collections
	Materials for fashioning products
	Means of distribution or communication
Market-segment oriented	Playground equipment
	Corporate-fitness equipment, guides, and programs
	Amusement park games, rides, prizes, and related items
	Residential pool auxiliary equipment, maintenance, additions, etc.
	Activity-defined products involved in engagement in any recreation activity
	Special population adaptations and aids

Any of these can be directed primarily toward the *provider*—the school, public recreation program, activity-oriented business, resort, service, instruction program, or any other agent offering resources for participation. Or the product can be aimed directly at the *user*—the recreation participant who is expected to provide a market for the product because it enables or enhances the recreation experience. Some products will be used by both providers and participants. Others will be distributed through providers to participants. Some will be the resource. A surface that permits summer or indoor downhill skiing becomes the basis for the program, whether offered by a public agency or a business. The possibilities are infinite, even without including innovative services among the products that call for the sequence of product development outlined here.

WHAT IS A NEW PRODUCT?

If a product is something that is designed, made, developed, and distributed, then there are at least three kinds of *new* products: A product may be new as an improvement, innovation, or invention.

Most products introduced to the market are *improvements* on others that are already available. In the recreation field the improvement may be in lower cost, increased performance, enhanced safety, greater flexibility, or general attractiveness. The redesign may be primarily aesthetic or functional. The product may look better or it may work better. However, it still does what others do. It does not alter the activity or the mode of doing the activity. A camping trailer may be lighter and less costly to produce. A sailboat may be easier to manufacture. A tennis racquet may have a different set of laminations in the frame. A court surface may dry faster. A snowmobile may use less gas. The main aim of product improvement is to gain a better market position. The improvement does not change the market but may give the firm some theme for promotion. Improvement is, in this sense, competition-directed.

However, some new products are *innovations.* An innovation is a different design, material, or combination that changes the way the activity is performed. A larger tennis racquet of new materials may not only be more durable than traditional wood but may actually make a difference in how some aspects of the game are played. The introduction of fiberglass in boats not only drastically reduced maintenance and prolonged life but also increased performance. It made boating quite different and more accessible. A new surface may transform the nature of an outdoor sport in rainy weather. Design and incorporation of new material may reduce the weight of weather-protection gear for backpacking by 70% and make possible the conquest of more difficult terrain. New types of materials may lower the cost of recreation equipment so much that the number who can afford participation is greatly increased. Or an innovative instruction technique like Suzuki string programs for the violin may open an activity to an entire new set of learners. Innovations do more than provide a better market share for a product; they employ different design, materials, or other resources that change the activity. In many ways innovations are the most attractive product developments because they build on current participation and still create new markets.

However, less frequently there are new products that are *inventions.* The invention, from this perspective, creates a new activity. The frisbee was an invention, even though it employed known principles of motion and techniques of manufacture. In its time any equipment that became the basis of a kind of activity not experienced before was an invention. The outboard motor was once an invention as was the roller skate, bicycle, and inflatable ball. An entire sport may be an invention, such as basketball. Electronic inventions have created games so different as to be more invention than innovation, especially when they can be packaged in home units. However, note how quickly an invention moves into the innovation phase and then to a proliferation of "improvements" to enhance market positions. In so many recreation product areas, the "latest" thing, not only this year but for the past twenty, has been just more of the same. The risk for inventions in recreation is great because it is impossible to predict just how successfully a new product can be introduced to the market and attract a number of people willing to learn new skills, recruit new partners, and make an investment in a new activity.

PRODUCT CYCLES AND COMPANY OBJECTIVES

The picture of the lone genius working in a garage to design something new and different is not irrelevant to recreation product development. Someone engaged in an activity may well be the originator of a new product. However, there is a full range of originators of new products: from the design or sales engineering department of the recreation products division of an international conglomerate to the lone craftsman in the home workshop. In the recreation field many mid-sized companies are involved in the development and marketing of products. Some concentrate on a technology. They may produce fiberglass items, for example, for many different recreation activities. Others manufacture and/or distribute items related to a type of institutional buyer, such as a school, or they cluster around a particular type of recreation, such as camping. Some sell primarily to dealers, such as the manufacturer of portable heads for boats or mobile homes. Others seek to market directly to users, such as the developer of a new ski rack for compact cars who advertises in participant-oriented magazines.

THE ISSUE OF SCALE

The size and scope of the business enterprise is a major factor in the mode of product development. For example, a cross-country skier may suffer from cold hands in the early stages of an outing but find that gloves warm enough at that stage are too heat-retentive after a half hour. One solution is a type of glove liner that can be worn for a time and then removed and compactly stowed away. The developer, sure of a market if the product can be developed, invests considerable time and several thousand dollars into designing and making up models of several different weaves and materials. The development may be a one-person operation until the time comes for manufacture and marketing. Then an established company is likely to be asked to enter into an agreement for manufacture and possibly marketing as well.

On the other hand, considerable product development, even in recreation, is accomplished according to corporation procedures and objectives.[1] A company may already produce a number of recreation-related products. As a result the firm already has certain manufacturing capabilities, a marketing and distribution network in place, and a corporate image. They are "known" for certain kinds of products. The product, usually a matter of improvement or innovation rather than invention, is in line with the company image and objectives and utilizes the on-line resources of the company. However, a new product line may be complementary to those already in the market rather than competing. For example, manufacturers of snowmobiles faced a downward trend in sales, indicating that the peak of the product cycle had passed. They already had their dealer systems and manufacturing capabilities for motorized vehicles. They were also known for snow-travel vehicles. The development sections of firms sought to develop a different motorized recreational vehicle that would complement their existing lines. In time they came up with the motorized large-tired tricycle that could be used for off-road play in the snow and in rough terrain in summer. It also could be marketed outside the Snowbelt as a complement to another line of products, the motorcycle. The product was initiated out of corporate aims rather than participation analysis.

And there are other dimensions of scope. One is geographical. A product may be designed and developed for a specific culture, environment, or even institutional type. For example, a type of paddleboat may be designed for rental operations in Florida amusement parks. The design may have little or no appeal elsewhere. At the other extreme, a multinational corporation has a division that does nothing but investigate and develop products for the international market. Their responsibilities include assessing the markets in different cultures for products developed within a national economy and also proposing product revisions that will make them more marketable in other countries. For example, the development, retrenchment, withdrawal, and eventual reentry of bowling centers in the United Kingdom from North America involved in a reevaluation of the cultural expectations of the British for amenities at a recreation facility. The standard package that had been successful in North America had failed in another English-speaking culture. One reason was the association of community recreation for male groups with access to a pub-type atmosphere.

Recreation is a major segment of business in every "developed" economy. Seeking possible development of markets in other regions, countries and continents is a natural progression from any localized success. However, such expansion requires an evaluation of the "fit" of the product into the resource and cultural contexts of another place. Leisure styles are not universal. Given adequate promotion, some products will make their own markets in almost any culture. Others have to be redesigned for the styles and value systems of other possible markets. Product development, then, is in touch with the potential user. Recreation products are based in recreation experiences.

CORPORATE AIMS AND IMAGES

For some corporations recreation products are only one line of many. However, even in those cases the recreation line usually has some special image identified by a brand name or trademark. Other firms are more specialized and market only in recreation or, more narrowly, in one type of recreation. A firm that specializes is most likely to be knowledgeable about the participation requirements and patterns of that activity. They have their own sales trends as well as a network of informants feeding back information that can assist in product development. Further, they have many ways of testing markets as well as products.

In the case of new or smaller firms the product may create or revise the image. For example, a firm that has produced one type of small recreational sailboat may develop a new competition craft that in time may alter the company image. In fact, the competition design can enhance the company reputation in ways that will expand markets for the recreational designs. Product specialization consists of concentrating on one type of product, for example, fiberglass fishing boats, composite skis, molded and inflated balls, running shoes, aluminum bats, or ballet training equipment.

A second approach is to organize product development around the activity context. The products themselves may vary. For example, a reputation for making good fishing rods may lead to lines of reels, lures, creels, and even clothing. The core concept may be the fishing market in general or one type of fishing such as surf casting or fly casting in streams. The examples of expansion from a single product are endless, including the company that began with oil lanterns and now has hundreds of camping products or the firm that began carving baseball bats and now has a full sports-equipment line.

A third approach is to have a central product and develop secondary product lines. A developer of a new type of exercise apparatus may add lines of gloves, portable exercise items, and special warmup suits. The secondary lines may be only the application of the trademark and utilization of distribution channels for products developed and manufactured under contract. Diversification is a common mode of business expansion, especially when one product has established a favorable brand image.

Most established firms have some marketing and distribution system in place. Diversification may be either encouraged or limited by the compatibility of a new product with those already being marketed. A product that adds a sales line for the off-season may be quite attractive to point-of-origin retailers. On the other hand, retailers of high-end merchandise may hesitate to take on any product line that would diminish the quality reputation of a store.

Product development consists of a series of integrated functions. The steps and decision processes may be rather different for the recreation-products divisions of diversified corporations and the local partnership that began to develop a single item for a specialized and local market. Nevertheless, there is at least one central common dimension. For recreation products that central theme is the experiential recreation base for product use. For the most part recreation products can be ignored. Their purchase and use is not necessary for economic functioning, household maintenance, or anything else that has to be done. There is no *necessary* market. The product, then, must appeal to those who are making choices about their investment of time and resources in their leisure. A new product not only competes with other products but must in some way be demonstrated to promise an enhancement of the experience to attract buyers. Those who are responsible for the development of such products had better know the nature of the activity as well as the characteristics of participants if the product is to succeed.

THE EIGHT STAGES OF PRODUCT DEVELOPMENT

There are several versions of the "eight stages" of product development. However, they all outline a process that begins with an idea, moves to evaluation, and then formulates a marketing plan.[2] The concepts involved have already been introduced in earlier chapters. They involve market assessment, market research, and promotion. The marketing strategies for recreation are based on an analysis of participation. Also, the complexity of the process depends in large part on the type of firm engaging in the product development. In the introduction that follows we will give examples from both the simple and complex ends of the scale.

STAGE 1: THE GENERATION OF IDEAS

What is the origin of a new recreation product? There are any number of possibilities:

- A tennis player with a history of invention and product development retires from his company but keeps his mind engaged. He tries a number of different frame styles and materials for tennis racquets. One morning he wakes up with a simple concept, a larger hitting surface. The product-development process leads through experimenting with a number of shapes and styles, but settles on what is essentially an enlargement of the traditional racquet. By patenting the size/shape, the inventor controls for a time an innovation that dominates the market and leads to a wave of innovation by competing manufacturers. The secret? Simply that the innovation does contribute to results in certain aspects of playing the sport.
- New materials can also make a difference. One of the drawbacks to sailing or power boating in mid-sized craft that stay away from land all day is the problem of toilet facilities. An ideal device would be compact, odor-free, simple, and not too expensive. The development of chemicals that decompose waste quickly, seals that control gases with minimal pressure, and a two-piece design enabled a manufacturer to meet a demand that not only already existed but could be enlarged easily through boating periodicals and marina operators.
- A large corporation knew what they wanted, a new product that could be distributed through their existing dealer network and utilize their present design and manufacturing capabilities. The problem was that the corporate structure got in the way. The assignment was given to their winter-sports research and development section. That limited the search even though the firm also manufactured motorcycles, boats, and several lines of sporting goods. The new product was to be a motorized winter-use recreation product. Some initial investigation included the employment of recreation

analysts. A review of research on snowmobiling revealed that there was an underdeveloped market among those who engaged in snowmobiling more as a family activity than as a high-risk and high-speed excitement.[3] At the same time, rapidly increasing fuel costs were making many recreation participants in North America concerned about motorized recreation equipment and activities that required traveling some distance for an environment. The consultants proposed that the introduction of a new motorized offroad device might be ill timed. However, if such a product were to be developed, research into recreation meanings and patterns suggested a lower-powered, easy-to-control vehicle that could be handled by older children, use less fuel, and be adaptable to a variety of terrains and surfaces. This was not the message that the research & development section wanted to hear. While they discussed this conflict between possible market segments and their development preferences, the competition introduced such a vehicle, one that could be used the year around, was simple, relatively low cost, and was based on the technology for motorbikes rather than snowmobiles.

What, then, are the common sources of product ideas?

First, there is participation. Often the idea comes from some difficulty experienced in participation. The backpacker cannot carry the weight of tinned food but finds that other types spoil on a two-week excursion. Hearing of new dehydration processes for space exploration, a group is put together that develops "space-age" dried foods for wilderness camping. The need discovered in participation is frequently the spark for the concept. The most common block is that few participants translate their frustrations and solutions through the eight steps to market the idea.

One possibility is that the idea may be introduced to an existing firm, usually one with product lines in the recreation field or with production techniques that can be easily applied to the proposed product. In most cases the actual product model will be developed only after a relationship with a possible manufacturer is formed. However, this raises a series of legal issues. The originator of the concept may want to patent the idea prior to shopping it around to possible manufacturers. If so, technical advice from product consultants and patent attorneys is usually necessary. Of course, it is much simpler to work out a contract with an existing firm that has design, model-building, patenting, and marketing capacities appropriate to the conceived product.

Second, there is the analysis of participation. One need not be a devotee of an activity to come up with a product idea. In some cases simple observation may turn on the thought process. In others an inventor seeking a product may analyze the participation meanings, contexts, and facilitating equipment to discover a gap or problem that might be solved with a new product. For a firm that is already in the recreation business, the analysis of participation may be done by in-house or consulting experts who are able to identify possible markets based on how participants engage in the activity. Latent markets may be identified that are currently limited by the lack of equipment or resources appropriate to their styles of participation, skills, financial resources, or available environments.

Third, product concepts may begin with the firm itself. As already suggested, the distribution channels, manufacturing technologies, and corporate image of a company may direct attention to certain kinds of products. Of course, improvement efforts are usually an ongoing part of the business. Innovation is likely to be based on what is already being done. Actual invention is the least likely kind of product development for an established firm. Yet the recreation product firm can identify markets, use its reputation and capacities, and begin with internal capital to engage in research and development. Generally, the development will be spurred by the needs of the corporation for new markets, diversification, expansion, or the replacement of product lines in decline. An improved technology or material can be adapted by the established firm more easily than it can be introduced by a new company. However, the same capabilities and experience that enable a firm to engage in product development within its institutional base also tend to place limits on vision and innovation.

Where are the inventors and innovators? Are they a special kind of person, haunting the laboratory or workshop while normal people are out there enjoying leisure time and engaged in the common round of life? Design improvements may emerge out of current interests or products:

- The improvement of a backpack design is accomplished by a pair of devotees who know just what they want to carry, which items need to be accessible on the trail, and how much weight can be handled on various kinds of terrain.
- The two-person motor scooter is a design improvement over the earlier models that lacked the power or load capabilities.
- The scaled-down racing car for children and adults to rent at "little Indys" is initiated by an innovator who identified a possible market among all those who follow auto racing but could never own a regular car.
- The new amusement park ride is designed in a combination of marketing and engineering skills to produce a new experience of vertigo that has a promotable theme.
- The aluminum bat or racquet is developed by a firm already in the business and whose designer recognizes the potential of a different material.

Some products come out of a development department and combine the ideas of several persons. Others are the result of a particular experience of one person. Most often the concept begins with someone whose attention is already turned, vocationally or avocationally, to recreation activity.

STAGE 2: SCREENING AND ANALYSIS

Most of the products that reach the market fail to secure a viable sales level. However, most ideas never become designs, most designs are never manufactured, and most products are never widely distributed. It is a long way from concept to successful marketing.

So, the second step is evaluation. How is it possible to decide whether or not the concept is worth pursuing further? What are the criteria for a development decision?

In general, the questions are simple enough: Can the concept be translated into a product? Can it be produced efficiently? Is there a market for the product? Can it be brought to that market at a viable price?

For an established company there are other criteria:

The idea must fit the corporate image.

It must be congruent with corporate management, manufacturing, and distribution capacities.

It must be within the financial capabilities of the firm.

It must offer some advantages of growth, diversification, or replacement.

For any product idea there are other criteria:

The product must be capable of being standardized, identified, and protected from duplication.

It must have an attractive sales and profit potential.

There should be a continued or repetitive demand, a long-term market.

It should be "special," offering a unique benefit to the user.

There should be the likelihood of a rapid return on investment.

There must be no major legal barriers to its development and marketing.

Investment costs must be within the capacities of the firm.

Servicing of the product should be feasible.

Such analysis has to be critical and ruthless. The enthusiasm that accompanies a new idea need not impede a careful evaluation of product feasibility, business capabilities, and market potential.

Product Feasibility A design for a light aircraft that can be carried on the top of a car, assembled in 30 minutes, and fly for over 2 hours at a stretch was there on paper. However, it was never produced. Why? The first problem was the high cost of a frame material light enough for the design. The second was that the alloy included a scarce "strategic" material. And the third was that the control system was so unconventional that learning to operate the craft required a pilot "unlearning" all the responses acquired over the years.

Feasibility includes issues of materials, tools necessary, manufacturing costs, technical problems, labor skills necessary, and other manufacturing questions. It also includes fundamental questions about whether the product will work in a version that can be produced in large quantities and the extent to which it can be made safe to operate, utilize available technologies, and be compatible with the other products of the firm.

Marketing Feasibility The fundamental question is that of demand. Is there a sufficient demand for the product or will the product create a demand adequate to support its development? What are projected sales? Is there competition now or will competition emerge quickly? Is the product patentable? What is its estimated product life cycle? What are the marketing advantages? Is the probable production cost low enough to permit a pricing structure that will reach a viable market? These are general rather than precise questions at this point.

For example, a fiberglass and graphite softball bat might offer advantages over wood or aluminum in performance and durability. However, its production costs would require a price level three times that of the aluminum product in order to recover costs plus a profit. The market for softball bats is not high-end but consists largely of children, youth, and middle- to lower-income adults. Unlike skiing, there is not a large high-income group of participants who will buy performance at almost any price. Therefore, the market feasibility test is failed.

Financial Feasibility There is the investment cost of developing, manufacturing, and marketing a new product. For complex equipment that cost may be quite high. Those costs must be estimated and compared to the potential market. If the two are out of balance without the likelihood of sales ever meeting investment costs, then the product concept is of little value to the company. Again, at this point in the analysis rather gross calculations are employed. Evaluation of feasibility does not call for elaborate market research but only for a general knowledge of costs and possible demand.

However, this screening and analysis stage is complex in that it includes assessment of production, marketing, and finance. The old engineering technique of the "best estimate" rests insofar as possible on data. Yet the critical element in such evaluation is knowledge of the business costs and the recreation uses. The "best estimate" is not good enough if the estimator cannot integrate the variables.

For example, the relative costs vary depending on the type of product. However, as a general rule, development costs may run something as follows:

Research design and engineering	5–10%
Product design and engineering	10–20%
Tooling and industrial engineering	40–60%
Manufacturing start-up	5–15%
Marketing inauguration	10–25%

At least all these factors have to be considered. If the product can be introduced to a local market through existing relationships, produced on a small scale in a small shop, and engineered in the basement, then the total may be small. Nevertheless, all the elements will be accomplished before the first retail sale is made.

STAGE 3: PRODUCT DEVELOPMENT

Of course, product development *is* the process in one sense. In most cases continual feedback within the process will stimulate ongoing attention to the product, its design and manufacture. However, there are elements of the process that comprise a distinct part of the entire enterprise.

The concept leads to design. For those engaged in the process this may be the most exciting phase of the project. Sketches are made, revised, and revised again. Different ideas may be incorporated. Aspects of fitting components together and redesigning them singly may make this a complex task. And it never ends since production, marketing, and financial analysis will continually feed problems and possibilities back into the design.

At some point in the design process, the decision is made to make a prototype. Especially if the product is to be vended to a corporation that may buy or lease it, a working model is usually necessary. Also, a prototype may be required in order to attract venture capital. The question "Will it work?" is difficult to answer convincingly without a prototype. Further, some flaws in the design usually are discovered only by making such a model.

The building of a prototype, testing, revision, and comparison may also lead to an attempt to patent the device. Differentiating the design from others and avoiding infringing on existing patents may be a tiresome and time-consuming task, but the working model has uses for more than patenting, design evaluation, and raising capital for development. The model may be used for comparison to see just how it operates in relation to competing products. This function is crucial for improvements and valuable for innovations. The model also enables the developer to assess the merits of different materials in laboratory or field conditions.

Is a bicycle tool kit best enclosed in a metal or fiberglass container? Models may provide the answer. How much vibration will the differently shaped racquet produce? Computer simulation offers an answer, but testing of a model is required to convince most developers. A more flexible mast seems to provide more wind-catching surface when sailing close to the wind, but can anyone know for sure until a prototype is tried in various conditions?

In recreation the purchaser will be the eventual user. The trying out of models by those who perform the activity is another useful purpose for the prototype. There are different modes and styles of doing almost anything in recreation. Until the product is tried and evaluated by a sample of the potential market, no one can be sure that its convenience, performance, and aesthetics will be appealing.

Product development may take two basic forms. Type A begins with the product. The concept leads to design, models, evaluation, and further development.

Type B begins with the market. The analysis identifies a need that might be met by a new product. Then the product is developed to meet that need and capture the related market.

The sequence of product development is somewhat different from the two types. A prototype may precede market estimation in the Type A approach. In the Type B approach a number of designs and models may be produced and then market-tested in some manner. Further, some contingency may interrupt the sequence in either approach. The stage sequence or the steps within each stage are not fixed. Rather a certain amount of flexibility lessens the chance of becoming locked into a design concept, corporate decision, or marketing technique too soon. There should be "feedback loops" built into the process so that any element may influence the program as well as the design itself.

CASE: "WHOOPS!"

Designers expert in construction and the architectural aspects of layout had consulted with exercise physiologists before designing a playground apparatus for motels, small residential developments, and schools. The measurements were based on averages for the age groups in the market and the physical movements possible yielded a variety of opportunities for stretching, climbing, strength exercise, and flexibility. However, when a prototype was built and placed in a playground for evaluation, the designers couldn't believe the problems that emerged. Some surfaces were dangerously slippery when damp. Height variation in the age groups was greater than estimated. Some of the moving parts could pinch when grasped incorrectly. And the overall layout created "traffic jams" when children didn't start in the places or move in the directions anticipated by the designers. So it was "back to the drawing board."

STAGE 4: BUSINESS ANALYSIS

Attention to the product is coupled with attention to the final aim: sales. Businesses expect a return on investment, at least over time. A business analysis consists of calculation of potential costs and returns.

Cost Analysis The variables are essentially the same ones included in the earlier screening and analysis stage. But now the viability of the product is established. The developers know that it will work, what materials and manufacturing procedures will be employed, and the unit costs at various production levels. In many cases actual manufacture will be contracted to one or more existing firms while the developers concentrate on marketing. In that case costs will usually vary by quantity. The first item may cost $10,000; the second, $500; and the next 1,000 only $20 apiece. That makes the first 1,002 cost about $30.40 each. But the next 1,000 might be manufactured for less than $20 each. Therefore, cost analysis is closely tied to estimated sales and the projected volume.

Cost estimates at this stage need to be rather precise. The design and engineering costs can be exact. Tooling and industrial engineering costs should be available from bids from manufacturing contractors. The manufacturing start-up costs are part of the contract or can be calculated by the engineers who are designing the manufacturing procedures and tools. These calculations are not informed guesses but are based on available data from either contractors or the firm's own industrial engineers.

In much the same way marketing costs can be estimated. These costs include packaging, distribution, promotion strategies, and servicing. They vary with volume, geographical scope of distribution, the type of wholesale and retail outlets involved, and the projected sales for the product.

Return Analysis Variables in return analysis are, of course, price and volume of sales. However, calculation of appropriate pricing and projection of sales involves many factors.

What are the channels of distribution? The number of outlets, their business volume, and the likelihood of their promotional cooperation will affect initial sales.

What is the potential demand in the marketing area through those channels? How many recreation participants who might use the product are in the area? How likely are they to use the product? How long will it take to get the product recognized? How many in the potential market will be reached through the retail channels? In some cases a strategy is to test the market in one or more limited areas before commitment to high production costs.

What kinds of packaging, promotion, advertising, and retail contacts will be needed to get the product introduced? Here the analysis of costs and of returns join. The question of levels of advertising, for example, that are likely to be cost-effective in each stage of product introduction will be related to estimates of sales income in the period of introduction and anticipated growth.

What is the best price strategy in the introduction of the new product? There are two main possibilities:

High initial pricing presumes that there is a kind of pent-up market for the product. Because of its evident desirability, the product will attract immediate response in the market. By beginning at a high price the aim is to "cream" the consumers who are not sensitive to price but will purchase at any price short of the outrageous. Then, in time as production costs per unit decrease, the price can be lowered to increase the market. When the good is quite innovative and attractive to an identified high-end market segment, high initial pricing may be a viable strategy.

Penetration pricing is more common in a competitive situation. The initial price levels are set recognizing that there are alternatives available and that most potential customers will be sensitive to prices. Such a strategy is most effective when the product has a production cost that drops sharply with increased volume.

In either case the pricing strategy requires a careful analysis of the market segmentation. Whether or not there exists a significant segment that is not price-elastic depends largely on an analysis of participation in the related recreation activity. Further, whether the product can be demonstrated quickly to be superior will depend on building a reputation over a considerable period of time will affect what is possible in pricing.

For recreation products the variations in the distribution system are also crucial. A product that is almost self-evidently attractive and that can be advertised in user media and distributed by mail may have quite low start-up costs and a relatively brief introduction period. On the other hand, an item that requires some alteration in mode of recreation participation and can be distributed only through pro shops to a limited market may take off very slowly and have a return far below costs for years. In general, a recreation product will have a snowballing rate of return if it is successful in market penetration. That is, every sale produces a potential salesperson who is demonstrating the product among other potential users. Customer satisfaction may lead to a rapidly ascending sales curve for products that do not require discarding other quipment in which there is likely to be a considerable investment. The snowballing will also be more rapid for a product that wears out and has to be replaced periodically.

All this business analysis is complex as well as of critical importance. Some of the costs can be estimated rather precisely. The potential markets that can be reached may also be calculated based on available participation estimates. However, the issue of channels of distribution may be overlooked at great cost to the developing firm. This is especially the case when the business is started to develop a single new product.

CASE: DISTRIBUTION PROBLEMS

The story of this game has become familiar in the annals of business. The basic sketch is simple. Two professors developed a new board game for at-home and school use that was not only challenging fun for participants but also had been demonstrated to increase the logical analysis skills of students who played it. Initial distribution was through personal contact at area schools. The price was just above cost in the introduction period. The originators wanted the game used and tested more than to gain a profit. The problem was that they were never able to get much beyond that first successful stage of marketing. School equipment sales representatives would not take on the new product because they feared it would alienate the big comprehensive suppliers they represented. Advertising other than in their university alumni magazine produced just enough individual sales to break even. Even television media attention did not seem to lead to any great increase in sales. Further, the game was considered too limited in appeal to be purchased by any of the games companies or publishers. After several years the two developers had actually lost some money on a game that had been recognized as both fun and developmental, widely acclaimed, and marketed in several different ways. The problem was that they were not able to identify and enlist any distribution channels that would make the game available to either retail or institutional buyers at a volume rate that would permit a discount to schools and widen the market for family sales.

STAGE 5: MARKET TESTING

How is it possible to estimate the probable sales curve of a product that has never been on the market? The answer is that it isn't, at least not without some market testing. Once a product has been designed, pretested, refined, and a pricing strategy decided on, the next step is to test both the product and the strategy in the market. In general, the method is to introduce the product in a limited area selected for accessibility and representativeness of target market. At least one full cycle of seasons is required for such a market test.

Any evaluation research requires a plan that integrates the program or product to be evaluated, its delivery, and measures of the elements to be evaluated. For market testing, the overall strategy is to identify the marketing issues that will determine the eventual success or failure of the product and incorporate measures and analysis that will test those issues. For example:

Question: Which target markets will be most responsive when the product is first introduced?

Evaluation: A code is developed that includes age range and sex of purchasers at retail outlets. Further, the sales by location of outlet and type of outlet will measure general economic level and participation locale of purchasers. For mail orders the order form will include a code for where the advertising was placed. Addresses for delivery and bank card names approximate a demographic index.

Question: Which kinds of outlets and promotion, mail order or retail, are most effective?

Evaluation: Sales source records can easily be compared.

Question: How price-elastic is the product?

Evaluation: Two paired but geographically separate test market areas can be chosen with different pricing strategies employed.

The kinds of questions that need to be answered are, for the most part, *marketing* ones:

Is the pricing strategy correct?

Which types of distribution outlets are most productive?

What advertising approaches attract buyers in the introduction phase of the product cycle?

Will sales be seasonal or steady?

What will be the pattern of repeat buyers, if any?

Which target markets are most responsive and how can they best be reached?

How large is the demand potential in various market areas?

What rate of growth can be anticipated?

Can the product yield a profit in the early growth stages? If not, is the potential there to justify longer-term financing?

However, there are also *product-related* questions:

Does the product perform as expected?

Are modifications suggested by users?

What is the experience with returns, breakdowns, and servicing?

Should a variety of models be developed for different types of users? If so, to what extent is price a factor in choices?

The main purpose of market testing is to avoid making a large investment before the demand is demonstrated. Remember that 40% to 60% of products that reach the market fail. Market testing minimizes the cost of such failure.

Within a test market area, conditions of introduction can be controlled and monitored carefully. The aims are to assess interest in the product from relevant recreation participation aggregates, evaluate how the product performs in actual use, try out a variety of sales techniques and outlets, and test the overall marketing plan. Most important, since recreation goods have to secure a market based on their contribution to the user's satisfaction in doing something, the performance of the product in use by a variety of consumers is the central issue. If they don't like using it, no engineering or scientific data will create sales.

This means that the market test will include a variety of means of feedback. Further, that feedback will go into the decision process of the producing firm so that revisions can be made. No one, inventor or promoter, can be allowed to veto arbitrarily the discovery that the product or the plan is less than perfect. To be reliable all the criteria or any research are applied to the feedback in the test period. Representativeness of informants is part of the feedback design so that a biased set of users does not send messages that are untrue for major market segments. Checks on the validity of the information, including sales figures, need to be made.

After all, the purpose is to reduce the down-side risk by trying out both the product and the market before large investment is made in inventories and promotion. A biased market test may be worse than none at all if it yields information that represents only a fraction of those who are likely to use the product.

CASE 1: PRODUCT TESTING

When a different-shaped racquet was designed for racquetball, the engineering tests demonstrated that it provided control over a larger hitting surface than conventional racquets. However, there were two questions: First, would the different shape be rejected by players on appearance alone? Second, would a variety of players at different skill levels find the new racquet equally satisfactory in use? If not, then should marketing be directed toward beginners, high-skill players, or a general market? The method employed was that of *paired comparisons*. A sample of players was developed with the assistance of public and business court managers. They were put through a series of hitting tests and matches with a conventional new racquet and the new design at two different times each. An instrument was completed after each session that elicited an evaluation of several dimensions of performance. The cost was small, consisting only of purchasing court time for the players.

CASE 2: MARKET TESTING

The big issue was that of distribution channels. The product was simple, an easily detachable carrier for skis that was adapted to small cars. The market test required producing 500 of the devices. They were then placed in two point-of-origin retail stores, two on-site ski shops, and advertised in two ski magazines with a mail distribution scheme. After one session both costs and sales were calculated and the decision reached to concentrate on the mail-order method. Why? It was cost-effective because it required no company representation to retailers, but had yielded 75% of the first-year sales.

STAGE 6: MARKET FORECASTING

Market forecasting is carried on throughout the product-development process. However, it is most precise and important after some test marketing has yielded specific information on markets and users. The central aim of market forecasting is to provide an estimate of production quantities and income probabilities. The central issue is the fit between the product and the recreation user. Further, some estimate of the product life cycle is needed in order to plan ahead for production and marketing.

What are the factors that need to be considered?

1. The size, composition, and location of the user populations.
2. The nature of the competition, both in products and distribution channels.
3. The price elasticity of the good and the purchasing power of the various market segments.
4. The singular versus repetitive nature of the product use. Based on rates of recreation participation, will it be purchased once only, once a season, or repeatedly? If participation rates determine frequency and quantity of purchase, then that information has to be included in the analysis of the user market segments.
5. The use patterns according to season, locale, resource availability, social timetables, and special events and periods.

Again, all these factors have been considered from the beginning, when the initial concept was screened and evaluated. However, now that some market testing data are available, it is possible to be much more precise about the forecast. And precision is important because the production quantity decision is one that involves considerable investment for most new products. Economics of scale and decreasing per unit costs are balanced by paying for storage and distribution of goods that do not sell. One significant element in the production decision is advance orders. However, retailers will usually be quite conservative about initial orders of a new product.

CASE: A BETTER PRODUCT

The invention was just a new kind of "goo" for repairing worn canvas shoes. However, for runners and court players who purchase expensive footgear and see the soles wear through while the uppers are still sound, the chance to prolong the shoe life by dabbing on some compound is a very attractive idea. The problem with earlier products was that they just didn't last very long. An application might have to be repeated after two hours of use. The new compound looked like the others and was applied like the others. However, it had been tested and found to last up to three times longer. Now, how could the market forecast be developed?

First, sales figures for the existing products were used as a baseline. Second, a market test was run that gave indications of about how the sales curve would rise in retail outlets as the product was displayed and word got around that it really was better. Third, the number of such outlets that could be supplied in the first two years was calculated based on the need to visit most in person.

Fourth, the market in each community was estimated by taking national figures on participation in running, tennis, racquetball, and basketball and comparing them to the population breakdowns for the selected market areas. Fifth, the repeated sales were estimated by taking an average of participation rates and likelihood of shoe repair per hour of playing or running time. This was a general estimate, but it suggested that few would buy more than one tube per four-month season.

Sales totals were then drawn by combining the sales rates with the figures for the market areas chosen for the first year of distribution.

CASE: A CONVENIENCE PRODUCT

Was there really a market for such a novel product? The idea was based on an experience the inventor, a clothing company representative, had shared with colleagues who traveled. The experience was having a very wet and smelly shirt to pack away after playing tennis on a trip. The idea was simple—a low-cost disposable shirt. A traveler could take one or a few on business trips, play a racquet sport or otherwise exercise, and then just throw it away. It wouldn't then damage the other packed clothes or impose its odor to the hotel room. The technology was there in a paper-based cloth developed some years before. But was there a market?

How do you forecast sales for something that does not yet exist? In this case the person with the idea began with his own market research. He asked as many fellow travelers as possible when he met them on the courts or while jogging. Then, having obtained an indication of interest, he completed the step up through the market test. Now the forecast was developed based on the market test that had been conducted for six months through a series of racquet clubs that sold travel togs.

CASE: HOW FAST WILL IT GO?

When the stellar sailing racers went into the business, they took their know-how and reputations as assets. But their design capabilities were relatively untested. The first boat they designed was now in prototype. The target market was the competition day sailor who wanted a boat that was fast, versatile, easy to transport, and challenging to sail.

The first step was for a number of sailors in the region to use the prototype in paired comparison tests. When it did well, there was a large obstacle: How could they forecast sales for a new product costing over $2,500 in a highly competitive field in which most participants already had commitments to other designs? Further, racing sailboats is best done in a "class" with several boats of the same design. A new boat has no official "class."

There was the conservative approach. Line up a few dealers, produce enough models to get one to each dealer, and let the sales determine production. After all, sailboats are not made by the dozen, but one by one. The cost of this was not low, however, due to the manufacturing start-up costs. The conservative approach meant a price level that might scare off competition. The alternative was to sell the design to an established manufacturer who already had in place the manufacturing, marketing, and distribution capabilities. Was there any other way than to just make the decision and see how it would come out?

STAGE 7: A MARKET PLAN

Once a forecast is developed, a marketing scheme has to be completed and carried out. To begin with, the marketing plan is related to the projected project life cycle. Will there be rapid growth and a rapid decline as with "fad" insignia, apparel, or games, or will the product have steady sales growth until the size of the market is demonstrated and competition causes a leveling and eventual plateau? Or will there be continued growth for an undetermined period as with products that lead to repeated purchases and have a high replacement rate?

The marketing plan integrates a number of elements: introduction, promotion, distribution and packaging, and pricing. It involves an overall plan that anticipates demand and supply, recognizes that the marketing aims change through the product cycle, and allows for ongoing evaluation and alteration.

Introduction is a series of announcements to the identified market segments. The details of how this is done depends on who those markets are and on the nature of the recreation activity. A product requiring specific commercially provided facilities will usually be marketed through pro shops who are contacted by company or wholesale reps. In other cases the announcement is made through participants or trade-oriented media as outlined in chapter 14. The introduction is specific to the primary markets that have been selected and tested.

Promotion includes all the elements of retailing that are designed to attract buyers and lead to sales. For a product, promotion includes packaging, display materials, and efforts to gain media attention as well as the advertising mix. At the beginning of a product cycle the focus is on getting attention and giving the product an image. One common method of doing this for recreation products is to secure the immediate use of the product by those who can influence others. Often key participants or professionals are given samples of the product, clearly labeled, for their use.

Distribution is critical for any product. For a new recreation product the link between manufacture and sales requires an identification of the most accessible, efficient, and prestigious channels.

Pricing, as already outlined, is central to the marketing plan. However, the plan should also take into account the expansion of markets, alternative approaches, and a step-by-step course of action for implementation. Further, the results of the plan will be monitored so that the sales can be related to the various promotional efforts and a cost analysis undertaken.

The Duke of Wellington was once reported to have said that his battle plans were made of rope and could be retied and rewoven when cut or broken. A marketing plan is more like a rope ladder than a scaffold. It is useful and efficient, but it is also flexible enough that it can be altered at any point in the campaign. Of course, there are other problems with scaffolds.

STAGE 8: PRODUCT INTRODUCTION

Reaching this final step is likely to take two years or more from the inception of the product concept. The product and the plan have been tested. An integrated system has been developed. Now all the preparation is about to bear fruit.

The product is announced. Outlets are supplied. Promotion appropriate to the product is under way to influence first sales. The competition, if any, is watching and preparing to make countermoves if their market is seriously eroded. What do you do except wait and hope?

First, introduction will seldom go without a hitch. The firm has to be ready to meet early emergencies, unanticipated contingencies that may be costly to retailer or consumer relations and to the company image if not handled quickly.

Second, market results will be checked closely and regularly. The sales will almost surely provide some surprises. Distribution channels, promotion, and even production may have to be shifted to meet unexpected sources of demand as well as disappointing slowness in some markets.

Third, production will have to be monitored and managed in this first period. Material costs, labor productivity, product reliability, technological breakthroughs in manufacture, and machine reliability are all aspects of manufacture that may become problems. Exclusive attention to marketing may produce a catastrophe if production is neglected. After all, the product must now make its own way in the market. There is no substitute for quality, and quality requires production control.

Production management is a topic in itself and far too complex even to introduce here. The processes of standardization, purchasing of materials, inventory control, planning and scheduling of manufacture, human resource (worker) management, and quality control are all part of an integrated process. While the stress in this approach has been on marketing, production errors can destroy the best concept, marketing plan, and evaluation system.

Investment and pricing are also significant aspects of the process that have only been mentioned here. A price analysis that does not take into account the need for investment capital and provide for a return on that investment in a reasonable period of time will fail as a business no matter how ingenious the new product.

CASE: SMALL CAN STILL MEAN VARIETY

The firm began because the founders were interested in a new kind of fishing common to the Midwest and South that employed special boats with high-powered motors, comfortable seating, and often fish-detection gear. These craft were a growing market. So the plant was opened to make fiberglass bass boats. However, cautious business managers as they were, the owners decided early to expand on the basis of their technology. They contracted to produce fiberglass sidecars for a nearby manufacturer who wanted to expand motorcycle lines without building a new plant. Then, also in contract, they began to make fiberglass TV disk antennas for rural areas and, rather outside the recreation line, liners for burial vaults.

Over a period of time the demand for the boats was reduced, partly by market saturation and partly by an economic recession. The other products, even though they also had quantities contracted reduced, were enough to keep almost all the production force at work to wait for better times. The diversification probably also saved the company itself because the loan obligations and fixed costs of doing business did not slow down for the recession. The rise of interest rates was forcing the closure of many less-provident manufacturing businesses.

SERVICE AS A PRODUCT

The chapters on retail business have introduced many aspects of recreation-related services as business. However, the development of new services has much in common with product development. The stages of conceptualization, assessment, planning, testing, and marketing are much the same. In fact, new businesses in recreation are at least as likely to be services as involved in making or marketing products.

CASE: POINT-OF-ORIGIN RENTALS

The new product was actually a service concept. At first it was just a brokerage. Then it became a multifaceted rental agency. The slogan was "It's a pleasure!" and the company image was one of the affordable leisure. At first the firm simply acted as brokers for those in the community with recreation and vacation equipment they were willing to rent. Travel trailers, snowmobiles, and other major items were listed with weekly and weekend rental rates. The managers made the arrangements, kept schedules, and kept 20% of the fee. Run out of a home, it was mildly profitable.

However, in time the business began to expand. Over a three-year period, demand for a variety of camping and travel items, both large and small, led to stocking many kinds of products that owners were reluctant to rent. What the business managers found was that there are many "occasional" and first-time recreation participants who want to do something special without investing in expensive equipment. While some things can be rented at destination areas, such as skis and horses, especially the en route items could only be borrowed or purchased at the residential location.

The next step was to include handling the rental of vacation cabins as well as recreation vehicles and camping trailers. The business became almost a full-service vacation center. The brokerage for cabins and travel vehicles remained a major part of the business but was augmented by carrying smaller, rental items in the store. At least in this community this recreation service had much of the same history as a new product. Beginning with a concept, the idea was developed, introduced, tested, expanded, revised, and augmented with complementary services and products.

CASE: POINT-OF-USE PROVISIONS

What do you do when you step into the airport for a brief vacation and find that the recreation resources in the area encourage activities for which you are not prepared? What about the business trip that stretches over a weekend but finds you without the recreation gear that would permit participation?

At a major urban airport the service was advertised: "Rent Some Fun!" Offroad vehicles and tennis racquets, camping equipment and bicycles, down jackets and cross-country skis, and even beach umbrellas, all were advertised for rent. Many of the items could have been assembled by going to several locations, but "Fun City" could put together a package for use at the beaches, lakes, mountains, and country clubs in the area. "One call would do it all!"

The question that emerged was one of expansion. The business began small and grew gradually with the demand. Advertising was extended to airline magazines for the major carriers. However, Los Angeles could be a special case. There was so much travel business there and so many recreation opportunities available the year around. How could a judgment be made on expansion? How big a city, how mild a climate, and how many recreation resources were necessary to support such a business? This product/service development required some careful evaluation in order to make such decisions. Maybe there was only one city with a market adequate for the business concept. How could they find out?

DEVELOPING SERVICES

The new service also begins with a concept. However, the concept, even more than with a product, is likely to begin with some experience with the recreation activity. However, from that point, the steps are similar.

First, it is necessary to study participation in the activity—who is doing it and how. The service has to supplement existing resources in some way that makes possible participation now blocked or enhances the experience for those already engaged.

Second, the current resources offer a context for participation. Is there evidence that those resources are in some way inadequate? Is there constricted access or playing time? Are some groups excluded? Do some limitations make the experience problematic or less than has been demonstrated to be possible?

Third, what are the costs of providing the service? Will there be a market at a feasible price, or are current resources priced at a level that open a market for a lower-priced resource? Is the current limitation a matter of quality, cost, or quantity? A new or complementary service is based on careful market analysis that begins with the current provisions.

Fourth, what is the likely return on investment? Some services may be used, but only at a price or with a frequency that does not produce enough revenue to provide the service and make a return on investment capital.

Recreation services may also be quite specialized. The most common specialization is in resources for a particular activity. The service is developed by studying fully the activity, its participants, resources, skill acquisition, equipment, and schedules. However, there are other kinds of service specialization. For example, a service may cater to the needs of beginners in some activity or set of activities, it may seek to supply those who are only occasional participants; or it may be directed only toward the devotees, the participants who are both knowledgeable and have made a commitment.

Who services the equipment and with what level of convenience?

Who cares for children while parents are engaged in the activity?

Who teaches the children, the older-than-average beginner, or those with particular learning difficulties?

In so many ways developing a recreation service can be something new: It can be an improvement on existing services; it can be an innovation that changes the mode of participation; or it can be an invention that creates a new realm of recreation for those who are attracted to the environment, companions, or experience.

SUMMARY OF ISSUES

New recreation products may begin with participation constraints or experiences as well as with corporate objectives.

In general, product improvements are competition-driven; innovations market-driven; and inventions based on technologies.

Corporate aims, images, and marketing and distribution systems are all factors in new product development.

The eight stages of product development are cumulative and should include the flexibility to respond to continual feedback loops.

Participation enhancement is the basis of new recreation product concepts. Therefore, markets are part of the concept from the beginning.

The viability of the product, efficient production, adequate markets, price versus costs, and corporate objectives are all involved in screening

Design and evaluation of a prototype recreation product has a use component.

Business analysis requires cost estimates in relation to volume, return analysis, price strategies, and marketing plans.

Market testing provides a basis for forecasting and planning.

Competition and price elasticity as well as user potential are part of market forecasting.

Anticipated adoption patterns determine the choice of high initial or penetration pricing.

While the stages of introducing a new recreation service are much the same as for a product, a service may be inaugurated and developed more slowly as demand is created and developed. Monitoring client patterns and characteristics is even more crucial than for a product.

DISCUSSION QUESTIONS

1. Give examples of current recreation products that are improvements, innovations, or inventions. How common are inventions?
2. What are the advantages of product diversification and of specialization?
3. Give examples of new products that have enhanced the satisfactions of a recreation activity.
4. Try to think of a new product or improvement for some sort of recreation par-

ticipation. Then subject it to the "screening and analysis" evaluation. What seem to be the most important questions?

5. What kind of recreation products have been introduced with high initial pricing? Why was this strategy chosen?
6. How would you develop a way to decide on the best production and marketing strategy for the sailboats in the "How Fast Will It Go?" case?
7. How could the owners of "Fun City" in the "Point-of-use Provisions" case determine whether or not expansion would be profitable?
8. Are there growing markets for new recreation products? For services? What are possible products for those markets?

PROJECT

Select a recreation product introduced 2 to 5 years ago. Write a case on its development and marketing by doing research on its history using trade journals, magazines for participants, company annual reports, and direct information from the firm.

REFERENCES

1. Udell, Jon C., and G. R. Laczniak. *Marketing as an Age of Change,* p. 241f. New York: Wiley, 1981.
2. Gitman, Lawrence J., and C. McDaniel, Jr. *Business World,* p. 285f. New York: Wiley, 1983.
3. Report No. 5. Champaign, IL: Social Analysis Associates, 1980.

12 RESIDENTIAL RECREATION RESOURCES

ISSUES

How are recreation provisions and community development related?

Are marketing aims and recreation planning sometimes in conflict? How may they be complementary?

How do marketing and recreation businesses differ in the different types of residential developments?

How should recreation planning be based on marketing objectives and target markets?

How are common ground and private space trade-offs central to neighborhood recreation planning?

What are the special recreation planning opportunities offered by a Planned Unit Development or New Town? How are those opportunities integrated with the business aims of the developer?

How can a life-course model be a basis for community planning?

How do the three types of recreation-based communities—retirement, mixed, and resource-focused—differ?

What are the particular recreation provision requirements of a retirement development?

To what extent are the recreation plans of a mixed community "real-estate driven"?

Does examining a resource-focused recreation community from a development rather than local business perspective raise issues different from those in the destination resort chapter?

What is the major obstacle to developing communities with a central recreation orientation?

Real estate is a major part of American business. The sales, rental, construction, and maintenance of housing is central to both the economy and to the context of life. Although some housing is provided by the public sector and some is subsidized in various ways, for the most part housing is in the market sector of the economy. Sales and resales, design and construction, and a range of services provide new residences through the market. Rentals and a variety of use agreements are also most often offered on an investment and profit-seeking basis.

Residence is related to recreation in several ways. First, most leisure takes place in the home. Reading, watching television, familial interaction, games and hobbies, entertaining, and a variety of child-oriented activities most often occur at home. Access to away-from-home activities is usually measured in time or distance from the residence. It is the geographical and resource center just as the household is the social center of leisure. Second, space in the residence is designed, allocated, managed, and maintained with such at-home recreation and leisure in view. Larger homes may have over half their total space allocated to leisure rather than the activities of eating, sleeping, food preparation, and bodily maintenance.

Third, both the residence and the surrounding environment are locales for recreation. Frequently housing is provided by businesses that develop more than one unit at a time. Land acquisition and planning, housing design and construction, and marketing and sales all have recreation resources as one element in the overall plan. Recreation provisions are commonly a major element in the promotion and marketing of new housing. Further, design, land-use planning, and recreation resources are usually developed with particular market segments in mind. Recreation is part of the total plan. The focus of this chapter is on the recreation dimensions of residential planning and marketing.

Just look through the real estate section of any major newspaper on the weekend. What aspects of housing are featured in order to attract purchasers and renters? There is housing design and quality. There is location. There is price. And there is often some description of recreation amenities on-site or nearby.

In fact, in order to differentiate the development from others, the recreation opportunities may even come first. After all, price is largely determined by costs and the market. Location is seldom unique. Competitors offer housing in the same general area. Design may be special, but it frequently represents a common style. Therefore, leisure amenities may be promoted as outstanding for the market segment addressed: families with young children, older adults, young singles and couples, or those with a particular leisure style built around sports, the arts, or natural environments.

The business core of considerable recreation planning is real estate. The recreation facilities, programs, and other resources are part of the total package in order to enhance sales and rentals. The investment return is not on the swimming pool, tennis courts, fitness center, or beach. It is in real estate sales, commissions, differences between development costs and sales prices, and financing arrangements. As a consequence the recreation opportunities may be sales-oriented more than participation-based. One issue is whether the two are in conflict.

It would seem that good sales incentives and good recreation planning should be complementary. Insofar as people know what they like to do, what they have found satisfying, and what resources have been difficult to locate or use, the provision of desired resources would be the best sales aid. However, in many cases the design is done by those whose interest in appearances outweighs their interest in or knowledge of leisure participation. Often they assume that a certain package of amenities is expected and need not be questioned or analyzed. They are reluctant to do anything different.

The time to plan for leisure is when a residential development is first on the drawing board. Then land can be used most efficiently, terrains adapted for recreation opportunity, interior space allocated for leisure uses, and the interrelated interests and activities of various household members taken into account. Planning for leisure involves knowing how specific recreation resources fit into the overall leisure patterns of those likely to live in the development. It involves knowing something about work and leisure schedules, timetable decisions and adjustments within households, transportation, and priorities. It involves time, space, and financial resources. In short, it involves more than placing a swimming pool by the sales office or a meeting center by the highway.

When developmental planners are first at work, they may or may not consult those who specialize in recreation planning. If their assumption is that appearance is primary, they are not always concerned about how well the plan will work once the development is complete and all units sold. However, if they wish to maximize long-term satisfaction with the community, they will attempt to bring together projected household composition with the results of leisure research in order to plan for participation.

RECREATION IN THE RESIDENTIAL DEVELOPMENT

There are a number of types of residential developments. Multiple-unit buildings can house hundreds or thousands of people in a single edifice. Clustered housing, whether or not walls are shared or units are detached, provides common ground for exterior environments and little or no private exterior space. *Planned Unit Developments* are designed for 5,000 to 20,000 residents in one contiguous area. *New Towns* also begin with a master plan for land use and housing but are designed for communities of 50,000 or more and include retail businesses and employment opportunities. And then there is the recreation-based community that emphasizes leisure resources in the image and planning of the community.

There are also communities and residential developments that are planned for particular populations—the retired, singles, child-rearing families, or some other segment. These developments usually take recreation opportunities into account in the initial planning. Other developments are located where they have access to some special recreation resource such as a lake, golf course, or urban theater district. In those cases the marketing begins with the leisure opportunity.

MULTIPLE-UNIT HOUSING

It has become increasingly common for the designers of multiple-unit residences, rental or condominium, to include recreation facilities in the plan. The most frequent provisions are for some lounge area by the entrance, an adjacent "conversation area," and some sort of exercise center. The exercise center may be no more than a 250-square-foot room with some weight and exercise equipment or may be a complex and elaborate facility. The size of the development is probably the major factor in the extent of such provisions.

However, developers who are seeking to appeal to particular housing market segments are more likely to provide extensive facilities. For example, in an urban area, the following may be offered:

- Indoor or outdoor (often rooftop) swimming pool
- Sun decks
- Poolside refreshment counter or bar
- Party rooms available by reservation
- Tennis, squash, or racquetball courts
- Special access to nearby resources such as golf courses, racquet sport clubs, or marinas (the development occupants are given a special rate for membership, guests, and fees).

In some cases the recreation provider may lease space in a large urban multiunit residential structure with the anticipation of capturing a large share of the residents as members. The key element is the planned market appeal of the development itself. If it is directed toward younger adults—single and childless couples—then the recreation stress will be on active sports and group entertaining. A pool may offer a relaxed and nonthreatening meetingplace. If, on the other hand, the design is for larger units and family groups, then recreation may be more oriented toward children and families, with outdoor playgrounds, rooms for a variety of arts participation groups and programs, and daytime opportunities for unemployed mothers. For retirement-age residents, there is more stress on game rooms, hobbies, and social interaction.

CASE: DESIGN FOR ON-SITE RECREATION BUSINESS

The developer was not only planning for two major downtown apartment condominium buildings within a half block of each other but also recognized that at least three other such structures were being planned for the block. Rather than each having a small exercise room and perhaps a racquet court or two, the plan was for one major facility. However, knowing that the management and operation of such a facility required expertise, the architects were instructed to consult with recreation planners about space needs. Then the needed space was included in the design for the first of the two structures.

Long before completion, a contract was negotiated with a chain operation that specialized in indoor fitness centers. They were to provide the equipment, operate the program, and maintain the space. In return for a renewable lease, they had to meet certain requirements: to operate seven days a week for at least eight hours a day; to offer a range of recreation opportunities including racquet sports, indoor swimming, exercise and weight rooms, special programs for women, adequate locker and shower facilities, and some instruction programs; to organize an advisory committee of residents who would report to the project management as well as to the recreation provider; and to provide audited financial reports yearly to the project management.

In return the recreation business received already constructed space including the swimming pool, freedom to develop attractive programs, access to several hundred young adults with relatively high incomes and education levels who lived in the building and worked nearby, and a location within a block of over 2,000 more potential members. Further, the facility was near enough to a number of restaurants, large hotels, and major corporate offices that nonresident use of the club was also possible.

The concept was that a program of extremely high quality would be offered. The location meant that it would be quite costly in both time and money for the residents of the high-rise apartments to seek alternative opportunities. Further, the market segment was perfect for such a business—young adults without private space for physical activity but the most likely to desire such an opportunity. In fact, the major competition turned out to be self-initiated running and jogging at a nearby lakefront park. However, the winter climate made the indoor environment quite attractive. After three years, memberships in the club were limited and used as an inducement to buy resales in the apartments that had entered into an agreement with the club.

The operation was maintained at a quality level with relatively high fee structures. Both staff and clientele were thoroughly coed, with full accommodation for women members. On the other hand, no programs were developed for children. After five years of operation a major question was whether or not to utilize more space for the "gathering area" in which members could have refreshments before or after their participation. The concept of a club that would provide a major resource for several adjacent multiunit residences in the city seemed to prove successful when it was planned from the beginning.

Facilities Who will live in the building? That is the critical issue. A multiunit residence is planned for a particular kind of resident. A few may have broad-spectrum aims, but most are directed toward clearly identified market segments. Location, size of the units, price, amenities, and promotion all yield a focused population. As a result, the recreation resources that will be attractive to prospective renters or buyers are based on the recreation interests of those residents.

However, stereotypes in relation to preferences by age or sex may become a problem. Older people now tend to be more active physically as general health improves and encouragement grows. Retirement-age people are of increasingly high education levels who are likely to desire more active involvement in the arts and community activity. Women exhibit much greater concern for physical competence and sports participation. Current participation rates need to be tempered with an understanding of trends. "Averages" from national surveys may be misleading in planning a building that will be occupied in twenty years by young adults now only five years old or by the "young old" who are now active at age 45 to 55. At least, designs should allow for flexibility as interests and activity patterns change.

There are two kinds of facilities. Some are on-site, in the building or on the grounds. The standard package for such offerings seems to be one party room, one modest exercise room, one swimming pool and deck in the courtyard, and perhaps two tennis courts in the rear. This package is maintained by the development management, with costs built into the rents or condominium fees. Personnel are minimal—janitors and possibly a lifeguard if the pool serves children.

The second kind of recreation facility is off-site but readily accessible. Advertising for the apartments may include references to the distance from the lake, golf course, public park, theater district, or even to public transportation to recreation areas. Residence in the building offers no advantages in obtaining access to the facilities except location. Nevertheless, location for recreation may be a major factor in selecting the building site, choosing the target market, and designing the structure.

For both on-site and off-site recreation, the resources become integral to the marketing plan. Seldom does the recreation plan come first and marketing follow. Rather, investment in facilities or in the higher-cost land near parks and beaches is made because of the marketing appeal of recreation resources. The costs are expected to be recovered in the price structure and in differentiating the product from similar housing.

Program In many such buildings there is no program. The facilities are just there and available to those who have a key. More often, there are some resident-organized programs. A committee will be formed, sometimes at management initiative, to have monthly parties, set regulations for pool or exercise room use, and generally oversee the operation on a volunteer basis. The role of management is to encourage and facilitate such organization as well as to make sure that no residents are arbitrarily excluded by the operation. There is always the danger of "takeovers" in which one group comes to dominate the use of a facility or to preempt prime hours with some limited-access program.

However, in major housing developments there may be at least one recreation coordinator. Such a person may hire seasonal or part-time assistants for particular programs. Or a facility such as an outdoor pool may be managed by a company that specializes in staffing and operating a number of residential resources. The recreation/social director is usually charged with multiple responsibilities of facility management, program development in sport and other areas, and some social events. Depending on the residents' interests and characteristics, there may be trips, special events, and other off-site opportunities offered.

CLUSTERED HOUSING OR DETACHED-HOUSING NEIGHBORHOODS

Most often in suburban areas housing developers include recreation opportunities as part of the total plan. In areas of clustered housing some common ownership of land and/or recreation facilities may be included in the deeds for each parcel. Then the land is managed by a homeowners' association after the developer has sold the lots. More often the developer attempts to arrange for a public agency to take over the operation of the park or facility provided in the plan. The aim of the developer is to maximize the marketable recreation offerings and still minimize front-end investment. As a result plot plans for a 200-unit development will contain squares with labels such as "swimming pool planned here" and "park dedicated here."

The following sections on planned unit developments and communities will deal with the inclusion of comprehensive plans and resources for recreation as part of the total investment and marketing package. However, much more common are the partial efforts of developments to allow for recreation without heavy investment. With clustered housing such as town houses that share walls and are arranged in court areas without any pass-through streets, the economy is achieved by using less space for housing. Density may be relatively high since each residence does not have a surrounding yard and garden area. However, there are generally expectations of some available outdoor space. Such space can be deeded to the property owners in undivided shares. The land will usually be landscaped and play areas laid out. However, the long-term maintenance and management will be the responsibility of the owners. As of yet there have been few attempts to develop businesses that serve the needs of such neighborhood groups. The exceptions have most often been the pool management companies who service a facility for a yearly fee.

In developments of detached homes recreation planning is more likely to be minimal. Since each dwelling has some private outdoor space, common ground may be nonexistent except for some set aside for public administration of park, playing field, or pool.

The issue is partly one of priority given to common or private space. The history of family housing in the Western world has stressed private environments outside the enclosed residence. However, the established ideal of the spacious garden and yard area is becoming increasingly prohibitive in cost for many households. As a consequence private exterior space large enough for children's games and entertainment events is available for a smaller proportion of the population. One alternative is to cluster housing and provide commonly owned ground that can be shared. Common ground for children's play that is still protected and accessible has many advantages. However, adults have been slower to give up privacy.

If there is common provision of outdoor space and recreation resources, then the planning has to take account of the characteristics of households more than has been necessary in traditional suburban or community neighborhoods. As in the city, more and more is shared and the residents of a neighborhood may be more and more alike. The probability of having children in the area and their number and age distribution is the most important factor in planning. The importance of accessible opportunities for group activity is primary.

Program mamagement may be provided by public recreation authorities. However, neighborhoods in which common ground is not accepted by the public sector may become more the rule. In such neighborhoods organization will be carried out by the residents whether or not there is an adequate plan in the developer's land-use design. What is needed is based on the composition of the households, not some standard package. Access, protection, compatibility of activities, flexibility in space utilization, and a means for cooperative planning and development are all necessary. A responsible developer will provide the initial planning and services that enable residents to develop the programs they need.

PLANNED UNIT DEVELOPMENTS

A Planned Unit Development (PUD) is considered a residential development of middle size, designed for 5,000 to 20,000 residents. It includes a complete plan for land use, transportation, housing, retail centers, services, and schools. The infrastructure of drainage, sewers, water supplies, utilities, and transportation access are part of the plan. However, the aim is to develop an overall design for the community that enhances the quality of life rather than just to stamp grids on the earth.

Recreation is one element of the plan for this type of development. As with other housing developments, recreation facilities are included both as a marketing attraction and as an element in the fabric of the community. However, some conflicting aims are possible. For example, the placement of major facilities such as swimming pools for maximum access and use may not be the same as location in a "showplace" recreation center by the sales office. Further, a concept of recreation that is based on neighborhoods and promotes localized interaction may not be the same as one that seeks to produce an edifice that will be impressive on brochures and in print advertising.

Facilities Again, the facilities needed should be determined by the projected composition of the population. Factors to be taken into consideration are:

Household size Larger households, generally composed of families with children, require a range of everyday and accessible outdoor facilities as well as indoor space in climates with a cold season.

Income range A PUD may have a relatively narrow spectrum of housing costs and attract a commensurate income range. While those with higher incomes usually have a variety of leisure investments outside the community, lower- and lower-middle-income households need more cost-free opportunities near home.

Housing density A high density of residential placement means that each household will have less private space for recreation. As a result a network of playgrounds and outdoor spaces will be needed. For small children such facilities may be at a ratio of one playground—preferably within sight of homes—for each eight households. Larger areas for games, sports fields, and other types of resources can serve larger numbers of households. The key is to anticipate the household composition based on residential size and cost and to lay out such resources to maximize access and safety.

Access and transportation There is often the architectural desire to consolidate recreation facilities in one impressive place. However, research on use patterns suggests that, especially for younger children, a neighborhood approach is superior. One reason is that transportation arteries are barriers for younger children, less mobile older persons, and any caretakers who must keep track of a number of children. Roads and play areas should be planned together, not one after the other.

Ecology The better PUDs take into account the ecology of the land in order to retain variety and as many natural features as possible. Established growth, natural drainage, and exceptional features add to the general environmental interest of the community as well as provide outdoor spaces that children and adults can adapt to imaginative play and personal interaction.

As will be outlined in the next section, planning for leisure begins with anticipating the participation and intents of the residents. Since a community is planned for specific markets, such anticipation is easier and more accurate than for a town that just grows without a plan.

Program A PUD is generally small enough for participatory development of recreation programs. Even though limited by the facilities planned and put in place by the developers, the program can be responsive to the ideas and interests of the residents. In some cases a recreation coordinator may be employed to supervise the maintenance of facilities, initiate program-developing mechanisms, and carry out some of the program ideas. In smaller PUDs the formulation and implementation of program may be done entirely by volunteers. In either case the program committees need to be representative of all segments of the community. The danger of space and facilities being preempted by organized groups can be reduced when young mothers and employed singles are represented as well as the tournament tennis players and the swim team parents.

CASE: SURPRISE IN AN "ADULT COMMUNITY"

The "adult community" was added as an enclave to a major new town in southern California. Housing was divided between condominium apartments, mostly compact two-bedroom models, and duplexes. Some designs allowed two singles to share one residence with some separation of living patterns. In general, the target market was the younger single adult and childless couples who were getting started in the housing market and whose life-styles would include considerable leisure at the beach, in the city, and at other locales outside the community. Provided in the middle of the plan was a set of eight lighted tennis courts and a clubhouse with a party room and an exercise room. Two pools were built, one on each side of the development.

The package was rather traditional except for the number of tennis courts. Again, the expectation was that residents would be engaged in active recreational and social lives. No residents under 16 were allowed. Children's play areas, school provisions, and organized sports programs would not be needed.

The surprise was that quite a number of sales were to adults outside the target market. Along with the "on-the-way-up" singles and couples, there were also retirement and preretirement couples, divorced and separated adults of all ages, and a sprinkling of young renters in units purchased for investment by nonresidents. The reason for the diversity was the relatively low cost of the units in the generally high-end Irvine area. A volunteer social and recreation committee made a useful discovery. Everyone was not a "swinging single" or a tennis buff. Many had come because of location and price, rather than life-style. When a Sunday morning brunch was inaugurated in the clubhouse by the prime movers of the social committee, the diversity of the development was demonstrated. Ages ranged from 18 to 78. Some were there in preformed groups and some came alone, hoping to meet neighbors and make new friends. As the tennis players adjourned to the courts outside, quite a number remained to drink coffee and juice and get acquainted.

The point is that even such a narrow target market for a PUD may mishit. People select housing for a number of reasons. Investment hopes, price, financing, location, availability, and aesthetics may override the projections and marketing strategies of the developers. As a consequence the best planning may be somewhat off-target when a community has its residents in place. Further, there will be changes from the profile of the first residents. Recreation plans and programs need the flexibility to adapt to who is actually there, to their changing life-styles, and to "surprises" produced by the market.

PLANNED COMMUNITIES

In several countries the term *New Town* has been used to refer to larger planned communities. Usually with final populations in excess of 35,000, New Towns are based on comprehensive *master plans* that include the full range of businesses, services, and residential development. The New Town is intended to be varied and integrated in population, at least partly self-sustaining in retail businesses and employment opportunities, and inclusive in life-styles and resources. A planned community, whether designated a New Town or not, will have an image to project of a superior environment for living. The plan is intended to enhance the quality of life and provide opportunities for personal and social development.

Recreation planning is an integral part of the overall plan. In New Towns in the United States the community image has leisure resources as a major focus. Enabling leisure is central to the concept and plan.

CASE: RESTON—PLANNING AND CHANGE

The New Town of Reston, Virginia, was the creation of Robert E. Simon, who attempted to implement the vision of a community that would incorporate a balance in ecology, population, and life-styles. Located 18 miles west of Washington, D.C., in a largely undeveloped woods and meadowland of over 7,000 acres, Reston was based on a master plan that followed the ideologies of European New Towns. It was to integrate work and leisure, residence and institutions, leisure resources and the natural environment into a total community that would enable residents to develop a superior quality of life. Integral to the plan was the centrality of leisure—a mingling and sharing of persons of various social backgrounds, the expression of the arts, physical development and sport for all ages, and immediate access to natural environments of walkways, woods, and streams. The terrain and its drainage contours were retained and made part of the plan rather than flattened for easy building. Further, up to 40% of the land was retained as common ground to be used for play, appreciation, buffers, and an environmental setting for community.

From 1962, when the special "Residential Planned Community" zoning was adopted, to 1982, there were several significant shifts. First, the founder discovered that financing such an enterprise required more front-end and long-term capital than he could muster. As a result Reston was sold to the Gulf-Reston Company with its energy-produced investment resources. Gulf in turn sold to the Mobil Land Development Corporation. The capital requirements along with a withdrawal of federal support has reduced the size of new planned communities more to the PUD magnitude since 1975. Second, fluctuations in the housing market and periodic recessions have put Reston's growth off schedule. By 1983 less than half of the originally projected 80,000 residents were in Reston. Third, a series of external factors related to transportation, schools, and federal housing programs had "unplanned impacts" on the planned community.[1] The master plan had to be adapted to a number of unanticipated factors.

Nevertheless, recreation remained central to the Reston vision of community. By 1983 there were 15 public and 4 private swimming pools, 40 community and 11 private tennis courts, a public and a private golf course, 44 ball fields, an indoor tennis and racquet club, a bowling center with 32 lanes, 4 lakes, 850 acres of open space, 5 miles of walkways and bike paths, 4 small community halls, and the community center. The Reston Homeowners Association (RHOA) operates most of the facilities except for the private clubs. However, it is not the number of recreation resources that is especially worthy of attention.

First, the New Town concept of a planned basis for community does not relegate leisure to the periphery of life. Rather, it is assumed that various expressions of chosen activity and associations are part of the whole of human development. Further, design can facilitate or impede participation in such activity and interaction. Leisure requires place and space as well as social organization.

Second, access to a full range of leisure places was part of the overall community plan. Rather than cluster all recreation resources in one "center," Reston was designed with the neighborhood foremost. Swimming pools, tennis courts, play areas, walkways, and meeting rooms were within walking distance of almost all residents. Further, such facilities were to be in place as locations for community interaction rather than lag behind housing construction. Major activity centers support the "adepts" of recreation, those who are competition-oriented and who prefer to associate only with those of similar skill levels. Neighborhood opportunities tend to attract children, learners, those with more social orientations toward participation, and those who do not schedule activity far in advance.

Third, while some desired resources are always missing or scarce, the attempt was to enable participation in a wide variety of leisure pursuits. As an integrated community with a wide span of ages and household composition, there was no single image of sport, arts, or nature appreciation sought. A shortage of indoor meeting space was evident within a few years. However, the aim was to schedule space for music and dance as well as Campfire Girls and religion.

Fourth, the concept was that most programs would emerge out of the community. The intent of the developers was to support an organization that would be responsive to the initiatives of residents. It may have been inevitable that some were more responsive than others and that special interest groups would become influential beyond their numbers. However, there has also been "counterorganizing" that has represented interests other than those on the RHOA boards and committees.

Fifth, as with smaller developments, recreation resources have been employed as marketing elements. Recreation has been featured in promotion from the first. One estimate is that housing in Reston has been 5% to 10% higher in cost than in ordinary developments in the area, but Reston has been marketed as a *community* that is a better environment for living, and recommended especially for leisure, the natural ecology, and design excellence. But the marketing has not dominated recreation design or location.

At first the stress was almost entirely on community facilities and voluntary programs. However, in time the mix of provisions has become much more varied:

1. When a second golf course was opened, the first became a private club offering the privileges and protection that come with higher cost.
2. The sprinkling of small businesses offering instruction in the arts developed into a major market sector for recreation. Now a commercial center in three adjacent buildings has the racquet club, gymnastics, a fitness club, a bowling center with an elaborate refreshment and meeting area, and a skating rink. The restaurant and bar offerings have been considerably expanded.
3. The community-organized arts festivals and events have also been augmented by a number of business-based entertainment offerings.

4. The total lack of truly "public" recreation programs and resources has been changed. For years RHOA, rather than the county, provided all recreation opportunities. However, identification of a number of shortages led to the financing and construction of a public community center with a theater, large indoor pool, arts facilities, and meeting rooms. There is a game room, a photography lab, a woodworking shop, dance studio, and theater facilities. Classes and activities include:

Drawing, painting, sculpture, printmaking, and weaving.

Performing arts with acting, ballet, jazz dance, guitar, jazz music, African dance, and tap.

Cooking, photography, woodworking, fiber, and ceramics.

Tryout groups such as "Ballet for Klutzes," a step at a time.

Aerobics and fitness, jazzercise, magic, square dancing, and yoga.

Aquatics for all ages and skill levels.

Special events for children, teens, seniors, and others.

Visiting performers and concerts.

It was discovered that some kind of public funding and development was needed as a part of the overall set of provisions. Now the community center fills some of the lack of indoor space, even though it is booked a year in advance by groups.

Leisure in the Reston plan was integrated into the total concept and design. While many changes and adaptations were found necessary, that integration has not been radically altered. From the beginning Reston was a business, and recreation a part of the concept. The complementarity of community, private, voluntary, and business organization of opportunities is seen in the planned community at least as clearly as in one that has just evolved through the decades.

Further, recreation planning is not just a matter of providing a set of facilities. For example, in the first decade almost all employment was outside the community, usually in or around Washington. Commuting time averaged two hours a day. This meant that recreation resources for adults and programs that attracted families had to be scheduled in limited periods and take account of the long work and travel days. Later, as employment in Reston rose to over 10,000, more variety in adult recreation schedules was possible. Businesses were able to exploit the lunch period as well as evenings for adult participation. Economic, political, family, and community institutions are all related to recreation planning.

CASE: LEISURE AND THE LIFE CYCLE

Like Reston, the New Town of Irvine, California, is too complex a story to present in detail. However, again like Reston, Irvine emphasizes recreation resources and styles in both its plan and marketing.

Irvine began with a unique opportunity, the ranch of the Irvine family located in Orange County, south of Los Angeles. The ranch encompassed 120 square miles, over 120,000 acres in the fastest-growing area in the country. It stretched from the coastal mountains to the Pacific Ocean and included desert and estuaries, orchards and fields, hills and valleys. In 1960 a master plan was developed for a New Town by The Irvine Company. One thousand acres were donated for a campus of the University of California, which opened in 1965. Although the original concept of integrating campus and community was abandoned, it was replaced by a plan with a unique combination of marketing and social sophistication.

The city was to consist of a number of "villages" that would each have a distinctive character. The life-style characteristic of households in various phases of the family life cycle would be the basis of the village design and institutional provisions. For example, a village primarily for families with young children would have ample schools, fields for team sports, play areas in the center of residential culs-de-sac, homes designed for family living, and protection from traffic. Outdoor recreation space would be reserved for child, youth, and family activity.

On the other hand, villages with apartments and smaller units for "never nested" childless adults would emphasive physical activity, social meeting places, and evening activity centers. A village for those at or near retirement age would have a community center for social organizations, the golf course, and easy-access housing with upkeep minimized.

The concept was that individuals or groups could remain in Irvine and yet have not only housing but a village designed for their needs as they progressed through their life courses. Again, leisure as a central element of life, requiring some community as well as residential resources, was integral to the concept. It was unique that the villages would be marketed for exactly the kinds of households for which they were designed. In time, an intact living unit might sell and move to the village most appropriate for its current household composition and life-style.

Dimensions of the overall plan were a graded network of roads that enabled efficient travel without arteries that divided neighborhoods, a mixture of employment opportunities with science and industrial areas, a network of schools planned in relation to the housing and transportation, shopping centers, and entertainment clusters at arterial intersections, and accessible recreation opportunities. Resources that are part of the city plan are provided by public agencies but are complemented by business operation of a major tennis club, theaters, and other leisure locales.

As with Reston, the Irvine plan was subject to amendment as the economic context had its impacts. A series of corporate clashes led to some changes. However, more important in the 1980s have been two economic factors. Both revolve around the investment dimension of residential real estate.

First, the cost of housing increased rapidly through the 1970s. In California prices rose two to three times the national average. Irvine became quite expensive, boasting a median home value of $168,000 in 1981. At the same time there was a scarcity of available homes in Irvine. Lotteries were used for a time to select those who would be allowed to purchase real estate. Prospective buyers lined up, not only for the chance to live in Irvine but, even more, to invest there. When the housing market collapsed during the 1981–82 recession, assumptions of such increasing values left many new owners in precarious financial positions.

Second, the investment aspect of a home purchase in Irvine then had its impacts on life-style. Couples postponed having children because they could not afford to reduce their dual-career incomes. Income and making first and second mortgage payments became a prime consideration in career decisions. The concept of moving to another village as the life-cycle period changed was stymied by high interest rates and slow resales. In short, the market had a powerful impact on the implementation of the life-cycle-based concept and on the life-styles of residents.

Nevertheless, leisure remained central to life-styles and marketing for the villages. The first descriptive page of the brochure for a family-oriented village has photos of sailing, running, swimming in a neighborhood pool, and children on play apparatus. It emphasizes parks close to home as well as housing styles, lakes for a variety of activities, beach and tennis clubs, and accessibility, followed by schools and retail centers. A more adult-oriented village stresses the interaction potential of the gathering-places in the clustered housing, shopping areas, and pools. On the other hand, a village of larger detached homes starts with private-space leisure for families as well as nearby parks and pools.

When research was done on new residents, the following ranking of reasons for buying in Irvine was found in the 1975–77 period:[2]

Highest:	Planned community
	Investment opportunities
Next highest:	Environmental—open and country
	Close to work
Other:	Weather and freedom from smog
	Close to beach

Elements of attraction to the planned community were recreation, beauty, transportation efficiency, and other amenities. However, these were considered to contribute to the investment potential of real estate in Irvine. The design features and concepts are not separate from the business of developing a community. Rather, leisure planning is always two-dimensional—for living and marketing. The two come together when satisfaction with the community produces an image that attracts other buyers.

Of course, Irvine has some special attractions such as the southern California climate and the unique expanse and location of the ranch property. Further, it has become almost totally oriented toward high-end markets. Its reputation as a high-cost place in which to purchase real estate is deserved. However, there is a lot to learn from the Irvine concepts of designing for life-style as well as from how the designs have worked out in providing a base for marketing as well as for recreation-oriented life-styles.

A MODEL OF COMMUNITY RECREATION PLANNING

In the book *Leisure Identities and Interactions,*[3] there is a model for community recreation planning. The approach is based on identification of the population segments of the actual or anticipated community. The developmental and social aims of leisure through the life course are outlined and related to the types of activities that provide such outcomes. Planning, then, begins with people and their overall life patterns rather than with a map of the terrain or an assumption that certain amenities are necessary for promotional purposes. At present many developers seem locked into plans with biases unrecognized by those who base their concepts on facility packages rather than on leisure behaviors and meanings.

Beginning with people provides a perspective on planning that can enhance satisfaction with greatest efficiency.

The order of planning would be as indicated in the diagram below.

A Community Recreation Planning Sequence

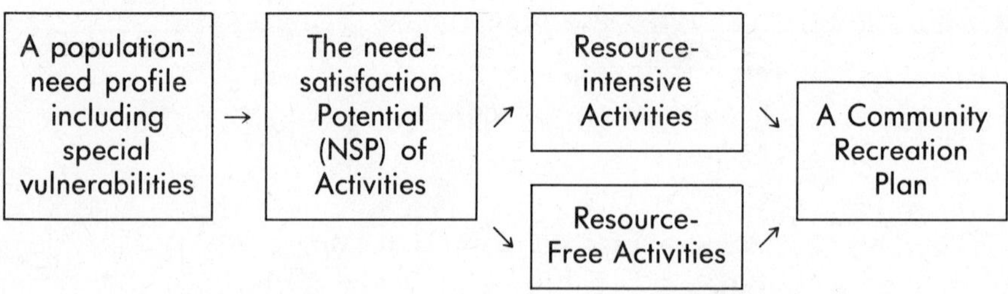

First, planning would begin with a simple analysis of census data or a marketing profile for the community. Particular needs of population groups, taking account of life-careers and temporary and lifelong limitations, do not vary greatly from community to community. Therefore, no new in-depth study is required once the basic need-satisfaction analysis is developed. Rather, the critical needs will be correlated with the population characteristics to produce a need profile for the community. In the community profile recreation needs will be listed by the size of population groups having those needs.

Second, the kinds of activities that tend to meet those needs will be listed under each segment of the population-need profile. Activities with the potential to meet such needs and which are either resource-free or for which there is abundant opportunity may substitute for some that are resource-intensive.

Finally, the planning can concentrate on providing opportunities for which special resources are required and that are important in the leisure need-satisfaction of groups identified in the population profile. Further, vulnerable groups will be noted and their needs given specific attention. The community recreation plan will then concentrate its resources on activities with the need-satisfaction potential to meet the critical needs of those who lack substitute opportunities and resources.

Although no one-to-one correlation is possible, a number of general relationships of activity to perceived or anticipated satisfactions can be derived.

There is no single satisfaction for each category of activities. However, some are perceived to yield greater proportions of particular satisfactions. For example, cultural activities such as reading, watching television, and going to the movies are most likely to satisfy needs for relaxation and escape from constraints. On the other hand, sports like tennis and cultural activities such as developing arts and craft skills satisfy needs for self-expression and the development of mastery and competence. Travel combines satisfactions but is weighted toward recuperation. Family activity also is mixed but tends to complement role relationships in positive relational satisfactions and in meeting the expectations of others. Conversely, further analysis of the reasons given for choosing particular activities provides a preliminary list of activities with the NSP for certain needs.

Note that all but one kind of satisfaction are oriented toward the self rather than being primarily social. Further, both relaxation and excitement are recognized by adults as desired leisure outcomes. Therefore, the likelihood of simplifying the multiple satisfactions to a single dimension seems unlikely. The crucial step is to find the needs that are especially salient for various groups in the population to be served. Both self-related and social reasons for selecting activities are important to adults and may be combined for the same activity. Ideally, activities with a multiple NSP might meet different needs for a variety of participants with a single set of resources. The most efficient use of resources for leisure opportunities would be based on such need-satisfaction analysis. Priorities would be developed considering those resource-intensive activities that are important to population groups and cannot be easily replaced in NSP by resource-free activities.

Leisure Needs and Corresponding Activities

	Activities	
Leisure Need	***Predominant Satisfaction***	***A Major Satisfaction Element in the NSP***
Rest, relaxation, work contrast	Reading for pleasure, watching television	Swimming, hobbies, concerts, family outings
Skill development and mastery	Arts, crafts, hobbies, adult education, tennis	Other sports
Self-expression	Arts, crafts, hobbies	
Personal growth	Reading for pleasure, adult education, concerts, museums, etc.	Hobbies, making friends
Excitement and a contest	Indoor and outdoor sports	Reading, arts, crafts
Exercise and health	Swimming, running	Other sports, family outings
Companionship and belonging	Family outings, meeting friends	Going to concerts and museums, eating out, sports

LIFE CAREERS AND LEISURE RESOURCES

The aim of a book by Rhona and Robert Rapoport[4] is to begin to delineate patterns of leisure in relation to employment, education, and family careers. They propose that at any stage in the life cycle persons have *preoccupations* derived from their basic biological, social, and developmental tasks. These preoccupations, in turn, lead to certain *interests* in the kinds of occupation and relationships that will predominate in that period. Through one's life career these interests change as preoccupations and social expectations change. Finally, the opportunity structures present activities that provide arenas to carry out these interests. The "preoccupations-interests-activities" scheme is one way in which to examine the secondary and flexible character of the specific activities that are intended to provide need-satisfactions related to the changing needs of a person moving through his or her life career.

The main point is that leisure interests are not some separate segment of life that may be altered at will. What a person "wants" in leisure complements identity and social-role development through the life career. Leisure is not determined by work, education, family, and community roles; but neither is leisure separate from them. Activities would ideally be chosen to satisfy needs integral to biological, personal, and social development just as employment, marriage, and community relationships may be chosen to enhance valued leisure roles.

The outline that follows is only suggestive. Both careful searching of available research and new programs of investigation can begin to fill in the blanks and lead to a fuller explication of the kinds of activities that have the greatest need-satisfaction potential (NSP) for the various periods and preoccupations of life careers.

FACILITY PLANNING IMPLICATIONS

Without going into detail, some suggestions of how this approach to planning might alter the development of a neighborhood park may illustrate the procedure for facility development.

Planning for a neighborhood park would begin with a profile of the population to be served. Then, with a need profile for the groups, activities requiring outdoor park resources would be identified. A crucial step would be the designation of those vulnerable groups with the fewest alternative resources. For a neighborhood park special attention would probably be given to children too young to go more than a few blocks on their own. Transportation possibilities and limits would also receive special attention.

Once the groups needing priority are identified and their park-related activities outlined, the use-potential of the site itself would be mapped. Space, terrain, soil, and access limitations of most sites do not allow for an infinite range of activity provisions. Activities that conflict in space, personnel, or other environmental resource would be weighed, and those with the lowest NSP and the greatest conflict potential eliminated.

Finally, provisions of space, access, separation, amenities, and schedule would be combined into a plan for the park. For example, the need for 10- to 12-year-old boys to gather for participatory games and sports in places open enough for possible participants to "scout the scene" and yet separated enough not to drive younger children away from their activity sites would determine the landscaping design of part of the park. Flexibility would be sought so that different groups could adapt the space to their needs at different times. The design process would then begin with the life-career need profiles of the neighborhood and end with horticultural amenities rather than vice versa.

Life Careers and Leisure Needs

Life Career Stage	*Preoccupations*	*Central Leisure Needs: Intrinsic and Social*		*Activities*
I. Preparatory				
A. Child	learning and expression	exploration and equilibrium needs in a cycling variety		games: negotiated and structured
B. Preteen	personal identity	exploration and testing		limited duration, developmental
C. Adolescent	social identity	independence and sexuality		experimental, group expressive
II. Establishment				
A. Student	life investments, role-testing	self-development	role anticipation	variety: physical, social, escape
B. Single	intimacy, testing, role-taking	self-development	relational: intimate	communal and unrestrictive

C. Preparental	intimacy development, role establishment	self-development	communicative	couple-oriented, mutual
D. Parental:	life investments	self-expressive	familial and institutional	family intensive, with "freedom opportunities"
Preschool	meeting demands			
School-age	nurture			
Launching	readjustments			
III. Re-integration	self-acceptance			
A. Postparental	redefining roles	expressive-experimental	intimacy renewing	learning skills, couple and self
B. Preretirement	security	maximizing self-satisfaction	consolidating	develop physical and social contexts
C. Retirement	self-acceptance	time-intensive	community building	variety, introductory
D. Widowhood	community	home, role-renewing		familiarity and friendship combinations

RECREATION-BASED COMMUNITIES

A major element in real estate development in North America is the recreation-based community. Planned communities with recreation resources as a central part of the plan are increasingly significant. Millions are also being invested in developments based on the projected leisure styles of future inhabitants. For example, the Mobil Corporation in 1983 was involved in 17 real estate developments in Florida, California, and elsewhere. Of those 17, about half are on sites with a special recreational feature around which the development is planned.

A recreation-based community can be defined as one in which economic productivity is not central. Rather, life-style resources are the primary dimension of planning. There are at least three types of such communities. *Retirement* developments are planned for those who have withdrawn from regular engagement in the economy and whose timetables are no longer dominated by work. *Mixed* communities may include retired residents, recreation-oriented visitors, second homes for those still having a regular economic relationship elsewhere, and full-time residents who are currently employed. *Resource-focused* communities exist because of a particular leisure resource at that location, but they are more than resorts.

All three types are important elements of the overall real estate development industry. Each of the three has specific characteristics in the planning for housing, recreation, community interaction, and location. And most recreation-based communities are found in the Sunbelt, in the Southeast or Southwest or in special resource sites such as the Colorado Rockies. In all three types recreation is employed as a significant element in marketing. In many, some attention is given to the leisure needs and orientations as well as personal resources of the likely residents. For the most part, previously established communities have served as models for those now being planned.

RETIREMENT DEVELOPMENTS

They are scattered across the southland from Florida to California. Their residents come from all states, but especially from those with severe winter climates. Those who purchase homes or apartments in such developments tend to be in the middle- to upper-middle-income range. Housing costs are too high for the lower half of the income range, and social institutions are not exclusive enough for the upper 5% of that group. However, there are very special developments for the wealthy where recreation opportunities tend to be quite private due to high entry costs.

What is different about retirement adults that requires a different kind of recreation planning?

1. In a retirement community they have left behind former social networks and need to establish new ones. The recent trend toward retirement

housing in or near former residences testifies to the importance of social integration to older people and the personal costs of having to begin again. Therefore, both housing layouts and recreation provisions need to be designed to maximize social interaction. There needs to be space for milling and mixing as well as sitting and talking at the pool, park, community center, and shopping areas.

2. Those who choose to move to a retirement community are most likely to be seeking a comparatively active life. They often have in mind being outdoors, engaging in physical activity, and being active socially. National participation figures for 65- to 80-year-olds engaged regularly in, say, swimming will not be representative of this population. They will be far above national averages in many such activities. Golf, the sport that has the least decline in participation with age, often becomes a regular activity even for those who have played only infrequently. In fact, except for high-income enclaves, the Sunbelt retirement community may be the only one for which a golf course can be justified on the basis of year-round daily use by a substantial proportion of residents.
3. Most of the residents will be women. As the community ages, more and more will be women alone. Leisure planning should not concentrate so much on the physically active "young old" male and couples that the "middle old" and "old old" women are neglected. Their leisure will be more social and require accessible places for formal organizations and informal meeting. Especially in the early period of widowhood, women need ways of reintegrating themselves into a society of survivors.
4. Stereotypes of the recreation of older people tend to be far too limiting. The communities with the highest satisfaction of residents are those that offer a wide variety of opportunities. Leisure is characterized by diversity and variety, among retirees as well as among those who are younger. Arts interests include participating as well as watching and listening. Sport interests include more than golf and shuffleboard. Social clubs are formed around interests in politics and archeology as well as poker and bridge. The biggest shortage of recreation resources for most such communities is likely to be comfortable indoor meeting rooms.
5. Older people can learn. The assumption that only previously acquired skills will be exercised in the so-called declining years is proven false whenever opportunities for new learning are available. One can want to sharpen a backhand or try a new kind of ceramic firing at 75 as well as at 15.

Taking into account these and other factors in retirement recreation, the planning of such a development becomes more complex than might have been expected. One key is to develop facilities and institutional mechanisms that can change. As residents are encouraged to take over the direction of their own recreation resources, they should not be stopped by rigid spaces and inflexible locations that made sense to some architect/planner working with paper and a drafting table. The mark of good design is adaptability. At the very least, it should be remembered that the population of such a development will continue to age, go through the later phases of the life course, and seek leisure adapted to current aims and competencies. Careful delineation of the demographics over time and not just of the target markets for initial purchase should be integral to the planning. Among the most famous retirement communities are Sun City, Arizona, and the Rossmore Leisure World of Laguna Hills, California. Both are the size of small cities. Both are now well established and have become models for other such developments. Both are the products of companies with residential development experience that predates their entry into retirement development. And both have a wide diversity of recreation resources built into their plans and programs.

While there are significant differences, there are also a number of important similarities between the two communities. The differences reflect both location and the visions of the founders. Sun City seems more conventionally residential, a suburb planned for older people whose life-style will continue to center around residential activity, entertaining, and interaction. The culture is something of the Midwest transplanted to the desert, where the sun shines, winter never comes, and air conditioning is a necessity. Leisure World, planned after the test case of an earlier community could be evaluated, provides an incredible variety of housing types, recreation facilities, and styles. Over the hills is Laguna Beach and the ocean, and now just up the road is Irvine.

Common elements include the following:

- Integration of recreation resources into the basic land-use plan.
- Recognition of the importance of location and access for use.
- Adaptation to the particular terrain and climate conditions of the site.
- Provision for expansion and diversification as the community develops and ages.
- A variety of housing sizes and styles so that residents can move within the community.
- In Leisure World, especially, provision for health care and maintenance as well as for the well and able.
- Provision for visitors and for linking the community to cultural and other resources outside.
- Concern for safety, both in internal design and protection from industry.

The planning of such communities now has enough history and experience that it is not necessary to guess about the future. However, those who will enter such residential environments in the 1990s and after the year 2000 may be significantly different from the pioneers of Leisure World in the 1960s.

CASE: "HIDDEN VALLEY"

A study by Nancy J. Osgood of retirement settlements included one referred to as "Hidden Valley."[5] Located about 25 miles south of Tucson, it grew in 15 years to a community of about 6,000 residents. Developed by the University of Arizona Foundation, its core area was comprised of fifteen hundred rental apartment units, a shopping center with ten stores, a community center, golf course, medical facility, and a municipal services building. Detached homes and town houses were built around this core, designed with a Spanish motif. After financial difficulties and government intervention the development was managed by a private company.

Social life is characterized by a proliferation of voluntary organizations including churches, fraternal groups, and interest-centered clubs. Organized recreation includes facilities for golf, swimming, shuffleboard, and arts, crafts, and hobbies. A tour of the recreation opportunities is part of the sales introduction given to prospective buyers. In interviews residents testified to the importance of recreation participation in making new friends. Recreation is often a context for interaction as much as for activity. Hidden Valley also has a history of concerted political action when changes in the development structure threatened access to the golf course and swimming pools.

Two recreation complexes are available in Hidden Valley. Each has a set of directors and committees that plan and manage much of the program. The East Center contains meeting rooms, a 25-meter pool, a therapy pool, shuffleboard and tennis courts, a par-3 golf course, and facilities for several types of craft and hobby participation. There are classes in painting, sewing, weaving, silversmithing, lapidary, drawing, rug hooking, bridge, Spanish, yoga, astronomy, desert history, and a number of games. The West Center has a theater along with various activity and meeting rooms.

Among the most popular activities are golf, ceramics, and home-oriented activities such as furniture refinishing. The parking lots at the neighborhood centers are often filled from 8:00 A.M. on. The smaller neighborhood centers are especially valued for providing places to meet and interact with others and to develop ongoing relationships. Dropping in for coffee is a common thing to do, and special events become a context for more organized interaction.

One major feature according to residents is the different social climate. There is a high value placed on leisure activity. No one is too old to engage in activity, be seen in swimsuits or sports attire, or try something new. Rather than leisure being valued primarily for its contribution to work or health, it becomes a legitimate and valued realm for the investment of time and self. Hidden Valley is a "leisure world" in the positive sense that it enables and encourages participation.

Are there problems? Of course, people can be lonely there, too. Especially when health problems occur or a spouse dies, adjustments may be quite difficult. People do die there as well as becoming tan and active. However, this self-selected group prizes activity and strives for involvement rather than withdrawal. Recreation planning and marketing is directed toward that orientation, the market segment of those who believe they will utilize resources as much or more than ever before.

MIXED COMMUNITIES

The mixed community is one that has a recreation locale and marketing thrust but is planned for a variety of temporary and full-time residents. These developments are found in the winter-free climates, near natural recreation environments such as seashores and lakes, and include a recreation theme in both planning and marketing. They are real-estate driven in the sense that the business aim is to sell real property for residence, tourist resorts, retail businesses, and recreation activity centers. They rely on retail entrepreneurs to provide much of the opportunity structure for those drawn to the area with recreation in mind. And in many cases the developers and design teams are truly interested in working out a plan that facilitates rich and diverse life-styles. However, the core of the business base is real estate.

A mixed community will be planned for two or more of the following residential markets:

Full-time residents from other areas, often at or near retirement age.

Full-time residents who are part of the local economy.

Part-time residents who come for "the season" but retain primary residence and economic affiliation elsewhere.

Condominium owners who are in residence for two weeks or a month and who rent their units the remainder of the year.

Time-share owners who come only for their assigned time period but who may be a market for other real estate sales.

Recreation visitors who rent in resort hotels, condominium units, or other residences available for periods of the year.

The mix will vary from one development to another, even in the same general locale. For the decade of the 1970s condominium sales of units that combined use and rental programs were the fast-growing market in recreation-based developments. More recently the time-share approach has become popular. Always there is the significant rental business for one-time tourists, first-time visitors, convention business, and other identified market segments.

As outlined in the case on interrelationship of businesses and services in a comprehensive ski resort town, the complementarity of resources and services in such a community is both vast and complex. In a mixed-market development, such provisions are a combination of planning and entrepreneurship. A master plan has to provide space and access for business and services as well as protect the prime recreation sites. Further, a gradation of businesses allows for relatively easy access to frequently required provisions and greater centralization of businesses that may be visited less than once a week. Further, some resources, such as golf courses, are space-intensive and have to be part of the initial land-use plan if they are to exist at all.

CASE: HILTON HEAD ISLAND

Hilton Head Island, just off the South Carolina coast and north of Savannah, Georgia, is the largest Atlantic coast island south of Long Island. It is about 12 miles long with 30,000 acres of land of which 2,000 acres are marsh. It has broad sand beaches, a moderate climate, and easy travel over a bridge to the mainland.

In 1982 the permanent population was about 12,000. However, the additional population magnitude is indicated by the recreation provisions: 175 tennis courts, 15 golf courses, over 100 restaurants, and a variety of other provisions. Planners estimate that up to 550,000 individuals visit the island each year, with the peak in the summer of about 25,000 at one time. Hilton Head is a year-round community *and* year-round resort with the high season beginning in March.

The first development, Sea Pines Plantation, covers the western "toe" of the island. However, there are five other "plantations" and plans for eventually covering most of the solid land with more. There is continual activity in the sales offices of the developers, emphasizing the sale of new units with 1983 prices beginning around $60,000 for small condominiums away from the water to the over $500,000 market for shore units in detached and multiple-unit designs. Hilton Head is clearly a high-end market development. The exception is the introduction of time-sharing that opens ownership possibilities to middle-income buyers. Rentals of apartment-style units run about the same as first-class motels away from the water, and considerably more for choice locations.

Sea Pines was begun by Charles Fraser on land already owned by his family. The concept was for an ecologically balanced plan that would preserve marshlands in the estuarial boundaries, reshape dry land for residences and recreation, mix multiple and detached housing neighborhoods, protect the development from crime, and offer a community in which leisure, residence, and services were self-contained. Neighborhoods within the total development would be keyed to housing type and leisure style. Some were oriented primarily toward the beach, others to golf, and others to tennis or a harbor. Some were more clustered and even semiurban. Others provided greater seclusion. However, the full range of leisure resources—beach, golf, tennis, shopping, eating and drinking, community events, spectator sports, cultural programs, and so on—were available within the development and no more than a few minutes' drive away. The 4,500-acre site is the largest such recreation-oriented development in the United States, with five miles of beaches, 40 miles of roads and bikeways, harbors, and a 600-acre forest preserve.

Some of the market segments identified for the overall planning were:

1. Convention trade with three conference locations.
2. The golf-inclined older household with enough wealth to build a high-cost home on the island whether or not they would live there for more than part of the year.
3. The eastern seaboard resident with second-home financial resources and willing to pay a premium for the environmental control and recreation opportunities.
4. The resort visitor escaping northern winters or seeking a summer beach and sport life.
5. Those attracted by special events such as major golf and tennis tournaments.
6. The investor ready to buy property in the special planned community, but with personal use as a secondary incentive.

In 1980 over $129 million in building permits were issued. Not only have several other "plantations" been started with Sea Pines as both a magnet and a model, but Charles Fraser has been in demand as a planner and concept-developer for numerous other resort and mixed developments. Employment on the island grew from 2,900 in 1972 to 9,500 in 1980. Property values have risen each year. And Sea Pines guests were found in 1980 to have an average income of almost $50,000 per family. The high-end marketing has reached its target.

Recreation in the "plantations" of Hilton Head is heavily oriented toward the beach, courts, and links. However, there are also equestrian opportunities, sailing, power boating, fishing, and a variety of games. Instruction centers for tennis and golf are integrated with the major clubs and courses. Instruction packages are one of the incentives for visiting the area as renters or guests in one of the resort hotels.

There is no doubt that location is a major attraction. Most of the Atlantic coast barrier islands are closed to business development. Hilton Head is the largest exception. Climate is a factor. However, the combination of environmental planning and recreation resources is a marketing feature. The market segments identified are willing to make major real estate investments to gain regular access to the environment—natural, built, and social—in which leisure is accepted, enhanced, and enriched. There are significant incomes to be gained from the operation of sports centers, retail establishments, restaurants and bars, and a variety of other services aimed at leisure. However, the major investment returns go to those who have been able to secure part of the real estate business where the demand has grown each year.

Like other recreation-based businesses, the draw of the business depends on recreation participation. There is no attempt to provide for all population groups, all cultural interests, or for the deprived and vulnerable. The interests and aims of particular market segments are analyzed. They are related to interests, self-definitions, life and leisure experiences, current leisure investments, recognized constraints and limitations, and hopes for the future. Planning brings together the natural resources of the location and climate, distance factors for potential markets, and the leisure commitments and dreams of those who can afford the time and investment for the development. Environmental protection and access are sales factors for Hilton Head markets. Protection against groups whose life-styles are seen as disruptive is purchased at a price. And the opportunities to *do* recreation without all the current limitations, frustrations, and inhibitions are attractive. Planning for the mixed markets of such a community is not simple. It is more than counting courts and tees per capita. It also involves a readiness to place the recreation investments at the center of planning and marketing the property investments.

RESOURCE-FOCUSED COMMUNITIES

The resource-focused recreation community exists in its location because of a single leisure resource. There may be secondary and complementary opportunities. Some attempts may be made to attract visitors in the off-season with other programs. However, Vail and Aspen exist because of Rocky Mountain skiing. Longboat Key is developed because of the Gulf beach and climate. Surfers Paradise exists for the water and the beach. They are recreation-based communities with a single resource as the primary reason for their existence.

This does not mean that business in such a community is solely aimed at the central activity. There are a spectrum of services and business-provided opportunities that surround and complement the core. Nor does it mean that real estate is not the basis of the investment potential for the site. The differences from a Hilton Head are, however, important:

- The focused development will plan, design, and market with a concentration on those who do or may want to do the particular activity.

- There is less emphasis on full-year residence than at the retirement or mixed development.
- Seasonality may be a more pronounced factor in marketing and for programs. Some may simply accept the off-season as given and concentrate on business during the peak participation periods. Others may seek to extend the season or develop a second season based on alternative resources and activities. Pricing may be adjusted to attract visitors to the well-known destination outside the activity period.
- The development is designed for a higher proportion of short-term visitors who stay one or two weeks. Considerable marketing offers lodging and activity packages for such visits.
- The image of the community is almost entirely linked to the resource focus. This can be useful if the image is one of high quality and success. However, it can be a problem for any attempt at diversification.
- Condominium development coupled with rental management services will be the major real estate format. However, time-sharing in which there is a rotation of use periods in and out of the prime season is also a growing market technique.

One dimension that all such communities have in common is the need for large amounts of front-end or development capital. More and more such capital is being supplied by corporations with other sources of wealth: energy companies, banking and insurance corporations, and conglomerates. The millions required to build a ski resort, even on leased land, and then operate the businesses for some years before reaching a business level that yields a profit makes such investment difficult for individuals. In addition, additional years are needed to assemble the land package, complete the master plan and design, and coordinate financing. Recreation-based development can yield high investment returns when well located and planned. However, the risks and delays are formidable.

THE COMMUNITY CONTEXT OF LEISURE

The ecology of leisure begins with the household and extends outward through private space to the neighborhood and larger community. In the same way the social context of leisure is centered in the immediate community of the household and expands through those interaction groups that are accessible to the more institutionalized and occasional contexts. Therefore, planning for leisure has the same starting point, not the farther reaches of the area but with the circles of availability centered in the residence.

Planning recreation resources for a community, however, cannot include a separate plan for every residence. Rather, distance and access to residences is approached in clusters of dwellings, neighborhoods, and natural residential enclaves. Further, in most areas there are natural resources, natural and built barriers, and other features that give some shape to the map of recreation access.

From the development perspective, recreation resources are one aspect of marketing. They are a sales incentive, amenities of attraction, and elements of distinctiveness. They are to be attractive, evident to the prospective buyer, and in line with expectations. However, the experience in the planned communities such as Reston and Irvine has been that good planning extends beyond marketing. Further, business success in the long run seems to be enhanced by planning that is more than the provision of superficial packages of amenities. Rather, combining objectives for market segments with a well-grounded understanding of recreation through the life span is attractive for both initial sales and for resales. How well a plan "works" is more important than how it looks to the casual observer.

As introduced in the planning-model section (page 384), this means that identification of the aims and meanings of leisure for the people expected to make up the population is the basis for the selection, placement, and design of particular facilities. Planning that touches the realities of daily living, that is responsive to the hopes and desires of those for whom the housing is being designed, will be recognized as a cut above the ordinary and commonplace package. Good planning is also good marketing.

Such planning takes into account factors such as:

- All likely members of the households, not just children.
- The changing patterns and interests as individuals and families move through their lives in the community.
- The aging of the community planned with the potential for change and adaptation.
- The possibility of developing new interests, learning new competencies, and making the residential decision a time for other new life investments as well.

In the long term thc aim is for satisfaction, to design and build a community that is a context for a full, expressive, and varied life together. A community is more than buildings and blueprints, but the plan can support the development of real community. It can provide resources for the freedom, expression, and social enrichment of leisure.

SUMMARY OF ISSUES

Real estate sales are the business base of the recreation elements of residential development.

Marketing aims and recreation planning may conflict when visibility is stressed over accessibility and short-term attraction over long-term flexibility.

Location and facilities for recreation may be a major marketing device in an urban multiunit development.

Maximizing outdoor space for a clustered-housing neighborhood requires careful location of usable common ground.

The narrow market segment attracted by most Planned Unit Developments should not obscure the need to plan for later adaptation as the households evolve.

In the master plan of a New Town, leisure is integral to residential and ecological planning as well as to the placement of facilities for activities and social gatherings.

The changing recreation orientations of individuals and households through the life course suggest leisure styles that may be incorporated in the marketing as well as planning of a residential development.

The recreation requirements of a retirement community should include settings for social interaction and opportunities for learning that are responsive to the active preferences of the "young old" who settle there and to those who stay during later periods of aging.

In a mixed recreation-based community recreation planning may be subordinated to a marketing image of the expectations of the high-end segment rather than to a full range of year-round opportunities.

In resource-focused community development as well as planned communities, the need for front-end capital investment becomes the overwhelming issue.

DISCUSSION QUESTIONS

1. How is the residence the base of recreation activity?
2. How might there be conflict between a recreation design for a development oriented toward sales and a design for use?
3. What would be the values in having a "recreation director" for a housing complex? What kinds of developments would benefit most?
4. How may the desired recreation opportunities of the "young old" of ages 65 to 75 be different in 20 years?
5. Can the recreation needs of preparental adults and households with young children be met in the same planned unit development? How?

6. How would you propose adapting the "adults only" recreation provisions to the more heterogeneous population actually there?
7. What is the place of private enterprise in the recreation provisions of a planned community?
8. Is the Irvine "life-style village" concept economically viable? Is it socially desirable? Why or why not?
9. What does the chart entitled "Life Careers and Leisure Needs" suggest for developing recreation businesses?
10. How can a retirement community be planned for later life? What are the implications of an "aging" retirement community?
11. What are the vocational opportunities for recreation-oriented adults in retirement and mixed communities?
12. What can someone with a recreation planning background offer to the community development company?
13. Why is good leisure planning also good marketing?

PROJECTS

1. Gather examples of real estate advertising from weekend newspapers that feature recreation resources and opportunities.
2. Design a common ground plan for a cluster of residences expected to house families with preschool children. How can the design accommodate the same families as they advance through the family life cycle?
3. Outline the principles, aims, and framework of a recreation plan for a New Town that would integrate a full age spectrum of residents. How would the plan enhance marketing efforts?
4. In your own community, find examples of how incremental planning rather than a master plan has led to access barriers and inequities of provisions among neighborhoods.

REFERENCES

1. Kelly, John R. "Planned and Unplanned New Town Impacts." *Environment and Behavior* 7:330–357, 1975.
2. Data provided by the Research Division of the Irvine Company, Irvine, California.
3. Kelly, John R. *Leisure Identities and Interactions,* chapter 7. London and Boston: George Allen and Unwin, 1983.
4. Rapoport, Rhona, and R. N. Rapoport. *Leisure and the Family Life Cycle.* London: Routledge and Kegan Paul, 1975.
5. Osgood, Nancy J. *Senior Settlers: Social Integration in Retirement Communities,* chapter 4. New York: Praeger, 1982.

13 EVENT MANAGEMENT

ISSUES

How are the aims and structures of promotional, institutional, and entrepreneurial events different?

Who are the parties involved in event marketing?

What are the steps in event marketing?

How are the functions of event management interrelated?

What are the criteria of location selection?

How are events scheduled?

What are the main logistical elements of event management?

How do legal considerations affect management?

What are the two special aspects of financial management of an event?

What are the particular business opportunities in event management?

From the perspective of business magnitude, entertainment events are a major kind of recreation. Rock concerts fill football stadiums as hopeful purchasers stand in line overnight in front of the ticket office. Cities build multimillion-dollar auditoriums. There are many such indications of very big business. In 1983 over 30 convention and auditorium centers were under construction in the United States. Altogether, there are over 5,000 such facilities for large gatherings, such as concerts, conventions, sports, and other performance events. Some are public, built by cities or universities; some are private and operate without tax support. However, all are in the business of putting paying customers in the seats.

Analysis of such events has usually been from the perspective of the type of event. Sports, fine arts, popular music, and other types of performances are approached as though a rock concert, basketball game, and touring musical are quite different entities. Here we will approach events as business rather than as art and entertainment forms. However, even from this perspective there are different types of events.

The *business form* includes three distinct types of events:

- *Promotional events* have some business or institutional connection. The central purpose is to promote the sponsoring institution rather than to make a financial profit.
- *Institutional events* are organized and managed by institutions such as universities, civic organizations, voluntary organizations and associations, or other institutions with multiple purposes. For example, a university may arrange for a circus in its fieldhouse with the multiple aims of providing campus entertainment, attracting community support, and paying part of the cost of maintaining the facility.
- *Entrepreneurial events* are those organized for the purpose of making a profit for the promoters.

The *attraction form* is based on an attraction or performance that can be any of a number of types. The most common are *arts, popular culture,* and *sports.* In any case, the entertainment appeal of the event is utilized to bring in the audience/spectators.

Finally, the *event form* encompasses the following:

- *Participation events* are organized for the active engagement of those involved. They are not primarily spectator events but involve at least a part of the assembly in participation in the performance.
- *Amateur performance* events are those performed by nonprofessional individuals or groups, those who do not make their living at the activity. They include basketball tournaments, softball playoffs, community orchestra concerts, community opera, school performances, and any kind of

performance activity done well enough that some will pay to come and watch, listen, and appreciate.

- *Professional performance* events are performed by those whose major occupation is engagement in that activity: the "big name" soloists and groups, top teams, traveling shows, and others known to do something so well that a number of people will pay to come.

Of course, there are also differences of scale. An event may be as modest as an intramural track meet in a grade school or as vast as the Olympic Games. For the most part we will be dealing in the middle range of events, those that require considerable organization and management but are something less than global in scope.

This brief chapter is an introduction to the nature of entertainment events and their management. Along with reading such periodicals as *Billboard* and *Variety* in the entertainment business and a number of trade journals, the details and idiosyncrasies of this kind of recreation business are learned on the job. Opportunities to apprentice informally in event management are found at almost any campus or urban meeting center. After an outline of elements of event marketing we will run through five other general functions of event management. Finally, there will be three cases, one from each of the business forms.

EVENT MARKETING

One problem with introducing event management is the variety already suggested. Therefore, in the functional analysis that follows the premise will be that the event is some sort of entertainment event or series of events that have the performer-audience format. There are many events other than concerts, but these will serve as models around which to discuss management. The parties involved then are:

The performer or performing group

The agent or agency representing the performer

The show manager who organizes the event for the performers

The presenter who is the local promoter/organizer/manager

The facility manager of the site for the event

The support staff including crafts, musicians, etc.

Marketing is often the joint task of the performer's representatives and the local presenter. Depending on the type of event, the agent will deliver a variety of materials that can be used in promotion at the local level. Further, the performers may agree to participate in pre event promotion such as interviews, appearances, or other attention-getting devices. However, the basic local job of developing a marketing plan lies with the presenter. What are the elements in a marketing plan?

Analysing the market: As with other marketing plans, the first step is to identify the potential market in terms of geography and access. Then, within that market area, what are the segments that are likely to be attracted to the event or series of events? Is there a history for such events in the area? Have there been population changes? Are there special aspects of the event that may have previously unrealized market appeal?

For example, for particular kinds of music the market segments are quite age-specific. The number of teens within the target range, their current economic condition, and access to the site are all parts of the initial analysis. On the other hand, defining the market for various kinds of fine-arts presentations requires examining education level as a significant variable.

Demographic indicators of markets are total population, age composition, income distribution, educational levels, and the spendable consumer income of households in the market area.

However, there are other aspects of this screening analysis: What are the current economic conditions and employment ratios of the target markets? What about season and climate? Is transportation or competition with other in-season events a problem? Does seasonality have an impact on what people expect to do that time of the year?

Analyzing the product: The nature of the event is, of course, the basis for the entire marketing strategy. The type of program defines the market segments. The schedule and location further shape the likely draw for the event. Whether the event is discrete or part of an established sequence of programs is a major factor in marketing. Further, the available performers or sources of attractions may be decisive in the overall marketing strategy if they determine time, pricing, and program format.

However, there are a number of local elements in product analysis. What is the history of such events in the area? What has been the amount and pattern of ticket sales? Have particular periods of schedule and specific times been most successful for a type of program? Are there trends in sales and attendance for types of events? The entertainment field, especially, tends to be quite specific to the attraction and the community. No details of the history of previous programs are too minute to ignore. Decisions to purchase tickets are specific to the time and the event. Part of the market may go to rock or opera in general, but to fill an auditorium usually requires a number of performance-specific decisions.

Pricing is also crucial to marketing in a price-elastic good. Past policies, price scales, discounts, group discounts, and the perceived quality of the performers are all part of the strategy. However, pricing has to cover the costs of the presentation at that time and in that place. That is, pricing is predicated on a particular site with a defined capacity for people.

Finally, the objectives for different events may vary. An institutionally or organizationally sponsored event may seek to bring a particular experience to the community rather than maximize profits. The aims may be more artistic than financial. On the other hand, a promoter may make business aims paramount.

The strategy is to gain as much revenue as possible for the single event rather than build up loyalty, attract interest to a facility or series, or advance the type of presentation in the area.

Analyzing the competition: There may not be another event on the same date or even on that weekend. However, there is always competition. The competition may be for the scarce resource of money. Ticket costs may preclude purchase of some other experience or even more durable good. Further, an event at a different time and place may be the competition for some segment of the market.

Or the competition may be other kinds of entertainment or recreation. In season some may choose between watching an athletic contest or engaging in some active recreation. An event that requires the commitment of an evening will compete with dining out, spending an evening with friends, or staying home as well as with some other event. Some research indicates that many leisure decisions are made very situationally with factors of the immediate social context as well as scheduling and sequencing involved in choices.[1] It is useful to have some sense of the overall leisure decision patterns for the target markets. Then the marketing strategy may be responsive to the real decision context of the potential ticket purchaser. For many performing-arts events the decision is a group one. People decide together whether or not to come, either by planning in advance or at the last hour. Marketing strategies for pricing, ticket distribution, and publicity can be designed to maximize commitment to the event. In any case, marketing plans should take into account that there are always alternatives for even the prime market segments—in the general entertainment offerings as well as in a variety of household-based activities.

Analyzing the target market: Knowing the market in general and defining the appeal of the event leads to a more precise identification of the target markets. To some extent markets can be identified from national profiles of those who attend such events.[2] However, that is too general unless the probable market clearly overwhelms the available facility at almost any price. Organizing a unique event such as a national championship contest or the last recital of a world-famous arts figure is quite different from bringing obscure artists to a community with a minimal population base and an erratic response history.

Some of the local variables may be:

Frequency of opportunity How often are such events offered? Is this event likely to be seen as very special or just one of many opportunities?

Cultural identification Is the presentation one that can count on the strong response of some part of the population, an ethnic group, or devotees of the particular kind of performance?

Organizational support Is the event one that can be promoted through existing membership organizations with enough coherence to draw large numbers of their members? Marketing that gives certain advantages to such organizations may also guarantee an adequate market response.

Community commitments Are there market segments who will usually feel a loyalty to the sponsor, performers, facility, or type of event? If so, how can they be employed in the overall market approach?

Program differences Just what are the particular features of the event that will differentiate it from past events and from possible competing opportunities? Reaching target markets requires a clear delineation of the appeal of the performers for that time and place.

Analysis of the total event: What are the strengths and weaknesses of the program and the potential market? Just how can weaknesses be addressed? In general, is this the right product for the reachable markets? Is there direct competition that must be dealt with? Can promotion, scheduling, location, pricing, or other factors overcome the competition? Are the target markets large enough for the necessary investment costs and risks?

Just what marketing strategies can capitalize on the strengths and cope with the weaknesses? Is there some type of packaging or organization that will cope with particular problems?

FUNCTIONS OF EVENT MANAGEMENT

The first question is whether or not an event is possible. The second is whether it is worth organizing. From the perspective of the aims—business aims of profit, institutional aims of enhancing the constituency, and recreational aims of providing a satisfying experience—is the event likely to yield adequate outcomes? The third question is one of marketing: How can the event be presented in order to reach those aims?

After all that analysis it would seem that there is little left to do except to let it happen. However, event management is not for those unwilling to attend to detail with persistence. Some versions of Murphy's Law seem to apply: "If anything can go wrong, it will." Event management may also follow the rules of several Murphy corollaries:

Everything takes longer than you plan.

If several things could go wrong, the one that will do the most damage will—and often at the last possible moment.

Left to themselves, things tend to go from bad to worse.

Human beings tend to regress toward being mean.

Every solution creates new problems.

Nature—and agents—seek the hidden flaw.

And, finally, the scientific consensus on Murphy's Law: Murphy was an optimist.

Of course, with a little luck nothing will go ƃuoɹʍ. Nevertheless, the functions of event management are eased with foresight and experience. Among these functions are site selection, scheduling, logistics, legal protection, and financial management. Some aspects, such as pricing, are also part of marketing:

Location For some events the site is preselected. There is one auditorium, stadium, or opera house. In an institution the event may have as one latent aim the use of an existing facility. However, in other cases there are options. Woodstock might have happened somewhere else. Outdoor events may be amenable to several sites. Many communities have facilities of different sizes and access to various populations.

The first criterion is, of course, availability. However, after that, size is usually most important. Will the size accommodate the anticipated gathering? And will that gathering be large enough to meet financial obligations? However, there are other criteria as well. Access and transportation are important. Can the target markets get to the site. If they come by car, is there enough parking?

A third criterion is cost. No matter how attractive, a site priced too high may make the event financially impossible. Along with availability, size, access, and cost, there are some more subtle aspects of selection. Does the site have an image that will attract the target markets? For example, a youth-oriented concert in an old opera house or a fashion show at the fairgrounds livestock pavilion might discourage attendance. Safety for the kind of people coming is both a matter of image and real protection. Auxiliary services may be necessary for a particular market segment. Neighborhood acceptance of the event may be a major problem if there are conflicting perceptions. And, finally, the recognition of the site by the target markets is significant. Holding the first film festival in a old theater that has been closed for many years may have nostalgia appeal, but it may present difficulties if most people under 25 don't know where it is.

Schedule In some cases there are no options. A regional promoter may call to offer a date for a particular performer. It may be the only one available. Or an arranger of arts-series programs for smaller communities will be dealing with an itinerary. If you want a certain artist at all, it will be on the given date. However, for events that can be scheduled, what are the main factors of selection?

First, there is the choice of the program itself. In the popular arts such publications as *Billboard* and *Variety* give reports of planned tours and of the results of past events. Regular reading gives an idea of which performers are doing well at the box office. Also, there are ideas for different types of programs and presentations that have been successful elsewhere. However, local interest is not just the same as that in New York or measured by nationwide record and music sales. There needs to be some local measure of likely appeal. For music, local record and tape sales can be checked. Past programs can be evaluated. In some cases the risk is simply too great when production costs will be especially high. Sometimes it is possible to reduce the risk by scheduling or arranging for a lower-cost presentation or event to test the market. Scheduling should be responsive to the tastes of the target markets and yet offer some variety from other events. Scheduling involves spacing to separate events from those that might be considered so similar that "either/or" choices will be made.

Second, the overall community calendar must be considered. There are seasons that are inappropriate: holiday times that are filled or vacation periods when much of the market is absent. Traditional dates for area events may have been scheduled far in advance and will not be changed. Any event has to fit into the overall calendar in both its cultural shape and local particularities. Especially the school calendars should be checked carefully for possible conflicts.

Third, specific competition must be assessed. No date is likely to be completely free from other events. The issue is their appeal for the market segments crucial to the event under consideration. Don't schedule a rock concert the night of the "big game" in which the local high schools play their great rivals. Don't schedule a road race the week of a major track meet. Don't expect an auto racetrack to be jammed at the same time that the Indianapolis 500 is being televised. And, to retain support as well as avoid competition, don't bring in a road company musical the same weekend that the community college or high school is having its own spring musical show.

Fourth, take account of seasonality. Many kinds of events have times of the year when they are considered appropriate. Counterscheduling sometimes works but should be undertaken only after recognizing both the risk and the kind of promotion that will be necessary. In some cases there may be a latent demand for an arts festival in July or an old-timers baseball exhibition in October. However, in general, for every kind of event there are established times and places that have been built up over many years. Prospective customers and participants *expect* to be engaged in recreation with some seasonal rhythms and variations.

Fifth, many events are part of a sequence. In some cases there will be a series of performances or presentations. The scheduling of any one is one element in the overall design. Generally, the aim is to space events widely enough to allow them to be fit into overall commitments. Further, a series may be planned so that there is some alternation of types of programs. In music, soloists may be placed between ensembles. In a community arts series the two dance programs will not be consecutive. On the other hand, the series should not be so dispersed or erratic that it is difficult to maintain continuity. The ideal is for a fixed set of dates, every first Saturday evening, for example, but that is seldom possible. Competition and program availability render this unlikely.

Sixth, another form of schedule is the *festival*. A number of events may be clustered at one time. They may be varied in content and form or monothematic. In either case the timing of the festival itself is critical. It becomes necessary for those who participate to clear the entire period of other commitments and engagements. Generally, such clustering of events is begun on a small scale and designed to build when the response is sufficient.

Sixth, and perhaps most important, there must be enough *lead time* for marketing and management to be accomplished adequately. Many events require a year or more advance scheduling. A long preparation period may give more time for Murphy's Law to take effect, but it also allows time for recovery. The building of support for a major event, especially if it requires considerable local participation, can seldom be done overnight. Often an otherwise attractive event proposition will be rejected due to inadequate lead time. On the other hand, the risk may be worthwhile if a low-risk financial contract can be negotiated.

Logistics: There are so many things that must be arranged for most events. Just a list seems formidable: transportation, seating, crowd management, safety, food and drink services, staging, service personnel, and meeting the unexpected contingencies. And that does not include marketing, legal elements, and finances. What follows are only a few examples of logistical considerations.

How do people get to the event? It may be necessary to arrange for supplementary car parking. Public transportation agencies need to add to their regular schedules. What about the concert ending at 11:30 P.M. when all buses stopped running at 11:00? Transportation may involve special arrangements for satellite parking and shuttle buses on a scale that escalates as ticket sales increase. Specialists in transportation management may be needed to design a plan for a major event in a site unaccustomed to such impacts.

Is there a place for everyone? Again, at sites not normally used for the particular kind of event there may be seating where an audience cannot see and hear the performance. Sound projection, line of sight, and other such audience placement logistics have to be planned and checked carefully.

Crowd management can be a problem. As has been well documented, people do things in crowds they might never do in smaller groups. Can the crowd-control problems be anticipated? They include protection of the performers and performance area, entrance and exit, direction to assigned seating, early arrivals and late departures, protection from crime, control of alcohol and drug use, and so on and on.

Entry is an especially critical matter. Large numbers tend to arrive at events at the same time. Can they be screened, admitted, directed, seated, and provided with necessary materials in the given window of time?

Food and drink services as well as comfort facilities may be critical for events that are of long duration. The site may have contracts that cover such provisions. Or separate negotiations may be necessary.

Performance support can be quite complex. What is needed in staging, sound, lights, and other support? Is the show largely self-contained or will local technicians, musicians, or entertainers be needed? Is it a "Yellow Card show" with the number of union workers specified in advance? Who arranges for property handlers, electricians, carpenters, and stagehands?

What about the unexpected? There are almost always contingencies. Some events may be canceled or postponed by weather. Illness of key performers may force changes. Any number of contingencies may arise that call for adjustment from replacement to cancellation. How are announcements of changes, adjustments, and possible refunds handled? Is the money available to refund ticket prices? Is the staff prepared to adapt to the unexpected?

These and any other kinds of logistics indicate that there should be some kind of *timeline* outline that presents tasks in sequence. In order for some arrangements to be made, others have to be completed first. Working backward from the actual event, it is possible to develop a planning timetable that clearly shows what must be completed in sequence if the event is to be carried out successfully. For example, the shortage of facilities in a city may require scheduling a convention years in advance. Preparing for a peak in advertising a unique event may necessitate planning the campaign with an agency in January for an October event. Even printing tickets must be specified some weeks prior to the time that they will go on sale. There seems to be no substitute for advance planning.

Legal Considerations There are a number of legal factors in event management. They include contracts, risk management, safety, and obligations for dealing with contingencies such as cancellation. In Washington, D.C., the *Journal of Arts Management and the Law* is published to assist with these and other problems.

Contracts are a central element of event management. For visiting performers such contracts are usually negotiated between the agency representing the performer and the local presenter. The contract specifies fees. Some involve a flat fee to be paid and some are a straight percentage of receipts. However, most common is the contract that guarantees a minimum payment to the performer, a fixed or cost-based sum then reserved for the presenter, and then a percentage division beyond those totals. The percentages to the performer are reported to have been escalating to the 65% level. In such a contract the performers might be guaranteed $25,000 placed in escrow before the event. The presenter might receive the next $25,000 to cover expenses. Then the split of receipts over $50,000 would be 60–40.

Contracts also include a series of other provisions. Just what is to be provided by the performers and what by the presenter? Show costs and local costs are specified. Talent demands for publicity, housing, equipment, transportation, or other amenities will be included. While there are standard form contracts, both performer and local peculiarities will make each contract different. Even when the contract is made with a major agency such as Columbia Artists or ICM, the items for a touring musical, a one-person drama, a rock concert, or a dance company have to be tailored for that kind of event in that time and place. Further, the contract may add the payment of royalties to ASCAP, BMI, or another copyright firm if music is included in the presentation. Finally, some accounting procedures will also be laid out in advance to prevent later conflict.

The major factor in risk management is insurance. However, some events are not completely insurable. There is always the possibility of employee negligence or error, of the unforeseen and unforeseeable, and of the unique "act of God" that involves damage or injury. Self-insurance for any but major institutions involves considerable risk. However, the risks may be reduced by management that anticipates possible threats to life or property and minimizes their likelihood. In some cases insurance firms will cooperate in such planning.

How many ways can people get hurt in the event? A simple checklist may be the beginning of risk management. It is important to remember that no signed disclaimers can relieve the presenter from responsibility for injury that could have been reasonably anticipated and prevented.

And, finally, what if the whole thing is called off? For many reasons almost any event may be canceled. What are the immediate and long-term legal responsibilities of the organizer? What promises have been made to participants and spectators, both explicit and implicit? What does state law require in refund policies? What about labor contracts and site rentals? The cost of contingencies needs to be calculated in advance in case Murphy descends catastrophically.

Financial Management Of course, there are financial issues involved in marketing, various logistics, and contracts. Further, there are the details of how payments are to be made, reserves and escrows for guarantees, accounting, and cash management. Having the money to pay the bills when they come due is often complex enough. However, there are two financial functions on which we will focus: pricing and investment.

Pricing policies vary with the kind of event, institutional sponsorship, and market analysis. Assuming that the preliminary analysis has determined that there is a viable market for the product at an acceptable price structure, contracts are signed and detailed planning is begun.

One initial decision involves the type and levels of pricing. In a site with a certain number of seats in fixed places, the process is called *scaling the house.* For example, an auditorium might have 1,000 seats, 700 on the main floor and 300 in the balcony. Costs of presenting a local amateur company's *H.M.S. Pinafore* would be estimated at $5,000 including music rights, costumes, professional orchestra, theater rental, and incidentals. That means that the break-even figure for a two-night presentation would be two half-full houses at $5 per ticket. However, more commonly, there would be some allowance for gaining capital for the company's overall program or next show. The aim might be for a $8,000 gross. Further, seats vary in the theater as to sound and sight quality. Therefore, it would be customary to sell prime main floor seats for $7.50, the better side and balcony seats for $5, and the rear for $3. Scaling the house involves assigning prices to the seats by location to produce the desired total revenue. Such pricing also includes questions of group discounts, late "rush" seats at half price on an availability basis, and other variations. Further, variable pricing is designed to reach the different markets that may be interested in the event, but for whom price is a determining factor.

Scaling the house precedes the ordering and printing of tickets. It follows, however, the development of a budget for the event. Pricing has to fit into the overall marketing plan and also promise to produce the gross revenue needed to finance the event.

One major factor in the overall budget is *investment* capital. Generally, it is necessary to have some investment up front in order to present an event. Performers, those who rent the site, and some staff will require that they have a guarantee of payment. No theater or auditorium manager will reserve dates and forfeit other possible business without some guarantee. Most other providers also want some assurance that they will receive the contracted payment. Further, the costs of management and promotion will not all wait until after the event. This is one reason why so many events are sponsored by some business or institution with financial stability and something to gain from holding the event. Sheer entrepreneurial event management requires that there be up-front investment capital from sources that are willing to engage in relatively high risk business.

THREE CASES

To give some idea of the variety of events, we will introduce three cases. The first is promotional, sports-based, and participatory. The second is institutional, popular-culture-based, and involves amateur performance. The third is entrepreneurial, arts-based, and professional. However, the three barely begin to touch the variety of possibilities, large and small, in offering special events as recreation businesses.

CASE 1: A LOCAL PROMOTION

The purpose was twofold: to attract attention and loyalty for the store and to provide a participation opportunity for local runners. The market was the "serious" runner who regularly ran at least 4 to 5 miles every other day, but who was not Boston Marathon caliber. There was no shortage of routes and trails for those who just wanted to run at their own speed for conditioning, exercise, and the experience of such disciplined physical engagement. But for those who had goals and approached running with more of a competitive orientation, there were few opportunities.

The promotional intent was also clear. The specialty retail store had only one line of products, the athletic shoes of one prestige brand. The store name referred to the brand trademark. Although they had important markets for sports such as basketball, tennis, and indoor court sports, running was important. Further, running shoes had become significant in their high-end trade since the stress on feet from regular distance running on hard surfaces often led participants to invest in expensive footgear. The store manager wanted to have his product identified with the best of the runners as well as to support the participation of those who were already regular customers.

One question was whether or not to sponsor a 10K (10 kilometer) race alone or to explore cooperation with the local public recreation agency. While either might have been feasible, the willingness of the agency to allow for the race to be named after the brand trademark in return for full financial backing was determinative. The "Four Stripe Road Race" was to be a cooperative venture.

However, the store manager did have some conditions. One was that the race be as inclusive as possible. Therefore, it was organized into classes divided by sex, age, and experience. There were men's and women's categories for youth, seniors, and open age as well as for novices and more experienced runners. The distances were set by class at 5 and 10 kilometers. A course was laid out by the recreation agency in cooperation with a committee of runners. This arrangement meant that the cost of prizes was mounting quickly for the store. Further, the manager decided to go all out and give every participant a T-shirt imprinted with the race title and date. Of course, worn around the community they would also advertise the store. This cost was shared with the shoe distributor.

The event proved that the planning had been well conceived. There was a latent demand for just such an opportunity, with participation by women and older men surpassing estimates. Costs were not inconsiderable, but the good will for the store was augmented by the direct promotional value. Every poster announcing the event, every news release, and all the postevent attention reminded the community that the store existed and contributed to recreation opportunities. Now the event is annual, participation has grown, and other such events have been added to the schedule. Further, the promotion was directed precisely at a major target market for the retailer.

CASE 2: A JAZZ FESTIVAL

There were a number of indications that jazz was beginning to break out of its obscurity. The jazz boom of the 1950s had subsided, but interest had not disappeared. Some of the local indications included:

- The popularity of a band of older amateurs who referred to themselves as the Sit-down Seven. They had become a group with over thirty members who were in regular demand as entertainment at meetings, conventions, community celebrations, and other events.

- The gradual progression toward stability of a small restaurant and club that featured amateur jazz five nights a week.
- The growth in the university of participation in jazz bands so that now three "big bands" gave regular programs.
- The packed house for Count Basie and other touring jazz groups on the rare occasions they had come to the area.

The concept was for a weekend jazz festival, a mini-Newport with all or most of the talent being amateur. Since the instigator of the idea was the music director at the local community college, institutional sponsorship seemed the way to go. When she contacted the community arts council, the university music department, the public-school band director, and the owner of the local jazz club, all were ready to cooperate in sponsorship within the limits of the organizational and financial structures. Within a matter of weeks, a number of decisions had been made:

- Cost would have to be kept low. Therefore, no featured talent would be brought in unless they were willing to come for expenses only. (As it turned out, several did just that.)
- There would be a variety of types of offerings—formal concerts, late-night jam sessions, informal presentations, and workshops for students and others who wanted to play jazz themselves.
- The main contribution of the sponsoring institutions would be in the time of key organizers and in space for the events.
- The arts council was able to secure a seed-money grant from the state. This was augmented by promises of donations of money and services from local businesses. As it turned out, the actual cash outlays would be quite modest for a festival that included: six recognized open jam sessions, four workshops for musicians, six special presentations in public schools, visits by musicians and groups to music classes at all three levels of institutions, and several unannounced meetings of musicians who played at the shopping mall, on campus, and even in neighborhood parks.

Of course, no one made any money. In fact, it was considered a small miracle that no one lost any. The business sponsors who were prepared to add to their donations to make up the losses were more than relieved to remain untouched. Attendance varied from a full house Saturday night at the high school auditorium to a waning interest on campus by Sunday evening as competing commitments took their toll. A postevent analysis was positive except for one item, the time that was required of the main organizing individuals, for whom a major interest had become a consuming commitment for several weeks.

CASE 3: WILL IT SELL?

Event management becomes even more complex when the announced aim is to make money. To begin with, attractions that are likely to draw well come not only at *a* price but at several prices. They require guarantees, contracts, suitable facilities, promotion arrangements, and all the marketing and management outlined previously. Further, they usually come when it fits their schedule.

The market is limited in a western town of only 15,000 isolated from other communities and surrounded by sparsely settled ranch land and National Forest and Grassland. The cultural and educational level is not high. There is no four-year college in the area. The auditorium is in the high school and seats only 900 people. Nevertheless, a committee has been formed to develop a concert series. In their fourth year of operation they have selected from available performers one young pianist, one veteran baritone of modest reputation, one chamber group from a West Coast university, and a cellist who finished third in a regional competition in Philadelphia two years ago. They are pleased with the variety. However, there is a major gap in the schedule with nothing available from March through April.

When a regional promoter called about the I Solisti d'Ravenna, it seemed too good to be true. They were on tour, had an open date, and would stop in Custer City for well below their normal guarantee. In fact, this Italian group had expressed interest in seeing "real cowboys." However, the subscription series was full and committed, the only possibility being that someone take on the opportunity as an entrepreneur.

What were the salient considerations for the young music store proprietor who now was considering launching his career as an impressario?

First, could the contract be negotiated and the house scaled to promise break-even receipts and perhaps a chance at a bit of profit? He calculated that he could manage $1,000 for local expenses and pay the performers close to their requested guarantee with a half-full house at $7.50 per seat. He then negotiated a contract with a performance guarantee of $2,000, 50% lower than their usual price. The presenter would take the next $1,000, and all receipts in excess of $3,000 would be divided 50–50.

Second, with the date set for March 28, the auditorium reserved, and newspaper announcements made, the marketing strategy began. Who were the viable markets?

- The almost 500 regular concert series subscribers. They would be approached and wooed by offering them a period of advance sales. They could retain their customary reserved seats for this performance or obtain better ones by committing themselves early.

- Junior high and high school students involved in music participation would be approached through posters, assembly announcements, in-school sales, and half-price tickets. The house scale and low guarantee permitted this method of trying to fill seats that might otherwise go empty.
- A special target market was then identified. In the community and in a subregion to the south there were Italian residents who numbered altogether about 200 adults and older children. He would solicit this group through a direct mailing with a mail-back coupon even though they did not ordinarily attend the series. The mailing would stress ethnic identification, traditional love of music, and the special social occasion.

Altogether, the new presenter calculated that if 80% of the regular series subscribers were augmented by 150 students and 80 members of the Italian subculture, he and I Solisti would divide up to $2,000 above the guarantees. It was not a lot for all the time and effort that he would have committed, but the risk seemed manageable. Further, by selling tickets at the store some business might be generated and the store image enhanced. Of course, there was always the possibility of a spring blizzard.

EVENT MANAGEMENT AS A BUSINESS

Are such events and others viable business opportunities? And what about career possibilities for those interested in this kind of management?

First, there are thousands of job opportunities for those with the organizational and entrepreneurial skills who develop appropriate experience. Trade organizations, community centers and convention facilities, arts councils, sport promotion hotels, commercial clubs, professional organizations, and fraternal groups do hold events. Their aims and structures may differ, but many of the skills required are similar. Further, there are consulting and service businesses that specialize in managing events. For those with experience in organization, working with people, business, and the entertainment-recreational aspects of events, opportunities do exist.

Second, the business viability varies with the location and the institutional structure and aims of the "home" organization. Further, the variety in market areas, type of attraction, financial undergirding, and aims makes it difficult to generalize. As business the risk is high. However, the returns may also be substantial.

Promotional Events Promotional events tend to be relatively inexpensive in financial cost, often labor-intensive, and involve considerable participation. Since their purposes are not entrepreneurial, the requirements do not call for a return on investment capital. They serve to draw attention to a business, organization, facility, or service. They usually seek wide participation from the public, either as participants or attenders.

Promotional events may depend on recreation commitments and interests. For example, many shopping centers feature weekend displays of recreation goods combined with some demonstration of skills or appearance of celebrities. A recreation event may be designed as the promotion of a particular business related to supplying equipment or other resources for the activity. A cultural event may showcase a facility or seek to gain support for some related organization.

This does not mean that promotional events can be designed without thought for marketing issues or carried out in a slipshod manner. They may bring discredit on the promoter as well as gain unfavorable attention. In general, the principles of good planning and management still apply to all the marketing and functional tasks.

One issue is just how direct or subtle the promotion element should be. In some situations there may be negative reactions if the promotional tie-in is too blatant or interferes with the sequence of the event. Nevertheless, the recreation aspects of many promotional events make them business-related recreation as well as recreation-related business.

Institutional Events The scale of institutional events varies widely. In major universities and civic centers the management is highly professional. After all, many of the major events in the entertainment world take place in the stadia and amphitheaters of major universities. For the most part, the performance centers of major cities are the premier sites for major presentations.

At the other end there are all kinds of institutional events that are intended primarily for those in the organization and that have minimal structure. A trio may simply appear at an announced time at a gatheringplace and play. A contest may be for the darts championship of a local pub. A dance presentation may be Ms. Jones's after-school group of unsynchronized stumblers. Such events also have their purposes for the institution and its aims, educational, or other.

However, if the presenter—whether a descendent of the legendary S. Hurok or Ms. Jones—wants people to come, then it takes some planning and execution. The scale may differ, but the process follows much the same outline. It still takes a concept, a product, marketing, managing, presenting, and accounting. There are still logistics as well as dreams, budgets as well as creativity, and schedules as well as expression. And it always helps to identify potential markets and to know their tastes.

Entrepreneurial Events There are many slogans in the literature for those who would be event organizers: "Know your markets!" "Be on time with the product!" "Promotion begins with the idea and never ends!" Differentiate your product!" "Connect with the real commitments of your target markets!" And even, "Tell the truth!"

However, all the promotional design, marketing sophistication, managerial experience, and financial wizardy in the world will not eradicate the risks from trying to bring together an attraction and a paying collectivity in an event. It is an act of creation because something exists, for that time, that never existed before. Of course, there should be a reliable break-even analysis and forecast. Of course, the cost analysis should be on a timetable of event planning and development. Of course, there is no substitute for the quality of the attraction and the event. But in the end the risk remains, and such a career is not for the timid.

SUMMARY OF ISSUES

Promotional events are intended to advance the interests of the sponsoring organization; institutional events serve multiple aims; and entrepreneurial events are designed for profit.

Event marketing involves numerous parties along with the presenter and performers.

The steps of event marketing include analyzing the market, product, competition for a price-elastic good, specific target markets, and the integration of the total event.

Other functions of event management are site selection, scheduling, operational logistics, legal considerations, and financial management.

Location decisions consider availability, size, cost, image, safety, and recognition.

Scheduling, when there are alternatives, involves analysis of the relation of the type of program to the community calendar, competitive events, seasonality, program sequencing, festival formats, and adequate lead time.

The logistics of event management require planning for transportation, seating, crowd management, entry, safety, refreshments, amenities, staging, service personnel, and contingencies.

Legal aspects of management focus on contracts, risk management, and contingencies.

The two special elements of financial management are scaling the house and up-front costs.

Business opportunities in event management include specialization in promotion, institutional programming, and the high risk and potential profit of entrepreneurial enterprise.

DISCUSSION QUESTIONS

1. What kinds of events are quite age-specific in their marketing? How does this shape promotion strategies?
2. How does pricing influence the projected audience composition for different kinds of events?
3. What kind of schedule conflicts would be most detrimental to a sports event? A pop concert? A dance recital?
4. What are the advantages and disadvantages of a festival in comparison with a series of events?
5. Work out how a local "house" might be scaled for a presentation? What are the advantages of a wide spread of prices?
6. How do the aims and marketing strategies of promotional and entrepreneurial events differ?
7. Outline the possibilities of organizing a shopping-center promotional event for recreation retailers. What are some of the market segments that might be drawn to the center?
8. What are some of the major dangers and problems in event management?
9. Are there "event gaps" in your area that might be filled by an enterprising presenter?

PROJECTS

1. Develop a timeline for the sequence of tasks that must be accomplished to organize an event. Which tasks are most critical because they must precede several others? When are the critical organizing periods?
2. Participate as a volunteer in the organization of an event on your campus or in your community. Trade your time for access to planning meetings and conferences.

REFERENCES

1. Kelly, John R. "Situational and Social Factors in Leisure Decisions." *Pacific Sociological Review* 21:313–330, 1978.
2. Kando, Thomas, L. *Leisure and Popular Culture in Transition,* 2nd ed. St. Louis: C. V. Mosby, 1980.

14 RECREATION MEDIA

ISSUES

What are the special employment requirements in the recreation media?

How do participant-oriented and trade-oriented publications differ?

What is the "first principle" of media finance?

How have the "Leisure and Life-style" sections of newspapers evolved?

What is the great advantage of advertising in participant-oriented magazines?

How do such periodicals and nonstore retailers depend on each other?

What are the most common recreation book types?

How do radio or television respond to and promote recreation businesses?

How are trade journals sponsored and distributed?

What are the main elements of trade journal content?

Who are the targets of trade journal advertising?

What is needed to evaluate the validity of market research for a recreation industry?

What is the basic function of recreation media?

Throughout this book there have been references to the media. Trade journals have been mentioned as an important source of market and management information for many kinds of recreation businesses. Print media as well as radio and television are part of the mix of advertising possibilities. Further, various publications are sources of information for the participants in recreation activities.

Such media are a specialized area, related to the spectrum of recreation businesses but generally requiring somewhat different skills and preparation. Nevertheless, such media are a significant aspect of the overall recreation business picture. And for some with interests and abilities in writing, graphics, and selling, they are a possible source of employment opportunities. The two main types of recreation-related employment in the media are in journalism and advertising. The skills required are writing and selling. Auxiliary skills are those of art and graphic design, photography, and all the other communications skills useful in the various media.

There are many types of media that incorporate recreation material in their content. *Magazines* include the travel-oriented publications such as those distributed on airlines and promoting the leisure opportunities of various locales that can be reached by air. There are also commercially distributed travel magazines, activity-specific journals such as those concentrating on camping, fishing, gun collection, flying, a particular sport, a particular type of boating, and so on. These magazines are supplemented by those that appear annually and contain lists of resources, presentations of new equipment, maps, and other handbook or catalog-type materials. And, finally, there are the trade journals that are seldom seen by participants and are distributed to those in the related businesses.

Newspapers are increasingly giving special attention to leisure and recreation. Not only is there a general run of recreation-related stories on sports, the arts, travel, and features on unusual or otherwise interesting people or events, but most dailies now have at least a weekly "Leisure and Life-style" feature section. Often appearing on Thursday or Friday in time for weekend planning, this section contains features on various recreation opportunities and engagements as well as concentrating advertising for recreation resources.

Recreation *books* are most often of the "How to" variety and frequently list a well-known adept as author. However, there are also a number of books that relate recreation experiences or histories and are aimed toward the participant market.

Radio and television not only are leisure-related media but also include some recreation-based programming. There are drill programs on exercise, instruction features on various kinds of activity, "human interest" features on news or other programs about recreation participation, and news about events and opportunities. Even more than for the other media, experience with radio and television has tended to precede the recreation background for program management. However, special recreation knowledge has often been the basis for employment when a station decides to target material for some part of the recreation participation spectrum.

In general, there are two types of recreation media, participation-oriented media and trade-oriented media. This chapter can in no way provide a journalism or advertising background sufficient for preparation for such specialized work settings. However, background in recreation plus the media training and experience may lead to opportunities in this growing aspect of commercial communication. Something of the place of media in the overall recreation scene is an important element in recreation business.

PARTICIPANT-ORIENTED MEDIA

Most of the books and magazines aimed at recreation participation markets are found on the shelves of retail outlets. However, the magazines depend heavily on regular subscribers not only for income but even more for the assured readership that is the basis for advertising sales. The "first principle" of the media in a market economy is that advertising pays the bill. This is just as true for *Field and Firearms* magazine as for television. Therefore, the medium product is always a use of participation interest and commitment to attract a market to the products and services advertised.

LEISURE IN THE NEWSPAPERS

Some local and regional newspapers contain news about recreation, especially sports events, arts and popular culture offerings, and organizational news. However, a more comprehensive view of leisure and its importance to readers has permeated the policies of newspapers.

The "Leisure and Life-style" sections of newspapers have developed from older sections on the arts and travel. In many cases they appear in a designated section of the newspaper on a given day of the week, usually just before the weekend or in a Sunday section. Major attention is given to events that have advertised in the paper. However, feature articles may be on modes of leisure that are presumed different or new enough to be interesting. The editors of such sections are more likely to have a journalism background than any other. As a consequence they are seldom prepared with any comprehensive view of leisure and recreation.

The primary basis for inclusion in such a "Leisure" section is its relationship to advertising business. Articles often accompany advertising. Announcements of plays, concerts, and special events in the arts may be on the same page as feature articles. Considerable attention is given to travel-related recreation. If the travel section is not separate, then the editor will incorporate material on destinations and modes of transportation in the "Leisure" section. Such material is available from the news services as well as from industry sources. Further, such editors receive many invitations to travel as the guests of some segment of the travel industry. The line between news and promotion becomes a thin one in such journalism. Further, the general prohibition against the purchase of favorable treatment by offering free goods and services is usually lifted in the case of recreation. The newspaper receives free tickets to events, transportation and hospitality at the resort, and other forms of persuasion in the guise of providing first-hand information.

Participant sports tend to be an underdeveloped area in newspaper coverage. In local papers there may be listings of scores from softball leagues and tennis tournaments. On occasion special events receive some coverage. However, in general, the kind of material directed toward participants in the specialized magazines is absent from newspapers. Again, the exception most often is recreational activity that is business-related, such as downhill skiing. However, increasingly public recreation departments are providing news releases on events, programs, and the opportunities they provide.

In larger urban newspapers the arts are covered in a special section. There is a trend toward a comprehensive section in Sunday papers. In either case news attention to the arts is of two types: First, there is the traditional review of new performances, which may or may not take a critical stance. In major cities such reviews are an important factor in the commercial success of theatrical runs. In smaller cities the attention given by newspapers may make the difference between a community theater or orchestra concert being noticed or not. Major exhibitions of plastic and graphic arts are usually covered. Attention to local arts participation and opportunities may be much less adequate. The stress is usually on the public performance and on evaluation or promotion rather than on those who are "doing arts" as leisure. However, figures on such participation and the increase of such participation in everything from dance to ceramics suggests that news coverage is lagging behind participation growth.

The exception to this lack of attention to leisure participation and to participation-oriented programs is the trend toward aiming newspaper features and sections toward particular population segments. When "women" are the target, material on careers outside the home and on expressive activity both at home and outside are usually included. When there is a special "teens" section, attention to leisure in the form of popular culture is inevitable. When "senior citizens" are given a special section, various forms of recreation and new opportunities are often featured. As a consequence participation in recreation and information on resources and opportunities may be found more in once-a-week sections for teens, older adults, or the family than in a designated leisure section.

RECREATION PARTICIPANT MAGAZINES

Almost any newsstand or supermarket magazine counter displays a staggering number of periodicals for recreation participants. The specialization is surprising to those who are not aware of distinctions between gun collectors and competition shooters, model airplanes and model racing cars, back-country camping and camping in recreation vehicles, or automobile restoration and road racing. Almost anything can be employed in recreation for either display or use. Almost anything can be collected or constructed. Almost any level of skill or financial investment can characterize some groups of recreation enthusiasts.

The magazine does more than provide information. It identifies those who have come to define themselves in part by their commitments to the activity. There is introduction to vocabulary, the offering of memberships and insignia, the latest in appropriate apparel, announcements of gatherings and opportunities to attain higher levels of skill, and, of course, advertising. In fact, for recreation in which equipment and apparel are important, the ads may be at least as important as the articles to subscribers.

The specialization of such magazines also offers to both readers and business interests a medium of communication exchange that is targeted and quite efficient. The advertiser knows that only those involved in marksmanship are likely to buy a magazine on that subject. Therefore, advertising goes to the intended market with a minimum of inefficiency and waste. In some cases the specialization is by product rather than activity. For example, a journal may be directed to the owners of light airplanes rather than to pilots in general. Or, even more selectively, it may be only for those who build and/or fly home-built ultralight aircraft, a small proportion of the entire flying market. In such cases the magazine is quite central to the entire process of developing a "subculture" around a specialized activity. The journal for amateur sky divers is required reading for those who gather not only to parachute but also to engage in exchange of ideas, experiences, and resources. In the magazine many of the group-identifying signs and symbols are introduced and made available.

The beginning of such a periodical is usually the identification of a number of devotees large enough to support such a publication. Often what is now a professionally produced monthly magazine began as a duplicated newsletter run off in someone's basement. As the participation base grew, the need for a major means of communication produced a market for the new magazine. The actual production history varies. In some cases publication firms identified a new market and approach a participant organization for an endorsement. In others, the organization combined with publication interests in beginning a journal for participants.

Content At least some of the content of such participation-oriented magazines rests on the expertise of writers and editors. There are features on or by "stars" whose recognized skill makes them authorities on the activity. Special events are reported and described. The content frequently combines material aimed at enhancing the skill or interest of recreational participants with attention to those who do it especially well. "How I won the tournament, conquered the obstacle, learned the new skill, entered the environment, or developed a new kind of equipment" approaches are the most common. The skill angle is central to recreation journalism for participants. Expertise from those who "know," the authorities in the field, is the staple of editorial planning.

However, there are also the articles that are more product-oriented. They may describe or evaluate equipment, introduce new or improved locales for participation, and in other ways offer a kind of catalog of resources. In fact, many recreation periodicals publish a special "buyer's guide" each year. The purported aim is to provide the potential user with information useful in making a selection. However, the frequency of negative evaluation or information about products is low. Also, the guide is packed with advertisements for the items that are listed and described.

Advertising The recreation periodical is a wedding of recreation-related content and advertising. As already suggested, the main source of income is advertising rather than subscriptions or newsstand revenues. The appeal of the medium for advertisers is the self-selection of the readership. In no other way can an advertiser be assured that those who see the advertising are so completely a market. In fact, purchase of the periodical is an index of even more than general interest in the activity; it suggests some commitment. The subscribers are already a target market.

The consequence of this selection is that advertising rates may be relatively high for the size of the circulation and still be a "best buy" for the firm offering goods and services. One aim of the publisher, then, is to increase circulation and resulting advertising rates. If the price of a subscription covers subscription handling costs and postage, that is enough. However, the cost must be high enough to demonstrate commitment to the advertisers.

For such a magazine the advertising staff may be at least as large as the editorial department. Such a department will be able to provide complete information on the readership—their incomes, geographical locations, age, sex, and often life and leisure styles. This is partly obtained from subscription information, but is usually augmented by some sort of reader survey that offers an incentive to participate.

The content of the advertising takes several forms:

Ads for products used in the activity

Announcement of competitive events for experts, other participants, and spectators

Advertising for resources: regions, committees, resorts, or other opportunities for participation.

Skill-acquisition programs and opportunities

Conferences, trade shows, and other public events

This advertising is all targeted at the participants. It presupposes some network of information, a set of business suppliers of resources, and some identified requirements for participation.

However, along with targeted advertising, the recreation magazine often carries correlative advertising. Those who participate in recreation are also consumers of other goods and services. Especially recreation with an upper-income set of participants will identify important market segments for goods such as travel packages, financial services, expensive cars, and alcoholic liquids. The most important correlative advertising market, however, is for various kinds of sportswear. The styles of recreation participation related to particular activities are frequently those that offer important market segments for the producers of expensive clothing.

Mail-order Business For many recreation modes that require special equipment or apparel that can be shipped by mail or parcel services, nonstore retailers are an important advertising segment in the specialized publication. The retailing appeal of firms that advertise lists of equipment for recreation is *price.* In most cases the mail supplier can offer goods at a discount from local retail prices. The reasons for this price advantage are evident:

- High volume
- Minimum or no cost for display space and face-to-face selling
- An efficient warehousing system
- A delay in shipping that allows for relatively low inventories when rapid and repeated orders from manufacturers are routine
- Possible reduced costs for merchandise due to volume orders
- Employment of specialized personnel who are efficient due to the lack of customer attention and waiting time
- Use of national bank credit systems to expedite purchases, maximize convenience for the customer, and avoid bad-check problems
- Most of all, the targeted national market through specialty magazine advertising

The reciprocity between the advertising department of the magazine and the mail-order firm is almost total. The supplier is a sure presold ad for each issue, and the periodical is a necessary medium for reaching customers. In some cases neither could exist without the other.

However, there are also some disadvantages to this type of equipment and apparel provision. The entire relationship between retailer and consumer is in the transaction. No loyalty is developed. No relationship such as the exchange of information occurs that leads to further transactions. It is just a matter of price and efficiency. For the residential retailer the problem is a considerable one.

Customers may inspect equipment at the local store, solicit information, and, in some cases, even borrow or rent it for a tryout. Then, when the purchase is made, it is through the discount mail-order supplier, who has not had to pay for display space, access, an inventory, floor selling costs, theft losses, local advertising, community support, or any of the other costs of doing business. While "rent-to-own" plans and immediate delivery and service are some protection against the out-of-state seller, the loss in revenue can be considerable in some product lines.

There are also other types of mail-order recreation suppliers. They do advertise in the specialized journals, but their merchandise is displayed primarily through catalogs that are mailed widely. Former customers are only one source of names and addresses of potential clients. Some firms purchase mailing lists as well as periodical subscription lists. Selling lists is a source of income for the publisher but may also divert potential advertising revenue. The mail-order firms that market on a selection rather than price basis, distribute expensive catalogs widely, and have heavy return costs on apparel, shoes, and other "fitted items" may have no price advantage over the local outlet. Their appeal is selection as well as presumed convenience.

The recreation base of the specialized magazines suggests that some knowledge of the recreation activities, equipment, locales, participants, and superstructure of participation is important for the development of the periodical, its editorial policies, design and production, advertising, and marketing. They may provide interesting career opportunities for those who learn the skills that are required for the editorial and advertising functions of publication.

RECREATION BOOK PUBLISHING

Other than textbooks for the college market, what are the book publishing opportunities related to recreation?

"How to" books often have a wide distribution through institutions such as schools, public recreation, and private teaching programs. The fundamental market is for low-cost books, usually in paperback, that clearly introduce the initial steps of learning how to do the activity. A second, and related, market is for handbooks and rulebooks for those within some instructional program. Often they have an assured institutional distribution outlet that encourages a commercial publisher to produce the book.

The second type of "how to" book is more likely to be distributed through bookstores and book sections of comprehensive stores as well as through specialized stores and media. They trade on the name recognition of some adept in the activity—whether indoor activity, the arts, or sports. Whether or not the book is actually written by the "name" author, it captures attention in the more general markets. Such a book is usually at a higher price level, in hardcover, and produced by one of the largest publishing houses and distributed through their normal channels.

A third type of book is the author-subsidized or "vanity press" book. In many cases an author will have a special approach to instruction or participation that has been demonstrated in one or more settings. However, a lack of author prestige or a presumed limited market will prevent the author from finding a commercial publisher. In such a case an author who believes in the approach or who has some built-in market for a low-cost publication may pay all or part of the publication costs. In such a case, the author will also gain quite a high percentage of the profits if the book sells well.

Along with the "how to" books, there are a number of other styles of recreation books. Some authors relate unusual experiences in the activity. Some base a book on the special environments for participation that are not likely to be visited by most participants. Some are biographical or autobiographical and are based on the experiences of well-known figures related to the activity. Some are based on the special knowledge of an authoritative figure in the activity.

In general, the publication of books has become more and more expensive. The author costs and expenses are the smallest part of the production, promotion, and distribution of books. As a result the likelihood of recreation participants being able to write such books full-time is very low. On the other hand, clearly identified markets for books—especially the "how to" type—can yield a good return on investment.

One of the problems in developing a book for the market is the cost of production. Along with the general printing costs, recreation books frequently call for expensive graphics, reproduction of photographs, considerable "white space" in the format that increases the paper costs, and other costs of illustration and layout. Further, the book may have to compete with the advertising-subsidized periodical for attention. The production costs of multicolor printing, graphics, and the gathering of attractive illustrations puts the book at a considerable disadvantage. The growing areas of recreation publishing are periodicals—the specialized journals for participants and for the trade—rather than books.

RADIO AND TELEVISION

The airwaves are full of recreation and leisure. There are news reports on a wide variety of events, public affairs specials on local or regional recreation opportunities and programs, and a variety of programs covering recreation experiences on both public and commercial radio and television. There are direct ads for recreation-related resources, opportunities, equipment, and apparel. There are innumerable uses of recreation environments and activities in the advertising and entertainment programs throughout the program day. And, of course, radio and television are major aspects of leisure in contemporary society.[1]

However, the assimilation of recreation into the life-styles and culture of developed societies has made almost everyone knowledgeable about forms and resources. In fact, one of the elements of being a regular spectator of sports or the arts is some presumed knowledge about the nature of the activity and requirements for skilled performance.

As media, radio and television are quite specialized. A writer trained in print journalism or in general writing has to learn a whole new set of techniques and aims when writing for those who will never see the words in print. Depending on hearing alone makes writing for radio especially difficult. However, combining moving visual stimuli with the spoken word in television has its own set of problems and opportunities. Neither radio nor television are transparently simple media open to the contribution of those who will not learn their particular forms and techniques.

On the other hand, specialized knowledge in recreation is often lacking among those with the technical media preparation. The employment of those who are skilled in an activity is common in the news or special-event coverage of radio and television. What has seldom been explored is the employment of recreation experts in the programming decisions of the media. With the evident importance of leisure to the overall life-styles and values of so many people, recreation-related programming may increasingly become an area in which media and recreation expertise may be blended.

Conversely, the coverage of recreation on the media that capture the greatest proportion of the nonwork time of American adults is critical to those in any line of recreation business. A few simple examples illustrate this relationship:

- Participation in many forms of recreation has increased dramatically following coverage of the Olympics, special attention-getting events, or fascination with a particular person engaged in the activity.
- Demonstrations and illustrations of a variety of recreation goods, opportunities, and environments are seen continually on television. In some cases the producer or distributor of such goods can only take such unsolicited promotion into account in marketing plans. In other cases the attention to a product or resource may be arranged as part of a promotion campaign.
- The more that attractive figures are found in various recreation environments in television programming, the more expectations for some similar participation may seep into the value structure of viewers. While there is no direct correlation between seeing a golf course, tennis club, beach, mountain, theater, restaurant, city, or great event on television and deciding to go there, the idea that such leisure is possible and desirable is planted and reinforced. On television, people are depicted spending an inordinate amount of time in recreation locales rather than at the kitchen table or on the sidewalk. And who gets caught in a traffic jam on television?

- Not only are recreation resources advertised on the air media, but recreation environments are used to try to promote an incredible variety of goods. Associating the product with health, fun, companions, sexual attractiveness and opportunity, and change often brings the advertising manager to place the user of any number of prosaic items in leisure settings.

This can be important to those in the recreation business in several ways. First, much of this attention provides free promotion, often much more subtle and effective than direct-selling schemes. The depiction of desirable outcomes from being in leisure places and using recreation equipment in order to sell cars or hair spray can be a powerful message, especially when repeated over and over. Second, attention in the media can be exploited in promotion campaigns. Third, it may be possible to gain explicit promotional value by making arrangements to provide some goods or services to the media in return for their visible use. Fourth, the media producers may respond to offers of providing free expertise in return for the simple announcement that it was provided by a business interest in the community. The association of expertise with recreation participation may draw clients to the business.

The basic point here is that the media often are in need of recreation programming ideas and assistance. Leisure is important to people and often is the basis for attractive programs. Recreation personnel can contribute to the media without becoming professionals. At the same time, knowing what is coming directly to consumers through the media experienced at home and in the car is significant to recreation marketing. Not only specific information but a general image of recreation as interesting, pleasurable, and socially attractive may be a major force in a long-term increase in recreation markets. The styles, environments, and accoutrements depicted on television may lead to many kinds of leisure investments as well as new interests.

TRADE-ORIENTED MEDIA

The main trade-directed media are the journals designed for those who are themselves resource providers. Trade journals are the immense hidden layer of business-related journalism. The periodicals are not seen on the newsstands or advertised for sale. In some cases only members of a trade organization are permitted to subscribe. They contain both information intended to be of value to those in the business and advertising for products and services. The formats range from quite expensive four-color magazines of over a hundred pages per issue to duplicated newsletters with blurry print.

Recreation business journals include those that are produced by particular retail product sales organizations such as marine products or sporting goods, those that are for the operators of recreation services such as campgrounds or bowling alleys, and those that have a broad-spectrum approach to a variety of users of recreation goods and services. Some are aimed at particular markets such as schools or community public recreation markets. Others are "insider" publications for those who compete for retail sales in residential swimming pools or prefabricated second homes. "Big-ticket" items such as highway recreation vehicles, powerboats, and vacation tours have more elaborate trade publications than producers of low-cost and replaceable items.

Most, but not all, such trade journals are associated with trade associations. Further, a major element in the content scheduling for the journal is the promotion of an annual national trade fair of some sort. In some industries regional trade fairs are on a seasonal timetable to anticipate peak sales periods. The services of the business organization, the journal, and the conference are all an integrated package for the retailer or public provider who is the link between the producing firms and the consumer.

TRADE JOURNAL CONTENT

The editorial policy of the trade journal is one of service to those who engage in the related recreation business. The journal is to provide information that will be of evident value to the reader who is running a business or program. When the journal is part of the membership package of an organization with dues in the three-figure category, it must be readable, attractive, and useful. When the trade journal is independent of an organization, it must have content that attracts subscribers or it will fail to develop a subscriber base for advertising revenue.

What is included in a recreation trade journal?

1. News about business climates: General economic analysis, aspects of economic change that impact on markets for the line of products or services, technological developments, and financial trends are all important. Further, data and analysis of sales trends of products nationally and by regions, seasonal forecasts, and shifts among major suppliers are generally reported. The data are obtained from government sources, market research firms, and the reports of members of the trade organization.
2. Government climate news is quite important in today's economy. Not only legislative proposals and actions on federal and state levels but the actions of regulative agencies, the program changes of recreation-providing agencies, and judicial decisions all impact on business. The trade journal may have an in-house source for such material if the organization has a legal staff and a government relations department. If not, the journal will have to allocate staff time to gathering such information.
3. Technology information is important to retailers of recreation goods and services in several ways. First, they need to know if some new development threatens the established markets for products. Second, they may profit from the efficiency of some new technology. Third, they may need

some relatively objective analysis of a product or service that is being promoted for their business. For example, just how a data computing service may be cost-effective in relation to business size may be vital for management decisions. Case studies related to technologies make interesting reading as well as provide useful information.

4. "How to" articles on operating the business, increasing sales, providing an attractive customer service, expanding product lines, obtaining financing, developing new kinds of promotion, and so on are valuable to the merchant or program manager. Such information may be based on the experiences of others in the business or may be the result of some type of research. In some cases such material will be provided by those with a financial interest in a particular method or service. The basis of content on "how to" or on technology is research, at least in the sense of having staff competent to evaluate material and to obtain information from those who can exercise independent and informed judgment. This means that research on techniques and technologies for the recreation activities requires those who know how to develop recreation research designs and who know the field.
5. Promotion is always one aspect of a business. In the editorial allocations of a trade journal, various kinds of promotion are a major segment of the overall plan. "Product news" is often based on information provided by those who manufacture or distribute the products. The advertising department of a journal frequently will propose a combined advertising contract with a "news" feature for the journal. The related organizations will expect promotion of their meetings, special workshops and training sessions, and trade fairs. Trade organizations also depend on their journals to inform the members of their services in relation to lobbying with government, representing the industry in court, and developing various kinds of market research.
6. Directories are often a major part of the trade journal program. The yearly directories may, in one volume or separately, list members of the organization, service organizations in the field, and those who hope to sell goods and services to members of the organization. Such directories may be in a special issue of the journal or in a separate publication. In any case, they are an integral part of the information content catering to the industry.

For recreation-related trade journals there are a number of special opportunities for contribution by those whose background and experience are from the recreation side of the business. Retailers are, after all, selling products and services that will be used in recreation. Those who know the skills, environments, social organization, and outcomes of those recreation experiences are best able to provide material about the "user climate" for the businesses. As previously outlined, the participation base of recreation businesses calls for an understanding of both the participants and the experiences from more than a purchaser perspective. The present and future markets of recreation goods are in the meanings, contexts, and resources for the activities rather than in the stores. Sales figures are only the beginning of understanding a recreation industry.

As a result, those who know recreation may be involved in editorial and writing *if* they have the skills required. They provide analysis of the business climate *if* they have the research and business analysis background necessary. They evaluate technologies and products from the perspective of the user rather than the promoter. They know *how* as well as *what, when* as well as *where,* and how any given recreation activity or resource fits into the overall leisure groups and aggregates in society. The recreation perspective is invaluable for the well-planned trade journal.

TRADE JOURNAL ADVERTISING

Again, however, it is advertising that pays the bills. Except for the organizational newsletter, trade publications tend to rely heavily on advertising revenues. The advantage they offer over almost any other promotional medium is a precisely targeted readership. For the most part every reader is either a retail recreation supplier or an institutional user. For those who produce and distribute recreation-related goods and services, the trade journal offers access to those most likely to buy early and buy often. The types of advertising run a full range from specific user products to correlative goods and services. However, the following kinds of ads predominate:

1. Products are advertised to the retailer and to the operators of programs. Such product advertising may feature recreation equipment, clothing, locales, or anything else likely to be sold or leased by businesses at retail. Manufacturers offer their new and established products in trade advertising to get them into the stores. The institutional markets are approached through such promotion. In some cases the business or institution is encouraged to contact a manufacturer directly to inquire about retail dealerships or bulk orders. In other ads the intention is to announce and promote the product in general when distribution is through wholesale outlets and regional sales staff. The special "800" phone numbers for free information are common in such ads.

   The exact nature of such advertising depends on the kind of product, intended markets, modes of distribution, and period in the product life cycle. Heavy informational and announcement advertising in the inaugural product cycle phases may give way to positioning and differentiating from competition in the later growth and maturity phases. In any case, the focus is less on the user than on the market potential of the product.

Trade advertising may simply replicate market advertising. However, more often trade-oriented ads extol how well the product will "sell" rather than how it will enhance the recreation experience.

2. Services to businesses are advertised heavily in trade periodicals. These may be operations services or financial management, maintenance services for equipment or real property, marketing services including advertising and research, or consulting services that offer counsel on some aspects of the business. Such services are aimed at providing to the retail business or the institutional recreation provider something that will reduce costs, increase efficiency, ease some operations burden, solve a problem, enhance programs, increase sales, or provide some new opportunity for the supplier.
3. Organizations that are in some way serving the readership of the journal often advertise their services. Seeking to increase membership or the use of their offerings, they often attempt to combine announcement in the "calendar" section of a journal with paid advertising. Some journals have special institutional rates for such advertising. Others coordinate their editorial functions with institutional advertising to give a feature complement to the announcement and ads. The politics of coordinating the support and cooperation of related professional and business organizations may require a clear set of policies to protect the journal managers from considerable pressure.

The advertising mix of a trade journal is closely related to its readership and to the product lines for the kinds of recreation involved. One periodical may consist primarily of advertising aimed at the community and school programs that purchase major items such as floors and artificial surfaces for sports, bleachers, uniforms, and buildings. Others are aimed more toward the retail outlets and feature product line advertising. Some are for the operators of facilities that cater to a specific type of recreation such as power boating, ski hills, or amateur theater. Many are designed for major business investors such as those who develop condominium apartment complexes or planned residential units. Some are directed toward the second-home builder, the music teacher, or the tour arranger. In each case the advertising is a mix of those goods and services likely to be needed by the readership. It may be surprising to know how many kinds of outdoor artificial surfaces are marketed for football or tennis, how many kinds of resin are sold for string players, and how many compounds are sold to sweep gym floors. The size and complexity of recreation business suppliers can be glimpsed only by examining the advertising in one hundred-plus trade journals in the field.

Some journals offer considerable assistance to advertisers. They not only give precise information on the subscribers but also provide format advice. Many include "reader return" cards that enable those interested in particular advertised goods or services to circle numbers on a single card, fill in their name and address once, and return it postpaid to the journal. Then the advertising department will transmit the list of those interested to the advertiser as part of the overall service. Other journals maintain lists of those providing particular goods and services in regions or metropolitan areas. The intent is to market a service to the industry rather than simply sell advertising space.

INDUSTRY MARKET RESEARCH

Almost witbout exception, the official journal of any trade association will publish statistics on salient kinds of sales. The dollars spent in a recent period on goods and services will usually be published in the journal along with some indication of trends. At the annual conference of members there is some analysis of sales trends and a forecast—most often guardedly optimistic—for the future.

However, this is only the beginning of the kinds of market research available at the industry level. Some such research is either done in-house by major firms in the field or is contracted by them with market research organizations. The results of such research are generally considered proprietary and not released to the industry in general. For example, a manufacturer may have completed research-testing the market for a new product or variation on an established one. Such research is used in making product decisions and developing marketing plans.

It is also common for trade associations to commission research intended to be of value to their members. Such research may be made generally available through the trade journal or may be offered on a subscription basis to those who support it. When research results are limited to subscribers, protocols are developed to restrict access to those who have paid.

Some trade organizations have their own capabilities in research. Others have entered into long-term contracts with research firms to do specified research at regular periods, most often once a year. In either case the research is for the industry and designed to inform business decisions, meet industry problems, or yield basic business environment information.

Market research is designed around the markets for industry products or services. For the most part it is designed to identify the present and potential purchaser for the products and services of the supplier. Who is the customer? Where are potential buyers to be found? How can they be contacted and informed? What are their "felt needs" that may be tapped? What are the constraints to their purchasing? How do they view the products and services in the field of competition? And how may current nonconsumers be persuaded to become part of the active market? Many such questions are not very different for the various participants in an industry. Useful market research can be done for all campground operators or Arizona resort managers that may conceivably enhance markets for all the industry.

The most likely organizer of such industrywide research is the trade organization. In the case of recreation organizations there may be two difficulties. The first is a general lack of expertise about the development of good market research. As a consequence a contractor with good sales technique but less than adequate research capabilities may sell an inferior package. Second, most market research organizations know little about recreation. They can compile sales figures or do participation surveys. However, the complex set of behaviors and attitudes that shape recreation participation are a foreign field to firms that have specialized in durable goods and home-care products, not to mention cosmetics and odor suppressors. The most cost-efficient course for the trade organization is to identify an organization with the capability of developing a useful, responsive, and reliable market research plan. Then a contract with enough stability to permit the firm to invest in the research is likely to produce more for the industry than a series of unconnected projects always let to the lowest bidder.

The design of such market research needs to take into account the actual decisions made by those in the industry.[2] These include product development strategies, promotional efforts, distribution operations, pricing strategies, and service programs. As introduced in earlier chapters, the nature of recreation business calls for more than the usual trade information. Recreation—so often seasonal, discretionary, social, experience-centered, and even experimental—is a special kind of human behavior. It has its own timetables and constraints, motivations and outcomes. Recreation is the organized part of leisure, requiring resources and organized opportunities from both public and business sectors of the society. It is integrated around desired experiences but includes in its resouce supplies the school and the shop down the street, the forest and the yard, the neighbor and the professional. Adequate market research may focus on the supply of resources, but always in the context of the meanings of participation.

SUMMARY

The recreation media, then, are an important part of the resource environment for recreation. They provide information and incentive, exemplars of activity and glimpses of opportunities. The media serve as links between participant and supplier, government and business, research and management, producer and distributor, innovator and user, services and operations, and personnel and employer.

Perhaps the basic link provided by the media is that between the participants and the supplier of resources. The media bring into a form of communication those who do and those who provide resources and opportunities. The mechanism of distribution may be the market for business suppliers, some level of government for public welfare, or private and voluntary organizations that organize groups of participants. In any case, there is the need for communication that informs both suppliers and participants of new possibilities, changed environments, and various modes of cooperation. And, in a market economy, the financial support of this communication is advertising, a type of communication directed toward profitable exchange.

SUMMARY OF ISSUES

Employment in recreation media requires skills either in journalism or the selling of advertising.

Trade-oriented media provide information to the suppliers of products and services rather than to the participants.

The basis of financing recreation media is that "advertising pays the bills."

The development of "Leisure" sections of newspapers is augmented by sections on population groups, such as teens or the retired, that include considerable recreation-related material.

Periodicals for participants in a recreation activity offer access to a targeted market with a demonstrated commitment to the activity. Even correlative advertising may be highly efficient in market focus.

The content of participant-oriented magazines is skill- and product-oriented.

"How to" books are based on recreation participation.

The specialized skills required for radio and television writing and production are not common among those with recreation knowledge.

Mail-order or "nonstore" selling depends on the medium of participant publication.

Trade journals are often associated with product and other trade organizations.

Content of trade journals includes information and analysis of business climates, government activities, technological developments, "how to" material on business operation and promotion, and directories of goods and services.

Production of trade journals requires knowing the recreation base for the businesses and having the competence to evaluate industry market research.

Trade-oriented media are supported by the advertising of products, services, and organizations.

DISCUSSION QUESTIONS

1. In the "Leisure" section of a major newspaper, what are the main types of content? How much of the material appears to have promotional sources or tie-ins?
2. Analyze the content and advertising of a participant-oriented recreation magazine. How much is devoted to products and service and how much to recreation experiences?
3. What kinds of newspaper features would be of most interest to recreation participants?
4. Whare are some books related to recreation that have been quite popular? What is the basis of their appeal?
5. How could you use regular television programming in the promotion of a recreation business?
6. Bring in samples of trade journals borrowed from local recreation businesses. How are they useful to business managers? What are the main similarities among different trade journals?
7. In periodicals studied, are the sources of product information clearly stated? How reliable are the evaluations?
8. What kinds of market research information are most useful to business managers? How can such information be misleading?

PROJECTS

1. Analyze the content of a recreation trade journal for a year. How much of the material is practical information and advice for the retailer? How much is promotion for the trade organization? How much reports research? How much is related to advertising and promotes products?
2. From a selection of trade journals, develop a catalog of the businesses and services that in some way are related to that segment of recreation business.
3. Interview a number of recreation business managers about the relationship of their management and marketing practices to the various kinds of media.

REFERENCES

1. Kelly, John R. *Leisure,* chapter 18. Englewood Cliffs. N.J.: Prentice-Hall, 1982.
2. Udell, Jon G., and G. R. Laczniak. *Marketing in an Age of Change,* chapter 8. New York: Wiley, 1981.

15 RECREATION BUSINESS AND SOCIAL CHANGE

ISSUES

What philosophy of business is most likely to lead to success in the recreation markets of the future?

What are the changes in leisure participation patterns that will impact markets in the coming decade?

How will schedule diversity, space limitations, ecological shifts, skill acquisition, and attitude orientations help create business opportunities in recreation?

What are the family, political, geographical, and value-orientation trends that will alter recreation business markets?

Will economic changes alter the climate of business in recreation?

What fundamental economic issues remain unresolved in the environment of American business?

What are the most likely market, product, and resource changes in North American recreation business? Will the competitive climate be significantly affected?

There are many kinds of forecasts of the future. The usual business forecast, especially from trade organizations, is "guardedly optimistic." The current levels of business are expected to improve, unless some factor outside the industry becomes a major impediment.

Popular journalistic forecasts are usually one-dimensional. The most common are based on some technological innovation that is alleged to transform everything. The hidden assumption is that technology is the source of change that will sweep all else before it. Almost without exception, historical analysis shows that most of life is rather resistant to change and the "third wave" of change is followed by a fourth, fifth, and so on. In the "information age" most jobs are still manual or service. In the "electronic age" most people still watch rather than "interface." In the "sexual revolution" most adults marry and have children. In the "leisure age" students are still preoccupied with getting jobs. The changes are real, but no single element sweeps all else before it. Most often, both people and institutions adapt rather than crumble.

There are several models of social change.[1] A *revolutionary model* presumes that internal conflict will lead to a replacement of the former power structures and a reorganization of social institutions. A *conquest model* proposes that external conflict will lead to an overthrow of the system and institutional reorientation to meet the demands of the conquerors. An *evolutionary model* points to the continual adjustment to inconsistencies in a social system leading to institutional change without altering the locus of power. A *technological model* describes the alteration of economic institutions due to technological innovation that in turn requires social adjustment throughout the social system.

In general, social change is defined as transformation of the institutional arrangements and value systems in a society. Such changes may be manifested in shifts in legitimized power, values, and world views by which people define their lives and interpret their world, and ways in which the economy, government, family, or other institutions operate. Looking ahead calls for sorting out and assessing a number of interrelated factors. The exceptions are the predictions of those with an ideology that purports to explain everything, a simple model of explanation, or a naive faith in some set of unchangeable values.

Radical change is possible. Economic systems do collapse, resulting in transformation of entire systems and the beliefs they have fostered. Ideologies do have impacts on political action. Suppressed peoples do rise up and overthrow ruling classes. And disillusionment can lead to people defining themselves and their societies differently. In the United States the depression of the 1930s had a variety of impacts on the bubbling optimism of the 1920s that still influence how many people today deal with problems such as unemployment.

However, in the short term general stability in the system and in the world views implicit in it have to be assumed. Further, there are a number of well-established trends that are unlikely to disappear within a decade. While there are debates about the relationship of population growth to resource scarcity, impacts of structural economic change, and crucial factors in world economic adjustments, looking ahead a few years—to the year 2000 or so—generally presupposes that the institutional structures will remain intact and that recognized trends will continue.

To examine the future of one element in a single economic sector, recreation business in North America, involves this assumption of processual change in a condition of fundamental stability. The likelihood of such stability is another issue and outside the realm of this discussion.

Further, the process is seen as systematic rather than unidirectional. Business activity is one factor in change and stability, neither always the initiating agent nor the end result of other variables. Recreation business, however, will be viewed as largely a consequence of the nature of business in general, the social system, and overall leisure patterns. This does not take into account that recreation business may also be a factor in changes in leisure patterns through the promotion of certain goods and services.

A diagram of the approach would look like this:

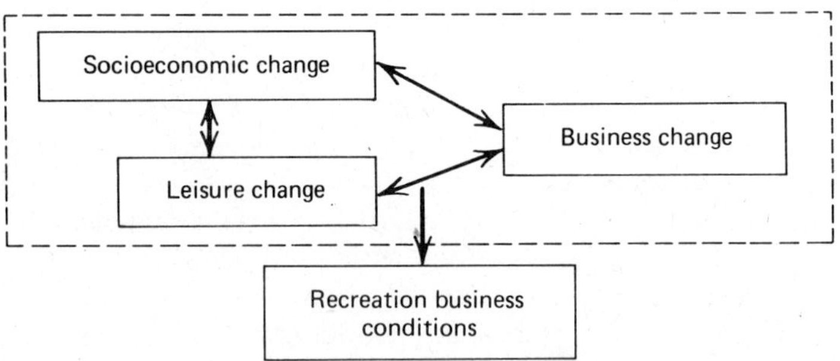

The dynamics of the socioeconomic system shape and in turn are affected by subelements, such as the market sector of the economy, and social spaces, such as leisure, community, family, and religion. A particular segment of the market segment of the economy, such as recreation business, exists in the larger context. The conditions in which businesses are formed, develop, and prosper or fail are set by the overall context. If that context did not change, then the probable outcome of a business venture would be highly predictable. However, the context is constantly changing, and businesses exist in an environment of uncertainty. The analysis that follows will not abrogate the uncertainty but is an attempt to identify some of the most probable directions of change and their implications for recreation business conditions.

CHANGES IN LEISURE

The business provisions for organized leisure, recreation, are only one part of the whole leisure framework for a society, community, household, or individual.

The demand for business-offered goods and services exists within the general patterns of leisure meanings and participation. The investment of resources in recreation is only part of all that people do to express and develop themselves and their social relationships in relative freedom. What are salient trends in leisure patterns in North America that may alter the context of recreation businesses?

LEISURE RESOURCES

The first is a shift of patterns rather than a major change. Resources for leisure are always limited. Further, those resources vary depending on the level of analysis. Here we will adopt the common economic level of the household as the unit of resource allocation. Household resources for leisure include the following:

Time: both individual and synchronized

Space: private and public

Money: cash and credit

Social: the interaction potential of regular relationships

Skills: learned competencies for recreation

Socioeconomic resources are those that can be utilized by the household, in this case for recreation. They include the infrastructure and superstructure of the economic system: transportation, energy, space, and all the organized operations that enable the commerce and intercourse of the society to be carried out. Changes in those resources can have dramatic impacts on leisure, as was found during the most acute periods of petrofuel shortages and price escalations. However, here we will focus on the household resource shifts.

Time The general leveling of average employment hours has been diversified with considerable differences among occupations. Further, service/retail occupations are characterized by more diversity and irregularity in work schedules with more "free time" being "off-hours." Time for leisure may be other than weekends and evenings for many who are employed by stores that never close, services that operate at night, and other organizations that require flexible or split shifts of some sort. Further, time as a scarce resource has been intensified for many who are single parents, in dual-career marriages, required to commute to work in crowded cities, or in businesses that attempt to increase productivity through pressure on a stable or reduced work force.

Space Housing and energy costs are reducing the proportion of the population who will live in detached homes affording considerable leisure-dedicated space. Multiunit housing, space-efficient design or lower costs, and other such trends will reduce the at-home space for leisure. At the same time metropolitan areas continue to grow, if at decreasing rates. The most accessible recreation areas are more and more crowded, especially if weather dictates and limits use periods. The high costs of real estate and construction also limit the expansion of both public and commercial space that can be provided for recreation requiring considerable space or high-price locations.

Money Household income remains varied, with acute limitations for a major segment of the population. Family income in 1981 included the following figures:[2]

10.1% of families in the United States totaled over $50,000 per year, 24.4% of the total aggregate earnings

53.4% of families totaled $20,000 to $49,999 per year, 61.1% of total earnings

25.1% of families earned between $10,000 and $19,999 per year, 12.5% of total earnings

11.4% of families earned less than $10,000 per year, 1.9% of total earnings

For that top 10%, discretionary income for leisure is an assured resource. For the bottom 10–25% it is a scarce or nonexistent resource. For the largest number, recreation expenditures are limited to the extent that any outlay is competing with other possible uses. These percentages and their related buying power have not changed dramatically since 1950. Further, the relation of income distribution to employment is clear and direct. Ninety percent of individuals with incomes under $15,000 do not have full-time, year-round employment. In 1981 the average family income was $24,656.

Social Smaller families, increased family dissolution, the separation of work and residential locales, geographical mobility increased by employment trends, and increased in-home entertainment have all had impacts on the development and maintenance of regular interaction associations and the availability of companions.

Skills Higher education levels have increased the opportunities and likelihood of gaining leisure skills, both activity-specific and those that can be generalized. However, opportunities are closely related to the socioeconomic status of households with persons socialized in families with higher income and education levels receiving disproportionate access to all kinds of skill-acquisition resources.

In general, there may be trends toward more resources for leisure. However, they are neither equitable nor consistent. The household with more income may have less time and vice versa. Resources in a market economy with great disparities in income are highly differentiated. Therefore, market segmentation may be more based on socioeconomic stratification when resources such as space, discretionary income, time autonomy, and skill development are crucial to participation.

LEISURE ECOLOGY

The ecologies of leisure are also affected by resource shifts. The social and economic incentives favoring home ownership in the United States together with the norm of detached houses in residential areas, usually urban outskirts or smaller towns, has spread the population over vast areas. Metropolitan residential areas are dispersed rather than concentrated. As a result, many kinds of leisure outside the home are quite time-intensive and require advance planning. Further, travel time to and from work tends to be a major time-use factor. Dependence on private transportation, the car, is basic to considerable away-from-home recreation participation. The ecology of leisure, like that of retailing, has more and more moved from the neighborhood to locations requiring special trips and schedules. This dispersion has, in turn, been a factor in an increase in at-home leisure that does not require the arrangements of dispersed recreation.

The ecology of leisure begins at the residence and spreads outward to shopping centers, playing fields, theaters, art centers, and outdoor recreation resources. The common weekend or vacation trip by car is supplemented by air travel to more distant locales. In terms of time use and regularity, most leisure takes place within 50 feet of the home eating area and television set. Leisure may also occur in other routines of work and travel. However, leisure as "occurrence" is home-centered with recreation "events" more often in market-provided settings to which travel is organized.

TIME

Time use for leisure reflects the priorities of home and family as well as the importance of regular interaction with intimates. While there are some differences among categories such as teens, singles, dual-career parents, traditional parents, single parents, and the retired, activities done every day tend to be consistent:[3]

Watch television	72%
Read newspaper	70%
Listen to music	46%
Talk on the phone	45%
Read books	24%

In general, at least eight of the ten most common activities in a 1982 survey are usually done at home. Exercise and jogging are often done from home or at home, and an evening of conversation is more often at home than away. Therefore, in time use, "leisure begins at home" and most days ends there.

However, that survey, like most such research, has major flaws. The assumption is that leisure can be identified as discrete activities with measurable chunks of time assigned. Of course, a review of most days shows that much leisure consists of informal interaction, imaginative inattention and daydreaming, and other minutes and moments interspersed throughout other contexts. A second flaw is that the list of activities omits the kind of interaction that is central to most leisure patterns, informal interaction with household members and other regular associates.[4]

Further, time use is not necessarily a measure of value. The leisure that is most important may not always be that which is most convenient. In the author's three-community research sequence, the order of activity types that adults were most reluctant to give up were as follows:[5]

Marital affection and intimacy
Reading for pleasure
Family conversation
Activity as a couple: talking, walking, shopping, etc.
Family outings
Visiting family and friends
Playing with children
Watching television
Outdoor sports
Eating out
Religious worship
Short car trips
Gardening and yard care
Home decorating and shop projects
Arts or crafts
Entertaining at home

There does not appear to have been a major shift in such priorities over the past twenty years. Further, comparative research in Britain and France now shows similar ordering. The events of recreation serve as punctuating highlights in the ongoing round of expression and interaction. While there are trends indicated by comparing different research efforts over the years, they are not dramatic. Since the advent of television revolutionized nonwork time use, the more recent trends have been more investment in exercise and fitness activities, especially by the young and more educated, a slight increase in actual participation in the arts, and a somewhat greater likelihood that women will engage in some activity outside the home. However, the home-and-household foundation of adult leisure remains essentially unchanged.

LEISURE ATTITUDES

What may be changing more are attitudes toward leisure. In the same media poll 91% agreed that "people should spend their free time as they please," and 65% said that "people should have the right to as much leisure time as they feel they need." However, about two-thirds also affirmed the priority of work and agreed that leisure is best when aimed toward goals and helping others.[6]

There are a number of indications that general quality of life is becoming more of a central value in the developed countries, and especially among the younger, university-educated populations.[7] However, for most, leisure has its place in life, important but not primary. Rather, leisure serves as one context for what is most important, relationships with intimates and especially family.

The fundamental shift in values seems to be one that accepts the legitimacy of leisure as part of the overall balance of life. It is considered more and more acceptable to include leisure as part of life's plans and priorities, not against others but as a complement to them. It is not work *or* leisure or the family versus leisure, but leisure as one accepted and even necessary dimension of freedom, expression, development, and community.

LEISURE MEANINGS

This developing acceptance of the legitimacy of leisure does not mean that there is a complete consensus as to the place of leisure in life. For example, there is conflict over both the forms and orientations of leisure that should be given priority. Just to look at driveways, residential storage, family rooms, and resort areas would suggest that American leisure was becoming quite commodity-intensive. There seem to be so many items of equipment, transportation, and entertainment in the possession of "Middle America" that leisure is dominated by the drive to own and use such market items. On the other hand, research on values and time use indicates that only television is a leisure commodity central to patterns of interest and participation.

According to most philosophical approaches to leisure, its aims should be personal expression and development, the enhancement of community in intimate and social interaction, the celebration and reinforcement of culture through creative and appreciative activity. More recently, the theme of health has emerged with attention given to emotional and physical benefits of leisure in building and maintaining health in conditions of stress and pressure.

Business orientations that presume that leisure is primarily a response to market provisions will run up against the definitions of leisure as more developmental and social. The market for recreation goods and services is not infinite, not only due to income limitations but also because of what many people seek in their leisure. Business provisions that enable and facilitate leisure consistent with the aims of those making decisions about the allocation of time and other resources stand a better chance of success than those that simply try to sell a product. Changes in meanings and aims of leisure, however gradual, will have their impacts on the demand for business-provided goods and services.

SOCIAL CHANGE

The social system is composed of a number of more or less integrated institutions. One line of understanding proposes that all the others are so dependent on the organization and accomplishments of the economy that economic change is the source of change in the other institutions. A second approach is more systematic in holding that change can begin in any institution, or even counterinstitution, and have effects throughout the social system. While the economy may be the most common source of change, anything new or different requires adaptation in all parts of the society, which in turn has reciprocal impacts on the innovation.

In any case, it is seldom if ever possible to analyze change in a simple formula, such as *A* causes *B*. More likely, *B* also reciprocally influences *A*. Further, their relationship is mediated and altered by social factors *C, D, E,* and *Z*. Analysis of social change is always selective out of all the interrelated factors. Nevertheless, there are a number of institutional trends that will have direct and indirect impacts on the conditions of recreation businesses and on the economy.

FAMILY TRENDS

Most of the family trends have already been introduced in some of the market analyses. In summary, structural trends for the remainder of the century as follows:

The two-parent single-worker family is expected to make up only 28% of the U.S. households by 1990.[8] This involves household composition with such distributions that over half will have no children at home, 29 percent will be headed by a female, and dual-worker households will be double those with one worker.

Later marriages and more divorces will increase the number taking adult roles without a marriage partner. This also means that more adults will be in some stage of transition, in or out of marriage, parenting, or employment.

The implications are manifold: Fewer adults will follow a regular life course with predictable transitions occuring "on time." Fewer will have the traditional age-normative familial context for leisure. Not only social but also financial and time resources will be restricted for many single-parent women. Adults without the nuclear-family context will experience more schedule freedom but also the strains of having to develop another intimate community.

Two-worker families will have greater synchronization problems in scheduling joint leisure, but will gain the possibility of greater economic resources. Just as important, women with their own incomes usually are in a different power distribution system within the family, which may affect leisure decisions. Women will be less available for recreation and community participation during weekdays and will compete with men for some recreation opportunities during weekends.

These family pattern changes are especially critical for leisure because leisure and the family have been so intertwined in modern Western societies. If intimacy in primary relationships is a major preoccupation through the life course, then disruption in the family has two implications for leisure. The first is that often new companions have to be found for social leisure. The second is that leisure will be oriented toward developing community and intimacy.

A set of family-related trends has been under way for decades. This is the trend toward smaller families, compressing the childbearing period and reducing the length of the parenting period. As a consequence more of adult life is lived without the constraints and opportunities of parenting children living at home. The central focus of leisure for parents tends to be familial. Reducing the parenting period opens to leisure what is now the longest period of the family life cycle, that between the time the last child leaves home and retirement. There will often be more time and money available for up to twenty preretirement years. Further, those entering these years will in every cohort be the most educated adults ever to enter that phase of life.

POLITICAL TRENDS

Judging the likelihood of political changes is hardly a task for which retrospect builds confidence. Even short-term political predictions seem to have a reliability of just about 50%. However, there are some general trends that will probably affect recreation business in this century.

First, there is a shift away from the concept of a service society. A number of demographic and economic factors including rising federal government debt burdens, increases in the proportion of the population retired from production-related incomes, consequent rise of the cost of various welfare and support programs for older people, and a failure to move toward full employment of those seeking work will increase the pressures on government budgets. Services that can be defined as secondary or unnecessary are not likely to gain vastly increased budgets at any government level. Combined with such factors is a philosophical questioning of the welfare society philosophy that advances the proposition that government should take responsibility for a wide range of provisions that support and enhance the quality of people's lives. Part of the attack on the welfare approach has been a disillusionment with the outcomes of programs that have been intended to combat poverty, urban problems, and a range of social ills. Public recreation, as part of the service sector of government, is not likely to expand rapidly unless economic conditions turn government deficits into surpluses.

Second, there is a general recognition that government bodies are operating in a condition of scarcity. Just because a service or program is desired or used will not be an adequate justification for its provision by the public sector. In general, opportunities that can be provided by the market sector will be left for private enterprise. It is likely that the dependence on business as a recreation provider will increase rather than diminish.

Third, one exception may be the area of the conservation of natural resources. Environmental concern seems to be firmly established in the public consciousness. While there will continue to be conflicts over both policies and practices, natural areas that are a resource for recreation will be managed for long-term conservation as well as current use.

Fourth, there seems little likelihood that recreation itself will become a central political issue. Although citizens are concerned about the quality and quantity of recreation resources in the particular, political discussion and decision making will continue to keep such concerns on the fringes of national debate. The present fragmentation of federal programs and management, with its lack of coordination or policy, is unlikely to be replaced by some "Ministry of Leisure" or supported by a senator known for his advocacy of leisure opportunities.

GEOGRAPHICAL TRENDS

The obvious geographical trend has been the move southward. Economic opportunities related to energy and the availability of low-wage workers, location of federal spending, and the obsolescence of older plants in the North have pulled industry southward. Life-style considerations of winter avoidance have also been a factor. The demographic shift has been intensified by the concentrations of high-technology industries in California and Texas.

To a lesser degree, the shift has also been leisure-related. The possibilities of outdoor activity through most winter months has been an attraction. Many people would rather employ air conditioning in the summer than cope with snow and ice in the winter. The relatively long seasons for boating and other outdoor activity have been one element in the migration.

Other geographical shifts have been more limited and specific. There has been movement back to the new and renewed neighborhoods in the cities, especially by adults not raising children. However, suburbs are still growing apace. There has also been some migration to smaller towns and rural areas within travel distance of metropolitan areas. However, most new housing being built is of the tract variety that pushes the urban sprawl farther out. Nevertheless, the alterations in residential distribution and location may be highly significant for the location of individual recreation businesses that serve particular market segments.

VALUE-ORIENTATION TRENDS

It is always hazardous to try to draw general conclusions about how people understand and define their world out of bits of evidence from statistics on attitude polls, affiliations, time use, and behavioral trends. However, there are a number of possibilities that may have considerable long-term impact on recreation business conditions. Coincident evidence suggests that the following *may* be possible:

- A diminishing of the influence of traditional voluntary organizations, especially the churches. Not only is it now socially acceptable in most communities not to go to church, but religious organizations do not seem to have the power to shape the values of the young, as once was the case. There are regional differences and the recurring emergence of growth sects. However, the idea that churches, Boy and Girl Scouts, and similar organizations are a major molding force in the society appears past.
- Social solidarity now seems more than ever based in the immediate communities of family and household. It is the face-to-face relationships that claim priority rather than the larger institutions. Life tends to be organized around places owned and controlled by the people to whom one has direct and immediate bonds. Community celebrations have dwindled or become, like Fourth of July fireworks, just a place where families and small groups continue their essentially private parties.
- A greater emphasis on personal expression and development is found among the educated and upwardly mobile younger population groups. Relationships, activities, investments, and even work may be chosen with personal gratification as a central aim. If they do not produce the personal satisfaction anticipated, they may be discarded. For example, marriage is to yield companionship, not just the security of home and family. Work is to offer opportunities for personal development, not just financial security and a place in the society. And leisure is to afford individual development and expression, not just a pleasant filling of leftover time. Whether or not the loss of social solidarity and commitment is a dangerous flaw in the society, the turning toward the self and raising of personal expectations seems widespread.

Such trends will have their effects on all social institutions. A readiness to delay or discard old relationships and commitments for activity directed toward the self may indicate a profound change in the motivation-and-reward system for social institutions. There is also the concomitant possibility that leisure, broadly defined, may become increasingly salient in the priorities of many people. If so, there may be an allocation of time and money toward recreation that will eventually enlarge the demand for recreation provisions through the market.

ECONOMIC CHANGE

The basis of this section is found in chapter 2. Here we will only draw together some of the analysis of trends and issues introduced in that chapter. However, the relative brevity is not an indication of the profound effects that such economic changes will have on the conditions for recreation businesses.

GENERAL TRENDS

The following summary is of what might be termed middle-range trends. We are not dealing with yearly or 24-month cycles in interest rates, money supplies, cost of living, capital investment, stock prices, business inventories, or employment. At the other extreme, we are also not attempting to incorporate long-term analyses of the potential survival or collapse of economic systems in the twenty-first century. Rather, in the framework of a decade or so, what are the changes that seem likely to persist?

First, growth in the world economy appears to be limited. There is the potential of undeveloped markets in the third world for all kinds of goods, including the basics of food and housing as well as the services of education and social infrastructure. However, limitations in investment capital, the relative paralysis of many national economies of both East and West, the continued spending on armaments with their economic dead ends in providing for economic growth, and the control of wealth in a few institutions do not provide the basis for enormous economic growth. Even the more optimistic scenarios suggest gradual and somewhat erratic growth in productivity and a similar uneven pattern of distribution and market development.

Second, in the developed economies of the West the shift toward services is likely to continue. Production, even in growth periods, will be less labor-intensive. Further, industries will continue to seek low-cost labor where the work force is just removed from peasant status or has components willing to work at substandard rates. The implications for the major segments of the work force in North America and Western Europe suggest that retailing, human services, and businesses such as recreation may not be able to absorb the labor surpluses. If so, the impacts on demand for service-sector offerings can cause a number of economic dislocations. Even in a generally healthy economy, there may be towns and even regions with high unemployment and costs of social support services. One demographic trend that can alleviate this problem is that fewer people will be coming out of school and into the labor market at the same time that more will reach retirement age. A growing economy may be able to absorb both the smaller number seeking work and the larger demand for social services.

Third, the trend toward a higher proportion of women in the work force does not seem to be threatened even by higher levels of unemployment. While most such employment remains in support roles and retail and public services, there is also some incursion of women into traditionally male occupations. This trend has implications not only for the distribution of income, but also for the relative autonomy and self-sufficiency of women, household schedules and time resources, family structure, child-rearing practices and the need for support services, and the timetables and demand for leisure resources and opportunities. Further, employment patterns will be more segmental rather than following a fairly simple hierarchy of the seniority of white males. The labor markets may be more open for support services, low-wage maintenance work with few skill requirements, and temporary employment than for stable jobs controlled by union organizations and professional certification.

The fundamental question is whether these and other trends signal a change to quite different economic conditions. Are there to be shifts gradual enough so that a viable economy can adapt to the change and buffer the transitions? Or do all the changes add up to something more profound, the development of a post-industrial economy that will require quite different definitions of work and leisure, different organization of economic means of production and distribution, and different systems of preparation and reward? For example, will fewer career paths run in straight lines with an integrated preparation, apprenticeship, advancement, and retirement pattern? Is the individual's work career more often to be a zigzag with periods of employment, preparation and retraining, and jumps from one sector to another?

The approach taken here will be somewhere between an assurance that "all is well," with all problems only temporary, and a prediction of radical change accompanying a series of collapses and traumas. The changes are not only real but profound. The economic world of the twenty-first century will not be just a growth extension of the twentieth. Further, the specific forms that will develop and the particular adaptations to change are not really predictable. Business will exist in a rather different economic world. What can now be identified are some of the issues, but not their resolution.

PRESENT ECONOMIC ISSUES

Again, introduced in chapter 2 are a number of issues that will not be resolved by the year 2000. Nevertheless, attempts to deal with them will have impacts on the basic conditions of doing any kind of business.

1. The investment balance between production industry and "human investment" will remain an issue. How much of the wealth within a society should be directed toward education, health, and other sectors of human

support and enrichment? On the other hand, what proportion of national wealth must be directed toward production that allows an economy to continue producing goods and services that can command markets? Goods and services that create wealth are necessary, as is support of human ingenuity and creativity, which is the key to economic innovation. The issue is more than an economic one. Even though education and leisure can be supported as essential to economic productivity, that is not the end of the argument. Life-enhancing services and opportunities, for human rather than economic ends, are valued in our culture. But what is the right investment balance?

2. The issue of the distribution of income also has its economic and social dimensions. Too great a concentration of wealth is counterproductive because it stifles venture investment and reduces internal markets. Employment and income for most of the adult population is the basis of markets for consumer goods and services. The ripple effects of a 30% reduction in automobile sales have been made clear enough in the early 1980s. Further, there is the equity question. Is a concentration of wealth among the upper 5% consistent with the values and goals of a democratic society? Is a persistent poverty class socially acceptable and economically endurable? The means of redistribution via taxation policies and public sector programs will also be debated. But the issue itself is fundamental to every aspect of the economy and society.
3. The time dimension of economic decisions is being increasingly raised. Major corporations are concerned about the long-term viability of business conditions, not just the yearly profit ratios. Attention to the environmental conditions of living has put in question many short-term policies of both industry and government. Problems such as the disposition of hazardous wastes from power production, chemical industries, and mineral extraction pose dangers for the "downstream children" of many generations to come. To what extent can current life-styles be supported at the cost of basic health conditions for our grandchildren? Again, the means of regulation and encouragement will be debated. But the issue will remain as each new technology produces its long-term yield of potential hazards.
4. Economic growth itself is also an issue. Is growth always good? What if one price is inflation? The consequences of a growth-inflation cycle are not the same for all. What may benefit those whose incomes are tied to growth may reduce the standard of living of those on relatively fixed incomes. Or, growth in one sector of an economy may come at the expense of another. Is there a rate of growth, a balance of growth sectors, and a shielding of those caught in the change that is optimal? If so, can a society plan for such measured growth or must it merely take its chances

in the world economy? What about growth in one energy-producing industry that bankrupts the national economies of twenty countries? What about new technologies that allow one industry to forge ahead and force others to the wall? Should there be national policy that supports "sunrise industries" with growth potential in world markets at the expense of "sunset industries" that are losing out in their competitive struggles? What are the economic and human costs when a sunset industry closes? Growth itself is an issue with more than a single dimension.

5. Economic and business scale is a related issue. In the market, is large always more efficient? One indication is that the world markets require large-scale enterprise in some sectors of both production and distribution. However, there are other areas, especially services, in which a small scale may be most effective. If so, the trend may be a dual one: toward large- and small-scale business with a loss of middle-size businesses. Others propose that both business and public scale have gotten out of proportion with their objectives. If the ends are human, smaller-scale operations and organizations, even if more labor-intensive, may be best adapted to their ends. Again, however, in the economic realms efficiency may be the deciding criterion in a world in which it is impossible to isolate peoples or places.
6. Finally, the issue of technological innovation pervades even recreation businesses. Some have proposed an inevitability to the adaptation of technologies. The theme is that "what can be done will be done." More sophisticated models of adoption and assimilation stress that a technology or its products have to have some compatibility with the institutional structures of a social system in order to attain adoption. A technology, however successful at accomplishing some function or task, requires that people at the decision-making level *want* to use it. It has to offer advantages in the existing world to gain acceptance. Even so, new ways of doing things, new products, and new processes do have their impacts on the economy. Old skills, traditional organizations, and stable markets may be rendered completely obsolete by a new technology of production, communication, or performance.

SUMMARY

The result of such analysis is that economic change is multivariate. There are many dimensions that have to be included in any model of analysis, many factors that may affect all others at every economic level. What is evident is that no one developing a business concept can safely assume that twenty years hence things will be much the same. Every aspect of the economy is subject to change in ways that will make a difference for the conditions of conducting a business. Even sorting out factors such as the cost of investment capital, labor, and population trends leads to problems that may not be solvable through former rules and approaches. Of course, change may also mean new opportunities for those who can adapt.

RECREATION BUSINESS CHANGES

Amid all these social and economic trends and issues, what is ahead for recreation businesses?

MARKET CHANGE

First, barring an economic collapse, there should be a general growth in recreation-related markets. A recurrence of the "stagflation" in which high unemployment in key industries is accompanied by inflation rates of over 10% a year will limit market growth in many business sectors. A more general recession in which major industries fail to meet international competition and high unemployment becomes a condition of the economy that affects 20% of households would, of course, cause a pullback in total recreation spending. However, overall growth taking the form of cyclical increases in production followed by adjustment periods will permit increased spending in several areas. The gradual shift in values toward the legitimacy of leisure along with orientations of younger cohorts that "expect" such opportunities and investment should support recreation businesses.

Second, the gradual increase in demand will create opportunities on two levels. The first is the major corporation level in which the finance, production, development, and marketing advantages of national and international scale will be combined to take major market shares. This will be the case especially for large-ticket items and major resort and recreation community developments. The second level of growth will be on a small and localized scale. The personal-service nature of so many recreation provisions suggests that relatively small and specialized businesses can establish themselves, build local reputations, and maintain a viable level of operation. Less certain is the future of middle-sized and diversified businesses. While the marketing advantages of franchises may prove useful in tourist areas, cooperative buying coupled with local ownership and identification would appear to be a viable compromise for most recreation retailing. The limitations of chain and franchise operations make it difficult to adapt to the special conditions of specific resources in a local market area.

Third, as already suggested, there will be a number of demographic changes in markets that will both open and close business opportunities:

1. The aging of the population means that greater attention to the 50-and-over segments may be accompanied by some reduction in the size of child-oriented markets. Again, it is important to remember that the cohorts reaching the older age levels in the future will be more secure

financially, have more education, and generally have experienced a broader range of leisure than previous generations. Their interests will create new markets in the areas of physical activity, the arts, travel, and various forms of recreation requiring the learning of skills.

2. The priorities given by child-rearing parents to recreation that is developmental for the children will also continue, even when the number of children levels and even shrinks. Further, family leisure, especially for home activity and vacations, will be important. However, the increase in single-parent families, the greater number of "reconstituted families," with the logistical problems of having children spend weekends in households different from their weekday contexts, and all the problems of marital transitions may increase the demand for daylong packages of recreation for adult-child groups. In any case, the importance of recreation that is seen by parents to contribute to intellectual and physical development will continue to create markets for many kinds of equipment, organized activity contexts, and learning opportunities.

3. The nature of recreation markets for women will also change. There will be more women whose employment does not permit them to have their recreation during the weekdays. Often service sector employment has irregular hours so that "free time" may come at almost any time of the week or day. On the one hand, women will be free of child-rearing responsibilities for longer periods of their adult lives. On the other hand, the present trend leaves more women as single parents with the dual demands of being breadwinner and caretaker. Leisure for such women has to be quite time-efficient. One factor yet to be explored is the shifts in demand that may be caused by more women having incomes that give them greater decision-making power in the household.

4. Income differentials and squeezes on some population segments are not new but may have somewhat different impacts from the past. The high costs of housing and other early establishment investments may have placed even greater restrictions than previously on the discretionary income of young families. As a consequence that market segment may respond primarily to low-cost opportunities and those that do not require the costs of travel. Recreation business markets may become increasingly differentiated, not by income alone but by *discretionary* income. It is the amount left to spend after primary financial obligations are met that is critical for recreation markets. This amount tends to vary according to the interrelationship of such factors as household income, period in the family life cycle, cost of living in the area, and expectations for housing, children's education, and other high-cost outlays. As a result of all this, market identification will require more complex analysis than merely segmentation by age and income.

5. Timetable variation also calls for more specific market segmentation. For example, dual-career families have to integrate the demands of the two employment schedules as well as social expectations that accompany two economic roles rather than one. The assumption that most households have one worker on the 8-to-5 Monday-through-Friday schedule will be true of a minority of households. Therefore, the requirements of transportation, available time, and common participation may be quite different for many adults and children. Timetables have to be analyzed in each locality in relation to employment patterns and household composition for that community.
6. New skills also alter markets. For example, the proliferation of electronic information-processing devices suggests the possibility of revised markets for various kinds of recreation requiring communication or other such functions. Assumptions of former learning likelihoods with the emphasis on traditional sports, especially for young males, may be changing faster than recognized.

PRODUCT CHANGES

As outlined in chapter 11, newly introduced products may be improvements, innovations, or inventions. What is significant here is that the introduction of something new for recreation use may be synergistic. A product may create new markets for a series of allied products, facilities, and services. The trick is to identify the products that have the potential of actually changing recreation participation patterns. In general, products with synergistic market potential are those that create opportunities for participation that are consistent with present patterns and orientations. A product that can enlarge an existing market by lowering costs, reducing skill-acquisition time and effort, or making an activity more accessible is more promising than one that calls for learning quite different skills, has a high front-end financial cost, or can be used only in some rare or distant environment.

However, technologies can alter participation. Electronics have made games more accessible and varied. Fiberglass has made boating more flexible and maintenance-free. Trails have opened areas for cross-country skiing. Short handles have made racquet sports easier to learn. Therefore, business opportunities may be grasped by being alert to such changes. In many cases the opportunity may not be so much in the production and distribution of the product but in some auxiliary or supportive service.

The other side of product change is obsolesence. How many times has a relatively inflexible retailer had to unload inventory at a loss because of a failure to recognize that an old design or material had been superceded? Wooden Nordic skis were sold for $12 a pair. Outmoded tennis racquets simply took up diaplay space at any price. Obsolecence can attack service and activity businesses as well as retail product distributors. Recreation markets may be quite volatile. People are more ready to experiment in recreation than in lawn care or gardening practices. Such experimentation enlarges markets for innovations. In another way, however, such markets become uncertain and difficult to predict. So much of the evaluation of products and their efficacy is within the networks of participants that local markets may develop quite differently from overall national sales figures.

What does seem certain is that recreation equipment will become increasingly subject to the impacts of technological development. All new products will not have significant market impacts. Some will be primarily promotional items that do not improve performance or satisfaction in participation at all. A reputation-conscious retailer will need to evaluate items critically before succumbing to the distributor's claims of market-capturing improvement. Nevertheless, technologies of design, materials, production, and use will probably arrive on recreation markets faster and faster as opportunities are perceived and older businesses lose their traditional markets.

RESOURCE CHANGES

At the present there are several indications of a likelihood of an increasing shift from the public to the market sector in recreation resource provisions. However, the shift will not be uniform. Public education will continue to take a major role in the introduction and development of interests and skills. Major land and water resources will continue to be managed for the public interest by government agencies. Efficiency and equity will still be adequate justification for the public provisions of pools, playing fields, local parks, and a number of other resources that have come to be expected and which cannot be made generally available through private means. It is also possible that there may be a trend toward greater investment in the public service sector that will enlarge the number and range of recreation resources provided through nonprofit means. However, more likely is the acute application of the question, What are the unique contributions of the public sector? A general pressure on public program financing will shift provisions to the market sector unless they are demonstrably worthwhile and cannot be offered at a profit.

In this case the provision of recreation opportunities by business may become a larger share of the total economy. A greater reliance on business for leisure provision will increase both the volume and diversity of market offerings. The other side of this trend, however, will make the factor of discretionary income even more salient. The financial resources available for leisure in the overall balance of household budgets will vary by both income and life-course obligations. Households with above-average income may be quite restricted in their recreation spending. As a consequence markets for goods and services that seek high-end spending will be extremely competitive. The less competitive markets may be found in providing resources for those squeezed by multiple obligations and with more limited discretionary financial resources.

Other resource shifts are more difficult to predict. Energy availability and costs are likely to undergo a sequence of cyclical periods of rise and fall. Some kinds of recreation spaces will become increasingly crowded while others may have a falloff in usage. In general, the resources near cities are most often used to an extent that will seriously affect the experience of users. The proliferation of in-home entertainment resources is expected to continue. However, former predictions of leisure patterns that concentrated on the home environment and private resources have not proven entirely accurate. Although most leisure is at the residence, there has also been a growth in the participation in activity in special environments. Further, recreation that begins at home but involves outside activity such as running, cycling, and gardening is important to many adults and children. Space not designed for recreation can be adapted for use when no special facilities are necessary.

The resource base of recreation and the relative availability of resources is a major element in participation. Overcoming the inertia of getting to a special locale keeps most leisure close to home. A business providing resources for activity that does not call for special trips, costs, and scheduling may have a number of market advantages. However, a willingness to invest in recreation that promises special experiences, including change, opens many business opportunities as well. In any case, it is essential that a business strategy take into account any changes in resource availability for market segments.

THE COMPETITIVE CLIMATE

The environment for many recreation businesses is likely to become increasingly competitive. There are a number of factors in this change:

1. Recreation is becoming recognized as a potential growth area when many businesses are experiencing sunset conditions.
2. The attractiveness of the conditions of many recreation businesses in locations, clienteles, and work experiences makes the sector attractive to many.
3. Business opportunities with low investment costs are hard to find.
4. Limited job opportunities in many human-services occupations, especially education, lead individuals to seek other opportunities related to leadership, learning, and direct contact with people.
5. Success breeds competition. One example is the proliferation of outlets for sport-and-recreation shoes. As the shoe portion of sales became more and more important to sporting goods retailers, the specialized competition emerged, and then doubled and tripled in a matter of a few years. In general, any successful enterprise concept can expect to encounter competition unless it is in a very limited market situation.

However, such direct competition is only the beginning. There is also competition at the individual or household resource-allocation level. Different resources, locales, times, and provisions compete for selection within a particular activity. One may choose to swim at competing resources or at different kinds of resources. In the decision there may be trade-offs among such factors as price, distance, resource quality, social climate, prestige, and familiarity.

Different activities are also in competition. Recreation decisions frequently are among activities as well as opportunities. The anticipated benefits of one activity may be duplicated by, or at least overlap with, another. There are many ways to exercise, meet other people, or relax. When the costs of one activity become too great, either on a particular occasion or in general, another activity may be chosen.

In some contexts choices may be not only among similar activities but among quite different ones. Travel may compete with an at-home activity, with different anticipated outcomes when both are valued.

The point is that the recreation business almost always exists in a competitive environment. Both direct competition from other providers and indirect competition from recreation commitments requiring other resources means that price, quality of service, perceived alternatives, and accessibility are always a consideration. Market monopolies, when they exist at all, tend to be temporary. Further, such competition may bring about a condition of market saturation or oversaturation in time. Especially for goods and services that do not need to be repeated or replaced regularly, a product life cycle may peak and decline quickly.

Differentiation of a business image, attachment to stable or growing markets, provision of goods or services necessary for participation, and some marketing advantages are necessary to survive competition. Good management and business practices, including the often unappealing tasks of accounting, critical analysis, personnel supervision, and attention to details of the condition of the place of business, may make a critical difference. The more competitive the climate, the greater the need that a business is operated well.

LEISURE AND MARKET RESOURCES

All of this is based in the context of the nature of leisure. Fortunately, there is now a wide and research-based literature on the meanings of leisure. We do have some good ideas of what people are doing, what their experiences are, and what factors draw them into further participation or send them hunting for alternatives. Remarkably, the fundamentals of this research have been consistent over time and among different cultures. Without going into detail, a final summary would seem useful.

Leisure has two related dimensions: the existential and the social.[9] One dimension has been the expression and development of the self. This existential dimension takes leisure as one context for the exploration and creating of the self, for the development of satisfying self-definitions and identities. The second dimension is social and has as its central theme the inauguration, maintenance, and enhancement of relationships with important others. Especially primary relationships of family and friendship are expressed and enriched in leisure times and places. While leisure is experience that differs for each person and each occasion, it most often combines these existential and social meanings. As a result leisure takes place in the real world of sight and sound, decision and intentioned action, physical and mental activity, competence and learning, and freedom and constraint.

Leisure, then, "takes place." It also takes time, personal decision and effort, and some combination of resources. One aspect of the overall spectrum of resources are those provided by the market sector of the economy. The variety and responsiveness to demand make such provisions a significant part of the overall resource spectrum. The basis of the demand for market resources is in the meanings and contexts of the intended recreation activity. While markets may be stimulated and even created by marketing, only demand grounded in the social and existential meanings of leisure promises a wide and enduring basis for recreation business.

The expressions and contexts of leisure change. The persistent meanings do not take the same form, even in the same environments, year after year. Rather, all the change factors outlined in this chapter combine to alter the particularities of leisure engagement. A business concept and strategy needs to be responsive to changes of all kinds.

Nevertheless, a valid business concept is based on the meaning of leisure in life. It offers a provision, a facilitation, or an environment for doing, for taking action that expresses our selves and who we seek to be among significant others. Recreation business is one kind of response to a call for enabling action that makes possible the being and becoming of persons who seek experiences of signifcance in their lives.

SUMMARY OF ISSUES

Recreation business is a response through the market to the need for enabling action that makes possible the being and becoming of leisure.

Adequate forecasting is not unidimensional or solely technology-driven, but incorporates many interrelated systemic variables.

Evident changes in leisure patterns include schedule diversity, residential space limitations, a greater range of education-induced skills and interests, ecological contexts of metropolitan sprawl, and a place for leisure in overall value orientations.

Family trends include diversity of structure with more dual-worker, single-parent, and transition periods that will impact on the resources and aims of leisure.

A political shift away from the service society may open new business opportunities in recreation.

Population shifts to the Sunbelt have not ended the "suburbanization" of urban areas.

Value trends include more attention to quality-of-life issues along with stress on immediate communities and self-development rather than social institutions.

Limited growth, employment shifts to the service sector, women's participation, and structural and segmented unemployment are likely to lead to more disruption of career paths.

Current economic issues affecting business environments are the investment balance, income distribution, long-term impacts of policies, growth outcomes, efficient scale, and the adoption of technological innovation.

Recreation business market changes include general growth, a competitive climate, new markets based on demographic shifts, stress on the large and small firms, and life-cycle sequences in resources.

Recognized growth potential, attractive conditions, and household resource trends suggest considerable competition in recreation business, especially for high-end markets.

DISCUSSION QUESTIONS

1. Which resources—time, space, income, social, or skill—are most critical for business-provided recreation? Why? Which seem most likely to change in distribution?
2. What factors are likely to increase at-home leisure? What factors may encourage more recreation involving travel and scheduling?
3. What kinds of recreation businesses will be responsive to changes in family patterns? What business opportunities may be increased?
4. How might recreation business opportunities be altered by restricted public-sector support of leisure resources?
5. What are indications of a possible value shift toward leisure priorities?
6. Can you identify technologies that may produce leisure resource changes that reinforce other changes such as in values, family, employment, or time use?
7. How many economic trends affect recreation business markets?
8. Identify possible recreation business growth and shrinkage areas related to demographic trends.

9. How may discretionary income be reduced in a period of rising income in general? How will this impact on recreation business markets?
10. Will recreation become more important in household budgets? At all income levels or just some? What kinds of spending may increase? Why?
11. How is the competitive climate for recreation goods and services likely to change? Are some viable markets less competitive than others? Which ones and why?
12. How can an analysis of the future of recreation business incorporate both the nature of leisure in life and the socioeconomic contexts of resource supply? Which is more important? Why?

REFERENCES

1. Kelly, John R. *Leisure,* p. 278. Englewood Cliffs: Prentice-Hall, 1982.
2. *Money Income of Households, Families, and Persons in the United States.* Washington, D.C.: U.S. Bureau of Census, 1981.
3. United Media Enterprises. *Where Does the Time Go?*, p. 34. New York: Newspaper Enterprise Association, 1983.
4. Kelly, John R. *Leisure Identities and Interactions.* London and Boston: Allen and Unwin, 1983.
5. Kelly, 1982:5.
6. United Media Enterprises, 1983:24.
7. Kelly, 1982:110.
8. Masnick, George, and Mary Jo Bane. *The Nation's Families: 1960–1990.* Cambridge: Harvard-MIT Center for Urban Studies, 1980.
9. Kelly, 1983.

AUTHOR INDEX

SUBJECT INDEX